AF361276

MARLOWE, SHAKESPEARE, AND
RELIGIOUS TOLERATION

IAN MCADAM

Marlowe, Shakespeare, and Religious Toleration

UNIVERSITY OF TORONTO PRESS
Toronto Buffalo London

© University of Toronto Press 2025
Toronto Buffalo London
utppublishing.com
Printed in Canada

ISBN 978-1-4875-6203-8 (cloth)   ISBN 978-1-4875-6205-2 (EPUB)
                                    ISBN 978-1-4875-6204-5 (PDF)

Library and Archives Canada Cataloguing in Publication

Title: Marlowe, Shakespeare, and religious toleration / Ian McAdam.
Names: McAdam, Ian, 1960– author
Description: Includes bibliographical references and index.
Identifiers: Canadiana (print) 2025012517X | Canadiana (ebook) 20250125242 |
    ISBN 9781487562038 (cloth) | ISBN 9781487562045 (PDF) |
    ISBN 9781487562052 (EPUB)
Subjects: LCSH: Shakespeare, William, 1564–1616. | LCSH: Marlowe, Christopher,
    1564–1593 – Influence. | LCSH: Religious tolerance in literature. | LCSH: Masculinity
    in literature. | LCSH: English drama – Early modern and Elizabethan, 1500–1600 –
    History and criticism. | LCGFT: Literary criticism.
Classification: LCC PR2958.M3 M33 2025 | DDC 822.3/3–dc23

Cover design: Val Cooke; Tamara Hawkins
Cover image: John Gilbert, "Richard II Resigning the Crown to Bolingbroke." Walker
Art Gallery, National Museums Liverpool; iStock.com/timonko

We wish to acknowledge the land on which the University of Toronto Press
operates. This land is the traditional territory of the Wendat, the Anishnaabeg, the
Haudenosaunee, the Métis, and the Mississaugas of the Credit First Nation.

This book has been published with the help of a grant from the Federation for the
Humanities and Social Sciences, through the Awards to Scholarly Publications Program,
using funds provided by the Social Sciences and Humanities Research Council of Canada.

University of Toronto Press acknowledges the financial support of the Government of
Canada, the Canada Council for the Arts, and the Ontario Arts Council, an agency of
the Government of Ontario, for its publishing activities.

Canada Council
for the Arts

Conseil des Arts
du Canada

ONTARIO ARTS COUNCIL
CONSEIL DES ARTS DE L'ONTARIO

an Ontario government agency
un organisme du gouvernement de l'Ontario

Funded by the   Financé par le
Government   gouvernement
of Canada   du Canada

Canada

MIX
Paper | Supporting
responsible forestry
FSC® C016245

To Wendy, Kate, and Sam

Contents

Acknowledgments

An earlier version of Chapter 2, "*Dido Queen of Carthage*, *Hamlet*, and the Transformation of Narcissism," has previously appeared as an article in *Marlowe Studies: An Annual* 5 (2015): 99–129. The discussion of *King John* in chapter 4, "The Shadow-King: Shakespeare's Development of Humanist History in *Richard III*, *Edward III*, and *King John*," appeared in an earlier form as an article, "Masculine Agency and Moral Stance in Shakespeare's *King John*," in *Philological Quarterly* 86 (2007): 67–95. I gratefully acknowledge permission to republish this material.

MARLOWE, SHAKESPEARE, AND RELIGIOUS TOLERATION

Introduction: Marlowe, Shakespeare, and Religious Toleration

This book is, in part, a study of influence. That the work of Christopher Marlowe significantly influenced the work of William Shakespeare is, of course, a critical commonplace, but the exact nature of the influence has been the subject of scholarly debate for decades – and, in terms of general cultural speculation, for centuries. In what amounts to a definitive treatment of Marlowe's influence on Shakespeare, Robert A. Logan has endeavoured to see clearly past the blurred line "that separates fact from speculation," and has consequently asserted that "Shakespeare shows himself primarily interested in the theatrical and literary techniques of Marlowe that made him a successful commercial playwright, and not in Marlowe, the Cambridge intellectual reflecting and moralizing on serious issues."[1] While I applaud such clear-sightedness, and find the position carefully and persuasively presented, I also respond with the desire to introduce a significant qualification. This qualification essentially emerges as the subject of my investigation in this study.

Behind Logan's assertion lies an acknowledgment of the radical differences not only in intellectual attitude but in artistic and even moral sensibility between Marlowe and Shakespeare, particularly evident when the playwrights appear to tackle similar subject matter (as in *The Jew of Malta* and *The Merchant of Venice*). In recognizing these differences, I (with Logan) am obviously not writing in support of claims, for example by the International Marlowe-Shakespeare Society, that Marlowe survived his presumed death in 1593 to author the works of Shakespeare. But I am also suggesting that the concern for commercial viability includes in this case cultural and psychological aspects of early modern self-fashioning beyond the purely professional or economic. While temperamentally highly distinct, the two playwrights undoubtedly also reveal intriguing affinities, arising from parallel drives towards social control and cohesion of masculine identity, what we might now call, with far less inclination to evoke a gender distinction, self-esteem. Logan emphasizes such affinity when he contests the applicability of the Bloomian paradigm of the anxiety of influence and the myth of "rivalry" or antagonism between Marlowe and Shakespeare, arguing instead that, while Marlowe was alive, "the awareness the two dramatists had of each other's work probably had the beneficial effect of heightening the desire of each to promote his creative individuality."[2] Harold Bloom's theory of influence, as well as his later criticism, have certainly undergone major critical reassessment in addition to Logan's – especially from the perspective of cultural materialism, which admittedly at times approaches categorical dismissal, doubtless invited by Bloom's comparable response to "the School of Resentment." Nevertheless, since this study proposes a radically humanist rather than post-humanist reading of the plays in question, I find a later development in Bloom's approach to artistic influence still relevant to my purposes, or at the very least intriguing: he admits in the preface to the second edition of *The Anxiety of Influence* that "to say, as I did in [the first edition of] this book, that Shakespeare swallowed up Marlowe the way a whale scoops up a minnow was to ignore the extraordinary case of indigestion that Marlowe caused the Moby-Dick of all playwrights."[3] In support of this revised reflection, I propose to explore why the Marlovian influence on Shakespeare should have such a potent and lingering effect throughout his career.

Bloom does not bother to explain his immediately subsequent assertion that "Marlowe never developed, and never would have, even had he seen thirty [or forty or fifty?]," which seems patently untrue. To paraphrase an enduring sentiment I first heard as a student in an undergraduate Shakespeare class, had Marlowe lived till he was fifty he might very well have become the greatest playwright in the language, and certainly would have completely altered the development of Shakespeare's career. Marlowe's history play *Edward II*, written under the influence of the *Henry VI* plays, not only shows his ability to develop and modify his own dramatic and poetic techniques, but the result is superior to its models, and in significant ways more emotionally compelling than the mature Shakespeare text, *Richard II*, which in turn employed *Edward II* as a model. Admittedly we must, with Bloom, consider the difference in social status between the playwrights: Shakespeare became "an actor before writing for the stage. Marlowe, though like Shakespeare the son of an artisan, had a university education and doubtless would have scorned acting, a socially ambiguous profession at the time."[4] Nevertheless Marlowe pursued some kind of service within the networks of Elizabethan espionage, which would certainly necessitate a talent for flexible self-representation.

The actual volatility of such role playing would depend on the extent of involvement, variously surmised in the critical and creative readings of Marlowe's life experience. Constance Kuriyama may offer a judicious corrective to the wilder speculations regarding this aspect of Marlowe's career: "However tempting it might be to concoct a spy scenario with Marlowe as its hero, the nature of his 'service,' considering his youth and inexperience, was probably far more routine. Marlowe was well qualified to be a messenger or letter carrier, and this is probably exactly what he was asked to do."[5] While Marlowe was not compelled like Shakespeare to develop a narcissistic complex under the ambiguous pressures of the acting profession – with its simultaneous encouragement of proud assertion towards, and abject dependency upon, an audience[6] – he nevertheless was involved ambivalently in a professional pursuit that both fuelled and restricted his ambitions and aspirations. Even in the absence of more romantic speculations, Kuriyama offers a persuasive reading of the development of Marlowe's explosive temper: "Marlowe was far too intelligent and practical to deny reality, but his humanist education, privileged status, and competitive spirit made him too proud to suffer frustration and adversity patiently."[7] In fact, Marlowe's "privileged status" as a university graduate may have paradoxically contributed to his social frustration. David Riggs points out not only that Marlowe spent a "fifth of his life" at Corpus Christi College, Cambridge, but also details the kind of hierarchical distinctions there that Marlowe (as evidenced by references in his plays) found galling. Riggs emphasizes, as well, the limited opportunities supplied by such education to the lower classes – "In the real world of Elizabethan society, a poor scholar's prospects of finding preferment at court were virtually nil" – although Riggs may slightly exaggerate this latter claim.[8] No doubt such frustration, and economic need, encouraged Marlowe's involvement in espionage. The exact or ultimate extent of his involvement will likely never be known, leaving forever unresolved the question of whether the playwright's death was a prearranged assassination (with Riggs the majority consensus in Marlowe scholarship), or whether personal "explosiveness" may well have played a contributing or determining role (with Kuriyama a minority opinion).[9]

But beyond the specifics of the professional differences between these two playwrights of decidedly low social origins, larger cultural considerations inform their psychological and material struggle within early modern society. A key element in Marlowe's self-construction that

Kuriyama underestimates in her biography involves the playwright's religious fascinations. Riggs emphasizes that "Seven of Marlowe's contemporaries refer in writing to his blasphemies; the number increases to eleven if we include writers who refer to him by pseudonyms." Marlowe not only becomes an important figure in the history of scepticism but in a sense heralds a whole new secular age: "Within the history of modern unbelief, Marlowe bestrides the moment when English atheism comes out of the closet and acquires a public face."[10] With regard to Shakespeare's religious concerns, recent criticism has tended to focus more conservatively on his relation to specifically Catholic or Protestant belief systems. My thesis is that Shakespeare – while he develops into a far subtler writer than the young Marlowe, and is temperamentally far more circumspect – produced play-texts more deeply implicated in, and indeed influenced by, Marlowe's religious radicalism than has previously been recognized. But I also wish to question whether the critical label "atheism," even in the historically qualified sense with which it is applied to the early modern context, mistakenly encourages the complete dismissal of the religiosity of Marlowe's private beliefs.

Of course Shakespeare has also, in a general way, been recognized as advancing secular concerns. Bloom intimates this broader context when in the revised preface to *The Anxiety of Influence* he anticipates his highly controversial claim regarding Shakespeare's invention of the human: "Doubtless Shakespeare, at heart always a player, conceived every part he ever wrote as a role for a specific actor, but it is an evasion to regard them as roles only, since they have become roles *for us*, whether we are players or not … We are fools of time bound for the undiscovered country, more than we are children of God returning to heaven. The issue is not belief but our human nature, so intensified by Shakespeare as to be his re-invention."[11] To many students of literature and of history, the assertion that Shakespeare "invented" the human appears questionable. *Shakespeare: The Invention of the Human* is in some ways unfortunate for the reputation of its author. Bloom is above all a scholar of Romanticism, one of the very greatest in the history of criticism. Among early modern writers, Milton (especially in *Paradise Lost*) anticipates Romanticism more directly than Shakespeare. Yet the Shakespeare canon ultimately emphasizes how *imagination* rather than "Spirit" plays a crucial role in the creation of human identity – through its (ethically fraught) dialectical engagement with material reality. Such an emphasis does render the playwright a prototypical writer in this tradition. If we consider the way his poetry has invaded our expression and our language, it is perhaps less outrageous to acknowledge that he has, at least for English-speaking cultures, helped to *consolidate* the "human," insofar as the term suggests a secular identity more or less stripped of an unqualified or culturally reinforced religious faith.

It must also be acknowledged, nevertheless, that the whole question of "secularization" as a key to the ideological development of the early modern period is now frequently interrogated as inadequate or simplistic. The "turn to religion" in early modern studies has certainly increased our sensitivity to an ideological context dominated by "biblical commentary and narrative," as succinctly described by Debora Shuger. While, by the sixteenth century, "certain fields, especially law and political theory, had already broken off to form separate disciplines, albeit shot through with biblical proof-texts and polemics ... the Bible remained the primary locus for a good deal of what we might classify as cultural, psychological, or anthropological reflection."[12] My focus in this study will be on how the specifically *psychological* is underpinned by the theological in early modern society. Consequently I must distance myself from a significant number of "turn to religion" scholars who, according to the currently hegemonic assumptions of cultural materialism,[13] maintain the ideological expression of the postmodern within the early modern, that is, an insistence on the same dissolving and inescapably unstable structures of subjectivity within both periods. Under the influence of poststructuralist assumptions regarding the fashioning and functioning of human subjectivity, they are themselves, I contend, willing to misrepresent and in effect caricature the masculine reaction I am intent on exploring. While I do not intend to engage exhaustively with this critical movement throughout the study, some key distinctions between our approaches will need to be clarified in the first chapter.

The Secular Christ

My translation of the theological into the psychological requires here a further clarification. While my own heterodoxy precludes a theologically focused consideration of Christological significance throughout, I will periodically invoke a concept I have designated the "secular Christ." Such a concept in Marlowe and Shakespeare curiously seems realized artistically in both parodic and ultimately intensely sincere ways, as this ideal of personal competence or mastery cannot be contained within any orthodox framework or dogmatic construction. The parodic elements suggest at times the potentially heretical emphasis, with comedy a convenient displacement or mask for ideologically dangerous reflections; the sincerity suggests that early modern self-conception indeed never fully escapes a theological concern. It may help to clarify this critical dilemma by taking up briefly a point I will consider more carefully in the following chapter. What I have termed Marlowe's religious radicalism takes the form most directly – as the surviving records suggest – of an interest in the Arian heresy. Thus a playwright notorious for his blasphemies appears to have entertained – not only from our own perspective but from the perspective of some of his more radical contemporaries – a legitimate interest in a compelling theological alternative to Christianity. As history indicates, one person's "heresy" can turn out to be another person's desire for a more pragmatic belief system.[14] I suggest that a significant component of Marlowe's influence on Shakespeare involves the latter's sympathetic understanding of the former's apparently reckless commitment (in its historical context) to theological revision.

The heretical potential of a "secular Christ," as already indicated, means this study will not be bound to trace orthodox Christological patterns in the plays. Neither do I intend simply to catalogue recurring Christ figures, parodic or otherwise. But I do intend to explore ways in which the drive towards spiritual self-realization reflected in the works of both playwrights ultimately challenges traditional ideas of Christian mediation and atonement. That is, I intend to trace what I regard as a legitimately spiritual impulse that dares to reclaim – significantly to a greater extent than Christianity has encouraged – one's *own* suffering as an essential part of, indeed the key to, spiritual process and personal growth. This challenge to the ideas of mediation and atonement ultimately leads, logically, to a direct questioning or at least serious qualification of one of the foundational doctrines of Christianity: Original Sin, what the Atonement was ordained to rectify. Yet oddly – or perhaps not so oddly – my approach simultaneously challenges the goal of much work in cultural materialism, which favours the argument that human suffering is very often gratuitous and almost exclusively imposed from without.[15] Consequently this study does not offer a cultural-historical exploration of masculinity in a sociological sense, as currently practised. It is fundamentally a work of literary criticism, not of cultural history, and focuses on a problem of ambiguous moral agency – and the difficulty of *owning one's agency* – which has continued to haunt us, in various and evolving forms, down to the present day.[16]

The spiritual process I propose to explore clearly remains paradoxical, contradictory, and at times morally problematic, from both the early modern and postmodern perspectives. Such striving towards a new kind of idealized, spiritualized masculinity involves not just a conflict between parody and sincerity in its artistic representations, but also a notable tension between violent assertion and morally sensitive social interaction, between destructive aggression and a more constructive if still revolutionary commitment to increased social and psychological competence. The secular Christ emerges as a riddle and a contradiction which is never fully solved or resolved within the religious radicalism of Marlowe and Shakespeare. However, at its heart lies, I think, a consistent "heresy" intimated above: the secular Christ, a *humanist* Christ, involves the attainment of a genuinely spiritual identity, but one whose agency is not subsumed in Christ-as-Mediator. That is, neither the necessary suffering, nor indeed the necessary assertiveness, is displaced beyond the individual experience or identification. It is in fact the assertiveness in the admittedly sometimes ruthless forms of masculine self-fashioning within this literature which most significantly highlights the less than "ideal" aspects – from the perspective of orthodox Christian morality – of this process of self-idealization.[17]

Imaginative Agency

Other critics addressing theological significance in Shakespeare have noted comparable aporias or contradictions. The kind of theological and moral ambiguity I propose to navigate differs from Sean Benson's interesting approach in *Heterodox Shakespeare*. Benson identifies both deeply religious and potentially atheistic significance in the same Shakespearean texts, yet at the same time challenges Alison Shell's conclusion that Shakespeare's writing "treated all religions, including the Christian doctrine of his time, as subservient to artistic unity and closure."[18] I agree with Benson that Shakespeare's art "does not merely subsume the religious," but, again, I hesitate to categorize major aspects of the playwright's work as atheistic. If my approach finds any kind of sympathetic alignment in recent scholarship, it is with Jeffrey Knapp's suggestion of Shakespeare's subversive, yet consistently "theological," artistic concerns; for example when he argues, "by framing his play [*Henry V*] as a sacrament whose real power lay in the minds of its spectators, Shakespeare represented his theater as a means not to 'fight against [God's] word' but to save it from papists and preachers."[19] In fact Knapp's identification of the sacramental purpose of plays, in which "real power" lies in "minds of spectators," brings me to identify a second crucial term which I will deploy in this study: "imaginative agency." This term designates a process in which spiritual and psychological growth is recognized as a function not of complete self-surrender to the Godhead, but of the playwright's own creative process and the kinds of audience response it encourages. Such "sacramental" purpose is I think more heretical than Knapp implies, and I will be concerned to consider carefully the crucial challenges inherent in the ideological and psychological entwinement of Christian mediation with the Protestant emphasis on *sola fide*, which rendered human agency for early modern individuals paradoxically both more potent and more problematic than for earlier generations. An elucidation of this paradox – that the radical theology of the Reformation both intensifies or encourages the drive towards individual agency at the same time that it undermines or problematizes the (social and psychological) coherence of such agency – constitutes a major rhetorical purpose of the discussion of theological contexts in the first chapter.

Chapter 1 therefore contains a relatively brief but necessary discussion addressing two closely related current controversies: the "new perspective on Paul" and the viability of human agency in the Protestant worldview. It subsequently traces how Pauline and Augustinian versions of a theology of grace were complicated by the reactions of Erasmus and Luther in the early modern period; and further how Calvinist responses in England were mediated by the theology of William Perkins, where a potentially weakened Christology may have informed Marlowe's interest in the Arian heresy. The conflicted nature of masculine self-construction under these theological influences is also traced in the writings of George Gifford, which contain an implicit or tentative disavowal of substitutionary atonement via Christ's mediation, and an accompanying Oedipalization of masculine identity. Gifford's response finds a more direct or emphatic expression in the hierarchical disciplines advocated by the (often misunderstood) Family of Love, whose presence and influence in early modern England has been underestimated, and whose symbolic or metaphorical readings of biblical figures and narratives at times correlates to, or suggests a version of, the imaginative agency defined above.

Chapter 2 begins by addressing the significance of not simply an allusion to *Dido Queen of Carthage* in *Hamlet* but in effect a glowing theatre review. With respect to Marlowe's play, previous consideration of contexts in Virgil and Ovid need to be augmented by the theological influence of Calvin. The failure or at least weakness of masculine, especially paternal, identification in Marlowe in effect catalyses *Dido*'s significance for *Hamlet*. Shakespeare, by subtly altering the action around the fall of Troy, emphasizes a key instance of imaginative agency, in which the narcissistic paralysis or the narcissistic aggression evident in Marlowe's characters is replaced by a more morally constructive and viable agency. That is, the "romantic" Shakespeare (in the sense considered above) responds to the theologically driven crisis of agency in Marlowe through the creation of an aesthetic space in which ethical reflection facilitates the acceptance of a more responsible imaginative (and imagined) self. In *Hamlet* this increased responsibility manifests through the culturally rather odd haunting of the play by a purgatorial Ghost, which points to a weakening emphasis on, or conviction of, atonement theology.

In chapter 3, I distance myself from recent claims of co-authorship of the *Henry VI* plays: the clear evidence of Marlovian influence here involves a growing tension between the two playwrights' admittedly comparable resistance to theological dependency as a form of emasculation. To clarify this distinction, I consider their differing responses to an authoritative, although vexing, literary representation of Pauline theology, atonement doctrine, and Original Sin: the first two cantos of book 2 of *The Faerie Queene*. Because of the greater deracination of his heroes from patrilineal identifications, Marlowe finds this Spenserian moment more disconcerting, a response again encoded within *Dido*. Conversely, Shakespeare's exploration of narcissistic self-fashioning in the first tetralogy, while repeatedly alluding to, even grounded in, Marlovian examples, especially from *Tamburlaine* and *Doctor Faustus*, reveals a greater level of emotional detachment and a greater potential for psychological growth or maturation, and results in some seminal Shakespearean versions of the secular Christ in the second and third parts of *Henry VI*. Such potential may partly be related to a greater respect for "pride" or self-esteem arising from Shakespeare's Catholic upbringing. Nevertheless both playwrights' interrogation of theological dependency leads eventually to a similar, existential emphasis on the ethical significance of human inwardness, an idea that crystallizes most clearly in a crucial passage of *Edward II*. This passage invests a familiar image pattern – the sun/shadow binary – with significance that transcends a simple distinction between divine essence and human performance, and suggests a more responsible, multi-faceted self-fashioning, which prepares for the exploration of humanist history in the subsequent chapter.

Chapter 4 begins by first focusing on how Shakespeare subsequently responds to this psychological and ideological complication in *Edward II* through the image patterns of *Richard III*, where the Marlovian influence remains persistent, although the influence of Kyd, and more tangentially Peele, is taken up in a brief consideration of *Titus Andronicus*. Thereafter Shakespeare develops, more independently of Marlowe, a rather militant image of a secular Christ in *Edward III*, again probably in collaboration with Kyd. In the remarkable *King John* Shakespeare then explores, through the contrast between John and the Bastard, political and psychological consequences so progressive that the playwright in a sense retreats from them again in the second tetralogy. The Bastard's more rigorous assertion involves to an extent a moderation of politico-religious commitments, although significantly not a complete rejection of spiritual concern. That is, this character's apparently secular energies, while pointedly excluding the more supernaturally sensational or magical, ultimately prove the efficacy of the irrational, and indeed of spiritual identification in general, by suggesting the need for the mobilization of emotional responses in the service of another version of imaginative agency, one which offers some intriguing parallels to Familist allegory.

Chapter 5 treats Shakespeare's return to a Marlovian effect that continues to haunt his writings, and traces the fitful, and ultimately unsuccessful or incomplete, containment of homoeroticism through a variety of works. While earlier plays, such as *Richard III*, foreshadow this problematic engagement, *Richard II* emerges as a key exemplar of Shakespeare's struggle with "subversive" sexual potential, a struggle which is clarified in this case through contextualization with a precursor text, the anonymous *Thomas of Woodstock*. This play thus emerges as a significant link between *Edward II* and *Richard II*, in terms of its portrayal of dissident sexuality. *Richard II*, in turn, emerges as Shakespeare's most ironic manifestation of a secular Christ. The psychological struggle is then further explored though a retrospective glance at *Venus and Adonis*, and a consideration of the latter three plays of the second tetralogy, which continue a subtle displacement of homoeroticism even as they suggest further parallels to masculine self-construction in Familist discourse. The chapter concludes with a discussion of *As You Like It* in conjunction with *Hero and Leander*, a poem (as has long been recognized) to which it significantly responds. *As You Like It*, as it also participates in the containment of homoeroticism, ultimately represents a notably melancholy limitation of, or restriction on, the power of imaginative agency.

The Conclusion explores Shakespearean "resolutions" by briefly examining two later texts that continue, somewhat more obliquely, an artistic response to Marlowe: *Antony and Cleopatra*, probably Shakespeare's most surprising portrayal of a secular Christ, and *The Winter's Tale*, an equally heterodox text that is almost literally haunted by Marlowe's continuing presence, even as it further asserts a potentially tragic containment of homoerotic desire. In fact the whole play in effect suggests the failure of the young prince Mamillius – who functions as a simulacrum of Marlowe within Shakespeare's late work – to achieve or effect imaginative agency. Ultimately both playwrights – not surprisingly in light of the ideological constraints of their historical moment – are unable to achieve a vision of masculine competence that can fully accommodate a recognition of the validity of such desire. Nevertheless their courageous engagement with a spectrum of powerful desire is one reason for the compelling interest which their work generates in a postmodern world.

In summary, this study offers the following central assertion: under the influence of Marlowe's depiction of a heroic struggle towards masculine self-cohesion, burdened by a self-thwarting and largely incoherent theology which nevertheless provides the main available mode of self-conception, Shakespeare attempts to recuperate the sanctity of not only the natural world but also the sexualized body itself, and dares to rework Christian myth in the service of a more productive, creative secular culture. My first book, *The Irony of Identity: Self and Imagination in the Drama of Christopher Marlowe* (1999), was motivated by a conviction that both sexual and religious conflicts need to be considered in order to trace Marlowe's artistic development. The second, *Magic and Masculinity in Early Modern English Drama* (2009), while adopting a broader focus, essentially followed suit, since a consideration of magical belief inextricably involved persistent attention to sexual and theological concerns. This study again suggests the necessity of a concomitant attention to religious and sexual themes, although the return to a closer focus on the psychology of the two playwrights assumes a more personal aspect of influence within a shared cultural context. I do not here claim anything approaching a definitive description of Shakespeare's artistic development. But if the exploration does not tell the whole story of his psychological concerns, I hope to at least illuminate a crucial aspect, by exploring an artistic intimacy which is one of the most fascinating in our literature.

Chapter One

Theological Contexts: Grace, Individualism, and Agency

The "Turn to Religion" and Masculine Competence

As the Introduction indicated, this chapter will clarify my argument's relation to, and crucial differences from, the current "turn to religion" in early modern studies. Ken Jackson and Arthur Marotti assert that "the deconstructive response to Enlightenment rationality has opened up religious culture and religious study to new (but perhaps also old?) forms of apprehension," and warn that we "should not turn to religion in our studies … the way that [an] earlier and more naive generation of Whiggish ethnocentrists or Catholic apologists did."[1] Commenting on Stephen Greenblatt's *Hamlet in Purgatory*, Sarah Beckwith writes, "despite these aims and intentions [of taking the play's medieval inheritance seriously], we seem to be left with a version of *Hamlet* and Shakespeare not so very different from the Whiggish, individualist protagonist of modernity present even before these investigations began."[2] John D. Cox, who casts some doubts on the tendency to identify Shakespeare more closely with traditional rather than reformed faith, repeatedly emphasizes "the [necessary] recognition of Whig liberal prejudice in the narrative of English history."[3] Although I wish to avoid partisan claims regarding the essentially Catholic or Protestant belief systems of the playwrights in question – I am more interested in heresy than orthodoxy – I do believe the dismissal of "Whiggish" constructions in particular seriously downplays the significance of the struggle for personal self-cohesion evident in this literature. While "Whiggish" assumptions imply an overly optimistic and liberal view of history that asserts inevitable progression and improvement, some attention to a moral emphasis on self-coherence and self-control remains crucial in any assessment of the development of secular forms of human subjectivity in the early modern period.

In a brief study which offers a helpful overview for readers attempting to navigate this theological and critical labyrinth, David Scott Kastan writes honestly and directly about how religion in Shakespeare "seems different," and has in fact *always* seemed different, from religion in, for example, Spenser and Milton. The distinction in this case admittedly arises partly from difference in genre:

> ... the theater's engagement with the [religious] reforms and the debates they occasioned mostly takes place ... only as they have filtered down, almost always unremarked and usually unobserved, into the terms and forms of connection that mark our social world. Crises of belief in the plays [of Shakespeare] are more likely to be provoked psychologically than doctrinally, functions not of soteriological uncertainty (*Hamlet* is perhaps the exception proving this rule ...) but of sexual uncertainty.[4]

By "sexual uncertainty" Kastan implies, presumably, a significant proportion of masculine anxiety – echoing the link between "crises of belief" and the cohesion of masculine identity that primarily concerns me. The nexus of theological and sexual concerns highlights the advantage of the Shakespeare-Marlowe critical pairing I propose, but admittedly also complicates the issues in hand. With John D. Cox, Kastan uses the drift of much "turn to religion" discourse to further intensify the critically "revolutionary" (that is, anti-Whig) nature of the current project: "A Catholic Shakespeare ... would ... not merely allow some to claim Shakespeare as a co-religionist but also force a reconsideration of his role in the Protestant triumphalism that has for so long largely determined what Englishness is and has meant."[5] Part of the complication that arises from such speculation is the necessary determination of what exactly Christian belief, whether Catholic or Protestant, entails with respect to masculine subjectivity. Kastan's identification of ubiquitous "sexual uncertainty" in Shakespeare evokes the now familiar trope of anxious masculinity in early modern discourse. But my resistance to the cliché of triumphal "Whiggish" assumptions emphasizes my concern with the challenge of a necessary individual, if in this historical context primarily masculine, competence and responsibility – an issue that has been seriously downplayed in criticism of the last several decades.

The "New Perspective on Paul"

This critical dilemma needs to be contextualized, briefly, with two more specific critical developments – both of which serve to distort and ultimately underestimate the psychological challenges posed by conceptions of Christian atonement in the early modern period. First, renewed attention in literary studies to the impact of Christian theology very often focuses, unsurprisingly, on the figure of Paul, who more than any other individual in history determined the development of Christian doctrine, and who deeply influenced Augustine and the neo-Augustinian figures of the Reformation, Luther and Calvin, in their creation of a theology of grace. Beginning in the 1970s, Pauline theology began to undergo a reassessment, eventually identified as the "new perspective on Paul," which has recently exerted an influence on literary studies. Julia Reinhard Lupton may be regarded as spearheading the neo-Pauline movement in Shakespeare studies; in a brief article, "Paul Shakespeare," she canvasses the theorists and philosophers involved in this theological reassessment, and, with respect to the narrower focus of literary studies, cites Gregory Kneidel's *Rethinking the Turn to Religion in Early Modern English Literature: The Poetics of All Believers*, which builds on the "classic" and indeed impressive study, John S. Coolidge's *The Pauline Renaissance in England: Puritans and the Bible*. Lupton significantly praises Coolidge as "no historian of inwardness." While investigations of this subject need to balance sociological and psychological concerns, the former may have begun to monopolize attention at the expense of the latter. Nearly all recent commentators recognize the complex and often confusing nature of Pauline theology; Lupton admits that "Paul's self-divided thought … continues to plague contemporary engagements."[6] While the "new perspective" has many, varied proponents, they tend to encourage a reception of a Paul who transcends such self-divisions, whose thought encompasses a broader acceptance of both Old Testament and New Testament viewpoints, and of both faith and works as integral to salvation. But the application of "the new perspective on Paul" to readings of early modern literature, by calling into question the Protestant emphasis on the doctrine of justification by faith, the Reformation's central principle of *sola fide*, not only downplays the particular struggle for self-cohesion of early modern individuals, but also threatens to short-circuit our understanding of a key, intensely traumatic moment in the history of human subjectivity.

For his part, Kneidel admits, "I am not arguing that the universalist interpretation of Paul that has come to the fore in recent years really did triumph in the sixteenth and seventeenth centuries, only that traces of it influenced the period's scriptural poetics."[7] Lupton's admonition to "use" Pauline epistles suggests something more aggressive: "the follies and fall-out shelters of the new Pauline Renaissance … aim to *make use of* – to seize and activate, profane and enjoy – the several legacies of Paul." To maintain the critical relevance of such an approach to the early modern experience, Lupton questionably asserts, "It is safe to say ... that a Western literature founded on a Paul deprived of his layers ... would not have delivered either a Shakespeare or a Milton,"[8] where a progressive Shakespeare and Milton constitute the logical proof or guarantee of this more comprehensive, universalized Paul, in which the (fatal) polarity between faith and works, divinity and humanity, "spirit" and "flesh," has been dialectically disarmed. But I see Shakespeare's and Milton's social progressiveness as a necessary reaction *against* psychologically oppressive Pauline dualities, at least as they were conceived in the Protestant culture of early modern England. And just how were they conceived? In the context of the Reformation, Luther clearly emerges as the key figure consolidating, if not instigating, the "old" perspective on Paul. In general Luther's status would therefore, to state the obvious, encourage a traditional view of Pauline theology at the time of the Reformation. Disagreement between Catholic and Protestant, from the early modern period to the present day, has centred on the debate over the efficacy of faith versus works, and thus focused intensely on the interpretation of Paul's writings: "Theologians of Catholic and Protestant persuasion have debated for centuries whether or not Luther correctly conveyed the apostle's thought ... until quite recently, Protestant scholars tended to affirm, and Catholic scholars, to deny, that he did a fair job of it."[9]

Whatever we may conclude about the ideological and political confusion arising from Paul's "self-divided thought," we need to acknowledge the serious psychological and cultural consequences of the spiritual idealizations at the core of Pauline doctrine and atonement theology: "I deliuered vnto you that which I receiued, how that Christ dyed for our sinnes according to [the] Scriptures, And that he was buryed, & that he arose the third day" (1 Corinthians 15:3–4).[10] Karen Armstrong's admission that "There is a potential danger" in the idea of a "single Incarnation of Christianity, suggesting that the whole of the inexhaustible reality of God *had* been manifest in just one human being,"[11] seems something of an understatement. In one sense, then, A.N. Wilson's astonishingly bleak conclusion to *Jesus* is certainly not gratuitous: "When the Church triumphed over the synagogue ... the deadly legacy of anti-Semitism remained embodied in the Christian view of the world."[12] The nightmare of the Holocaust will forever remind us of this fact. However, in recognizing the darker manifestations of prejudice and persecution in the evolution of the Christian church, we cannot ignore the more positive contributions attributable to the Christian transformations of Jewish religious culture in human history.

Elaine Pagels in *Adam, Eve, and the Serpent* significantly interrogates the mythology of the creation story in Genesis, offering in the process a persuasive critique of Augustine's promulgation of the doctrine of Original Sin. Indeed, there is in my opinion no great ideological leap from Paul to Augustine, with respect to this doctrine; Heather Hirschfeld points out that "The doctrine of original sin grew out of second- to fourth-century exegesis of Romans 5:12 ('In Adam we all die, because through one man sin entered into the world and through sin death, and thus it passed unto all men …') and was strongly associated with Augustine's writings against the Pelagians."[13] As A.N. Wilson dares to summarize: "Many have observed, from Paul's day to our own, that [Paul] essentially distorted the message of Jesus, and that he conjured up a strange new cult, 'Cross-tianity,' … out of his own teemingly energetic imagination."[14] Nevertheless, in her study Pagels also observes the church's role in the promotion of a universal belief in the sanctity of individual life, something which must remain our social and spiritual responsibility to continually assert:

> About twenty years after Justin [Martyr] had been beheaded for refusing to worship the Roman gods, Clement of Alexandria took the statement that God had created humanity in his image as evidence of human equality – and as an indictment of the imperial cult. From such beginnings, in open defiance of the totalitarian Roman state, and often met with brutal violence, Christians forged the basis for what would become, centuries later, the western ideas of freedom and of the infinite value of each human life.[15]

The more one learns about the brutality of social interaction in the ancient world, the more one senses the vital importance of the role of various Christian teachings in the cultivation of universal charity and compassion in Western culture.

Logically this leaves Paul one of the most ambiguous figures in human history. Of no other figure is it so crucial to distinguish misjudgment from true spiritual insight. It is my committed belief that, in spite of (or because of) all he suffered, Paul did *not* manage to consistently maintain a "spirit of power, and of love, and of a sound mind," whether or not he actually wrote those lines. My ultimate response, then, to the proponents of the "new perspective on Paul" is to question why we are now so eager to reestablish him not as an interestingly conflicted mystic or seer but as a social and moral *authority*? For implicit in all this discourse seems an attempt to recover the Pauline text as sacrosanct, or at least, one might say, instrumentally directive.

The very impetus behind this apparent longing for more social control or power embodied in an institutionalized textual code involves a kind of orthodoxy I struggle to comprehend. Equally incomprehensible to me is Slavoj Žižek's assertion in *The Fragile Absolute – or, Why Is the Christian Legacy Worth Fighting For?* that *"there is no Christ outside Saint Paul."*[16] My own assumption that "Christ" can be understood to take on metaphorical meanings not limited by the doctrinal debates of the first centuries of the common era, or of later theological debates, leaves me with one possible speculation: such a position arises from an academic ego so in love with its own theoretical constructions, so in love with what it perceives as the necessity of working through its own histories and systems, that it declares the freer or more intuitive positing of a truly spiritual understanding – *or even the human, moral approximation of such an understanding* – as anathema.

Rewriting the Reformation

This personal admission brings me to a consideration of the second, closely related critical controversy, which again raises indirectly the question of "Whiggish" historical assumptions. At the beginning of an important 2008 article Debora Shuger announces:

> A survey of recent Shakespeare scholarship indicates a growing critical consensus that the Reformation was "the defining event" of postclassical European history, the cutting edge of "the fundamental long-lasting schism in Western consciousness." The influence of Eamon Duffy's erudite and powerful *Stripping of the Altars* (1992) – a postmodern remake of nineteenth-century nostalgic idealization of the Middle Ages at the expense of the early modern period – has meant that this transformation is almost always understood as loss ... where the "Catholic values of the sacred ... the ritual, the communal" give way, in a "cascade of cultural destruction[,]" to the "Protestant values of the individual, the critical mind, the subjective," and hence to "an interiority unleashed from old sacred shared sources and launched onto a sea of interpretative chaos."[17]

Shuger compares this reading with the one it has now presumably largely displaced: "Like the opposing myth of Protestant triumphalism, the narrative of the Reformation as Fall remains compelling. In no small part this is because both are good stories: stories of transformation, glorious or tragic; the kingdoms of this world becoming that of our Lord, or vice versa."[18]

The argument subsequently becomes primarily an interrogation of James Simpson's characterization of "the profound delusions of evangelical [that is, Protestant] theology." Shuger counters, "Tudor Protestants, like medieval Catholics, repeatedly affirm that our good works and our repentances, both of which are themselves God's gifts, do have, in Simpson's words, 'a real purchase on God,' that the future remains open to human effort'."[19] But Simpson responded to this interrogation, arguing (with some minor qualifications with respect to English Protestantism) that Luther's account of soteriology fails to confirm this claim.[20] Simpson has now offered a broader rewriting of the Protestant Reformation, *Permanent Revolution: The Reformation and the Illiberal Roots of Liberalism*. As the title suggests, this study again undercuts the "Whig" reading of the Reformation – "the growth of individuality and interiority … liberty of conscience … rationality … equality through the democratic priesthood of all believers" – with the assertion of the movement's darker realities: its "absolutist, cruel, despair-producing, humanity-belittling, merit-rejecting, determinist account of salvation … its closely related account of an exclusivist, invisible, ahistorical Church of the pure." Although Simpson initially insists on the correctness of both these descriptions, the more positive features really only emerge later – much later, in fact, in the seventeenth century – through either a kind of historical accident or a historical necessity: "Cultural systems are hydraulic. In the short and medium term they displace cultural energies; only in the very long term do they expel them. The proto-Enlightenment is less a clean break with, than an unintended transformation of, older evangelical materials." But this wider diagnosis would seem to downplay, or give inadequate attention to, the various experiences of *individual* repentance and conversion within the early modern age, both sixteenth and seventeenth century. The argument that "English Calvinist Protestantism necessarily produced its opposite cultural formation (… the proto-Enlightenment), against the punishing, crushing, violent, schismatic logic of the evangelical Reformation"[21] raises the question of whether the process was so *simply* a reaction formation, or whether it gradually or ultimately involved, more positively, the acquisition by the individual believer of a stronger, more integrated independence of thought and a more freely acquired and therefore more deeply felt understanding of religious faith. From my personal perspective as a scholar, Simpson's historical description seems to elide numerous readings in the archives – primarily from the later sixteenth century – which have demonstrated to me not only interesting, significant, and reasonable political concerns and scruples by Protestant writers, but also deeply moving and psychological viable spiritual commitments. But my questioning of Simpson's reading of this transformation is not meant to imply the process was easy.

Subsequent to the initial exchange between Shuger and Simpson, Heather Hirschfeld produced a book-length study on the relation between theological conceptions of penance and early modern drama. While she acknowledges that Shuger "has argued strenuously for the continuities between Catholic and Protestant penitential practices," she insists that "Protestants of various stripes themselves had to emphasize the radical difference of their model of repentance and its connection to solifidianism." The result is to render the Protestant position in some sense pathological, since plays produced by Protestant cultures depict "their suspicion of penitential satisfaction not as a theological triumph but as the opening up of a conceptual vacuum. The power of this vacuum ... is to turn cherished mechanisms of repentance into forms of aggression, so that the possibility of atonement by taking vengeance on the self always includes turning on the other – and vice versa. One's own repentance ... is never enough."[22] That this debate over apparently archaic theological distinctions is now heating up in a postmodern critical context should surprise no one, since it takes us to the heart of the crucial question of responsible individual *agency* in human social interaction.

That question is specifically addressed in another recent study, Timothy Rosendale's *Theology and Agency in Early Modern Literature*. Like Shuger, Rosendale defends the viability of human agency within Protestant doctrinal contexts; his position is in part personally motivated, and clear as early as the moving reference to the memory of his father in the Acknowledgments: "His example taught me, among innumerable other things, that Calvinism, grace, and a vigorously good and accomplished life are by no means irreconcilable." Apparently rising above partisan concerns, Rosendale ultimately emphasizes the universality of the question of agency, and rightly points out that the vexing debate concerning free will and determinism, in some form or other, has haunted both pagan and Judeo-Christian discourse for millennia. With respect to early modern studies, however, Rosendale launches his most pointed attack on Greenblatt's almost complete marginalization of the religious in general, in terms which I find significant: Greenblatt's "cursory nod to (and then abandonment of) theology is a decisive indication of what really matters to him – and as Debora Shuger and others have influentially and correctly argued, this kind of analytical hierarchy gets its object all wrong: for early modern Christians (that is, virtually everyone), religion was the foundation, horizon, and primary language of their existence, not just an allegory of their psychosocial lives."[23]

From Literal to Allegorical Self-Wounding

While I also find Greenblatt's materialist assumptions limiting, this study suggests that for some interesting and key early modern individuals the radical *questioning* of their religion was indeed "the foundation, horizon, and primary language of their existence." This claim may justify a brief survey of relevant playtexts before the detailed explorations in subsequent chapters. Marlowe's contemporary reputation for blasphemy renders him the obvious example of a radical mindset, but Shakespeare offers another compelling instance. Shakespeare in effect builds on but also attempts to recuperate or resolve the narratives of trauma and wounding that he finds, presented ironically, in Marlowe.[24] That is, Shakespeare rewrites the (ironic) "possibility of atonement by taking vengeance on the self" which Hirschfeld observes in this drama by transforming more completely the urge into containable allegory. *Contra* Rosendale, Shakespeare's religious references do often come close to constituting "an allegory of the characters' psychosocial lives." Certain recent efforts in "turn to religion" scholarship seem to me too intent on reestablishing psychologically limiting Christian orthodoxies that underestimate the radical potential of the early modern period. For Paul Cefalu, to take another instance, the current attention to Pauline thought is not theologically focused enough; his recent "revisionist" study emphasizing Johannine influence on early modern literature concentrates on devotional writers but nevertheless suggests in an "Afterword" that its thesis can be fruitfully extended to dramatists such as Shakespeare and Marlowe. Cefalu's final assertion in his book is that many early modern writers "found that they could abide in Christ through an emulation of John's very intimacy with the Savior. They leaned on John the way John alone, the beloved disciple, could lean on Christ's breast."[25] Here it is impossible for anyone with even a passing familiarity with Marlowe not to recall the blasphemous claim from the Baines Note that "St John the Evangelist was bedfellow to Christ and leaned alwaies in his bosome, th[at] he used him as the sinners of Sodoma."[26]

With a reminder of Kastan's emphasis on "sexual uncertainty," I contend that Shakespeare's ideological and psychological position is in significant ways closer to the heretical Marlowe than to Cefalu's apparently pious summation, as both dramatists engage in a subtle interrogation – although often masked through comedy and parody – of the mechanism of Christian mediation. When Falstaff in *1 Henry IV* exclaims, "*ecce signum* [behold the sign]," pointing to his sword "hacked like a handsaw" as evidence of his valour during the Gadshill robbery (2.4.166–7), we *could* receive this as simply light-hearted ideological displacement, a parody of Eucharistic practice. The moment, then, playfully echoes Robin's same exclamation to Rafe in *Doctor Faustus*, in reference to the doctor's conjuring book, after they have purloined a silver goblet, and just prior to their bestial transformation at the hands of an enraged Mephistopheles, who has presumably been unwillingly conjured (A 3.2).[27] Nevertheless, such moments need to be taken more seriously; there has in fact been surprisingly little critical response to David Bevington's editorial suggestion that both these exclamations of *"ecce signum"* echo the language of the Mass. Jay Zysk's recent *Shadow and Substance: Eucharistic Controversy and English Drama across the Reformation Divide* does not take up the significance of either of these allusions. Admittedly this specific objection may seem unfair, since Zysk's study, like much other recent scholarship, downplays the Protestant Reformation "as a decisive [in the sense of implicitly positive or liberating] epistemological shift from the sacred to the secular."[28] Yet Zysk's approach results at times in surprisingly orthodox and ultimately improbable readings. For example, he argues that *Doctor Faustus*'s deliberate confusion or equation of magical and religious discourse – which Gareth Roberts has established as highly typical of early modern conjuring books in general[29] – means simply, in Marlowe's case, that Faustus suffers from "priest-envy."[30] Surely the play more powerfully explores, through dark comedy and tragedy, the hero's failure of "manly fortitude" through the desperate (and narcissistic) fantasies inherent in magical thinking.

Such trauma may be summarized with a brief survey of Marlowe's four major tragic protagonists, as a prelude to the more controlled or contained comic parody of Eucharistic concerns in Shakespeare's second tetralogy. I begin with two examples of self-wounding in Marlowe that are rarely linked critically (and will be more closely examined in chapter 3). In the second part of *Tamburlaine*, act 3, the hero cuts his arm and invites his sons to search his wound with their fingers, in what Greenblatt terms a "zany parody" of doubting Thomas.[31] In *Doctor Faustus*, act 2, the hero cuts his arm in order to sign the pact with Lucifer in his own blood, before echoing Christ on the cross: "*Consummatum est.*" The *imitatio Christi* here apparently runs the gamut from a fantasy of omnipotence on the part of a world conqueror who incredibly claims he has never previously felt a wound, to the panicky impotence of a magician terrified by the apparent miraculous discursive effect of his own blood: "*Homo, fuge!*" The Jewish anti-hero of *The Jew of Malta*

surprisingly blends or conflates Christ and Antichrist roles.[32] He ratio-
nalizes his rejection of the governorship of Malta with the reflection:

> For he that liveth in authority
> And neither gets him friends, nor fills his bags,
> Lives like the ass that Aesop speaketh of,
> That labours with a load of bread and wine,
> And leaves it off to snap on thistle tops. (5.2.38–42)

Scholars have failed to identify the specific fable in Aesop, although
Renaissance depictions of donkeys laden with gold and riches as
emblems of self-defeating greed certainly seem relevant, and chime
with the necessity of "fill[ing] bags." But then why does Marlowe
designate "a load of bread and wine," if not to suggest subversively
a Eucharistic "burden," which potentially and paradoxically conveys
the more selfless responsibilities of a religious, specifically Christian,
authority? Even more significantly, the self-wounding of Barabas earlier in the play becomes metaphorical, not literal, as he runs through
the night to regain, from his daughter, the riches he has hidden in his
former home:

> The incertain pleasures of swift-footed time
> Have ta'en their flight, and left me in despair;
> And of my former riches rests no more
> But bare remembrance, like a soldier's scar,
> That has no further comfort for his maim. (2.1.7–11)

In the theatre such a speech may suggest in passing Barabas's equation
of his heroic struggle for survival to the phallic assertion of a courageous
soldier; but a brief reflection on the imagery surprisingly suggests a connection of the "pleasures" and "comfort" not to phallic aggression but
in fact to penetration. Such darkly fantastical "pleasures" anticipate the
notoriously "symbolic" implications of the death of Edward II, which
one of the first critics to address honestly the homoerotic implications
of the play describes as an "anal crucifixion."[33] This description might
seem less gratuitous in light of Sara Munson Deats's reading of the play's
Actaeon analogy as "a dramatization of … the cleansing of the kingdom
and the restoring of order through the hunting down and killing of the
scapegoat king"; Deats notes "the frequent allegorizing of both the stag
and Actaeon as types of Christ."[34] From the perspective of postmodern
readings which link the horror and savagery of Edward's murder to
the intolerance of a homophobic society, such a death can hardly be

construed as "self-wounding"; yet the Revels edition of the play from the 1990s provocatively concludes that "there is something in Edward that invites the fiery spit even as he fears it, and the monarch's conduct of his own affairs, as of his kingdom, is rooted in a curious intermingling of wilful assertion and abject dependency."[35] As we shall see in chapter 5, this description of Edward's narcissistic dilemma – and his "symbolically" significant death – have implications for Shakespeare's depiction of the narcissistic Richard II, and his concomitant inability to entirely contain the homoerotic implications of *Edward II*. Lightborn's spit is reduced in Richard's imagination to the "little pin" that penetrates and implodes the "hollow crown" of his kingship, which he has managed to maintain only through fantasized identifications with the persecuted Christ. Finally, Richard's little pin anticipates the spear-grass which Falstaff recommends to Peto and Bardolph, to facilitate nosebleeds that can be used to "beslubber" garments as a completely fraudulent testament to martial courage and heroic self-sacrifice. Behold the sign indeed. Thus Shakespeare develops the parodic versions of *imitatio Christi* and atonement theology in Marlowe, but significantly in ways that critique a more specifically humanist self-fashioning – rather than mirroring the apparently inadvertent but ultimately tragic *collapse back into orthodoxy* so characteristic of Marlowe's plays.

The increasingly dark and disturbing versions of atonement motifs in Marlowe invite – from Shakespeare's perspective – not a correction or readjustment within doctrinally orthodox terms, but a radical psychological revision that allows more *space* for viable self-creation, a broader arena in which individuals can establish their own social or sexual integrity. With Hirschfeld, I have often in my scholarship observed a decidedly pathological element in Reformation self-construction. Historically, such pathology may indeed arise in part from the fact that the Protestant version of Original Sin is "unrectifiable by baptism"; hence "this doctrine calls special attention to the transgenerationally infectious consequences of the Fall, emphasizing both the permanent, deadly nature of parental fault and the sexuality that is both its punishment and source."[36] Nevertheless, while I am therefore clearly not embracing Protestant "triumphalism," I also cannot escape the deep conviction that the Reformation played a crucial role in the emergence of modern consciousness, as a necessary rather than regrettable chapter in that story. By attempting in effect doctrinal readjustment, not revision, much "turn to religion" commentary appears to me ultimately to offer theologically improbable but also obscure readings – such as Zysk's reading of "priest envy" or indeed Hirschfeld's reading of Faustus as a version of the medieval harrowing of hell[37] – and I intuit the obscurity of these readings not only from a postmodern perspective but from an early modern one as well. What so much "turn to religion" commentary appears to underestimate is the crucial energy of self-empowerment released by the dislodging or unloosing of individual agency from patterns of penance and good works, as defined strictly through the corporate structure of the medieval church. The Reformation both problematized and intensified this crucial and historically fundamental drive towards individual agency and self-determination – and the two effects remain inextricable.

The Psychological Revolution of Luther and Erasmus

Let us accept then the not illogical proposition that the "old" perspective on Paul, with its Lutheran emphasis on *sola fide*, dominates theological understanding in post-Reformation England. Clearly an assertion of a "traditional" view of Pauline theology cannot – as the above discussion has emphasized – be taken as a licence to simplify the ideological context or deny the complexity and intensity of conflicts and debates that ultimately defined the course of history. If the "battle of the books" between Luther and Erasmus, for example, had had a different outcome, we would now be living, presumably, in a very different world. Erasmus, as Brian Cummings summarizes the confrontation, argues that "Sometimes the Bible urges us to higher moral effort; sometimes it rebukes our moral pride and humbles our presumption. Rather than contradiction Erasmus finds rhetorical and moral coherence." However, "Erasmus's attempt to make both assertions – that we have free choice, but that we can 'ascribe' it to God as the ultimate source – is for Luther proof of the duplicity at the basis of Erasmus's [argument]."[38] It might be sentimental, and certainly useless, to lament here the historical or ideological defeat of the more enlightened, less pathological, opponent – and, at any rate, Erasmus's anti-Semitism apparently didn't fall much short of Luther's,[39] making the description of a more humane, theologically inspired humanism overwhelmed by an overly aggressive or dogmatic theology somewhat difficult to maintain. Cummings, for whom "Theology and [Renaissance] humanism are uncomfortable bedfellows rather than sworn enemies,"[40] regards the debate between Luther and Erasmus as an instance of the new predominance of grammar over dialectic. Primarily under the influence of Romans and of Augustine, Luther's theology of grace focused crucially on an interpretation of *"iustitia"* which attributed complete agency to God and complete passivity to humankind – as the requisite faith for salvation comes only through the grace of God. Luther was therefore able to refute the quasi- or semi-Pelagianism implicit in Erasmus's position, and, in a purely spiritual or soteriological context, Luther "logically" has a point.

For Cummings the Reformation's obsession with "grammar and grace" raises intriguing parallels with our postmodern dilemmas:

> In their entrapment within language, the writers of the Reformation were no different than us. It should come as no surprise in the twenty-first century to find such extremes of abstraction and violence, of skepticism and belief, of desire and anxiety, within the exercises of language. If Luther's religious language seems alien, his sense of alienation from that very language should not. And if one characteristic of sixteenth-century linguistic usage is a lurch into insatiable violence against itself, another is an endless aspiration to escape from itself, to reach out for grace. It may be that in this act of hopeless faith it [that is, presumably, linguistic usage] finds its own redemption.[41]

What I don't share in this vision is a faith in the accessibility or even advisability of "grace" in this particular form, too closely tied as it is to a theoretical obsession with the power of discursive formulation. What needs greater emphasis are the other, crucial issues of experience, in particular the whole role of *embodiment*, not just in terms of sexuality but in all the manifold activities of human life, partly but not wholly culturally prescribed. Cummings does at one point acknowledge this role in his consideration of Montaigne's response to Luther. For Montaigne "Luther expressed absolute faith in language, when Luther himself made such faith in language impossible. Luther is denigrated as the apostle of literalism ... Luther has promised the ultimate linguistic fiction of a language without fiction, of words which really do render things. In the process he has apparently destroyed all confidence in any language which appears to do less." In effect, at least in a linguistic sense, Montaigne denounced the theological as the magical, and there is no doubt that much of the artistic energy of the early modern period is devoted to interrogating magical thinking. Whatever Word God created the world with, and whatever Word achieves the incarnation of human individuals, it is clearly not equivalent to the word or words of human reflection and communication. While both Luther and Montaigne reject "a division of language and experience," Montaigne "held it to be the height of wisdom not to reject the one final given of one's life, the gift of the body."[42]

The opposition in this case might encourage us to seek a resolution to the magical thinking of word-obsessed Protestantism through a return to a more comprehensive Catholic balance between faith and works, spirit and flesh. But of course the (ideological and psychological) situation is not that simple, and indeed the accusation of magic frequently went the other way around, levelled by Protestants – most notoriously through attacks on the doctrine of transubstantiation – against Catholic forms of ritual and idolatrous belief.[43] The Renaissance has traditionally been described as a period rife with paradox, and this assertion seems particularly clear with respect to not only its doctrinal debates but also the personalities of its major figures. Even the definitive opposition that gradually emerged between Erasmus and Luther is difficult to maintain when we recall the famous accusation that Erasmus laid the egg that Luther hatched.

Indeed, Erasmus like Luther introduced crucial retranslations of ancient texts. Diarmaid MacCulloch highlights as "notorious" Erasmus's

> retranslation [in his 1516 edition of the New Testament] of Gospel passages (especially Matthew 3:2) where John the Baptist is presented in the Greek as crying out to his listeners in the wilderness: *metanoeite*. Jerome [in the Latin Vulgate] had translated this as *poenitentiam agite*, "do penance," and the medieval Church had pointed to the Baptist's cry as biblical support for its theology of the sacrament of penance. Erasmus said that what John had told his listeners to do was to come to their senses, or repent, and he translated the command into Latin as *resipiscite*. Much turned on one word.[44]

In opposition to "doing penance," "coming to one's senses" creates a lot more space for humanist, and therefore (in the Renaissance) predominantly masculine, self-fashioning. Together with the radicality of Luther's *sola fide*, Erasmus's retranslation offered a kind of "gateway drug" of theology that opened up a far wider range of issues, and opportunities, than simply a revision of penance. Erasmus's whole program of humanist reform, like Luther's direct communication with God, challenges clerical pomposity and privilege, and encourages the self-disciplined ethics of individualism. The patriarchal edge of Erasmian humanism is intensified by his disdain for the cult of the saints, in particular for Marian devotion, and he certainly anticipates a kind of Protestant inwardness through his devaluation of outward ceremony and ritual in favour of inner contemplation. In fact, with his respect for the dignity of human free will, he might, theoretically, seem a better champion for heroic self-fashioning than Luther, though the latter came to detest Erasmus's lack of fortitude and of political and doctrinal assertiveness.

Perkins and English Calvinism

While it is obviously difficult to regard Luther, ideologically, as a champion of humanism, such is not the case with the theologian who exercised the greatest influence on early modern England. Calvin, although "[r]emembered by history as the narrowest of theocrats ... was known in his own time as a prince of learning and of humanist literature," and modelled his scholarship on, among other writers, Erasmus. He was also enlightened enough to acknowledge that the "text of the Bible is *a human production in human words*, through which God 'communicates' with man" (my emphasis), although he also asserted that, while "there are many Bibles in many languages there is only one word of God," which must always be the same and "is therefore innately translatable." Unsurprisingly, then, Cummings adds that "Derrida's ultimate 'metaphysics of presence' is found in Calvin."[45] Indeed, it is difficult not to be struck, as one peruses the religious pamphlets of early modern England, by how rigidly invested the Protestant and Puritan writers are in the absolute authority of Scripture – somewhat surprisingly, considering what they ought to recognize (especially since the invention of the printing press) about the production and translation of texts over time, under various kinds of ideological and political pressures. Moreover, the obsession of early modern English writers with the text is accompanied by a sometimes astonishing impulse to *logically* extricate its meaning. English Protestant culture, at least officially or consciously, often seems to hold little sympathy with Luther's famous dismissal of reason as the devil's whore. Luther, as Cummings points out, "asserted all men are sinners, including the righteous, so that his theology resolved itself only in the paradoxical formula *simul iustus et peccator*." On the other hand, "Calvinist logic dictated that it is a necessary truth about a person that *either* he is saved *or* he is condemned. A man must be one or the other, and if one not the other." Thus forms of Ramist logical reasoning, with its structure of repeating syllogisms, became popular within English Calvinism: "Ramist logic was seen as instrumental in serving two fundamental purposes of puritanism: propagating the gospel through preaching and confounding Roman doctrine through religious controversy ... its discursive basis ... meant that both purposes could be achieved through ... rigorous attention to the signification of holy scripture." One of the most important Calvinist theologians in early modern England was William Perkins. Although he did not directly acknowledge Ramus as an influence, "The dichotomous principle of Ramus's method, whereby every proposition is divided into two more, is found everywhere in Perkins's systematic works."[46]

It would be difficult to overestimate the influence of Perkins himself on the late Elizabethan theological context. Educated at Cambridge, Perkins was elected to a fellowship at Christ's College upon his completion of the MA in 1584. According to G.M. Pinciss, Marlowe's arrival in Cambridge in December 1580 "coincided with the period when William Perkins became known by his preaching as the most popular and effective spokesman for the extreme Calvinists,"[47] but Perkins's influence may have emerged as more mainstream than this assertion suggests. Ian Breward reminds us to question the "tendency to see Hooker as *the* theologian of the Elizabethan church, despite the fact that his *Ecclesiastical Polity* was a worst seller and appears scarcely to have been noticed until later in the seventeenth century." Perkins, on the other hand, "succeeded because of a clear style, ability to popularise and summarise, enormous industry ... and above all through a piety which contemporaries found compellingly attractive. It was this more than anything else which pushed him towards the top of the religious bestseller lists in Elizabethan England." Breward compellingly describes Perkins's appeal to the "socially mobile," with their concerns for "personal security" in a period of rapid social change: "Many were seeking a haven of certainty which did justice to the changing society and world in which they lived and yet satisfyingly preserved their memories of what had been good in the past," a process which combined "[d]irection about the exercise of personal freedom and responsibility" with "a strong sense of the need for political and social order."[48]

While the tension between obedience to conscience and obedience to external authority within Perkins's worldview represents a familiar opposition within Protestant cultures, this study is concerned with a deeper and more vexing psychological and ideological dynamic that emerges within the contradictions of Perkins's Puritan self-fashioning. Both Cummings and Breward interestingly remark upon this dilemma from, I think, slightly different perspectives. For Cummings, "Perkins appears to be on the point of hermetically sealing God off in a world outside language, before instead engaging him inextricably in its every jot and tittle. The resulting strain on Perkins's linguistic theology is intense."[49] Breward observes that, while "It was not new for protestants to emphasise the authority of the Bible ... the works of Perkins contain distinct signs that revelation was being accommodated within a framework of rationalist apologetic which could be a distinct disadvantage if the philosophical climate was to change, or christology became weakened."[50] The most profound paradox inherent in Perkins's brand of Calvinist theology emerges through the fact that an assiduously logical attempt to control scriptural interpretation actually results in a heightening of awareness of the potential for illogical or irrational impulses. As Perkins argues in his *Treatise of Mans Imaginations*: "We must know that these two thoughts, *There is a God*, and *there is no God*, may be, & are both in one & the same heart: the same man, that by light of nature thinketh there is a God, may by that corruption and darkness of minde that came by *Adams* fall, think there is no God … we may easily deceive our selves therein, for a man cannot always discerne what be the thoughts of his own heart." In the face of this assertion of inherent mental instability, the reader is struck by Perkins's insistence that "those who submit themselves to the ministrie of the word, must bee of this minde, not onely conformable thereunto in word and action, but in every thought of their minde … howsoever with men we say *thought is free*, yet with God it is not so. And indeed hee which hath effectually received the grace of Christ, will endeavour to yield obedience as well in thought, as in word and action."[51] The apparent result of such a program of religious self-control is a notable tension between conscious and unconscious impulses. Again, what might be considered the most appallingly dogmatic or doctrinaire in Perkins leads surprisingly to the most psychologically complex or subtle. Through the "doctrine inferred by Calvin and elaborated by Beza that God wills the reprobation of the wicked as certainly as he does the election of the blessed," Perkins "collapses entirely the distinction that might be held to exist between what is contingently possible and what God wills, something Calvin at least is careful not to do." As a result, "the 'simplenesse' of God's linguistic integrity is exposed to the arbitrary processes of human mood," and "God's true purposes are revealed only through the minutest examination of human motivation."[52]

It is this psychological intensity in Perkins's theological explorations that renders him a still underappreciated influence on Elizabethan modes of self-construction. He likely made a significant impression on Marlowe. It is an easy assumption that Marlowe, perhaps most obviously in *Doctor Faustus*, engages in a radical critique of the Calvinist doctrine of predestination and would therefore, presumably, vehemently reject Perkins's theology. But it has also been noticed that Marlowe seems to offer a fairly sympathetic portrait of Ramus in *The Massacre at Paris*. The Duke of Guise accuses Ramus, as a "flat dichotomist," of logical superficiality – "[thou] never [did] sound anything to the depth" (9.28, 25) – yet Ramus defends himself eloquently; it is the Guise, with his megalomaniacal assumption that his authority gives him the right to murder, who seems morally superficial. In his assessment of Marlovian response to theological uncertainty, Pinciss wishes to preserve the tension between Calvinist and anti-Calvinist belief systems within the ideological context of *Doctor Faustus*, as it upholds the moral ambiguity of the tragic protagonist; but the critic identifies the source of the anti-Calvinist influence on Marlowe with emergent English Arminianism at Cambridge. I suggest Marlowe would likely have even less sympathy, or find even less congenial, the Arminian emphasis on "the hierarchical nature of both church and state in which the office not the holder was what counted," and in fact would be at least residually drawn towards what Nicholas Tyacke identifies as "the incipient egalitarianism of Calvinism."[53] Marlowe's challenge to social orthodoxy takes, I contend, the form of an intensification, not a dialectical dilution, of Calvinist doctrine.[54] In fact Breward's concern (above) with a weakened Christology in Perkins's theology moves us closer to the kind of heretical thought for which there is certainly direct historical evidence: Marlowe's interest in Arianism.

Marlowe and Arianism

In light of the dire consequences in his own life and in the life of Thomas Kyd, the episode of the misplaced Arian tract, and the tract itself, has received surprisingly perfunctory treatment in Marlowe studies. In the wake of the Dutch Church Libel,[55] Kyd was arrested (and later tortured) after "atheistic" material was found among his papers in May 1593. The papers consisted of copies made from an anonymous Arian treatise, passages which are reproduced and confuted in a book by John Proctour, *The Fal of the Late Arrian*, published in 1549. In his book Proctour refuses to identify the Arian, since, he explains, he has heard of the heretic's recantation. Kuriyama repeats John Bakeless's speculation that the Arian was John Assheton, "a priest arrested for heresy in 1549," and also Bakeless's theory that the manuscript found among Kyd's papers was one of the copies made in 1549 and circulated among those investigating Assheton's heretical claims. Kuriyama concludes, quite sensibly, that "Proctour's book was more widely available and is therefore a more likely source," although a manuscript that faithfully copies the Arian viewpoint and does not mention the context of Proctour's refutation, if that indeed was the source, seems dangerously likely to increase suspicions of heretical thought, and deliberately ignores a handy qualification or cover for its own heretical interests. Kuriyama's observation that "Kyd seemingly had no idea where the manuscript originated, because if he had known about Proctour's book, he could have claimed that the manuscript derived from a perfectly orthodox source,"[56] may also indirectly strengthen Bakeless's speculation.

At any rate Proctour's book provides us not only with extensive quotations from the Arian treatise but also an interesting window into the concerns of an Edwardian, that is, a quite early English Protestantism. Although Proctour praises Henry VIII for freeing the English from Roman bondage, he clearly has serious reservations concerning the effects of Reformed theology on his compatriots, to the point of truly regretting the psychological influences of the Protestant access to vernacular scripture: "ye have … abused that comfortable treasure of Gods sweete worde. The nature wherof is, to make such as doo acquaynt them worthely with it, les proude, less vicious, lesse dishobedient, lesse contencious, lesse malicious, lesse covetous. But in that ye are more in all, and less in none: it appeareth, ye dyd more proffytte therin, when ye had lesse knowledge therof." On the one hand, Proctour encourages virtuous self-control, in good humanist fashion: "No man is hurt but through him selfe: it was a wyse and true sentence of Tully [Cicero] … [The devil] is of no power, but where no power is: Never overcometh, but through our owne prodicion [unnaturalness]: Our weakhertinesse, cowardnesse, and impotensye, is his onlye might." On the other hand, such virtue certainly does not come through the exercise of reason, which is soundly repudiated in favour of a mystical (and feminine) self-surrender: "Aske not how with Sacarye [Zacharias] lest ye receave punyshement for your incredulytie. Aske how with Marye the most blessed virgin, and mother of Jesus Chryste: then ye shall receave fruite of your question. She asked howe, but beleved firste, and therefore she receaved an Aunswere that contented her … suspect your reason, for it wanteth right judgement: mistruste your wyt, for it lackethe wysedome, condemne your sences, for they have not experyence, to deride, judge, and determine any one jote of gods misteries."[57]

From Proctour's perspective, the Arian could be said to fall into the trap of a too logical and too individual approach to Christian doctrine, with the unavoidable consequence of insinuating a daring challenge to key assertions of Paul, and of John the Apostle. Proctour is repeatedly, rather monotonously thrown back on the theory of Christ's two Natures, both divine and human, to explain what the Arian terms the "impiety" of positing an omnipotent God who could experience human suffering and limitation. The Arian clearly attempts to render scripture comprehensible through metaphorical readings: "[Christ] is called nowe and then the Image of God: for that I suppose, his lyfe is as ye wolde saye, the glass of the devyne wyl towarde us … He is called the Worde also: verelye because he was nerest unto the father. And as ye wolde saye the orgen or instrument of the devine voyce: For the worde is made fleshe, what els doth it signifye, then that the fleshe receyved the worde." Proctour vehemently counters: "He is therefore called the word, not for that he was the orgen or instrumente onelye of the devyne voyce as ye saye he was: But for that he was in verytye the devyne voyce it selfe, and the true worde it selfe."[58] There is in fact significant scriptural support for the Arian's theological position, as he himself observes, and as many "Christians" before the establishment of the Nicene Creed would probably agree: "if oportunitie served to searche the Scriptures accordingly, it shulde easely appeare that Christ is not of the same substaunce or nature, neither equall with God the father."[59] Clearly the political stakes are high in the Arian's attempt to dilute the authority of Christ, since logically this move results in the potentially unlimited empowerment of any believing individual, any "receiver" in faith of the word of God.

The Arian's deep respect for Jesus cannot hide this dangerous implication: "shortly thus I thinke of Jesus Chryst. Verely that he was the most electe vessel, the orgen or instrument of the devine mercy, a Prophet and more then a Prophete, the son of God, but according to the spreete of Sanctificacion, the first begotten but emongest many brothers." Proctour responds, "Here is Christe defined as unchristienly as ever I herd," and labours to distinguish Christ from other spiritually endowed individuals:

Now (sir) although the Prophetes & other dyd veraye great miracles, yet the maner of doynge so dyverse betwene Christ and them, well proveth him to be God, and these not to be goddes. For as thei dyd nothing of themselfe, so dyd Christ absolutly all of himselfe. They ever used invocations and prayer er they were able to do any miraculous matter. But Jesus Christe dyd all of hym selfe, never prayed, never invocated the father what tyme he wolde shew any miracle, but of his owne devine power, and with his onlye worde he wrought miraculous wonders.[60]

The assertion that Jesus "never prayed" certainly strains the rationale of this defence of Trinitarian doctrine, and logically raises doubts about the orthodox assertion that Christ represents not a model for emulation but a necessary spiritual Mediator, in effect a divine salve for the futility of human moral effort or amelioration. I began this section with the assertion that Arianism represents a radical but not entirely illogical development of psychological tendencies in Calvinist belief. It will therefore be helpful to explore further how the apparent moral futility of a dependency on a mediator figure is intensified or exacerbated by the Protestant doctrine of *sola fide*, which facilitates a sometimes fantastical and an often violent struggle for self-transformation but also a radical sense of personal inadequacy.

English Reformation Mediation

We have recognized that the position of Reformed theology does not deny the necessity of human effort, struggle, and discipline. But the pathological potential is there: that effort often seems intellectually torturous or ideologically constrained, rather than as "productively" emotional – that is, as leading to mental and doctrinal coercion rather than moral maturation. In early modern England, personal access to vernacular scripture not only increases the danger of an "inward," spiritual warfare, but in effect increases the possibility of internecine social struggle, in a metaphorical foreshadowing of the violence of the Puritan revolution. Proctour observes in his preface:

> Even so we must use our adversaryes, the devyl and the wylde beastes his ministers, not only that we be not hurte of them: but also that we be advauntaged by them: as the more vehemently to be sturred up to the studye of Gods comfortable worde, the more strongly to be confirmed in the faith of Jesus Christ ... in this hurlye burlye of Christis religion ... it behoveth us nowe especially to pley the men, to go stronglye armed.
>
> God no dout permitteth us to be thus persecuted with suche sismicks [presumably schismatics] and blasphemous opinions, partly for our wickednesse and dissolute lyvying past ... [but] chiefly to trye and prove our faythe and constancy towarde him by the same; no otherwise then we trye our pot or vessell by puttynge lyquor in to it, whether it be sounde, or not.[61]

Human "soundness" or integrity therefore is finally only realizable as a fit vessel for the divine substance, with the added – and inescapable – challenge that the vessel itself is only achievable through an appropriation of Christ's righteousness. In the context of later Puritan thought, such spiritual wholeness seems a precarious intellectual and ideological achievement underwritten by emotional instability, as in Bunyan's *Pilgrim's Progress*, where Christian's most memorable victory, after ignominiously abandoning his family, is over a frightening demon in the Valley of Humiliation, who really represents his own carnal ego or (more positively) his own self-cohesion or self-esteem; and even more disturbingly, where Ignorance is consigned to Hell for daring to rely not on the pathologies of a self-thwarting, self-torturing doctrine of ineradicable human sinfulness but on his own (clearly healthier) intuition of a loving God.

Marlowe's apparent fascination with the Arian perspective so vehemently (if not entirely consistently) refuted by Proctour suggests a somewhat desperate search for a more humane theological alternative.

Although my approach will not pretend to "resolve … all [the] ambiguities" (A 1.1.82) of Marlowe's most theologically notorious play, I do suggest that Mephistopheles' assertion in *Doctor Faustus*, "Therefore the shortest cut for conjuring / Is stoutly to abjure the Trinity" (1.3.53–4), takes on increased significance in light of the playwright's Arian interests. At the very least, the devil's claim indicates a high level of both aggression and anxiety inherent in Marlowe's challenge to orthodoxy. David Riggs very helpfully if somewhat cynically explains that the schoolboy Marlowe could not have avoided Alexander Nowell's *A Catechism or First Instruction of Christian Religion*, which "drilled in the key concepts of Calvinist theology – bondage of the will, predestination, election and reprobation. These lessons taught Marlowe what the state Church expected of its educated élite: in a word, obedience." Somewhat pragmatically the *Catechism* refers to "the visible Church of England rather than the invisible Church of Christ" when it recognizes that "Many by hypocrisy and counterfeiting of godliness do join themselves to this fellowship, which are nothing less than true members of the Church." But while a certain percentage of reprobation is expected, indeed inescapable, in human society, the *Catechism* required such reprobates "to retain a 'general' or 'dead' faith in the God who had doomed them to everlasting torment. Since the only God the reprobate could ever know was a God of wrath, they had a strong incentive not to believe in Him."[62] In the context of such culturally enforced hypocrisy it is easy, from our own perspective, to project a sense of cynical detachment onto Marlowe.

But while the scepticism in his work it undeniable, it is a mistake to attribute to him a postmodern sense of atheism or pure disbelief.[63] Marlowe's scepticism is rather fuelled by a deep desire to realize the true implications of spiritual belief in human experience, *a process in which self-cohesion can be recognized or achieved not by eradicating but by clarifying the individual's relationship to his or her divine source.* That is, for Renaissance England and, despite his remarkable heterodoxy, for Marlowe himself, there is no adequate way of coming to terms with reality without some crucial reassessment of the divine. While postmodern commentators sometimes make radical assumptions about early modern atheism,[64] an absolute dismissal of immaterial causes seems highly uncharacteristic of this period. In fact, until the hegemonic materialism of recent criticism, such a dismissal seems highly uncharacteristic of people in general, as David Hawkes observes: "Despite [Gabriel Egan's] claim that 'most people' find it impossible to conceive of an autonomous non-material subject, the vast majority of people throughout human history have found no difficulty whatsoever believing in such a phenomenon."[65] Criticism of early modern literature needs to consider more closely the tension between, not a projected postmodern atheism, but an "intense religious feeling" and the ruthless (even sometimes violent) drive towards self-definition and self-empowerment.

This paradoxical suggestion of spiritual independence, even spiritual aggression, may again have some connection to English Calvinism. While the doctrine of Christ as necessary Mediator potentially evokes a narcissistic dependency, I observed in *Magic and Masculinity* that William Perkins rather surprisingly uses the doctrine of the Trinity to resist what he regards as dangerous human fantasies of an overly indulgent and protective deity:

> God is to be conceived as he reveales himself unto us, and no otherwise: if otherwise, God is not conceived, but a fiction or idol of the braine ... when the mind abstracts the Godhead from the Father, Sonne, & holy Ghost, God is transformed into an Idol ... *for he that denies the Sonne, hath not the Father*. And the unitie of the Godhead is to be adored in the Trinitie of persons. Here then behold the Idol god of the greatest nations of all the world; of Turkes, or Jewes; yea of many that pretend Christianitie, who upon ignorance, worship nothing but an absolute God, that is, God absolutely considered, without any relation to Father, Christ, or holy Spirit. Yea the multitude in all places set up unto themselves, a god that is all mercy, and no justice: because they content themselves with the light of blinde nature, and frame God according to their owne desires and affections.

For Perkins the concept of the Trinity, and in particular the distinction between Father and Son, are necessary for an understanding of the Law, and in effect for a sure grasp of what we now call, mainly thanks to Freud, the reality principle. Religions without this doctrine, according to Perkins, have no protection against the fantasy of an all-merciful, loving God, who fails to impose (self-) discipline. Such fantasy recalls the "oceanic feeling" that Freud dismisses in *The Future of an Illusion* and *Civilization and Its Discontents*.

What remains difficult to determine is how Perkins imagines the imposition of discipline, on humankind, within his Trinitarian structure. He clearly attacks, in a subsequent passage, the Catholic Eucharist as a degradation of the manliness of Christ:

> [Christ] in one person is perfect God and perfect man: our only redeemer al sufficient in himselfe, and therefore perfect king, priest, prophet; without either partner or fellow in the work of mans salvation. And he which otherwise conceiveth of him, turns him into an idol or forged

> Christ. This doth ... the religion that stands in force by the late Councell of
> Trent. For it presenteth unto us Christ indeede, but yet a poore disguised
> and deformed Christ. For it spoileth him of his manhood, and degrades
> him of his offices. He is spoiled of his manhood by the presence in the
> sacrament ... it is supposed to be included and contained in the quantitie
> of a small round cake.

Although the Protestant position traditionally attacks the Catholic theory of transubstantiation as a kind of excessive literalism, an inability to read the sacrament metaphorically or symbolically, the latter part of this passage seems to attribute a narrow literalism to Perkins's Puritan objections. In objecting to the spoiling of Christ's manhood, Perkins seems surprisingly fixated on the physicality of Christ, although he subsequently clarifies his position regarding specifically *idolatrous* behaviour: "it is not unlawful to make or to have the image of Christ, two caveats beeing remembered. The first, that this image be onely of the manhood: the second, that it be out of use of religion. For if otherwise it be made to represent whole Christ, God, and man; or, if it be used as an instrument or a signe in which, & before which, men worship Christ himselfe, it is by the former doctrine a flat Idol."[66] But if Christ cannot be worshipped in the form of a sign, it is a pressing question how, or in what form, his mediation works at all, and even Perkins's Trinitarian emphasis paradoxically takes us to the verge of an Arian denial of the divinity of Christ, at least of Christ as the direct object of worship.

We can perhaps fall back on explanations offered by Debora Shuger: "all Reformed theories of the Eucharist presuppose a sort of rationally organised space, since they begin from the claim that because Christ is 'in heaven' He cannot be 'in' the Host. On the other hand, they also constantly speak of Christ ... as being 'in' the soul, as the radical center of personality and Holy Ghost in the machine, a notion that both defies spatial location and disclaims the sense of individual autonomy traditionally ascribed to the Renaissance."[67] We are left here, however, with the doctrinally tricky equation of Christ and the Holy Spirit, and the question of the exact mechanism of mediation. The Eucharistic controversies of the Reformation are notorious, and dangerous to oversimplify – anyone who has investigated them can testify to a level of subtlety, nuance, and complexity at the least the equal of any of the most rarefied theoretical debates of recent years. But through all the myriad forms of the Protestant refutation of the doctrine of transubstantiation – by Luther (consubstantiation), by Zwingli (purely memorial symbolization), by Calvin (some rarefied, subtly distinguished approximation of Zwingli), by the various English Calvinists (which for the most part seem versions of the Zwinglian position) – it is possible, even likely, that early modern English worshippers would be at least as bewildered and confused as postmodern historians and theorists. Can we then identify or outline at least a general or common form their anxiety would take?

In a compelling chapter of a subsequent study, Shuger takes up not theological tracts but the literary form of the Calvinist passion narratives, which "seem to encode some sort of cultural disturbance involving manhood, violence, and urban decadence." Shuger classes such narratives as "end myths": "If, following Durkheim's influential thesis, the function of dominant myths is to provide normative values and ontological solace – to relieve anxiety by grounding social experience in sacred order – then disintegrating myths … 'end myths' … can be characterised by their failure to effect this … [In this context t]he agony of Christ becomes a locus for the articulation of strange desires and moral uncertainties, disclosing rather than resolving cultural paradoxes." Whereas "Patristic theology [had tended] to envisage Christ's humanity as largely impersonal," the Calvinist passion narratives "[un]fortuitous[ly]" build on the personalization of Christ, the "production of an unstable, internally riven selfhood" in late medieval Christology – and then potentially intensify their traumatic effect through the *internalization* of Christ's sacrifice under the pressure of Calvinist Christology: "The church has the duty, 'by bringing men into the obedience of the Gospel, to offer them as it were in sacrifice unto God,' Calvin explains, 'and not as the papists have hitherto proudly bragged, by the offering up of Christ to reconcile men unto God'." Thus Shuger concludes that these narratives "construct a new male subjectivity, one formed not by identifying with ideal types – the rhetorical mode of the medieval passions – but by internalizing the whole *drama*, by restaging the Crucifixion in the theatrical subject. The end myth produces and mirrors a conflictual, decentered, and chimerical manhood."[68]

Gifford and Protestant Discipline

What I find so significant to the energy of the early modern dramatic production, as opposed to the Calvinist passion narratives, is a powerful and prolonged *resistance* to this conflicted and decentred masculinity, which will become the essential focus of the ensuing chapters. But such resistance can also be found, interestingly, in the period's religious debates, theological tracts, and struggles against heretical thought. One of the most appealing, disciplined but humane early modern Protestant writers, George Gifford (1547/8–1600), is worth examining on this score. In at least two tracts Gifford takes up his pen against the Brownists, whom he labels "Donatists" for their insistence that moral imperfection of individuals vitiates the holiness or integrity of the church to which they belong:

> Faith and regeneration being unperfect, in all that live upon the earth, it is hereticall, to say [as do the Brownists], that is no Church of God, which holding the sounde doctrine, hath sinnes and great abuses in it.
>
> The stablenesse of Gods covenant towarde the Church, being founded onely upon his free grace, it is detestable impietie, to hang it upon the works of men, as the *Brownists* do, when they affyrme, that where there is any open sinnes suffered in an assemblie, the covenant is disannulled with them all. And if men consider well, they shall finde that the whole *Brownisme* resteth uppon the heresie of perfection and Anabaptisticall freedom.

The moral imperfection of humanity necessitates external law, and Gifford attacks the Brownist denial of the authority of "Christian Magistrates," as well as this heresy's criticism of "prescript formes of prayer" within the liturgy. Thus Gifford (not without some suggestion of social snobbery) supports the return of a kind of reasoned hierarchy in church government, which "requireth men of the greatest wisedome, learning, experience, and sobrietie that may be, for to guide it. Now when the common Artificer, the Apprentice and the Bruer intrude themselves, and they will guide the same, being ignorant, rash, and headie, what worldlie wise man will not take it, that discipline her selfe is but a bedlem?"[69] Interestingly, the measure of decency and of moral approbation here, "worldly wise man," is the very figure Bunyan will later demonize in *The Pilgrim's Progress*. Gifford in fact echoes Proctour when he complains, "men receyve not the holy Word of God in humilitie, with fear and trembling, with conscience to practice, but are puffed up, and swell with opinion of their knowledge, as soone as they can utter a few words." Clearly Gifford asserts here that there is such a thing as spiritual *infancy*, which correlates to a certain extent with intellectual and moral immaturity. Yet Gifford might render Proctour somewhat uneasy in his (more radical) recognition, with the Brownists, of a universal Spirit that empowers the elect: "I professe unto ye, that I hold it a wicked opinion, to deny that the same spirit doth nowe teach Gods children to pray, which taught the Prophets."[70] While the mechanism of mediation of such "spirit" may again suggest a somewhat weakened Christology, Gifford's most interesting argument focuses on the ostensible and disconcerting difference between Paul and Christ, which for his subject position as an early modern Christian cannot be tolerated in a doctrinal sense:

> We are most sure that Saint Paul in that hee saith, dooth not differ from our Saviour Christ, and yet in shewe hee seemeth to speake quite contrary. For where one saith: No man can serve two Maisters. The other saith: I my selfe in my minde serve the lawe of God, and in my flesh the lawe of sinne. How shall this bee reconciled? is there no waye but to fall upon the rockes of Brownisme, and to imagine that the regenerate are so freed, that they be in no captivitie unto sinne, nor give place unto evill thoughtes? Yes, verelye: The regenerate doo fall into sinne, not onelye in thoughts but in deedes: not onelye in ignorance, but even against theyr knowledge, as David, Peter, and manye other in the holye Scriptures.[71]

Gifford in this passage raises – inadvertently but crucially – the disturbing question of Pauline dualism, a worldview in which "the wisdome of the flesh" (Geneva Bible) or "carnal mind" (KJV) functions as "enmity against God" (Romans 8:7). Paul's famous assertion does not merely suggest that spiritual modes of perception supersede material attitudes or beliefs, but that there is a real, and deadly, antagonism between "spirit" and "flesh." In my reading, Gifford's position identifies a tension between the two which does not represent an intense dualism, with its concomitant spiritual and psychological warfare, but which is better summarized by the recognition that the "spirit" is willing while the "flesh" is weak. That is, Gifford describes again the sometimes difficult and challenging process of spiritual maturation:

> we are taught every where, that regeneration which consisteth in putting off the old man, and putting on the new, is by degrees wrought in Gods elect. Wherupon the holy Ghost compareth the spirituall birth with the naturall. A man is borne a poore weak babe, not able to go alone, or yet stand upright: hee is nourished and fed with milke, and so in continuance, dooth grow up by degrees unto mans estate. We are born againe, not of mortall but of immortall seed, even the word of God which indureth for ever … wherefore he willeth, that laying aside all maliciousnes, deceipt, hypocrisie, and such like, we covet the sincere milke of the word, that we may grow thereby.

There is thus an interesting connection, and a not altogether clear distinction, between growth/maturation and conversion. When Gifford turns to 1 Corinthians, the distinction seems closer to conversion: "Let the Church of Corinth be for an example in this point, even the teachers and people together, unto whom S. Paul writeth thus: I could not speake unto yee brethren, as unto spirituall men, but as unto carnall men, as unto babes in Christ."[72]

The distinction between "teachers and people" reactivates the hierarchical assumptions in Gifford's worldview, which becomes clear in his refutation of the Brownists' contempt for academic learning: "there be many in the Universities, and not above the degree of Bachelour of Arts, unto whome the principall Maisters of Brownisme are inferior: if we respect either the Liberall Arts, or the knowledge of toongs, as of Hebrew, Greeke, and Latine, or a sound judgement in Divinitie ... Some do abuse the liberall Arts: but to condemne Logike, Rhetorike, and the rest as vain and curious ... is a very beastly error."[73] Gifford's motivations do not simply include the snobbery of class or education, but centre more humanely on the helpful functioning of a spiritual community, in which the strong or spiritually mature lend aid to the weak or spiritually immature, where again his condemnation falls on the cold exclusiveness of the Brownists' perfectionism: "Shall the strong, when all are to take the journey together, runne away, and leave the babes and the feeble behinde them? nay, rather let them leade them by the hand ... Let the Brownists alone, who, as if they were ayrie spirits, disburthened of all lumpe of the flesh, mount up aloft, and leave poore heavie loden sinners crawling uppon the earth."[74] But Gifford does not want to emphasize only a sense of mutual support and human charity. In another tract against the Brownists he explains how a more spiritually mature or disciplined minister can serve as a necessary role model for those still struggling against their lower, carnal tendencies: "it is better, that the minister be godly, because the infirmitie of man, to whome without an example it is laboursome and difficult to doo that which God commaundeth[,] may more easily by the imitation of a good minister be raised up and supported unto good life."[75] Crucially, through this "imitation," spiritual growth remains the responsibility of each individual believer.

Yet there also emerges in Gifford's argumentation a somewhat less benign sense of the need to maintain political control. He is, for example, willing to compromise or qualify the radical individualism of evangelical Protestantism in his insistence on liturgical discipline: "First, ye say, God in his law commaundeth every one to seeke the place where he putteth his name. Christ in the Gospell commaundeth to seeke the kingdome of God, and to take his yoke uppon them, &c. I aunswere, that if a man from these places shoulde conclude, therefore private men are commanded to preach the word, and to administer the Sacraments, it were ridiculous."[76] Gifford introduces a rather disturbing idea of necessary discipline that takes a concern for liturgical discipline into a potentially oppressive mode of church government; he thus appears to perfunctorily pass over individual liberty of conscience, the essence of the Protestant position:

> Indeed the kingdome of God is spirituall: all the power of kings in the world, cannot convert one soule unto Christe: that is done by the Holy-ghoste, through the livelye word of faithe. Neverthelesse, the civill power is an outward meane to drive men to heare the Gospell preached, and to obey the discipline … before men bee converted, compulsion, even with penalties, is a meane to bring them to that, whereby this regeneration is wrought: & after conversion to God, there remaineth still a great lumpe of corruption, which is to be kept in and bridled with some force.

Gifford, like Perkins, here evokes the political dilemma common to Protestant states, where liberty of religion competes sometimes desperately with concern for social order. What interests me most is the analogy that Gifford offers by way of clarification:

> I will make the matter cleere, by the chastisement which the Scripture willeth Parents to use to their children. A father hath a sonne which is dissolute and proud, whom he cannot reclaime by anye instruction or exhortation. He correcteth him with stripes, and forceth him to heare the word of God diligently being preached. It pleaseth God so to blesse this indevour of the Father, that his Sonne is converted, and dooth become a right godlye man. Shall we saye he is none of Christes subjects, because at the first he came not willingly? The king is the Father of all his Subjects, and by fatherly correction laboureth to bring them to goodnesse.[77]

We have moved a relatively short but significant distance from Perkins's evocation of the Trinity as a necessary antidote to the narcissistic fantasy of a deity of unlimited benevolence. Gifford's vision of discipline and correction, through the appropriation of divine authority by both church and state as controlling parents, in effect leaves the mystery of the mechanism of Christ's mediation behind, and brings the idea of spiritual maturation more clearly into what may be termed an Oedipal framework. In doing so, Gifford reflects a larger, and crucial, pattern of discursive energy and endeavour in early modern English culture.

The increasing focus on classical literature and mythological narratives in the literature of this culture often serves as a vehicle for the idea of generational competition and succession, an interest intensified by the increasingly energetic individualism of the Protestant Reformation. Marlowe's *Tamburlaine*, for example, qualifies its uncertain Christian theological concerns with pagan self-determination: at one point Tamburlaine famously evokes the precedent of mighty Jove's usurpation of his father Saturn's throne to justify his military aggression, and at a later point encourages his own sons' assertiveness by inviting them to penetrate his self-inflicted wound in the odd Christ and Doubting Thomas episode we considered above. I suggest that the peculiarly nightmarish quality of *Tamburlaine* and other Marlowe plays is not at all gratuitous, or simply the product of his eccentric genius, but owes much to the theological and psychological incoherence of Christian doctrine, particularly in the face of increasing pressure on masculine self-fashioning, not only in the context of militant Protestantism but in general through the intensifying drive towards patriarchal self-authorization at various levels of early modern society.

Indeed the significance of Tamburlaine's martial aggression struck not only the more secular-minded: in *A Treatise of True Fortitude*, dedicated to the Earl of Essex, Gifford also considers Tamburlaine's example as he attempts to explain the necessity of heroic masculine assertion within the Christian nation-states of Europe. The pagan heroes, Gifford reasons, "gloried of a vertue, that they dyd all for their Countrey, when all theyr valiant courage did spring and growe from ... beastly vices" such as pride, vainglory, ambition, and cruelty. Thus "A more valiant and expert souldiour then this *Tamberlaine* could not be found, and yet withal, as cruell a Tyrant as ever did breath." Yet Gifford paradoxically denies that such courage on the part of the pagans was entirely a vice, asserting rather it was the gift of God: "as God in hys high providence had before ordayned the great Monarchies or kingdoms, so also hee prepared the instruments that should erect and uphold them. He put that skill for the warres, and that heroycall courage into them."[78] From this perspective, martial fortitude is clearly divinely inspired, indeed a holy attribute, even if human foibles such as pride and ambition so often pervert it.

The Spiritualization of Oedipus

That Gifford must refute "thys perverse opinion, that a man cannot bee both godly and valiant," and attacks those who assert that "Hee that will studie the Worde of God to followe and to practise it, let him be chayned up on the Church like a moopish foole or a milk-sope,"[79] suggests that many of Gifford's contemporaries *did* hold doubts about the inherent manliness of the deeply religious or piously committed.

Such anxiety about spiritualized masculinity suggests that the particular currency of Oedipal constructions in early modern culture needs further consideration, especially in forms where the myth appears in conjunction with Judeo-Christian mythologies. Patrick Grant begins his *Transformation of Sin* with a consideration of E.R. Dodds's theory of a transition from shame culture to guilt culture in ancient Greece: "the most widely received solution to the problem of evil in the archaic age … lay in the belief that a successful sinner should be punished in his descendants … The effectiveness of such a belief … depended in turn on a strong conviction of family solidarity … In such a situation, sins against the father or the family group are especially horrifying."[80] This formulation consequently invites a significant parallel between the myths of Oedipus and Genesis, as between the great periods of tragic drama in ancient Greece and Renaissance England, where in both instances a guilt culture historically encounters an emerging Enlightenment. Richard McCabe asserts that "The myth of Oedipus is powerful precisely because it is a myth of self-discovery, or questioning one's origins," and implies a conceptual link between these classical and biblical narratives when he poses a crucial point of contention: "Whether mythography be an art or a science remains very much an open question. Lord Bacon's appropriation of the Oedipus story to the cause of scientific advancement is a case in point. Natalis Comes's detection in the same material of an arcane theology akin to Christianity is another."[81]

Bacon's appropriation of the Oedipus myth in *The Wisdom of the Ancients* in fact offers a highly imaginative allegorical reading:

> Sphinx is said to have received from the Muses divers difficult questions and riddles, and to propound them unto men, [who while] remaining [only] with the Muses are free … from savage cruelty: for so long as there is no other ende of studie and meditation, then to know; the understanding is not rackt and imprisoned, but enjoyes freedome and libertie, and even in doubts and variety findes a kind of pleasure and delectation: but once these *Ænigmaes* are delivered by the Muses to *Sphinx*, that is, to practise, so that it bee sollicited and urged by action, and election, and determination; then they beginne to be troublesome and raging; and unlesse they be resolved and expedited, they doe wonderfully torment and vexe the minds of men, distracting, and in a manner rending them into sundry parts.

Those who confront the Sphinx earn for themselves either madness ("distraction of minde") or a kingdom, "for he that knowes that which he sought to knowe, hath attained the end he aimed at, and every artificer also commands over his worke." Success thus comes in the form of Oedipal mastery over the external world, but Bacon is alive enough to the ambiguity of the myth to point out that there are two kinds of kingdoms or "emperies," one over nature (the objective world), and the other over man (the subjective world): "But that Aenigma propounded to Oedipus (by means of which hee obtained the Thebane Empire) belonged to the nature of man: For whosoever doth th[o]roughly consider the nature of man, may be, in a manner, the contriver of his own fortune, and is borne to command."[82]

Thus mastery of the external world is inextricably tied to self-mastery, and self-mastery depends precariously on things one may not or cannot know about oneself; as Perkins points out, "a man cannot always discerne what be the thoughts of his own heart." Debora Shuger has described Calvinist anthropology as deriving "from Erasmus's tripartite division of the psyche into sinful flesh, self-protective maternal nature" – which is presumably close to the tendency to fantasize an overly indulgent and protective deity which Perkins refutes (as observed above) – and "the spiritual law of the Father." Such psychic structure "seems less an early version of Cartesian dualism than a precursor of the Freudian allegory of id, ego, and superego. In the Calvinist passion narratives, the divided and discontented urban male who struggles to repress 'nature' out of obedience to the interior sacrificial command is an early victim of the civilizing process."[83] This assertion in a sense develops observations Shuger makes in an earlier study: "Descartes ... differs from earlier thinkers not by distinguishing soul from body but by insisting on an absolute distinction, whereas his predecessors generally made a more fluid and partial separation between the corporeal and incorporeal." The more fluid model of the self, or rather an anxious response concerning it, admittedly led, in the Renaissance, to "the obsessive desire for systematic order evident in the compulsive symmetries of Ramist dichotomizing" and "the visceral hatred of 'mixture' that pervades Calvinism."[84] But the more fluid model also illuminates the anxieties of our post-Enlightenment world, where the Freudian model itself has re-introduced or re-emphasized the mysterious indeterminacy of the exact border between the psychic and the somatic. Is the unconscious physical or metaphysical? Who can tell? Part of the problem here is that Freud, who insisted that he was a scientist and a materialist, was really a mythographer, an analyst of discourse with a predilection for its moral and metaphysical meanings – although this recognition admittedly returns us to the question posed by McCabe about mythography itself. For me the uncertain ontological status of the human mind renders such questions unanswerable. But the crucial point is that we need to admit that the mystery is necessary, inevitable – and that the particular anxiety over our inability to decide these questions is, at least in one sense, futile.[85]

If we are prepared to accept the validity of Shuger's claim regarding Calvinist anthropology's resemblance to a Freudian model of the psyche, we need to look more closely at the dyad of Heavenly Father and Heavenly Son. In her extended analysis of the Calvinist passion narratives, Shuger traces a highly complex pattern of both emotional expression and reader response:

> [These narratives] depict Christ's relation to this Father as an unstable compound of dependence, self-assertion, obedience, and subversion … The Son who meekly obeys the Father at the same time attacks him, the demand for submission itself eliciting a repressed anger. Christ is simultaneously child, champion, dutiful son, and aggressor … As the reader turns out to incarnate both the victim and the torturer, so Christ ends up, as most oedipal sons do, becoming *like* his Father. Although the crucifixion scenes are structured by the contrast between the harsh patriarch and the desolate child, the apocalyptic Christ depicted in the same passion narratives burns with paternal wrath.[86]

While speculations about peculiar emotional identifications within scenarios of hypothesized reader response often seem highly problematic or tendentious, I suggest that within this particular historical context we can offer the following generalization: if Christ ends up becoming *like* his Father, the main political and psychological ramifications revolve around the mechanism through which the reader or audience member – in this case early modern, English, and to at least some extent under the influence of the dominant Calvinist theological ethos – ends up becoming *like* Christ.

In Marlowe I see a response to the radical individualism inherent in Calvinist theology which approaches the dangerous limit of the Arian heresy. The danger is evident not only in Marlowe's interest in a particular document which was instrumental – to what degree it was also accidental is probably impossible to determine – in his premature death. Such danger, we should recognize, was not limited simply to the circumstances surrounding the Dutch Church Libel and the unfortunate consequential searching of Kyd's lodging and papers.[87] Park Honan points out that in the early 1580s Marlowe was dining in hall at Cambridge with Francis Kett, a "shy, introverted man" who in 1589 was – shockingly in the reign of a queen who famously did not wish to make windows into men's souls – burned to death as an Arian heretic: "that such a man had been a Fellow is one index of an atmosphere in which deep feeling, along with eccentricity, folly, and intelligence, had thrived at Corpus Christi."[88] Kett's fate also serves as a stark reminder of how threatening the Arian heresy was to the Elizabethan ecclesiastical authorities, and how early modern individuals heroically paid with their lives for daring to inquire into the logic of the Christian doctrine of the Atonement, for even speculating on issues we can now debate calmly and safely in our intellectual exchanges and historical investigations.

Shakespeare, characteristically more circumspect than Marlowe, probably embraced the possibilities of radical Protestant self-conceptions less directly and emotionally due to a natural detachment arising from his likely Catholic upbringing. Kenneth Graham argues that "the idea of a consistently Catholic Shakespeare has not met with widespread acceptance," even though the best scholarship devoted to this particular investigation has not "claimed to find such a consistency."[89] My position is that, in his conception of the possibilities of masculine self-fashioning, Shakespeare as an artist may be understood as responding to, not against, the Reformation, in spite of his social origins within a Catholic family.[90] But while fate granted Shakespeare a much greater length of time to develop as an artist, and therefore a broader range within which to conduct his dramatic explorations, the final position he reaches with respect to Christian theology seems, to repeat my central assertion, at least as unorthodox.

Shakespeare and the Family of Love

For Shakespeare there is admittedly no personal involvement with an Arian treatise to consider, but I offer another possible source of Arian heretical influence, as a concomitant to his own artistic response to Marlowe's dramatic examples. In *Magic and Masculinity*, at the end of a discussion of the second tetralogy, I hazard the speculation that

> the extreme inwardness of Hal's quest for perfection, coupled with a disturbingly duplicitous tolerance/contempt for his (secretly) despised, less disciplined companions, may have some connection ... to the "radical" sect known as the Family of Love. This sect was characterized by a deeply hierarchical vision that, while it stressed human perfectibility, distinguished spiritual novices from elders and ranked membership according to spiritual maturity. The Family of Love was harshly condemned by some Puritan writers, perhaps partly because of its ability to insinuate itself, through what was considered a hypocritical conformity, within the political hierarchy of Elizabethan England.[91]

I must here emphasize, and clarify, the tension – in fact the serious clash – between Puritans and the Family of Love. A deservedly influential study, Kristen Poole's *Radical Religion from Shakespeare to Milton*, offers an essential reading of Shakespeare's portrayal of Oldcastle, renamed Falstaff, as consistent with late sixteenth-century representations of grotesque Puritans living in carnivalesque communities. Yet Poole's subsequent treatment of the Family of Love unfortunately, and I think mistakenly, tries to fit this sect too readily into the same ideological mould of antinomian excess and carnal indulgence.[92] To make her argument, Poole questionably conflates responses to the sect from different historical moments within the early modern period, responses which Christopher Marsh, author of *The Family of Love in English Society, 1550–1630*, more carefully distinguishes.

My description of the ideology of this sect is drawn primarily from the Familist Crisis of 1576–82, and the attacks of the Elizabethan Puritan writers John Rogers, William Wilkinson, and John Knewstub. A later crisis was indeed catalysed in 1604 when "the Family's spokesmen ... broke a fifteen-year silence to speak up in defence of their fellowship," motivated probably by fears that King James would renew the earlier Elizabethan campaign. Unfortunately for the Family, the resultant *Supplication* was printed two years later in Cambridge "with the addition of lengthy and vitriolic editorial 'Examinations'." The anonymous Examiner's

> conscious motivation for attacking the Family was less theological than had been the case with Wilkinson, Rogers and Knewstub. He was predominantly impassioned by the positions the Familists had successfully taken up in this world, rather than by their views on the next. It was their talent as upstarts that really rankled, and the Examiner was far more intent than the three Elizabethans writers upon alleging that the Familists were sexually immoral [and] subverters of earthly authority.[93]

For another more recent and succinct treatment of why the intense Elizabethan attacks on the Family so abruptly and mysteriously ceased in the early 1580s, readers may consult Christopher Carter's "The Family of Love and Its Enemies." Carter observes that Familist doctrine "revived a positive Pelagian view of the capacities of the human will, one which came into conflict with the more Augustinian view of English puritans on the home island of Pelagius." Expanding on Marsh's discussion, Carter argues that "reformers made [their] attack on the Family a key battle with conservatives ... The reformers tried to transform the Family from a menace to religious peace into a threat to civil peace and to portray Familists, like Catholics, as a subversive group of potential traitors." But to a significant extent this attack under Elizabeth backfired: "Through their actions, the reformers created an illusion of danger in this period [1577–82], which then evaporated when the conservative faction [at court] triumphed and silenced the reformers' attacks."[94] This local and temporary "triumph" led, I suggest, to an increased interest in, if not respect for, Familist doctrine in the second half of Elizabeth's reign.

My intention with respect to the Family of Love is not to offer proof of Shakespeare's actual membership in this sect, but rather to argue that he was familiar with the theological thinking of the movement, which possibly influenced his own perceptions. Such familiarity at least is not surprising. As David Wootton observes, the sect was not, as is sometimes asserted,[95] only distantly marginal in Elizabethan England: "In 1581 … the Jesuit Robert Parsons wrote that there were four, not three, religions in England. They were Catholicism, Protestantism, Puritanism, and the Household of Love"; and Wootton adds in a footnote, "So too *Leicester's Commonwealth* (1584) takes the three major religious groupings in England to be 'Papists, Puritans, Familians'."[96] Wootton claims in this essay Donne's membership in the Family of Love, citing William Empson as a "distinguished precursor" in this theory. In another, earlier essay Wootton very interestingly argues for the inclusion of Abraham Fleming, editor of the posthumous edition of Holinshed's *Chronicles* (1587), and Reginald Scot, famous author of *The Discoverie of Witchcraft* (1584), within this theological group.[97] The former author, certainly, and the latter author, in *A Midsummer Night's Dream* and *Macbeth* at least, were sources for Shakespeare. Wootton cites the work of Marsh, and, in the later essay, of Peter Lake,[98] and offers claims that range from very persuasive, to somewhat persuasive, to occasionally questionable.[99] It is not for me to judge this strategy too harshly, however, since I attempt a similar "accumulation of detail, an intellectual [and literary] microhistory to complement the social microhistory of Marsh's work"[100] in order to suggest a possible influence on Shakespeare.

The daring and remarkable Scot, and other sceptical writers such as Samuel Harsnett, had a significant influence on Shakespeare, as well as on other early modern English playwrights.[101] Despite his fairly virulent anti-Catholicism, Scot's humaneness and pragmatism would, I think, increase his appeal for Shakespeare. Yet Scot's supposed affiliation with the Family of Love does pose an interesting problem, or apparent contradiction. Like Sydney Anglo before him, Wootton objects to the omission of the final section of the *Discoverie*, "A Discourse upon divels and spirits," from editions of Scot's work and therefore from scholarly consideration. Anglo calls this section the *"sine qua non* of Scot's work, for it makes clear ... the extent to which the author was prepared to go in his denial of the supernatural ... [Scot] can find nothing in the Scriptures to support the view that either angels or devils have any corporeal existence"; hence their appearances in biblical narratives constitute primarily metaphorical expressions.[102] In that final section of the *Discoverie*, however, Scot also condemns the Family of Love in the course of his insistence on metaphorical readings of the Bible, in this case of Genesis:

> And yet, if the divell should have entred into the snake ... I cannot see in what degree of sinne the poore snake should be so guiltie, as that God, who is the most righteous judge, might be offended with him. But although I abhorre that lewd interpretation of the familie of love, and such other heretikes, as would reduce the whole Bible into allegories; yet (me thinkes) the creeping there is rather metaphoricallie or significativelie spoken, than literallie ... Wherein the divell is resembled to an odious creature, who as he creepeth upon us to annoie our bodies; so doth the divell there creepe into the conscience of Eve.[103]

Wootton acknowledges this passage, but notes the "paradoxical sentence, in which the views of the Family of Love are simultaneously condemned and adopted."[104] Given the Family of Love's notorious support for Nicodemism, an ethical position in support of politically defensible or necessary dissembling, Scot's rhetorical position may be explicable. But Wootton does not raise the issue at this point in his argument, likely because the composition of *The Discoverie*, while courageous and daring, was also voluntary, and theoretically does not involve Scot unwillingly in a position where he must misrepresent his beliefs. Still, in spite of his expression of abhorrence at heresy, Scot must have been aware he was expressing opinions that many of his contemporaries would regard as heretical. Thus while an exact reading of his motives is difficult here, he is clearly expressing radical theological opinions shared by a distinct subculture of his time.

In addition to the speculations of Wootton regarding Donne, Scot, and Fleming, Margaret Healy has more recently considered Shakespeare himself in light of Family of Love influences. Healy interprets Shakespeare's use of alchemical imagery as a kind of refusal of binaries which she relates to ecumenical tendencies of H.N. – the Dutch mystic Hendrick Niclaes, the Family's founder – who welcomed both Protestant and Catholic believers.[105] Healy cites the following passage in Marsh to make her case: "H.N. was deeply troubled by the confessional divisions and religious violence that had come to mark his age, and his message was designed to transcend all other conflicts. The shedding of innocent blood was to cease, as Christians, Jews, Muslims, Turks and heathens all responded to the call." But Marsh also adds the following disturbing qualification that Healy ignores: "This peaceable intent, however, sometimes seemed to evaporate in the fiery heat of H.N.'s insistence that no hope of salvation existed for those outside the Family of Love."[106] Healy pursues a line of argument that downplays the possibility of Pauline dualism: she suggests a "Pauline authority [citing Ephesians 2:14–19] for the alchemical aversion to binaries" that she detects within the matrix of Shakespeare's allusions to Hermetic syncretism. I question this interpretation, since Pauline Christianity at its core – at least in its Reformation expression – directly contradicts what I believe to be the crux of the Family of Love's influence on early modern English writers. According to Marsh:

> In the England of the 1570s, H.N.'s understanding of the part played by Christ in the salvation of humans (soteriology) was highly distinctive. The Christ of protestant theology was inimitable in his perfection while on earth; the salvation of sinful humanity could come from believing in his sacrifice, but not from copying his example … For H.N., in stark contrast, the passion of Christ seemed almost meaningless without the positive belief that it could be directly reproduced within the spirit of the believer. Christ was to be imitated in all that he had gone through – crucifixion, death, burial, *resurrection* and *ascension*.[107]

The idea of human perfectibility, what the Family of Love refers to as becoming "godded with God," potentially plays a significant role in the historical undermining, or at least interrogation, of the Pauline emphasis on the necessary mediation of a personal Christ to deliver suffering humanity from the "body of this death."

In short, the writings of H.N. and his followers offer Shakespeare (whatever his personal involvement) a significant precedent for his critique, throughout his plays, of the masculine *incapacity* inherent in Pauline theology. The question arises, what then is the difference between the doctrine of the Family of Love and the Arian heresy, and what distinctions need to be made between these heretical influences? Indeed, Wootton describes the first missionary of the Family of Love in England, Christopher Vittels, as an "Arrianizing mechanic preacher,"[108] although Marsh documents how Vittels, unlike Francis Kett, successfully deflected and denied the charge of Arianism when examined by Archbishop Grindal,[109] perhaps some proof of the sect's promulgation of Nicodemism. Peter Lake's exploration of later conflicts in the 1620s between a Puritan divine, Stephen Dension, and a layman with decidedly Familist leanings, John Etherington, contains descriptions of the latter's belief that potently evoke Arian belief. Although in his initial comparison of these men's theological positions Lake does not directly identify the Arian component, he does recognize that Etherington, by including the following passage in one of his publications, effectively transforms it "into a full-blown familist manifesto":

> And is that angel, flying in the midst of heaven, having an everlasting gospel to preach to them that dwell upon the earth, saying Christ is not nor was not a man, as ye suppose, but holiness is Christ. And he that doth believe it is possible to keep all the ten commandments hath the right faith in Christ and they that do attain to the perfect keeping of them are risen from the dead, according to the scriptures, and as holiness is Christ and the son of God, so sin is Antichrist and the son of the devil.[110]

In spite of this radical, and (historically) clearly lingering, theological potential, Family of Love doctrine in the late 1570s was identified by the Puritan reformers as "a dangerous crypto-Catholic force," as Christopher Carter's argument indicates.[111] In her speculations concerning the various "crossovers" between sects promoting a mystical but socially progressive sense of spiritual community – Familists, spiritual alchemists, and Hermetic writers and philosophers – Healy cites Alastair Hamilton's supposition that while "the Family of Love seems to have initially attracted more Catholics, Rosicrucianism possibly had a greater affinity with Protestantism," although the expression of the assertion is vaguer in Hamilton, and it is unclear whether he is addressing, through this claim, the continental or the English context.[112] Apparently, clear-cut doctrinal distinctions become more different to maintain when one delves deeply into heretical contexts of early modern Europe. Shakespeare's Catholic upbringing *may* have predisposed him to an interest in Familist doctrine, but the same argument might be made concerning the radically Protestant Marlowe, who was notoriously noted by Baines as sympathetic to Catholicism: "That if there be any god or any good Religion, then it is in the papistes because the service of god is performed with more ceremonies, as Elevation of the mass, organs, singing men, Shaven Crownes, &cta. That all protestantes are Hypocriticall asses."

Such a claim recalls Jeffrey Knapp's crucial description of Shakespeare framing his plays as sacraments "whose real power lay in the minds of its spectators." Marlowe and Shakespeare are particularly focused on the power of the audience's imagination, and thus resistant to a doctrine, like solifidianism, which, by its insistence that such faith comes only through the grace of God, inhibits or distorts humanist self-integration. This point, as it connects to the concept of imaginative agency defined in the Introduction, will be of the utmost importance in the subsequent exploration of play-texts. It is, conversely, also possible to argue that the Protestant reading of the Eucharist as purely symbolic actually encourages a more internalized, independent, and psychologically comprehensive self-fashioning than does the doctrine of transubstantiation; that is, if anxiety about election – and about the mysterious (and mysteriously *limited*) Atonement of Christ – can be allayed. Such an argument would also draw us closer to the kind of symbolic or figurative readings of spiritual process, and a weakening of a belief in (literal) atonement, that characterizes Familist thought. Therefore I am reluctant to make any hard and fast generalizations, with respect to their specific role in the generation of heretical interest, about the Catholic and Protestant tendencies of the two playwrights. In the end, Shakespeare provides a broader, more constructive or systematic critique of theological constraints because he had more time to develop, artistically, a comprehensive sociological vision within his plays. Nevertheless both playwrights set a course that interrogates, and attempts to circumvent, a more traditional Christology.

H.N.'s distinctive soteriology may in fact explain the odd contradiction between his ecumenicalism and his fiery exclusiveness. The doctrinal structure of the Family of Love apparently makes a necessary distinction between individual psychological concerns and larger sociological ones. There is presumably a distinct focus on "personal" spiritual resources during the journey through which H.N.'s followers "are growen-upp obedientlie in the Service of the Love; from the Youngnes of their Understandinge, till unto the Olde-aige of the Man Christ."[113] Such a conception places the Family of Love's belief in the gradual perfectibility of humans in a decidedly different context from the "heresie of perfection" that Gifford complains of in the Brownists and other Puritan separatists, who (he believes) ignore necessary hierarchies within church government and within society at large. It is not therefore surprising that in England the Puritans turned out to be the Family's most vocal critics. Perhaps supporting Hamilton's claim above, Marsh observes that "Although [H.N.] was criticised both by Catholics and by protestants, his theological position and his hostile attitude to the Reformation combined to ensure that his most vehement opponents espoused the new religion rather than the old."[114]

I offer a brief sampling here of comments by John Knewstub, whom Marsh identifies as the most "zealous" of H.N.'s opponents. In his *Confutation of monstrous and horrible heresies*, Knewstub initially objects that

H.N. "expoundeth the doctrine of our resurrection Allegorically, and taketh it to be nothing els: but to ryse in our judgemente and affection, from the liking of all other, too the embracing of his doctrine and religion. And therefore the day of judgement which wee looke for, is in his opinion, already come, because the troumpe of his doctrine now soundeth, which worketh this his spiritual resurrection." Not only does Knewstub resent H.N. setting himself up blasphemously as a kind of Christ figure, but his doctrine, and his scriptural interpretation, clearly leave little room for Christ's singular sacrifice or essential mediation, and Knewstub anticipates Etheridge's later radical vision in the following passage: "Adam with H.N. is no man, but an estate of men, yet subject unto sinne: and Christ likewise is with him no man, but a combination of men altogether void of sinne. Therfore al his young disciples be Adams, [and] all his illuminate elders be Christs." Moreover, the Family of Love clearly opposes the Protestant doctrine of *sola fide* in addressing expectations of a true spiritual-but-human agency among its followers: "faith is nothing but deeds in [H.N.'s] opinion: Love is beliefe: believing is working: and loving or working, is become beleeving. For he will have our woorkes and obedience unto the lawe to get and give unto us the name of beleevers, that in so doing we may be accounted faithfull, and the same should be not a fruite of faith, but faith it self." Finally, anti-papist sentiment clearly fuels Knewstub's dislike of H.N.'s apparent sympathy with Catholicism:

> … speaking of the offices, and functions that were in the Churche of Rome, whereof he sheweth great liking, as beyng figurative services of that trueth which H.N. hath newely started, he saith of the parishe Priestes: Therefore they were joined with others, in the service of the holy worde, because they let passe the childhood, or the yongnes of the holy understanding, & grew up according to the requiring of the service of love, unto the manly agedness of Christ, that is, unto the true being, of the oldest & holiest father.[115]

Not only does the Family's doctrine resist the infantilizing potential of a theology of grace, but the implicit or tentative disavowal of substitutionary atonement via Christ's mediation which we observed in Gifford's Oedipal identifications is here made explicit.

Contrariety and Individuation

Thus, from our later historical perspective it is possible to see past Knewstub's partisan Puritan outrage to discover a serious psychological and sociological critique at work in H.N.'s theological positions, and to understand the careful structuring of individual maturation within the hierarchies of the Family of Love as the basis for the coherence of the larger spiritual society, which otherwise threatens to degenerate into what Christopher Lasch, in an analysis of our own contemporary malaise, has termed a culture of narcissism: "The achievement of selfhood [involves] the acknowledgement of our separation from the original source of life, combined with a continuing struggle to recapture a sense of primal union by means of activity that gives us a provisional understanding and mastery of the world without denying our limitations and dependency."[116] Healy commendably encourages our review of the "voices of toleration, peace and social cohesion" among the "Christocentric spiritual-philosophical movements that flourished in the late sixteenth and early seventeenth centuries," but somewhat naïvely castigates present-day scholarship's obsession with "binaries" and "the strident voices of intemperate extremes" as an obstacle in our path to fully realizing such a utopian social vision.[117] It may be more realistic to suggest that a truly tolerant society will have an investment in establishing structures of discipline and expectations of individuation which discourage narcissistic identifications, in order to avoid the kind of nightmare that Freud describes, with prophetic intensity, in *Civilization and Its Discontents*: "When once the Apostle Paul had posited universal love between men as the foundation of his Christian community, extreme intolerance on the part of Christendom towards those who remained outside it became the inevitable consequence."[118] Freud describes here not only the dreadful course of anti-Semitism in human history, but (potentially) the effects of any kind of excessive human idealization as a political force that, in seeking a radical purification or a magically precipitous instantiation of its vision, posits the extermination of, rather than the courageous confrontation of or dialectical interaction with, its ideological opponents or demonized "other."

We must therefore, I contend, acknowledge the groping towards a kind of necessary Oedipalization of social structure in the theological tracts and heretical theological formulations of early modern England. The uncertainty, the anxiety, and the sometimes violent struggle inherent in the ideological contradictions I have been exploring may explain the tragic nature of much of the literature produced during this period. Thomas McAlindon has powerfully described Shakespeare's "fundamentally traditional" understanding of nature as a reflection of a pre-modern cosmology which "construed the world not only as a hierarchical structure of corresponding planes but also as a dynamic system of interacting, interdependent opposites." McAlindon contrasts a Heraclitean worldview of clashing opposites with a Pythagorean worldview of harmonious blending opposites, and suggests that an Empedoclean model – which "combined these two theories to produce the pluralist doctrine that nature is governed by both Love and Strife" – established a philosophical precedent which would eventually help Shakespeare regard both the vision of harmonious hierarchy and that of endless conflict and competition as "polemical simplifications." While the critic implies that dialectical explorations of inherent contrariety offer a richer, more truthful reflection of human experience than facile assumptions of unruffled hierarchical order, he also, as he attempts to come to terms with the more sceptical philosophical movements of the twentieth century, challenges the assumption of much recent criticism that the binary structure of "Shakespearian complementarity resists all resolution."[119] I agree that the inherent instability of the created cosmos, of the physical manifestation of human experience, does not necessarily result in an artistic vision that can only confirm the instability of all meaning and moral value, and I would further emphasize McAlindon's crucial questioning of the postmodern assumption that Shakespearean complementarity is "essentially phenomenological rather than onto-logical, a product of consciousness rather than of nature." I therefore pointedly return here to my earlier emphasis on the reality of not just nature but "embodiment," and my critique (via Montaigne) of the tendency towards magical thinking in the Renaissance, which is ironically reflected in certain postmodern theoretical tendencies. But I also contend that McAlindon, while he commendably reasserts the importance of the role of time and temporal development, and therefore of physical and psychic processes, in early modern cultural depictions, underestimates the centrality of Christian conceptions of human identity and human agency in the often tragic struggles that Shakespeare, as well as Marlowe, depicts. In our pursuit of "resolution" and meaning, the tension between hierarchy and conflict needs to be further explored in psychological terms – that is, through the more specific tensions between love and discipline, control and relinquishment, identification and succession, self-mastery and (partial) mastery of the external conditions of life – even as they contest traditional Christian formulations.

Chapter Two

Dido Queen of Carthage, Hamlet, and the Transformation of Narcissism

Hamlet's Allusion to *Dido Queen of Carthage*

It is sometimes observed that Phoebe's couplet in *As You Like It* – "Dead shepherd, now I find your saw of might: / 'Who ever loved that loved not at first sight?'" (3.5.81–2) – is the only occasion in which Shakespeare directly acknowledges and quotes the work of a contemporary author. But it pales by comparison to the even greater compliment Shakespeare bestows on Marlowe in *Hamlet*, where the surviving playwright actually incorporates what amounts to a highly positive theatre review of Marlowe's first play.[1] And such praise arises, apparently, even in spite of the lack of enthusiasm with which *Dido Queen of Carthage* was greeted by its initial audience. As Hamlet states to the First Player:

> I heard thee speak me a speech once, but it was never acted, or if it was, not above once, for the play, I remember, pleased not the million; 'twas caviar to the general. But it was – as I received it, and others, whose judgments in such matters cried in the top of mine – an excellent play, well digested in the scenes, set down with as much modesty as cunning … One speech in't I chiefly loved: 'twas Aeneas' tale to Dido, and thereabout of it especially when he speaks of Priam's slaughter. (2.2.434–48)

The review is strikingly specific in its rhetorical praise: "I remember one said there were no sallets in the lines to make the matter savory, nor no matter in the phrase that might indict the author of affectation, but called it an honest method, as wholesome as sweet, and by very much more handsome than fine" (440–5). If we accept Bevington's editorial suggestions, this analysis apparently approves the play's avoidance of "spicy improprieties," commending its "well-proportioned" rather than "elaborately ornamented" language. While Shakespeare's fiction here may not necessarily reflect an accurate record of the playwright's assessment of Marlowe's rhetoric in *Dido*, these remarks by Hamlet are in fact curiously literary, or literary critical, observations for the prince of Denmark to make at this moment in the tragic action.

The meaning of the allusion must be assessed, then, not only in the general, and profound, mythical context evoked by the constellation of Virgil, Marlowe, and Shakespeare, but also in the more specific critical and psychological responses of Shakespeare to his dramatic precursor. With respect to the mythical resonance of the Troy narrative, historicist critics remind us that the fall of Troy, which now "seems important ... because of its 'literary' merits," was one of the "foundational myths" of medieval and early modern European culture. Alan Shepard and Stephen D. Powell argue that the myth was crucial in justifying aspirations "toward empire, or at least toward cohesive notions of national identity."[2] For early modern society in particular, I would add that the myth was also crucial in consolidating – and conversely, also undermining – cohesive notions of a new masculinity participating in the foundation of the nation-state. It may not be an exaggeration to suggest that in the Renaissance the narrative in many ways carried comparable significance to the creation story of Genesis. Tracing the significance of the myth for Spenser, James Carscallen provocatively argues that the Elizabethan poet's story of "Troy becoming his own England is ... a kind of scripture" which mirrors "the Trojan scripture that Virgil had produced for Rome."[3]

Classical and Christian Influence on *Dido Queen of Carthage*

We might temporarily simplify our approach to the question of influence by asserting that, while Shakespeare is clearly responding both to Virgil and Marlowe, Marlowe at least can be understood as responding primarily to Virgil. Yet such an approach would itself be oversimplification, and I wish to begin by considering a significant critical attempt to account for the oddness or ambivalence of tone in *Dido Queen of Carthage*, the perennial question of whether Marlowe is offering a seriously tragic, or rather a comical-satirical, version of Virgil, which in some crucial ways echoes a perennial question concerning Marlowe's art in general.[4] Timothy Crowley in fact wishes to assert that the supposed ambivalence of tone arises from a misunderstanding of Marlowe's artistic purposes regarding "the play's self-consciousness about its own theatrical parody rooted in compound *imitatio*." While earlier commentators have recognized a "generally Ovidian spirit" within the play, Crowley suggests a more controlled deployment of Ovid: "The play's imitation is not merely 'eclectic,' nor does it rhetorically suspend in a noncommittal way the Vergilian and Ovidian foundations upon which the ideological legacy of Troy stands. Rather, it consistently critiques the *Aeneid* and deploys Ovid for its unique parody of Vergil."[5] I wish to complicate this claim for an Ovidian interrogation of Virgil's Aeneas by adding a further layer of analysis, a consideration of a "Christian" Marlowe to Crowley's classical Marlowe. In doing so, I observe again a simultaneously parodic and serious treatment of imagery which circulates around the manifestation of a secular Christ (in this case, potentially, Aeneas as founder of a new order). This return to a more dialectical adjudication of the tone and morality of Marlowe's first play will elucidate the reasons that the early Marlowe held such a fascination for Shakespeare at the height of his career. Marlowe's implicit recognition of Christianity's, and in particular Calvinism's, psychologically constricting, even traumatizing tendencies, and an intensifying, more explicit recognition and subsequent amelioration by Shakespeare through the promotion of what I have designated "imaginative agency," together represent the real essence of the thematic and ideological link between the two plays.

Like previous commentators, Crowley must account for the surprisingly tenuous masculinity of Marlowe's Aeneas, "who remains both aware of and controlled by the power of language … Dido's hold on Aeneas has less to do with erotic attraction than with rhetorical persuasion." After his announcement of his dream from Hermes and his first attempt at departure in 4.3, Aeneas feebly resists Dido's attempt in 4.4 to ensure his continuing commitment to Carthage by exclaiming:

> How vain am I to wear this diadem
> And bear this golden scepter in my hand!
> A burgonet [small helmet] of steel and not a crown,
> A sword and not a sceptre fits Aeneas. (40–3)

For Crowley, "the play's audience could not escape the impression that Aeneas simply regurgitates the soldier's rhetoric impressed upon him in 4.3." The critic eventually observes that "Marlowe's Dido (and Marlowe as playwright) treats Aeneas like a blameless puppet," citing Rick Bowers to assert that Aeneas's "impetus for leaving Carthage is the same as that for staying: someone else is always 'organiz[ing] his desire'." Thus, Crowley can conclude, "In this radically non-Vergilian fourth act, Marlowe's pseudo-Ovidian Aeneas remains constant only in his impulse toward personal metamorphosis."[6]

While Aeneas's lack of genuine erotic attraction for Dido may certainly be relatable to a homoerotic displacement at work in the play and thus connected to the "high camp" that Bowers observes there, I suggest that Crowley's "pseudo-Ovidian Aeneas" and his susceptibility to discursive construction needs to be reconsidered as at the same time a "Calvinist Aeneas," with a theological basis for his uncertain masculinity and his treatment as a "blameless puppet."[7] In Reformation England the Virgilian theme of Roman destiny with which Jupiter assures Venus – who in Marlowe has anxiously speculated that "religion has no recompense" – would certainly carry overtones of Calvinist predestination:

> Content thee, Cytherea, in thy care,
> Since thy Aeneas' wand'ring fate is firm,
> Whose weary limbs shall shortly make repose
> In those fair walls I promis'd him of yore. (1.1.81–5)

The very Virgilian emphasis on "walls" in this passage, as the ultimate establishment of a new phase of civilization and of masculine ego boundaries, finds in Marlowe the very un-Virgilian repetition of the image in the form of quasi-maternal protection in a female embrace,[8] as Marlowe's Aeneas (unlike Virgil's) succumbs to Dido's pleas and asserts, "This is the harbor that Aeneas seeks, / Let's see what tempests can annoy me now" (4.4.59–60). As Crowley observes, Aeneas "now priz[es] her love as a 'harbour' that protects him from his 'wayward' destiny."[9] Thus Marlowe's version combines, provocatively, the desire for masculine self-authorization and for feminine nurturance. On a theological level, such combination may suggest Debora Shuger's intuition that in the Renaissance "fathers, especially divine fathers, are deeply endowed with what we call maternal attributes."[10] Indeed, in the opening scene Marlowe's Aeneas laments the vanishing of his mother Venus in terms which echo Christ on the cross: "Stay, gentle Venus, fly not from thy son! / Too cruel, why wilt thou forsake me thus?" (1.1.243–4). The conflicting desire for divine authorization and divine nurturance evoked in Marlowe also recalls, as we observed in chapter 1, William Perkins's surprising application of the doctrine of the Trinity in his attack on idolatrous religious conceptions, where the distinction between God the Father and God the Son staves off the apparent fantasy of an all-merciful God, framed according to that all-too-human desire for protection and nurturance, which Perkins wishes to repress.

Shuger in *Habits of Thought* considers whether "current notions of gender differentiation," specifically ones that attribute to fathers more despotism and control and less tenderness and nurturance, "may postdate the Renaissance." Perkins's Calvinist position would in this sense seem to anticipate more modern, less affectionate conceptions of father-hood.[11] Certainly forms of feminine, and maternal, identification are crucial in a consideration of the intertextuality of *Dido* and *Hamlet*, and I will attempt, below, to come to terms with their function within the plays. Nevertheless both plays suggest that the absence or the uncertainty of a viable paternal identification, exacerbated by theologically inconsistent conceptions of divine fatherhood, constitutes a significant, seemingly pivotal source of trauma for the vexed process of masculine self-fashioning. In the context of the intensification of secular culture which concerns Marlowe and Shakespeare, "Virgil's proclivity for building his theme around the loss of fathers and sons, thereby highlighting the problem of continuity," would have constituted a powerful attraction. Indeed, Anthony Dawson's consideration of "memorial repetition" in the two playwrights essentially defines the Reformation as an Oedipal moment, a "historical shift" involving "the growing sense … of England's global, Protestant destiny, combined with the nagging feelings of loss associated with the demise of Catholicism … the disappearance of embodied comforts before the mastery of a more rigorously austere religious aesthetic."[12]

Martial Masculinity and Christian Compromise

This general but powerful description of the period perhaps casts some doubt on Crowley's thesis of the "overall effect" of *Dido* as a satire of "Marlowe's contemporaries' investment in the Troy legacy." Crowley does end with an emphasis on Marlowe's "delightfully ruthless humour," and indeed the definitive study of humour in Marlowe, which recurs oddly and unexpectedly throughout the canon, probably remains to be written.[13] Yet the satire here takes on some darker overtones. Crowley's most intriguing point involves the consideration of another Shakespearean text: "King Henry's threat to the Governor of Harfleur in *Henry V* amplifies violent details from *Dido* 2.1.190–9: it provides a parallel image of old fathers' heads bashed in, changes the image of virgins skewered by pikes to that of virgins violated by soldiers, and intensifies that of infants bathing in their parents' blood to become 'naked infants spitted upon pikes' (3.3. … 27–41)." To an extent, Marlowe's parodic imitation of Virgil can be seen as a Renaissance critique of military aggression and martial *virtus*, since, "as in Marlowe's *Dido* and *Tamburlaine*, the anachronistic detail of pikes no doubt would evoke an impression of contemporary militarism. The King's speech containing this threat marks a divergence from Holinshed's *Chronicles*, Shakespeare's main source, and it conveys the brutal nature of 'impious war' (3.3.15) to much the same theatrical effect as the description of

Troy's fall in *Dido* 2.1."[14] Crowley's reading is undeniably attractive to the postmodern mind, filled to overflowing with the horrors and catastrophes of the history of modern warfare.

That Shakespeare would share or sympathize with this vision has been plausibly suggested by Robin Headlam Wells in his important study *Shakespeare on Masculinity,* where he argues that Shakespeare himself "probably" shared the critic's own view that "the 'ethic of heroism' has no place in the modern world." Wells outlines two idealized poles of early modern masculinity represented mythologically by Hercules (the warrior) and Orpheus (the divinely inspired creative artist), and argues that through the Shakespeare canon as a whole the playwright gradually subsumes the former in the latter. Wells's doubts concerning the viability of the heroic ideal are based in part on a distinction between Aristotelian "moral virtue, which consists in a mean between extremes, and heroic virtue, which is a kind of greatness that defies description, an excess … of virtue." Thus "Tasso gets closer to the truth about the peculiar fascination of the epic hero when he admits that heroes defy conventional morality,"[15] a claim that invariably brings to mind a figure like Tamburlaine. Wells's reasoning, and his preference for moral over heroic virtue (according to these definitions), is persuasive, but his thesis may in a sense oversimplify or too easily downplay Shakespeare's ambivalent admiration for the Herculean hero, which (at least in one case) is clearly reflected in the notorious ambiguity of his Henry V. While it may be easier for the postmodern reader to regard Marlowe as a cynical satirist of martial values, a consistent equation of Marlovian soldiers and martial motifs with an inevitably pathological masculinity is also critically problematic.[16] Anti-war commentary within *Dido* through anachronistic military allusions and Shakespeare's subsequent imitation of this method are plausible as one aspect of the artistic intent in these dramatic texts, but inadequate as a blanket explanation for either or both playwrights' portrayal of, and obsession with, uncertain masculine self-construction. Moreover, an exposure of the brutal nature of "impious war," as Crowley's reading of *Henry V* intimates, does not preclude, perhaps tragically, the positive valuation of a potentially "pious" one. As chapter 1 observed, the Protestant clergyman George Gifford, in *A Treatise of True Fortitude,* attempts to argue that the existence of men "both godly and valiant" does not constitute an ideological contradiction. Indeed, the Virgilian source for both *Dido* and the Player's scene in *Hamlet* includes the most famously ambiguous of epic heroes (prior to Satan in *Paradise Lost*), with Aeneas torn psychologically between the values of *pietas* and *furor*. Clearly the ideological effect of the classical sources on both early modern plays needs to be considered in deeper psychological and even religious terms.

Martial masculinity holds a powerful attraction for early modern writers, and in some contexts at least may in fact function, imaginatively or symbolically, as an expression of valid and necessary – that is, not gratuitously violent – masculine assertion. Such artistic attraction needs to be read in the larger context of the dramatic portrayal of masculine self-fashioning within the theological and historical uncertainties of an emergent Protestant state, as described by Dawson. Hamlet recalls from Marlowe's play the specific description of the fall of Troy – the climax of the war, which easily invites an interpretation involving a symbolic expression of early modern psychological and political trauma. Yet the accounts of Marlowe and Shakespeare, as has been noted, contain significant variations. Ending any questions concerning Shakespeare's direct allusion to *Dido*, James Black observes that the Player's speech "uses details that are in *Dido* and not in the *Aeneid* (2:559–728): Priam's feeble attempt to struggle with Pyrrhus at close quarters; Priam being blown over by the wind of Pyrrhus' sword; Pyrrhus being interrupted – in *Dido* by Hecuba's attack on him, in *Hamlet* by the distraction of Troy crashing down in fire; the prolongation of the butchery of the old man; Pyrrhus standing like a statue (*Dido*) or a painting (*Hamlet*)."[17] Clearly the figure of the patriarch Priam, and his "desecration" by Pyrrhus, compels the artistic imagination of both Marlowe and Shakespeare. The element of ekphrasis – the description in literature of a visual work of art – in both playwrights probably derives from Virgil: the memorialization of human suffering, and martial competition, in art occurs significantly in the *Aeneid*, where the walls of Carthage's Temple of Juno are, oddly, already inscribed with the "historical" images of Trojan war (including the actions of Aeneas himself) when Aeneas and his men arrive. The close, tearful perusal of these scenes by the epic hero thus suggests a potential for narcissistic self-reflection even in the classical source.[18]

Marlowe appears to replace this episode with simply a statue of Priam, although the exact nature of the image to which his characters allude has been debated by critics – Priam's figure is arguably meant to represent one aspect of an expanded frieze or relief sculpture in stone. Nevertheless Aeneas's response to Priam's image is highly significant:

Achates, though mine eyes say this is stone,
Yet thinks my mind that this is Priamus;
And when my grieved heart sighs and says no,
Then would it leap out to give Priam life.
O, were I not at all, so thou [Priam] mightst be! (2.1.24–8)

In *The Irony of Identity* I suggested that the scene involving Priam's statue "involves an attempt at 'transmuting internalization' of an idealized self-object by which Aeneas can fill in a missing psychic structure."[19] In more general psychological (and theological) terms, Aeneas's rhetoric obviously displays a deep and desperate need to recover a source of masculine identification in the form of the patriarch Priam, whom Dawson nicely terms the "ur-father."[20] The desperation and tenuous self-image reveal a kind of weakness that suggests narcissism. The parallel to the psychological situation of the young Hamlet, who expresses suicidal urges consequent upon his father's death and mother's hasty remarriage even *before* the trauma of the Ghost's appearance, seems irresistible.[21] Hamlet expresses a highly similar binary of excessive, externalized idealization and striking personal inadequacy: "My father's brother, but no more like my father / Than I to Hercules" (1.2.152–3). Yet there is something about Aeneas's heroic self-surrender – the desire to revivify Priam through self-sacrifice – that is not quite consistent with the clinging dependency evoked through psychoanalytic theories of narcissism. There are Eucharistic overtones to Aeneas's response before the statue of Priam, recalling the gesture to self-sacrifice before the altar in the liturgy of the Communion: "And here we offer and present unto thee, O Lord, ourselves, our souls and bodies, to be a reasonable, holy and lively sacrifice unto thee."[22] That is, Aeneas's response suggests the vexed combination of personal inadequacy, desire for personal empowerment, and uncertain or shifting identification that characterizes masculine self-fashioning in a Reformation or Calvinist context, where the church has the duty "by bringing men into obedience of the Gospel, to offer them as it were in sacrifice unto God."[23]

In fact the generally more theological character of Marlowe's account can be underlined by considering one detail he includes during the butchery of Priam that is found in neither Shakespeare nor Virgil. When the king falls to the floor, recites Aeneas painfully,

> Then from the navel to the throat at once
> [Pyrrhus] ripp'd old Priam; at whose latter gasp
> Jove's marble statue gan to bend the brow,
> As loathing Pyrrhus for this wicked act. (2.1.255–8)

Priam's status as "ur-father" certainly renders this action on the part of Pyrrhus as nightmarishly Oedipal and patricidal, even while Pyrrhus completes the revenge for his own father Achilles' death. In Marlowe the assault magically affects the whole symbolic order as, in another brief ekphrasis, a statue of the father of the gods himself registers the abomination. In Shakespeare the violation is in a sense humanized. Rather than evoking a *higher* symbolic or metaphysical order, Shakespeare emphasizes the violation of Priam's own physical and political integrity.

One of Black's key claims, a very crucial one for an understanding of *Hamlet*, is that the Ghost's story of his murder by Claudius becomes, through the play's repeated representation of "the individual as microfortress," "a precis of Troy's last hours" which "culminates in the brutal slaughter of Priam in his domestic and religious sanctuary": "the Ghost's description of how poison invaded his system is only one instance among many of a recurring figure – the individual as beleaguered and embattled in mind and body."[24] Black emphasizes that, while attention to imagery of warfare has long been central to readings of *Hamlet*, the *kind* of warfare, specifically siege campaigns, needs more critical attention, since "Hamlet's [psychological and political] struggle has the elements of a siege war." In a subtle but provocative claim, Black observes: "Coming as it does after a long passage of prose in this scene of *Hamlet*, the florid style of the Player's speech suggests that Hamlet's experience – including the Ghost's story – is 'real,' even though – in fact, because – the Ghost's story has the same *topos* as the account of Priam's murder."[25]

This coincidence of the "reality" of experience and heightened imaginative reception draws us into one of the most crucial questions regarding the text of *Hamlet*, and in a sense the function of Renaissance dramatic art. In the case of *Dido*, the question of psychological realism raises the apparent conflict between the supposedly burlesque nature of the play, or its failure in evoking a truly tragic pathos, and Hamlet's claim that the play he recalls was "honest," not given to excessive rhetorical ornamentation, with "no matter in the phrase that might indict the author of affectation." Indeed, rereading Marlowe's play never fails to surprise me in terms of its psychological interest and poetic intensity. In spite of the awkwardness of the triple suicide at the end, the speeches, especially Dido's, are frequently deeply moving and poetically powerful, persuasively delineating conflicting emotional responses, as when Dido cannot refrain from expressing a mixture of deep love and deep hate in her response to the desertion of Aeneas:

> I hope that that which love forbids me do
> The rocks and sea-gulfs will perform at large
> And thou shalt perish in the billows' ways,
> To whom poor Dido doth bequeath revenge.
> ...

> Why starest thou in my face? If thou wilt stay,
> Leap in mine arms: mine arms are open wide.
> If not, turn from me, and I'll turn from thee;
> For though thou hast the heart to say farewell,
> I have not power to stay thee. (5.1.170–83)

If anything, Dido's responses – while set in a simpler register of characterization or psychological complexity – seem more genuine at times than the manipulative rhetoric with which Cleopatra plies Antony, in the tragedy which often features in critical analyses as, on one level, Shakespeare's response to *Dido*.[26]

That Marlowe's characterizations seem more innocent than Shakespeare's in *Antony and Cleopatra* may relate not only to the appearance of the play at the beginning of Marlowe's career but also to its status as a production by child actors, and indeed the sense of not only pervasive immaturity – of a decidedly narcissistic intensity – but also the very theme of constrained maturation[27] may help explain why Aeneas stands out as the most disturbing, unnerving presence in the play. Of the correspondences between characters in Shakespeare and Marlowe (and Virgil), Black focuses on the most important, highlighting "word-play" which, as far as I am aware, has occurred to no one else: "In the Player's speech from the old play, Hamlet, by speaking the first thirteen lines, casts himself as the tale-teller Aeneas, the looker-on who saw Priam killed and did not intervene (it is tempting to hear word-play on 'Aeneas' in his soliloquy just afterwards when he rages at himself for silence and inaction and says 'Why, what an ass am I!' …)."[28] Marlowe's version of Troy's destruction heightens the observer status of Aeneas in a way that suggests the voyeurism associated with narcissistic disorders.[29] Such voyeurism develops full-blown in the dramaturgy of Marlowe's subsequent creation, which replaces the tentative and oddly detached Aeneas with the cruelly rapacious conqueror Tamburlaine.

Shakespeare in *Hamlet* responds to the sense of psychological paralysis in Marlowe's Aeneas. Black, among many other critics, draws some significant parallels: "Lucianus [more word-play?] in 'The Murder of Gonzago' is both Claudius and Hamlet, poisoner and [as nephew to the king] avenger, just as Pyrrhus in the Player's speech was murderer of Priam and avenger of his father Achilles. [Harold] Jenkins and others note that Pyrrhus is also imaged in Hamlet standing over Claudius and '[doing] nothing'."[30] But that notorious phrase "Did nothing" from the Player's description of Pyrrhus "as a painted tyrant" also echoes Marlowe's lines, where Aeneas describes Pyrrhus's response after the slaughter of Priam: "So, leaning on his sword, he stood stone still, / Viewing the fire wherewith rich Ilion burnt" (2.1.263–4). As Richard Wilson keenly observes, "Marlowe's murdering idol 'stood stone still' ... *after* the massacre, contemplating [the effected] genocide with the pitilessness that excites Hamlet" (my emphasis). But *Hamlet*'s Pyrrhus pauses before the act of patricide, "extending the life-saving interim 'Between the acting of a dreadful thing / And the first motion' ([*Julius Caesar*] 2.1.63–4) into the eternal stasis of a picture." Thus "Pyrrhus' hesitation opens space for the *aesthetic*, as a hiatus within which a reckoning is endlessly deferred. Its caesura is not ... just a signal for the prince of indecision, but a template for art itself."[31]

The Development of Imaginative Agency

I propose to build on the difference in the moment of stasis in Marlowe and Shakespeare to make a major case for the production of imaginative agency in Shakespeare, which, as it emphasizes a sense of artistic responsibility, will qualify Wilson's assertion of an "endlessly deferred" artistic reckoning, as well as "pitilessness" as the source of Hamlet's excitement in *Dido*.[32] Like many critics, Wilson ultimately suggests Shakespeare's refusal or surrender of "Marlowe's pact with power" – as exemplified most obviously in *Faustus* – a surrender clearly rendered in *The Tempest*. Harold Bloom offers a similar reading of the nature of the influence on this point: "Shakespeare clearly is not an exalter of power: even Henry V is presented equivocally, and it is not sentimentalism to affirm that Falstaff, both in his glory and when he is rejected, meant more to Shakespeare and his audience than did England's hero-king." Yet there seems some kind of sentimentalism at work in Bloom's unending admiration for Falstaff, whom Shakespeare, as early as the latter stages of *1 Henry IV*, casts in a decidedly chilling light: "Tut, tut, good enough to toss; food for powder, food for powder. They'll fill a pit as well as better" (4.2.62–3). It is unclear to me how post-Holocaust readers can ever really recover from these lines from the mouth of the supposedly greatest comic creation in English literature. Bloom does add, significantly, "Yet without Marlowe, Shakespeare would not have learned how to acquire immense power over an audience."[33] Because Bloom believes Shakespeare's art is "beyond political ideology," he fails to perceive how the artistic responsibility to which he alludes here is but one facet of the larger networks of responsibility within human social interaction. In the course of his career Shakespeare revises, not surrenders, Marlowe's vision of imaginative control and domination, through analogies suggesting progressively less narcissistic and more productive forms of psychological and political influence.

Wells's theory of a gradual replacement of Herculean with Orpheus-like ideals of masculinity, as it elevates the artistic over the presumably coarser, violent temperament, remains therefore highly attractive, but even still may represent an oversimplification. The first necessary stage in the process of masculine individuation remains the development of the will towards heroic commitment of action, of some kind, even the risky or potentially violent kind.[34] That Shakespeare qualifies the "pitilessness," the odd but undeniable sadistic quality that recurs in Marlowe's writing, can be seen even in Crowley's consideration of the amplification of violent details from *Dido* in *Henry V*, quoted above. Shakespeare "changes the image of virgins skewered by pikes to that of virgins violated by soldiers": without in any way downplaying the savagery and brutality of rape, Shakespeare at least avoids the complete eradication of the female body that features in some of Marlowe's cruellest moments, such as Tamburlaine's nightmarish consignment of the Virgins of Damascus to excruciating and merciless execution in *1 Tamburlaine*: "there sits Death, there sits imperious Death, / Keeping his circuit by the slicing edge" (5.1.111–12). Even less directly violent moments in Marlowe contain this unexpected eradication of femaleness, such as when Aeneas's lament before the statue of Priam in *Dido* embellishes Virgil with Ovid through an allusion to the myth of Niobe, but in this exclusively male "elegy" the devastated mother weeps only for "her sons' death" (2.1.4) and not for her daughters', though she had seven of each slaughtered by Apollo and Diana.

While it is often observed that Marlowe has Aeneas fail to save three women (Creusa, Cassandra, Polyxena) in a row – thus building on the martial inadequacy of Virgil's Aeneas, who stands "unmanned" (2.731)[35] after witnessing the murder of the patriarch Priam – Marlowe significantly deletes the extremely moving encounter between Aeneas and the ghost of Creusa in Virgil. Whether this moment of pathos in any way anticipates the invention of heterosexual romantic love that C.S. Lewis famously dates to eleventh-century Provence,[36] it likely would not appeal to the more cynical reading of sexual passion which often characterizes Marlowe's work, with perhaps the most infamous example from *The Jew of Malta*: "Thou hast committed – / Fornication? But that was in another country: / And besides, the wench is dead" (4.1.40–2). But perhaps the most telling change that Crowley identifies in Shakespeare's modification of *Dido*'s rhetoric of atrocity in *Henry V* is the rendering of Marlovian infants bathing (literally "swimming") in their parents' blood as "naked infants spitted upon pikes." While Shakespeare's deliberately horrific image may anticipate British propaganda during the First World War concerning German troops parading with babies on their bayonets, it nevertheless lacks the nightmarish lack of *affect* that characterizes Marlowe's indifferent offspring, which underlines the potentially psychopathic emotional paralysis that recurs in Marlowe's writing, as for example in Tamburlaine's repeated and unfeeling acts of cruelty, or Lightborn's cool pretence of concern before the sadistically savage murder of Edward. (The specific lack of affect here, as the next chapter will develop, carries even more profound significance for the religious attitudes of Marlowe and Shakespeare.)

While an attribution of psychopathic tendencies to Shakespeare's Henry V himself would admittedly not be beyond the realms of critical credibility, the distinction remains that the king's ugly threat to the governor and the citizens of Harfleur effectively forecloses the imagined violence; it does not revel in its fulfilment like the rhetoric of Tamburlaine, or memorialize its horror in strangely unempathetic ways, as in *Dido*. We need to consider more closely, then, Wilson's claim for Shakespeare's Pyrrhus, pausing before the slaughter, as emblematic of the opening of "a space for the aesthetic." As everyone knows, Laurence Olivier's film version of *Hamlet* attempts to cut the Gordian knot of centuries of critical debate and baldly identifies the play as "the tragedy of a man who could not make up his mind" – still not a bad point with which to introduce the play to undergraduates. The point frequently leads to a consideration of Aristotle's concept of *hamartia* in the *Poetics*, often explicated as "tragic flaw" but more accurately translated as "error in judgment." But in *Hamlet* we may indeed see Shakespeare deliberately working through Aristotle's more "existential" emphasis on action and transforming it into a principle of self-reflexive contemplation – self-fashioning not just as external action but as intellectual organization and, in keeping with the literary product of a Christian culture, spiritual reflection.

Andrew Hiscock very helpfully reminds us of the combined classical and Christian impetus behind the early modern project of humanist self-fashioning through a carefully planned program of education:

> if Roman theorists concentrated upon the oratorical experience requisite for success in the *civitas*, Christian theologians, at least as far back as St. Augustine, had recognized the significance of memory and the skills of public performance in coming to understand some of the mysteries of spiritual interiority … From the perspective of this Church Father, memory is frequently linked to the gaining of self-knowledge and ethical understanding, and indeed to spiritual commitment. In *De Trinitate* … Augustine envisaged an analogue to the Holy Trinity in memory, understanding and

will … However, throughout the development of all these various philosophical traditions, the stress returns regularly to the notion of translating
learned knowledge into significant human action.

Hiscock links the emphasis on memory, both individual and cultural,
in humanist education to the artistic interest in the story of Troy during the late sixteenth century. His most interesting critical suggestion
involves a reconsideration of what is in effect Hamlet's direct response
to the Player's speech. In consequence of his famous reflection, "What's
Hecuba to him, or he to Hecuba" (2.2.559), Hamlet arrives at an idea –
the staging of the Mousetrap – which is central, I suggest, to Shakespeare's art: we can paradoxically arrive closer to the truth of any aspect
of experience by strategically adding to it one more layer of illusion.[37]
As Polonius has already (unconsciously) made clear, "By indirections
[we can] find directions out" (2.1.67). Hiscock identifies *The Murder
of Gonzago*, since it constitutes "the *mimesis* of revenge," as a kind of
displacement of Hamlet's apparently reluctant project of personal vengeance which, in terms of audience response to *Hamlet* itself, encourages us "to collapse the boundaries between *doing* and *telling* in order to
diversify our understanding of cultural intervention." More than a test
of Claudius's guilt, the Mousetrap "offers the prince the possibility of
[ethically acceptable] empowerment."[38] That the ethical nature of Hamlet's actions and the stability of his identity remain, until the fifth act,
highly questionable is part of the tragedy of the play; the further irony
of the Mousetrap is that, while Hamlet comes to perceive more clearly
the state of Claudius's conscience, the reverse is also true.

Though not explicitly stated, Hiscock's argument concerning the
conflation of doing and telling, and Hamlet's "movements back and
forth from biological to textual fathers," has, through its suggestions
of the "talking cure," psychoanalytic implications – in this case ones
to be read, I contend, in terms of the psychological disadvantages
arising from the theological context which Shakespeare has inherited
from Marlowe. In the most obvious sense, the action of both *Dido* and
Hamlet recalls Nietzsche's admonition that "if one hasn't had a good
father, then it is necessary to invent one."[39] This requirement should
be considered in a more broadly cultural as well as a directly familial
or biological sense. Although in classical and later culture the Virgilian emblem of Aeneas bearing his father Anchises on his back as he
escapes the ruins of Troy became a notable encapsulation of patriarchal
dedication to patrilineal duty and inheritance, Aeneas's self-effacing
and self-immobilizing gestures before the statue of Priam in Marlowe
both shock his companions and underline a desperate psychological

need, even abject weakness. In *Hamlet* there is a notorious incongruity between the hero's extreme idealization of the memory of his father – compared with Claudius, as "Hyperion to a satyr" (1.2.140) – and the Ghost's tale of excruciating suffering in Purgatory as a result of "the foul crimes done in [his] days of nature" (1.5.13). More recent criticism has understandably wrestled with the Ghost's injunction to Hamlet, "Remember me," and its echo of the liturgical function of the Protestant Eucharist, in essence a memorialization of Christ's sacrifice.[40] What then is the exact meaning of Shakespeare's attribution, to a deified father (from his son's perspective), of the agonies of purgatorial imprisonment, in the apparently Protestant context of the Danish royal court, to the certainly Protestant audience of late Elizabethan London?

The Catholic Subtext of *Hamlet*

The ostensibly anomalous allusions to Purgatory in *Hamlet* have been a concern in Shakespeare scholarship since at least J. Dover Wilson's *What Happens in Hamlet*, which still functions as a helpful introduction for readers interested in the question: while Hamlet and Horatio, as students of the University of Wittenberg, are "Protestants," and while Hamlet never names Purgatory and only hints at it once, the Ghost on the other hand is clearly "Catholic" and comes from Purgatory. Because of these theological contradictions, Dover Wilson asserts, "the Ghost in *Hamlet* was a far more arresting and prominent figure to the Elizabethans than he can ever be to us."[41] Of the more recent historicist attempts to reconstruct something of this peculiar perception, Greenblatt's *Hamlet in Purgatory* constitutes the most significant effort to come to terms with the "afterlife" of Purgatory. According to Protestant polemic, the Catholic church invented, without any scriptural authority whatsoever, a "poet's fable" between Heaven and Hell – that is, between the irrevocable destinations of the elect and the reprobate – as a means of psychological and political control, and with an enormous financial benefit to itself. Thus Protestant writers "charted the ways in which certain elemental human fears, longings, and fantasies were being shaped and exploited by an intellectual elite who carefully packaged fraudulent, profit-making innovations as if they were ancient traditions."[42] But can the idea of imaginative agency which I have raised be employed to suggest that Shakespeare in *Hamlet* concerns himself with something more than simply a parody of Purgatory, or even, as Greenblatt goes on to suggest, a lingering attachment to a mechanism for assuaging fears and longings associated with human mortality and grief? In spite of the fascinating and illuminating contexts explored in *Hamlet in Purgatory*,

Greenblatt fails to push home a point about human *integrity* that seems implicit in much of his explorations.

At one point Greenblatt considers the emotional, even in a sense spiritual, paucity of the Protestant worldview concerning the life of the soul on earth, by focusing on Donne's *Devotions*:

> Donne began his work by imagining himself as his own ghost, an image he now immeasurably deepens. But where do these ghosts – all of us, in effect, or at least all of us who have heard the bells toll – reside? ... In a special place set aside for purgation? No, here in this world, a world that is an enormous charnel house, where we await resurrection. "Where Lazarus had been four days," Donne tells God, "I have been fifty years in this putrefaction; why dost thou not call me, as thou didst him, *with a loud voice*, since my soul is as dead as his body was?"[43]

Intriguingly – as this observation might support David Wootton's (and Empson's) claim for Donne's membership in the Family of Love – Greenblatt's reading of Donne's spiritual metaphor misses the possibility of Familist influence. According to Lynnewood Martin, H.N. approved of the nurturing power of certain "holy signs," such as "the Catholic mass, the veneration of saints, the sacraments and their doctrine of purgatory, but substituted his own idea that the suffering in this life was to be the purgatory of the Familists."[44] In his subsequent chapter Greenblatt considers more closely, in some hair-raising detail, the horrific nature of a *literal* purgatorial suffering – a horror nicely if briefly intimated by the Ghost in *Hamlet* – and begins his subsequent reflection with a fine sense of black humour:

> This is, let us reiterate, the good news. These are souls destined for Heaven, but they cannot enter its sacred precincts with the burden of even relatively minor sins upon them. Why did God's sacrifice of his own Son not suffice to clean the slate of each soul? Because that sacrifice did not erase individual moral responsibility. If all actions are significant ... if individuals are accountable for their own behavior, then the principle of retributive justice absolutely required that each and every sin ... be counted, weighed and punished.[45]

This passage highlights the profound challenge the "invention" of Purgatory ultimately poses to the doctrine of the Atonement: "Because that sacrifice did not erase individual moral responsibility." That is, Greenblatt's reading of *Hamlet* does more than complicate a comparison of Catholic and Protestant eschatology; it comes very close to undermining the central doctrine of Christianity. If *Hamlet* presents a very odd incongruity between Hamlet's intense idealization of his dead father and his father's purgatorial suffering, the play also intimates the necessity, indeed inescapability, of an earthly agent or role model for the young man's self-constructions within the social community, by having his less than ideal father return from the grave with the still very human motive of a desire for personal revenge: Remember me, not to surrender your sense of personal agency, but remember me, in order to perpetuate my legacy of masculine control and authority. But such remembrance involves not only an assumption or questioning of moral responsibility but an assumption or an acceptance of paternal guilt and imperfection.

The confusing and conflicted religious allusiveness of *Hamlet* does not so much parody Purgatory as it parodies the lack of any sufficient or viable masculine role model in the Protestant scheme of salvation – the fact that the atoning Christ remains inimitable, for men's agency in the world. In Marlowe, Aeneas's voyeuristic participation in Pyrrhus's assault on Priam, a gesture which conflates revenge on behalf of the personal father with the act of cultural patricide itself, recalls Debora Shuger's description of the experience of the reader of the Calvinist passion narratives, which "present violence (both acted and endured) as the site of self-division and subjective contradiction." Shuger observes that while such texts "stress the trial of obedience, where, to use Erasmus's terms, the Son must reject 'mother nature' – the instinct of self-preservation – in order to drink from the Father's cup ... their emphasis on the Son's meek submission to this economy of sacrificial suffering, which quantifies moral value in terms of pain, only partially conceals traces of filial aggression *against* the Father." Shuger reminds us that in "Calvinist piety, as students of Herbert will recognize, self-control usually implies a covert resistance to the 'Lord of Powre'; the attempt to withstand the torturer is itself a suspect assertion of inner autonomy."[46] The cultural context of Calvinist devotion – "by bringing men into the obedience of the Gospel, to offer them as it were in sacrifice unto God," in Calvin's own words[47] – therefore results in a reaction formation, an impetus towards a creative search for a major revision of the image of divine fatherhood. In order to avoid a facile participation in a cycle of violence for which personal responsibility is endlessly denied or deferred, the true Son needs a true Father who has himself, *in his own experience*, accepted the risks and the suffering of self-assertion and self-surrender, of human self-fashioning and the limits of self-fashioning. Shakespeare in *Hamlet* struggles to replace the voyeuristic, narcissistic paralysis of Aeneas – haunted by his own masculine inadequacy – with a subjectivity containing at least the potential for a more viable, creative agency. That Shakespeare's Pyrrhus hesitates before the destruction of Priam emblematizes the playwright's search for an "aesthetic space" which is really an acceptance of an imaginative, and imagined, self, one prepared to accept the responsibility for its triumphs and failures, not to blindly embrace, out of desperation or unthinking reaction, a purely narcissistic aggression against its own emotional being or the being of others.

The Struggle for Protestant Moral Coherence

Thus, while the purgatorial "subtext" established by the Ghost helps bring the necessity of individual moral responsibility to the fore, the *agency* through which such responsibility can be enacted or realized builds not on a model of a sinless Christ but on a productive if flawed masculinity. The play then must radically redefine the nature of Original Sin, a process recent scholars have engaged but also struggled with. Considering this critical problem, John Gillies in "The Question of Original Sin in *Hamlet*" has identified a series of "levelling readings" in which Shakespeare's protagonist fails to transcend the doomed biblical figures to whom he becomes analogized. Among such readings, I agree with Gillies' recognition that Heather Hirschfeld's earlier, trail-blazing reading "is the most comprehensive original-sin reading of *Hamlet* that we have and ... the most thoughtful," but also with Gillies' reservation, "Insofar as it sees Hamlet's awareness of original sin condemning him to repetition, it too is a leveling reading."[48] Hirschfeld's article, "Hamlet's 'First Corse': Repetition, Trauma, and the Displacement of Redemptive Typology," points out that the pairing of Cain's murder of Abel with Adam and Eve's transgression emerges as a "Renaissance commonplace," and indeed proceeds to argue that "*Hamlet* first holds out hope for, and then dramatizes the failure of, any recuperation from the trauma of Original Sin and its realization through a brother's murder."[49] I suggest nevertheless that the "levelling" aspect of Hirschfeld's reading can be challenged by questioning the conservative or orthodox nature of its typological assumptions: "typology defines antitypes, second events, as more powerful, since they simultaneously underwrite and redeem, even nullify, the first."[50] I intend to pursue some "fundamental questions" concerning heretical potential that Gillies proposes, in particular his supposition, "Is original sin a mental illness or an ideology?"[51]

Before doing so, however, I take up another significant attempt to render the *imitatio Christi* as conformable within the Protestant context of early modern England. Nandra Perry's compelling discussion "*Imitatio and Identity: Thomas Rogers, Philip Sidney, and the Protestant Self*" begins by taking up the Protestant Thomas Rogers's 1580 translation of Thomas à Kempis's *Imitatio Christi*, a text traditionally associated with Catholic devotional practice. Perry argues that "Rogers' revision is a useful starting point for examining the tensions in the period surrounding the practice of *imitatio*, both as a traditional devotional paradigm for saving the soul and as an emerging discursive strategy for shaping the self."[52] The analogy that Perry constructs between more secular forms of early modern self-fashioning – involving imitations of classical models – and the *imitatio Christi* may seem strained as an attempt to bridge a rather gaping ideological divide. But such tension in her eventual recourse to Sidney's *Defense of Poetry* serves to highlight the very point of my critical consideration here. Perry takes up Sidney's engagement with that crucial subject of Reformation piety, the penitential David of the Psalms: "Not only does David's sinfulness fail to compromise the sacred character of the Psalms, it actually contributes to their success as poetry." This realization brings Perry to the following conclusion, one that I believe carries us some distance from an imitation of Christ, and threatens or rather *promises* to relieve atonement theology of its tendency to short-circuit human psychological development:

> the ordinary or "right" poet [according to Sidney] cannot and need not entirely transcend his limited human perspective. David's example would suggest that the primary object of poetic imitation is not some half-glimpsed transcendent reality, but the poet's private experience of inadequacy in relation to that reality. Only by exposing and exploring the depths of his own depravity does David come to appreciate his reliance on God.

Sidney "sees David as defined by his struggle to negotiate between sinful and godly desires."[53] Perry's description of Sidney's interpretation might offer a parallel to the experience of the Redcrosse Knight in book 1 of Spenser's *Faerie Queene*, a hero who definitely only succeeds by "exploring the depth of his own depravity." But this interpretation potentially implies that more is at stake than just the (creative) individual's – in this case specifically the poet's – limitations, since we are implicitly invited to consider as well his or her competency and personal power: "Good poetry 'deserveth not to be scourged out of the Church of God,' not because it succeeds in delivering us a golden world, but because it fails *in ways that teach us who we really are*" (my emphasis).[54] The process that Perry describes vis-à-vis Sidney's argument in the *Defense* opens the way for more complex explorations of identity in the epic and dramatic literature of the period. Despite the eventual surrender of individual will to the godhead in such a process, the absolute necessity of human agency and self-assertion undoubtedly remains.

Perhaps this is why the text of *Hamlet* makes so much, in response to the Ghost's initial appearances, of its warlike attire – a spectral image quite unusual for the Elizabethan stage, according to Dover Wilson, which manages "to lift the whole ghost-business on to a higher level, to transform a ranting roistering abstraction into a thing at once tender and majestical," and quite "overwhelming in its realism."[55] The play clearly still honours the manly, martial image, an essential aspect of the dead king's nobility, but qualifies it as well. Every reader notes the apparent foils to the indecisive Hamlet, those other, more assertive sons – Pyrrhus, Laertes, and Fortinbras – who so energetically pursue revenge for their wronged fathers. But Shakespeare seldom uses foils so simply. For example, as the calculating Caesar in *Antony and Cleopatra* shows up Antony's lack of "manly" control of his Dionysian, predominantly sexual passions, so also does Caesar underline the limits of such control, the cost of Apollonian self-mastery to one's humanity; thus the tension between the two characters gradually reformulates, in essence renders more urgent, the question of what should, or could, constitute real manliness in the play.

Likewise, a figure like Fortinbras ironizes not only the purely martial image of masculine assertion but the whole meaning of the political resolution of *Hamlet*, with Hamlet's "prophecy" of Fortinbras's election. The play's complexity, indeed its centrality within the Shakespeare canon, is borne out by its careful inclusion, after the male-dominated political world of the second tetralogy, of the feminine perspective, not just as competing voices in the political context but as an artistic exploration of a more comprehensive psychological spectrum for the emergent secular self, incorporating both active and contemplative, "masculine" will and "feminine" emotional well-being.

Hamlet's Dialectic of Gender

Tanya Pollard, in a recent investigation of Hamlet's profound response to the Player's description of Hecuba, argues that "we have not yet acknowledged or understood the significance of the period's engagement with a predominantly female-centered canon of Greek tragedy," and suggests that "there is more than one ghostly parent haunting this play." When Hamlet describes himself "Like John-a-dreams, unpregnant of my cause" (2.2.568), he is technically "comparing himself with the player, but Hamlet's curious indictment of himself as 'unpregnant' suggests that it is Hecuba herself against whom he fails to measure up."[56] Pollard considers related passages in the play which associate Hamlet with the "brooding" state of pregnancy; such imagery certainly links the tragic hero with a feminine state which, as in the case of Marlowe's Barabas, could suggest a potential for narcissistic self-fixation.[57] But Hamlet presumably compares unfavourably to Hecuba not only for reasons of her astounding fertility – she is "identified by Euripides as a mother of fifty" – but because of her final assertiveness, and in describing Hecuba as "a bereaved mourner who seeks revenge," Pollard cites the action of the classical precedents she considers, specifically Euripides, where Hecuba manages to "transform grief into violence."[58] Considering collectively a series of Shakespearean allusions to Hecuba, Pollard argues that for the Renaissance playwright himself "Hecuba represents not ... passive suffering ... but active responses to wrongdoers, the possibility of transforming grief into the satisfaction of revenge."[59] But the case is different in *Hamlet*, and Pollard fails to clarify the distinction: there the description of the barefoot Hecuba "threat'ning the flames / With bisson rheum" or blinding tears (2.2.505–6) seems meant, poetically and pathetically, to underline not her vengefulness but her overwhelming impotence and distress. It is surprising that, among Shakespeare's sources, Pollard fails to consider *Dido* at all, since she seems to confuse Shakespeare's Hecuba in *Hamlet* with the "frantic Queen" in Marlowe, who, after Pyrrhus strikes off her husband Priam's hands, "leap'd on [Pyrrhus's] face, / And in his eyelids hanging by the nails, / A little while prolong'd her husband's life" (2.1.244–6).

I thus wish to add an important qualification to Pollard's historicization of *Hamlet*. In light of the "remarkable popularity" of Euripides' *Hecuba* in the Renaissance, Pollard argues, "early modern English responses to Hecuba suggest that the play's popularity derived especially from its combination of passionate grief and triumphant revenge, each of which embodied a crucial aspect of what the period's writers found compelling in tragedy."[60] While undoubtedly building on the popularity of this particular combination, Shakespeare at the same time explores his intimation that a coherent masculinity, and indeed a coherent *subjectivity*, needs to temper both; that is, he seeks a dialectical resolution of too much passive and too much aggressive emotion, in the containment and coherence of imaginative agency, and not – as Marlowe in his earlier work at times apparently offers his audiences – in the indulgence of narcissistic fantasy. Pollard does ultimately argue that *Hamlet* introduces innovations in the genre of tragedy that challenge tragedy's previous, classical culmination in triumphant revenge: "Presented as audience and mirror to the play's female figures, Hamlet takes the choral role from its characteristic position on the play's margins and moves it to the center, reversing its relationship with the grieving women to whom it responds." The artistic result is to refocus "the genre on the experience of the audiences who watch and respond to it."[61] Thus Pollard's reading aligns with Richard Wilson's "opening up of an aesthetic space" and my idea of imaginative agency.[62] But if Shakespeare "transforms women's place in the genre," as Pollard suggests, he does so by in fact reducing the agency of his female characters in comparison to their precursors in classical drama, whose grief led to active and satisfying revenge.

In *Hamlet* women's role in grieving, or not grieving – in the case of Gertrude's response to her husband's death – is certainly highlighted, but in a sense tragically contained within the process of achieving a more integrated masculinity. Mark Sweetnam interestingly accuses Gertrude of "idolatry as a type of spiritual adultery" with the help of Paul in 1 Corinthians 10:16–20: "The cuppe of blessing which we blesse, is it not the communion of the blood of Christ? The bread which we breake, is it not the communion of the bodie of Christ? ... *Nay*, but that these things which the Gentiles sacrifice, they sacrifice to deuils, and not vnto God." According to Sweetnam, Gertrude "has failed to learn [Paul's] lesson ... that there can be no equivalence between God and the demon, between King Hamlet and Claudius. One cannot feed on the true spirit and on the false bread." Thus Gertrude "remains immune even to [the] powerful visitation" of the Ghost in her bedchamber in 3.4.[63] But Sweetnam's Christian analogies oddly entangle Gertrude in Hamlet's own questionable idealizations contrasting Hyperion and satyr, reanimating questions about this spiritual father's sufferings in Purgatory. Indeed, the formerly martial Ghost's odd entrance "in his nightgown" here apparently underlines the domestic and narcissistic dynamic of Hamlet's distraught behaviour in this scene, which has led to generations of speculation concerning its Oedipal or pre-Oedipal character.

I suggest rather the critical necessity of combining Pollard's classical contexts with a consideration of the psychological pressures on Christian subjectivity, and not just in the sense that "revenge" is more morally problematic in a Christian context.[64] Crucially, classical self-conception does not present a core of subjectivity internally riven by the moral contradictions of a Christian guilt culture, and the resulting shifts and complications of gender identification, which problematize not just (violent) revenge but *any* kind of agency and moral discipline. "Passionate grief" can now no longer issue directly in "satisfying revenge" but must undergo a vexed and apparently tortuous masculinization – in

Pollard's terms the masculine appropriation of the choral role – that tempers suffering with a painful but inescapable moral objectification, achieved only by effectively challenging the terms of its own supposed inadequacy and dependency. That is, Shakespeare must establish a psychological and ideological context which interrogates the potential for narcissism in a theology of grace, its inherent inhibition of masculine self-integration, even while such theology paradoxically increases the spiritual burden of moral responsibility towards others.

This attempted transformation of narcissism may be related to classical and biblical mythological allusions involving the tragic objectification of female figures in the service of masculine self-idealization, for example Jephthah's daughter, beloved only child in Judges 11, tragically sacrificed by her father because he has promised God to offer up the first thing that emerges from his door in exchange for military victory over his enemies. Pollard notes that "Between hearing of the players and watching them represent Hecuba … Hamlet is … thinking about a female sacrifice linked to classical tragedy: his meditation of Jephthah's daughter [2.2.403] … foreshadows that Ophelia – who, like Iphigenia [Agamemnon's daughter], is sacrificed by her father for matters of state negotiated between men – will both mirror Hamlet and compete with him for the play's tragic center." This observation is linked in Pollard's argument with the claim that Hamlet's choric status, while effeminizing in terms of being "marginal, passive, and observing," nevertheless "strengthens him by giving him the leverage of an external vantage point."[65] The reference to Jephthah, who in the Renaissance imagination was frequently linked to Iphigenia, interestingly recalls Barabas's protestation of deep love for his daughter Abigail in *The Jew of Malta*: "one sole daughter, whom I hold as dear / As Agamemnon did his Iphigen: / *And all I have is hers*" (1.1.136–8, my emphasis). Besides the obvious irony in the foreshadowing of Barabas's actual "sacrifice" of his daughter later in the play, the rhetoric here also directly echoes the love of God the father in the parable of the prodigal son, underlining the potential for a fatal narcissism in "divine" love, especially since Barabas later vows to sacrifice Abigail "on a pile of wood" (2.3.53), alluding to the story of Abraham and Isaac, which was read as a type or prefiguration of God's willing sacrifice of his only Son. The text of *Hamlet* engages in a careful reconsideration of the necessity and the nature of human "sacrifice," in psychic or subjective terms. The Eucharistic potential I noted in Aeneas's self-effacement before the statue of Priam is in Shakespeare renegotiated by an implicit challenge to, or subtle correction of, the detrimental psychological effects of the doctrine of Atonement, through the notorious but (as it turns out) not entirely illogical appearance of a

Catholic ghost amidst a disordered Protestant state. In essence Purgatory becomes an emblem of the psychic readjustments activated within the Shakespearean unconscious.

Hamlet's meditation on Jephthah certainly reflects Shakespeare's recurring concern with unusually close father-daughter relationships, with perhaps incestuous potential,[66] and also contributes to Hamlet's quasi-Oedipal, ongoing critique of Polonius. In spite of what many readers have found Hamlet's fairly appalling treatment of Ophelia, his final protestation of love for her after her death – ironically while fighting over and around her corpse – seems a significant attempt to recognize her as a cherished, but distinct "other," even while her personal and social agency has been tragically subsumed (in effect like Gertrude's) within the psychological trajectory of his own trauma. The whole rest of the Shakespeare canon in effect shows the playwright's continuing attempt to resolve the dilemma of the narcissistic possession of women by men, through a reconceptualization of a viable masculinity as a necessary prelude for, in effect, human psychic integrity in both male and female characters. Janet Adelman has pointedly observed that the mother figure "returns with a vengeance" in *Hamlet*,[67] and even those readers unsympathetic to psychoanalytic interpretation must admit that in this central work Shakespeare begins a serious renegotiation of the power and the nature of the feminine in his imaginative world. In light of Pollard's argument concerning the secret affinities between Hamlet and Hecuba, it is probably significant that Marlowe, unlike either Virgil or Shakespeare, dares to depict if not the murder then the disposal of Hecuba at the fall of Troy – "At last, the soldiers pull'd her by the heels, / And swung her howling in the empty air" (2.1.247–8) – an image disturbing but consistent with Marlowe's savage and sadistic eradication of femininity and the female (or feminized) body.

Contingency and Independence

I have suggested that Marlowe's *Dido* served as catalyst for the development of Shakespeare's renegotiation of the feminine, but only by highlighting a failure and a lack of an integrated masculinity that the dead playwright underlined. Indeed it may seem a contradiction that the eponymous hero of Marlowe's first play is, after all, a woman, and therefore the play could be said naturally to fulfil the expectation of heightened female emotion that characterizes classical, especially Greek, tragedy, whose influence in the Renaissance has been underestimated (according to Pollard). But Marlowe's Virgilian context highlights a disjuncture between an erotic desire and the "necessity" of political conquest; the Christianization of this context further complicates both the desire and the political subjectivity in ways that clearly emphasize challenges to early modern masculine self-authorization and self-coherence. The pathos of Dido in Marlowe is certainly moving, but what Hamlet significantly recalls is Aeneas's speech about Priam's slaughter. Indeed, Rick Bowers's reading of *Dido* as "high camp" might support, as I suggested earlier, the claim for a displacement of homoerotic desire, but the idea has I think more serious artistic and moral consequences than Bowers ultimately suggests, when he concludes that Marlowe turned the "cultural artefacts" of classical culture into "something newly reconstructed, something hilarious and outrageously off-kilter, and yet something immediately recognizable in terms of extreme emotional behavior. Perhaps only his hairdresser knew for sure."[68] While perhaps not simply a projection of postmodern predilections, the aspects Bowers underlines are not, apparently, the "honest," "wholesome," and "sweet" qualities that attracted Shakespeare to Marlowe's play, as reflected in Hamlet's speech to the players.

If the effective pathos of Dido's speeches has something to do with a part of the consciousness of the playwright that shares both her desperation and her desire, it might be tempting to suggest that such a possible displacement also resembles a recurring pattern in Shakespeare's art.[69] This claim requires a separate discussion, significant aspects of which I take up in chapter 5. My main point here is to demonstrate that Shakespeare saw and remembered a moving human dilemma in *Dido*, one that related directly and deeply to crucial challenges facing self-conception in late Elizabethan England which were intensified by the theological and political upheaval of the Reformation,[70] and attempted in his own art to transform the trauma and paralysis he observed there into a more viable model of secular self-fashioning for his society and his age. That is, he saw the wonder, the wit, the brilliance, and indeed the humanity in Marlowe's art, but sensed at the same time something irrefutably (from his perspective as well as our own) pathological.

I thus finally question Lucy Potter's reading that *Dido* successfully enacts a sixteenth-century version of Aristotle's catharsis, and that after the telling of his tale of Troy, Aeneas "is entirely different."[71] In support of her claim, Potter quotes one of the play's most central artistic statements, Aeneas's exclamation, when he re-encounters the woods where he first landed destitute upon Carthage's shores, "O, how these irksome labours now delight / And overjoy my thoughts with their escape! / Who would not undergo all kind of toil / To be well stor'd with such a winter's tale?" (3.3.56–9). Potter certainly offers a detailed and carefully structured argument – in this reading and in earlier and later discussions[72] – describing the way "dramatic theory is constructed in drama as well as exegetic theory."[73] The problem remains that – for any reader struck by the consistently compromised agency, the subjective inadequacy of Aeneas's character – Marlowe's male protagonist does not appear "entirely different" after the telling of the Troy tale. That is, despite the elaborate nature of Potter's theoretical apparatus, her claim does not seem *psychologically* true within the play. Rather than a real working through, a transformation of an emotional burden, Aeneas's speech concerning the willingness to "undergo all kind of toil" signifies at best only the infantilization of a necessary reconstitution of experience, a reduction of the process of maturation to a child's fantasy, a delight in story-telling. Indeed, even its *intimation* of the challenges of individuation is enough to make Dido petulantly respond, "Aeneas, leave these dumps and let's away," which emphasizes the narcissistic refusal of reality that characterizes the play as a whole.

But Shakespeare keenly perceives, even while it fails here, the power of human imaginative production to facilitate a more practical and socially responsible self-fashioning – as does, I believe, Marlowe himself, even while in his art he specializes in exploring what could justly be described as primarily negative exempla, tragic versions of cautionary tales. Perhaps the Aristotelian concept that needs to be addressed here is anagnorisis rather than catharsis; Potter's claim, unpersuasively attached to Aeneas, does seem compelling with respect to the fifth-act Hamlet, who famously asserts, "There's a divinity that shapes our ends, / Rough-hew them how we will" (5.2.10–11). Admittedly Hamlet in the same scene overrides his apprehension concerning the upcoming duel with Laertes with the dismissal, "we defy augury. There is a special providence in the fall of the sparrow" (217–18), which has invited scholars such as Alan Sinfield to revisit the Calvinist underpinnings of the play. But the artistic effect is not simply, I contend, that the play's "action remains ambiguous."[74] While sceptical readings of Hamlet's final transformation predominate among scholars, William Kerrigan compellingly argues:

> We may now pause to consider the divinity that preoccupies our hero in the final act. Many have found it a barren and etiolated Christianity, hardly distinguishable from the stoic love of fate. They are surely right that it lacks the fullness and cultural ambition of the Christianity one associates with Augustine, Aquinas, Luther, and Calvin, though ... it borrows from Calvin a special notion of providence. Hamlet's narrowed faith has ... no

> set of virtues and vices, no answer to the general problems of mankind, no
> liturgy, no commandments, and no Christ ... [In the final analysis Ham-
> let's] divinity can only be understood in the context of his individuality.[75]

Shakespeare's tragic hero achieves in the final act a sense of viable agency, and real emotional freedom, with respect to what he can and cannot control. In this sense *Hamlet* anticipates the darker dialectical energy in *King Lear*, embodied at the outset in the tension between the facile astrological credulity and determinism of Gloucester and the murderous aggression of the sceptical Edmund. The vision is darker than conventional Christianity cares for, but "if Hamlet is to [finally] succeed as a revenger he must succeed as a thinker of contaminated thoughts, finding strategies of cooperation for a divided conscious-ness."[76] Hamlet frees himself from the haunting of his father only when he embodies the whole legacy of paternal *imperfection* within himself.

At stake in my final comparison between Aeneas and Hamlet is the crucial distinction between "real" or "true" and specious or (in effect) voyeuristic performances as acts of self-fashioning, a differentiation that certainly requires the consideration of the choices one makes, and the goals one pursues, as ethical or unethical, but depends in the first instance on whether legitimate choice is believed to be possible. Such judgment or assessment ultimately represents, in effect, an ideologi-cal challenge to much Reformed theology, from Luther's bound will to Calvin's doctrine of predestination – to what, as the previous chapter indicated, was the source of great ideological and psychological uncer-tainty and trauma in early modern England. That so much theoretical emphasis in poststructuralist and postmodern criticism has ironically tended to dismiss the distinction between an essence-who-performs and the nature of the performance as bogus, as an ideological and oppres-sive (not liberating) fiction, means that the moral catalyst Shakespeare perceives in Marlowe needs in this case further clarification through an honest admission of personal cohesiveness or self-coherence as a historically legitimate goal for early modern writers, in terms of their own humanist endeavours.

Chapter Three

Marlowe and Shakespeare's Early Histories: The Attenuation of Grace

Marlowe and Shakespeare: Co-authors?

The artistic relationship between Marlowe and Shakespeare has recently certainly been enhanced, and Marlowe studies in general have received an apparent boost, by the attribution of the three *Henry VI* plays to both Shakespeare and Marlowe in the *New Oxford Shakespeare*. Such a "discovery" might give an immediate (and humorous) lie to the not uncommon critical claims, such as my own in a previous study, that Shakespeare in the first tetralogy could be described as "still producing, periodically, bad imitations of Marlowe."[1] Yet the claims of the *New Oxford* editors created at the outset great controversy, and (it is fair to claim) are likely to remain highly controversial. In response to the *New Oxford* announcement, Darren Freebury-Jones in 2016 initially asserted, "As an attribution expert who has devoted years to examining the authorship of the *Henry VI* trilogy, I am uneasy about these headlines [trumpeting Marlowe as co-author with Shakespeare]. Unfortunately, while statistical analysis, like literary analysis, can aspire to an objective viewpoint, it also relies upon subjective interpretation."

I will not here directly enter the now increasingly contentious debate regarding the different kinds of computerized textual analyses, and their supposed, or competing, validity or accuracy. I do, however, note Freebury-Jones's further observation that "Kyd is very much the ghost at the feast here," and Kyd's ghost – in spite of the focus of this study – will briefly haunt the treatment of Shakespeare's relationship to Marlowe in the next chapter more than I had originally intended.[2] While I remain doubtful of a direct attribution to Marlowe of substantial passages of the *Henry VI* plays, enough to justify the designation of "co-author," I work here under the following assumptions. Shakespeare's early history plays raise most acutely the issue succinctly voiced by

Charles R. Forker in his 1994 introduction to Marlowe's *Edward II*: "We have long been aware, of course, of how much Shakespeare must have learned from his shorter-lived contemporary ... [but] What is less widely recognized, although we have become increasingly cognizant of it in recent times, is the almost equally formative impress of Shakespeare upon Marlowe."[3] And the *Henry VI* plays figure prominently in any critical speculations concerning Shakespeare's influence on Marlowe. While it seems likely that *1 Henry VI* was written in collaboration with Kyd and perhaps also Nashe,[4] I take Shakespeare (following Freebury-Jones, see n. 2 above) to be prime author of *2 Henry VI* and *3 Henry VI*, both of which are certainly more stylistically and thematically consistent than *1 Henry VI*. Together these three plays represent a kind of dramaturgy highly distinct from the dramatic patterns established by Marlowe, if admittedly still deeply under Marlowe's poetic influence. Structurally they seem to me to challenge, significantly, the monodrama of *Tamburlaine*, *Doctor Faustus*, and *The Jew of Malta*. As such, they constitute a significant influence on Marlowe's composition of *The Massacre at Paris* and *Edward II*.[5] Unlike Forker, I make the assumption that the final play of Shakespeare's first tetralogy, *Richard III*, postdates *Edward II*, and this chapter will offer a combination of poetic, textual, and psychological evidence to explain this speculative chronology.

From "Holy Family" to Human Family

I begin with a less controversial claim, that Marlowe's first play, *Dido Queen of Carthage*, led him directly to the composition of his next, possibly his most influential text, *Tamburlaine*.[6] While the composition of *Tamburlaine* constitutes one of the most important moments both in Marlowe's oeuvre and the history of the Elizabethan theatre, it also constitutes an important catalyst in the Marlowe-Shakespeare relationship. That Shakespeare at the height of his career in *Hamlet*, as the previous chapter explored, turned to *Dido Queen of Carthage* and not *Tamburlaine* as the focal point of influence underlines the importance of the paternal (father and ur-father) dynamic of the earlier play, as well as the significance of its absence, or its strangely belated relevance, in *Tamburlaine*. While Aeneas in *Dido* experiences dislocation and alienation in Carthage, as he struggles both with his own anxieties and his attempt to fulfil the will of the gods, in *Tamburlaine* Marlowe creates his rather more characteristic artistic scenario involving an apparently deracinated hero aggressively fulfilling the terms of his own grandiosity – and the pattern repeats in *Doctor Faustus* and *The Jew of Malta*. One of Greenblatt's earlier critical pronouncements on Marlowe seems still relevant here: "The family is at the center of the period's economic and social structure; in Marlowe it is something to be neglected, despised, or violated." The effect is to "dissolve the structure of sacramental and blood relations that normally determine identity in this period and to render the heroes virtually autochthonous, their names and identities given by no one but themselves."[7]

This claim can certainly be criticized as an accurate generalization of early modern drama as a whole. Middleton, for example, could be cited as another dramatist who neglects, despises, or violates traditional family structure. Middleton's ideological roots in Calvinism might serve as an intriguing foundation for an explanation of his similarity to Marlowe on this point.[8] Yet the process in Middleton suggests a fulfilment of, rather than a desperate resistance to, Calvinist theological strictures. Adrian Streete, in a discussion of Middleton, uses a passage from one of Calvin's sermons to illustrate this radical denigration of merely "human" bonds: "The name *father* is so honorable, that it belongeth to none, but to God onely ... And therefore, when we say, that they which have begotten vs, according to the flesh, are our fathers, it is an vnproper kind of speech." According to Streete, "the role of Father is only grudgingly bequeathed to fallen humankind. Because it is only ever a fallen, fleshy and immanent copy of God's patriarchy, the name of Father represents, at best, a surrogate title, and at worst, traumatic abandonment."[9] In Marlowe's case, on the other hand, the neglect or violation of sacramental, familial relations seems less a tragic or darkly comic version of a rather bleakly realized theological status quo than an attempt to critique the pathological assumptions undermining such relations. Marlowe's work therefore in essence paves the way for Shakespeare's ultimately more humane and constructive psychological explorations.

Greenblatt's claim in *Renaissance Self-Fashioning* regarding familial influence cites a paper by C.L. Barber later incorporated into the chapter "The Family and the Sacred in Shakespeare's Development" from *The Whole Journey*, where Barber significantly notes Shakespeare's evocation of "the sacred-in-the-human." Barber's assertion that "Shakespeare's extraordinary relevance to the modern age ... comes partly from his having so consistently done without any religious supernatural" challenges assumptions of the current "turn to religion." Yet his argument that Shakespeare "dramatizes the search for equivalents of the Holy Family of Christianity in the human family" deserves continuing critical attention:

The major tragedies come late because ... [Shakespeare's] sensibility is shaped by a constellation of family relationships in which, initially, female or maternal power is more important than paternal. The classic Oedipal confrontation, with its possibility of atonement by identification with the father, is postponed because for him there are alternative ways of achieving identity. After the effort to shift the prime allegiance to heroic manhood in the great tragedies, the romances again show the female as predominant; with the exception of the artist-dominated *Tempest*, male identity is lost when relationship to women is lost, and regained as their gift when relationship is recovered.[10]

Barber's thesis involves an unusual conception of the Sonnets, where "we can see most clearly the recourse of incorporating the cherishing parental role to cope with a problematic relationship to the maternal." The critic asserts that the poet's "identification with the young man and passive dedication to dependence on his love are far more visible than the poet's identification with the cherishing parent, because for the most part the parenting is expressed or embodied in the process of creating the sonnet." While this reading, involving the poet's appropriation of maternal nurturing, may interestingly suggest a reason for the metamorphosis of the initial sequence of procreation sonnets into a longer narrative of, evidently, more purely (homo)erotic obsession, it is doubtful that in Shakespeare's earlier artistic development "the adoption of a cherishing role permits a reception of heritage and the maintenance of a self grounded in it, without confronting centrally the problem of manliness."[11] This generalization cannot persuasively be extended to the plays, where the problem of manliness looms large in the very earliest works.

Manliness in the Early Histories

The opening scene of *1 Henry VI*, begins, at least rhetorically, on a decidedly Marlovian note:

> Hung be the heavens with black! Yield, day, to night!
> Comets, importing change of times and states,
> Brandish your crystal tresses in the sky,
> And with them scourge the bad revolting stars
> That have consented unto Henry's death –
> King Henry the Fifth, too famous to live long!
> England ne'er lost a king of so much worth. (1.1.1–7)

Regarding this speech, Bart van Es remarks, "the distinctive voice, if there is one, is that of Christopher Marlowe. The archaic imperatives, the outlandish and resplendent images, the recourse to cosmic forces in the light of an imperial superman – all these draw redolently on *Tamburlaine* and other Marlovian works." But van Es also argues that "the conspicuous borrowing in these opening lines is not the reason for doubting they are by Shakespeare. Throughout the *Henry VI* plays Shakespeare echoes Marlowe in just this way."[12] The particularly Marlovian flavour of these opening lines arises in part from their emotional echo of the final moments of the second part of *Tamburlaine*, where the loss of the "superman" father particularly traumatizes his two remaining sons, who seem inadequate to succeed him. After Bedford's speech, Gloucester's rejoinder evokes Tamburlaine even more emphatically in the description of the dead Henry V:

> His brandished sword did blind men with his beams;
> His arms spread wider than a dragon's wings;
> His sparkling eyes, replete with wrathful fire,
> More dazzled and drove back his enemies
> Than midday sun fierce bent against their faces. (10–14)

The resemblance to Tamburlaine might be considered uncanny, until, that is, Gloucester adds, "What should I say? *His deeds exceed all speech. /* He ne'er lift up his hand but conquerèd" (15–16, my emphasis). While not directly a criticism of Tamburlaine's characterization, which took the Elizabethan theatre by storm, the line nevertheless constitutes a pointed challenge to, even inversion of, the "working words" and the narcissistic fantasy that fuels the dramaturgical structure of Marlowe's two-part play.

The subsequent speech in this opening scene introduces an even more intriguing, and vexing, possible parallel between Marlowe and the early Shakespeare. In response to Gloucester, Exeter laments:

> We mourn in black. Why mourn we not in blood?
> Henry is dead and never shall revive.
> Upon a wooden coffin we attend,
> And death's dishonorable victory
> We with our stately presence glorify;
> Like captives bound to a triumphant car.
> What? Shall we curse the planets of mishap
> That plotted thus our glory's overthrow?
> Or shall we think the subtle-witted French
> Conjurers and sorcerers, that, afraid of him,
> By magic verses have contrived his end? (17–27)

The fleeting, potentially suicidal suggestion in the first line of this speech seems quickly subsumed in the aggressive tone of the later lines, which identify the French – effeminized through magic – as a possible target of vengeance, a less abject alternative than cursing the astrologically determined suffering of the English – which itself constitutes, symbolically, a violent rejection of Calvinist predestination.

But the possibility of Marlovian intertextuality emerges most emphatically in the descriptions of mourners "Like captives bound to a triumphant car." The line closely parallels Gaveston's boast in *Edward II* that, while he enjoys King Edward's love, he will think himself "as great / As Caesar riding in the Roman street / With captive kings at his triumphant car" (1.1.171–3). The image may again recall *Tamburlaine*, where in part 2, 4.3, the hero's chariot is actually *pulled* by two captive kings – thus literalizing the status of Tamburlaine, who bears a whip, as scourge of God – but the inversion of the order of the figures in the first tetralogy, implying symbolically the necessity of a pre-eminent male role model, likely originates with the descriptions of the mourners in *1 Henry VI*. Intriguingly, the passage from *1 Henry VI* also echoes a moment in *The Massacre at Paris* when the inflated Guise misinterprets the solicitations of King Henry, and boasts to himself:

> So; now sues the King for favour to the Guise,
> And all his minions stoop when I command.
> Why, this 'tis to have an army in the field.
> Now by the holy sacrament I swear:
> As ancient Romans over their captive lords,
> So will I triumph over this wanton king,
> And he shall follow my proud chariot's wheels. (21.48–54)

Here the secondary placement of the captive kings is more clearly emphasized. In this case the Guise's presumptuous identification with imperial Rome – as the Catholic villain of the play, he is undercut by his dependence on the "holy sacrament" magically transformed through transubstantiation – evaporates in his immediately subsequent murder.

1 Henry VI certainly emphasizes this sense of theological dependency, but only to attempt a radical divorce between theological substantiation and the sources of masculine strength within homosocial networks. While the Bishop of Winchester, underlining the connection between Henry V and Christ, trumpets, "He was a king blest of the King of kings … The battles of the Lord of hosts he fought; / The Church's prayers made him so prosperous," Gloucester violently objects, "The Church? Where is it? Had not churchmen prayed, / His thread of life had not so soon decayed" (1.1.28–34). The curious double negative in Gloucester's objection strongly implies that Henry's destruction has actually been brought about by the prayers of English clergy, in addition to the magical incantations of the French; the two forms of "religious" dependency appear an equivalent threat to the survival of (English) manliness. Gloucester then implies that the "churchmen's" main interest is simply political manipulation and domination: "None do you like but an effeminate prince, / Whom like a schoolboy you may overawe" (35–6). The lines indeed foreshadow much of the political struggle of the rest of the *Henry VI* plays, where the artistic focus remains on the hierarchical trauma brought about by the premature death of Henry V, leaving a nine-month-old infant to inherit the throne.

In spite of the intensity of his enemies' opposition, Gloucester emerges as a kind of surrogate father, and a very necessary (if tragically foreshortened) one, for the young prince. But this Oedipal emphasis is augmented by another crucial artistic and psychological development in the first tetralogy. The Bishop of Winchester's initial rebuttal of, and attack on, the nobleman – "Gloucester, whate'er we like, thou art Protector, / And lookest to command the Prince and realm. / Thy wife is proud. She holdeth thee in awe / More than God or religious churchmen may" (37–40) – is also highly significant, as it foreshadows the notable secular agency demonstrated by women in the *Henry VI* plays, significantly greater than the female characters who appear in *Tamburlaine*, *Faustus*, and *The Jew of Malta*. Indeed, the question of domination raised through the image of captive kings recurs in part 2 in the context of Gloucester's ambitious wife, who, punished for witchcraft, earns the commiseration of her humiliated husband in terms that now only ironically and pathetically recall Tamburlaine:

> Sweet Nell, ill can thy noble mind abrook [endure]
> The abject people gazing on thy face,
> With envious looks laughing at thy shame,
> That erst did follow thy proud chariot wheels
> When thou didst ride in triumph through the streets. (2.4.11–15)

It is as if the eradication of the spiritual dependency, the clearing of the way for greater masculine autonomy and agency, inevitably increases the possibilities for female agency – both constructive and potentially tragic – in competition or cooperation with masculine assertion. In this sense the *Henry VI* plays seem to be attempting something quite different from Marlowe's tragedies of the late 1580s, in spite of their frequently Marlovian rhetorical formulations.

Jeffrey Knapp observes, consistent with the drift of the immediately preceding argument, that with respect to the first tetralogy "One could hardly imagine English history introduced with a more anti-prelatical slant."[13] Chapter 1 offered the general description of the sometimes desperate nature of masculine self-constructions under the strictures of a theology of grace in Marlowe and Shakespeare, but also suggested Shakespeare's greater degree of emotional detachment. In an important article, Robert L. Reid has examined such an ideological and psychological difference between not Shakespeare and Marlowe but Shakespeare and Spenser.

Like all Spenserians, Reid emphasizes Spenser's Protestant credentials, established by the poet's portrayal of his first hero Redcrosse, who ultimately achieves the virtue of Holiness through, essentially, radical self-effacement; yet the portrayal of the subsequent virtues, which descend "ever more deeply into materiality ... seem increasingly tolerant of self-approval in the quest for glory." Pride therefore emerges in Spenser as an unqualified error, an unmitigated psychological danger:

> In the subtle combat with pride, a major problem for Spenser – as part of Leicester, Sidney, and Essex's Protestant party – lay in the conflict between their militancy ... and the harder quest for a Christlike "gentleness" that extends the beadsmen's charity [in book 1's House of Holiness] to all: Irish as well as English, commoners as well as gentlefolk. In arousing the highest power of scripturally-fed Intellect as a basis of faith, the Legend of Holiness uses troubling metaphors: the Pauline "armor of God" (Ephesians 6) and Revelation's apocalyptic "warfare." If these militant tropes are taken literally (as increasingly occurs in Books 1–6 of *The Faerie Queene*), the tandem evils of Errour and Hypocrisie may be endlessly reborn.

Conversely, Reid argues, Shakespeare explores more positive aspects of pride or self-esteem, and "portrays self-love as morally ambivalent but deeply attractive. This radical difference from Spenser points to an alternate tradition, more Roman Catholic than Protestant, which views self-love positively."[14] Reid's exploration of this alternate tradition is interesting and relevant, considering Shakespeare's familial background. Shakespeare's "Catholicism" may indeed have rendered him less susceptible to the instability or uncertainty of the Protestant Marlowe's struggle with the militant and imperialistic political agenda he perceived in the Protestant Spenser.[15]

In Shakespeare therefore an apparently calmer degree of self-discipline can be linked to the self-mastery that emerges as a major theme in his work, especially the histories. Such a theme might seem typically Shakespearean not only in the sense that Gary Taylor has suggested in his oft-cited argument, comparing Shakespeare to Middleton: while Shakespeare's portrayal of the nobility "is not always flattering ... his many royal protagonists are almost always the focus of intense psychological engagement and empathy. Their dramatic presence and power is unmistakable. In Shakespeare's works, kings matter."[16] As Annabel Patterson has reminded us, Elizabethan history plays, by Shakespeare and other early modern playwrights, are the artistic creations of middle-class men, as are the chronicle histories on which they are based: Holinshed's *Chronicles* "came from and were directed toward the already large and largely literate middle class ... [and] are an expression of citizen consciousness, though one that could imagine the entire nation as within the civil society."[17] Such narratives attracted the great interest of such men at this point in English history since they crucially serve as a rehearsal for male competency in a rapidly changing society. These plays, collectively, implicitly answer or elucidate Hilary Gatti's perplexity that, "given that one of the main leads in [the direction of a parliamentary principle] would so soon be offered by the England of the following century, it remains a curious cultural phenomenon that so meagre a mediation on the parliamentary alternative was developed by the culture of the sixteenth century."[18] It is in a sense a psychic necessity which causes the historical delay observed by Gatti. The history plays of the 1590s employ the figure of the king as archetype for the masculine self, using it to test and codify the potential of the new man for psychological, political, and ideological control; hence the subversive, indeed sometimes tragic nature of these historical protagonists, such as Richard III, the Bastard in *King John*, and the more pathetic Richard II, as a somewhat belated reflection of the more pathetic Edward II. Even Hal, the hero of the second tetralogy, appears justified not through divine right or metaphysical appointment but through his own talent for political machination.

I do not wish to oversimplify the complexities of these issues, especially as they have raised challenging political questions concerning monarchical and republican affiliations among various early modern writers, both epic and dramatic. I will, however, return to Robert Reid's psychological distinction between the ever-present threat of pride in Spenser, in opposition to the more favourable attitudes towards self-love – what I prefer to call self-esteem – in Shakespeare. I suspect a progressive, possibly republican potential in the (originally) Catholic Shakespeare and the (subversively) Protestant Marlowe more so than in the (imperially devoted) Protestant Spenser, but my main interest in this particular artistic triangle concerns theological and psychological (rather than specifically political) differences with respect to Calvinist and – most crucially – Pauline contexts. Reid's essay, in keeping with all the discussions in the volume where it occurs, focuses on the "attractive opposites" Shakespeare and Spenser, but as the introductory essay by J.B. Lethbridge admits, "Marlowe's borrowings from Spenser are so much more apparent, those we have noticed at any rate, than Shakespeare's."[19] It is difficult not to believe that the rate of critical *notice* of such allusions is inescapably linked to the actual intensity of the reaction or response by Marlowe in this case, who has a greater stake, or experiences a greater challenge, in separating himself from his Protestant poetic model than does Shakespeare. To bolster this claim I offer here another, I think crucial, moment of intertextuality not observed by Lethbridge, but pointedly connected to my analysis of imaginative agency in the previous chapter.

Contrasting Responses to Spenser's Pauline Framework

Since this study is ultimately concerned with a literary interrogation of a theology of grace and of Original Sin, it is worth asking what specific Elizabethan poetic contexts would figure in such a project, as "authoritative" examples that nevertheless invite a significant contestation of Pauline theology. Surely the transition between books 1 and 2 of *The Faerie Queene* constitutes such a textual moment, since this crucial juncture in the epic highlights Spenser's configuration of the tension between salvific grace and the more classical or pagan demands of self-discipline in the natural and temporal worlds. Such ideological competition not only would have spoken to the psychological concerns of Elizabethan readers but has remained a controversial topic of debate for later scholars and readers. David Lee Miller begins a recent article treating Pauline influences in Spenser with the observation that

> The allegorical relation between Holiness and Temperance in Spenser's *Faerie Queene* has puzzled many critics since A.S.P. Woodhouse in 1949 tried to sort the orders of nature and grace. Guyon and his Palmer seem nominally Christian. The Palmer's name indicates that he has made the pilgrimage to Jerusalem, and Guyon recognizes "the sacred badge of my Redeemers death" (i.27.6) on the shield of Redcrosse, yet together they give Mortdant and Amavia a pagan burial, and their conception of Temperance seems more Aristotelian than Pauline.[20]

Having long attempted to solve this puzzle, I unapologetically cut the Gordian knot by again suggesting that theologically sensitive

Elizabethan readers were ultimately no more likely to understand or to resolve the central ideological issues raised here than later scholars. There is no magical critical answer to these issues since Spenser (tragically) replicates the confusions and contradictions of Paul.

While I continue with the significance of the transition between books 1 and 2 of *The Faerie Queene* below, I briefly address here one of the most intriguing textual cruxes which may consolidate the linkage between Marlowe, Shakespeare, and Spenser, on the issue of human agency and grace. When Aeneas relates Pyrrhus's attack on Priam in *Dido*, he observes that Pyrrhus, disdaining the injured Priam's attempts to resist, "Whisk'd his sword about, / And with the [wind] thereof the King fell down" (2.1.253–4). H.J. Oliver rejects the common emendation to "wind" here – as Frank Romany and Robert Lindsey point out, "The received emendation of Q's *wound* emphasizes Priam's frailty."[21] Oliver's rationale is worth consideration:

> Collier's emendation to "wind", the most famous in Marlowe, is ... one of the silliest. It depends not only on the premise that Shakespeare remembered those lines when he wrote the Player's Speech in *Hamlet* ... but also on the assumption that the Shakespearian text preserves a correct reading that the *Dido* Q gets wrong. The first premise I accept ... the second I reject: Shakespeare was not quoting Marlowe but half-affectionately pushing over the verge of absurdity what was only trembling on the brink of it, and so he converted "whisk'd his sword about, / And with the wound thereof the King fell down" into "Pyrrhus at Priam drives; in rage strikes wide; / But with the whiff and wind of his fell sword / The unnerved father falls". The point of the joke *is* the alteration; and perhaps it was Shakespeare, if anyone, who remembered Spenser's lines "Yet so exceeding was the villeins powre, / That with the wind it did him ouerthrow." (*F.Q.*, I.vii.12)[22]

But Oliver's remarks also require expansion, since significantly the passage he quotes but does not further consider from book 1 of *The Faerie Queene* involves Orgoglio's defeat and capture of Redcrosse, weakened through his dalliance with Duessa:

> The Geaunt strooke so maynly mercilesse,
> That could have ouerthrowne a stony towre,
> And were not heauenly grace, that him did blesse,
> He had beene pouldred all, as thin as flowre:
> But he was wary of that deadly stowre,
> And lightly lept from vnderneath the blow:
> Yet so exceeding was the villeins power,

> That with the wind it did him ouerthrow,
> And all his sences stound, that still he lay full low. (1.7.12)

Here Redcrosse is *almost* destroyed by a figure whom scholars have plausibly linked to the concept of Spiritual Pride, and saved only through a peculiar function of heavenly grace. Human "frailty" in Spenser paradoxically ensures the eventual salvation of Redcrosse, but in Marlowe and Shakespeare underlines the tragic failure of the patriarch, and of the masculine ideal. That is, a "gracious" accident that in Spenser preserves the hero's life and soul (while ironically prolonging his suffering) becomes in Marlowe and Shakespeare a striking example of *the failure of the father* to serve as an adequate model of strength. In light of other contexts I consider below, it seems to me likely that both playwrights recalled this passage from book 1 of *The Faerie Queene*.

David Lee Miller asserts that, in the transition from book 1 to book 2, "Spenser calls both [theological and secular] perspectives into play, narrating [in book 2] the struggles of a hero from the world of pagan epic who has wandered into a Reformation allegory he cannot comprehend."[23] This critical approach implies that perfect understanding will become available to the reader who correctly identifies Guyon's limitations, whether intellectual or spiritual. But as Miller indicates, Spenser has already (partly) Christianized Guyon, and therefore the interpretative dilemma is clearly more complicated than he implies in this description of Spenser's ideological balancing act. I propose therefore not a secular dismissal of disconcerting theological obsessions or concerns, as a way of clearing away the puzzle completely, but rather a reading that attempts a critique of the flawed theological formulations that Spenser unfortunately replicates from Paul, which I believe more closely reflects the process in which Marlowe and ultimately Shakespeare were engaged.

While scholars have agreed that the action in cantos 1 and 2 of book 2 of *The Faerie Queene* "point to a Pauline allegory of Mosaic law ... their accounts do not explain why an allegory of the Law and the flesh should be personified as a dying husband and wife, nor why the Law's generative effect, creating the knowledge of sin, should be drenched in the pathos of Dido's death-scene from the *Aeneid*."[24] In some sense we return to the status of the Troy narrative as a kind of creation myth in Renaissance culture. The *Aeneid* is most obviously evoked in the rhetoric of 2.1.45, where Amavia's lamentation echoes Virgil's description of the death of Dido; yet there are a series of contradictions throughout this account – traceable in A.C. Hamilton's annotations[25] – which multiply to the point of incoherence. Amavia oddly claims, and the text supports (1.58), that her suicide is not sinful, as she instructs her young child, "whom frowning forward fate / Hath made sad witnesse of [his] fathers fall," to "attest" to her innocent state (1.37). The oblivious baby, however, is presumably too young to register either his "father's fall" or his mother's suffering:

> Pittifull spectacle of deadly smart,
> Beside a bubbling fountaine low she lay,
> Which she increased with her bleeding hart,
> And the cleane waues with purple gore did ray;
> Als in her lap a louely babe did play
> His cruell sport, in stead of sorrow dew;
> For in her streaming blood he did embay [bathe]
> His litle hands, and tender ioynts embrew. (1.40)

Guyon's attempt at the beginning of canto 2 to wash the blood from the innocent baby's hands fails utterly, the ineradicable stain presumably indicative of Original Sin. As Miller observes, "[Carol] Kaske has rightly dismissed the idea that the washing of Ruddymane's hands in canto ii is baptismal, but this does not mean that baptism has no bearing on the allegory: in Paul's account, the struggle between sin and the Law both precedes *and* follows baptism." The paradox of the innocent but defiled baby for Miller actually clarifies the relationship between books 1 and 2 of the epic: "No sooner do we glimpse [in Redcrosse's betrothal to Una] the consummation that awaits the faithful than the narrative steps back, relocating us in the moment between baptism and resurrection, the interval in which the Pauline 'inner man' struggles with the law of his members."[26]

Yet the greatest contradiction of the narrative emerges through the terms of the destruction of Mortdant. Apparently rescued by his wife Amavia from the "vile Enchaunteresse" Acrasia, the witch leaves the departing knight with a cursed cup or chalice: "*Sad verse, giue death to him that death doth giue* [the warrior Mortdant], */ And losse of loue, to her that loues to liue* [contradictorily, the suicidal and despairing Amavia], */ So soone as Bacchus with the Nymphe does lincke*" (1.55). Using the cup to drink at the well, Mortdant falls dead in fulfilment of the incantation, although the mixing of wine and water, Bacchus and the Nymph, is traditionally, and reasonably, an emblem of temperance. As Hamilton points out, Erasmus in the *Colloquies* had emphasized such an emblem, but Spenser inverts Erasmus's meaning. Spenser's poem therefore suggests not only that a *humanist* reliance on personal control of the passions, that is, on a specifically human morality, is ultimately a fatal response to experience, but (if we recall Erasmus's theological position), more disturbingly, that even any reasonable cooperation of human effort and divine assistance or inspiration is likewise equally fatal. Such a reading might partly explain the very vexing contradiction that "Perfect concord and harmony are the topoi of *in*temperance in Book II, lovingly elaborated both times the narrative visits the Bower of Bliss [5.28–31, 12.51, 70–72]."[27] Such contradiction could be interpreted as Spenser's Protestant undermining of a more Catholic, Thomistic vision of harmony between the orders of Nature and Grace. Nevertheless, more subversive implications arise. Hamilton further suggests in his annotations to 2.1 that "Mortdant's drinking from Acrasia's poisoned cup corresponds to the Red Cross Knight's drinking from the enfeebling fountain [in 1.7 during his dalliance with Duessa, the very source of the controversial "wind" image]. Both acts parody the mingling of wine and water in the Communion chalice."[28] In the case of Mortdant especially, however, this reading appears, under the pressure of religious orthodoxy, to insist on a parodic inversion where an *ironic mirroring* seems, subversively, the more logical interpretation; that is, Spenser's narrative unconsciously but powerfully encourages a suggestion of the enervating, potentially fatal effects of a psychological investment in Eucharistic practice and therefore in atonement theology.

Marlowe likely perceived this more subversive suggestion. Marlowe's description in *Dido Queen of Carthage* of "Young infants swimming in their parents' blood" (2.1.193) during Aeneas's voyeuristic description of the atrocities of the fall of Troy occurs in a passage having no precedent in Virgil,[29] and deliberately echoes, I suggest, Spenser's description of the "cruel sport" of Ruddymane's bathing in his mother's blood. It constitutes the first major signifier in Marlowe's work of the emotional paralysis stemming from the doctrine of Atonement and a theology of grace that he will spend the rest of his short career attempting to work through.

Spenser even more definitively than Marlowe creates a poetic world of deracinated heroes, with apparently little interest in upholding "sacramental and blood relations that normally determine identity in this period." At the very least, *paternal* identifications seem extremely tenuous in Spenser, as Tom MacFaul observes in a somewhat broader literary context: "In allegorical interludes such as *The Marriage of Wit and Science* (c. 1569), as in Spenser's *The Faerie Queene*, the hero who must realize his virtue tends to have a mother but no father, as a father would represent the virtue as already achieved."[30] In *The Faerie Queene* specifically, "Bastardy is used principally [as in the case of the central hero Arthur] as a narrative trope which enables the unfolding of identity, in that characters' uncertainty as to their paternity allows them to learn their legal identity as they develop in their virtues; characters who are not bastards have often been stolen from their parents (like the Redcrosse Knight)."[31] The suddenly orphaned Ruddymane can hardly serve as "sad witness to his father's fall," since he apparently has as yet no clear ego boundaries, no consciousness of his father's separate existence.

There seems to me, moreover, a greater issue than the absence of paternal identification at stake; the Pauline influence on Spenser apparently traumatizes attitudes towards human physicality, and human sexuality, in general: "For ye are dead, and your life is hid with Christ in God ... Mortifie therefore your members which are on the earth, fornication, unclenness, the inordinate affection, evil concupiscence, & covetousness which is idolatrie" (Colossians 3:3–5). The "consummation" that Miller identifies above, in the joyous conclusion to book 1 of *The Faerie Queene*, is not, even in a purely allegorical or spiritual sense, a consummation, but only a betrothal. In fact sexuality all through book 1, though presumably predominantly a metaphor for "spiritual fornication" (a term which recurs in witchcraft pamphlets), is distorted and demonized through often highly misogynistic imagery which itself seems intensely pathological. And the beginning of the descent "ever more deeply into materiality" at the beginning of book 2 is marked by the heroic action of a wife saving a husband from, or forgiving a husband for, infidelity or fornication or simply intemperance, which ironically leads only to the horrific destruction of them both, a complete desecration of their marriage and their married life.[32] This inability to psychologically *process* even married sexuality is, admittedly, a striking claim to make of a poet who is also the author of the most famous epithalamium in the language, but it is nevertheless extremely difficult to deny Spenser's poetic embodiment, "in all its weirdness, [of] the distinctive Protestant understanding of sin as an existential condition rather than the will's deliberate consent to evil."[33]

Shakespeare as well, somewhat later in his career, responded directly to this ideologically crucial moment in Spenser, according to Miller, but the emotional response is far different from Marlowe's: "Shakespeare apparently recognized the [allusion to Virgil in] Spenser ... for his knowing mockery of the elder poet in *A Midsummer Night's Dream* includes a parody of Mortdant and Amavia's death scene in the deaths of Pyramus and Thisbe."[34] Such a parody, with Shakespeare's comic sensibilities at this point in his career still partially aligned with a tone of aristocratic disdain which fuels his social-climbing tendencies, seems less invested than Marlowe's response in the Pauline tensions that otherwise concern Miller: "The horror of Dido's suicide strains against the scripture's need to affirm the Law in its death-dealing aspect, much as in the *Aeneid* it strains against the uncompromising demands of imperial destiny."[35] Shakespeare's response in *Dream* appears focused on Virgil's description of Dido's suicide rather than the fall of Troy, as a means of testing or critiquing audience response to depictions of tragedy – another potential version of imaginative agency. For reasons of theological difference, the core problem of masculine incapacity makes this Spenserian moment more disconcerting for Marlowe, who invents in his description of the sack of Troy a striking image of amoral indifference, as a mirror of emotional and intellectual paralysis – the very behaviour in Ruddymane that so appals Guyon, even as it moves him to pity (2.2.1–2). Therefore in Marlowe the immediate response to Spenser's Virgilian version of a creation myth, artistically, is an intensification, rather than a circumvention, of the psychological ramifications of a theology of grace.

Developing Parody of Grace and Atonement

After *Dido Queen of Carthage*, Marlowe's *Tamburlaine* in fact pushes the traumatic implications of atonement theology, especially in the context of Calvinist views on predestination, to the ideological limits of the Arian heresy. When Cosroe, astonished at his military and political betrayal at the hands of Tamburlaine, rails against the protagonist's presumption, the Persian lord Meander observes, "Some powers divine, or else infernal, mixed / Their angry seeds at his conception; / For he was never sprung of human race" (part 1, 2.6.9–11), a description that insinuates a most radical version of Protestant divine election. Upon Ortygius's assertion that, whether deity or demon, they bravely oppose Tamburlaine, Cosroe replies,

> Nobly resolved, my good Ortygius;
> And since we all have sucked one wholesome air,
> And with the same proportion of elements
> Resolve, I hope we are resembled,
> Vowing our loves to equal death and life.
> Let's cheer our soldiers to encounter him,
> That grievous image of ingratitude,
> That fiery thirster after sovereignty,
> And burn him in the fury of that flame
> That none can quench but blood and empery [conquest]. (24–33)

While the rhetorical formulation here has, not surprisingly, challenged scholars, the general description of "natural" men banding together is clear; the martial bonds and vows are clearly homosocial, but without the incipient homoerotic valence that emerges in Tamburlaine's own rhetorical appeals to his allies and comrades. Yet no natural or worldly force succeeds in opposing the astonishing singularity of Tamburlaine's magical prowess. After imprisoning the Turkish emperor Bajazeth in a cage, Tamburlaine dismisses his curses with the boast, "The chiefest God, first mover of that sphere / Enchased with thousands ever-shining lamps, / Will sooner burn the glorious frame of heaven / Than it should so conspire my overthrow" (4.2.8–11). Using Bajazeth as a footstool to mount the Turkish throne, Tamburlaine justifies himself with exactly the same astrological predestination that will haunt the terrified Faustus at the conclusion of Marlowe's subsequent tragedy: the grandiose imperative, "Smile, stars that reigned at my nativity / And dim the brightness of their neighbour lamps!" (4.2.33–4), becomes the desperate, "You stars that reigned at my nativity, / Whose influence hath allotted death and hell, / Now draw up Faustus like a foggy mist" (A 5.2.89–91).

In the transition from the portrayal of an arguably "Christ-like" Scythian shepherd who becomes world conqueror to the exploration of the notorious exploits of a German necromancer, the dream of divine substantiation becomes a nightmare. This theological and psychological transition – a striking fantasy of absolute control collapsing directly into absolute *loss* of control, abject personal dependency – constitutes, perhaps more than anything else, the core of Marlowe's profound artistic influence on Shakespeare. The persistent attempt at a dialectical resolution of this binary summarizes in a sense Shakespeare's entire artistic response to Marlowe's work. Indeed the *Henry VI* plays allude repeatedly and alternately to both *Tamburlaine* and *Faustus*. Such allusions often involve more than simply rhetorical echoes, like the ones I considered at the beginning of this chapter.

In part 1, there are intriguing parallels between Talbot and Tamburlaine, but their meaning resides primarily in their ultimate distinctions or differences. For example, 4.5 briefly parallels an uncharacteristically quiet, paternal moment in *Tamburlaine* (part 2, 3.2). Talbot tells his son John that he originally brought the youth to the siege to teach him "the stratagems of war," but with the sudden and unexpected military danger he wishes, unlike Tamburlaine, to sacrifice himself to save the life of his son, rather than sacrifice a son to maintain his own vulnerable self-image, as Tamburlaine subsequently does, shockingly, with Calyphas in 4.1. In Marlowe the hero lectures his three sons on the art of war,

with surprisingly pragmatic and extensive details lifted from Paul Ive's
Practise of Fortification (1589, possibly read earlier in manuscript),[36] as
apparently a way of distracting them from the grief they feel over their
mother's death. But it modulates quickly into parody of the Gospel of
John's doubting Thomas episode which we briefly took up in chapter 1:

> View me, thy father, that hath conquered kings
> And with his host marched round about the earth
> Quite void of scars and clear from any wound,
> That by the wars lost not a dram of blood,
> And see him lance his flesh to teach you all.
> He cuts his arm.
> A wound is nothing, be it ne'er so deep.
> Blood is the god of war's rich livery.
> Now look I like a soldier ...
> ...
> Come, boys, and with your fingers search my wound
> And in my blood wash all your hands at once,
> While I sit smiling to behold the sight. (3.2.110–28)

This moment represents Marlowe's play at its most bizarre: a world
conqueror has never felt a wound or lost a drop of blood? I suggest
the later playwright(s) of *1 Henry VI* wish to anchor the "magically"
realized but curiously passionless and apparently painless moment of
Tamburlaine's only gesture of "self-sacrifice" in a more realistic, albeit
rhetorically stilted,[37] depiction of human suffering, and of the inescapable consequences of courageous self-sacrifice. The parallel thus
appears to constitute an artistically awkward but genuine attempt to
reclaim a "real" rather than a fantastical masculinity. The apparently
painless gesture of the seemingly robotic Tamburlaine recalls the
response of Ruddymane to his parents' death, echoed in *Dido*'s "infants
swimming in their parents' blood." It is as if, in Marlowe, genuine process and legitimate suffering are effectively narcotized.

Interestingly, Tamburlaine's gesture of cutting his arm also clearly
anticipates the moment Faustus stabs his arm, in order to write the
"deed of gift" to consign his soul to Lucifer, at Mephistopheles' request
(A 2.1). One imagines the action in this case as less robotic, and more
painful – intriguing questions directors and actors must decide –
especially since the panicky Faustus's blood apparently naturally
coagulates, even while he succumbs to the temptation to look for supernatural wonders to explain such "staying" of blood. But a wonder then
does occur, when Faustus blasphemously appropriates the most sacred
moment from the life of Christ:

Consummatum est. This bill is ended,
And Faustus hath bequeathed his soul to Lucifer.
But what is this inscription on mine arm?
"Homo fuge!" Whither should I fly? (74–7)

Ironically, however, there is nowhere to flee within Faustus's Calvinist ideological dilemma. The signing of the demonic pact renders Faustus essentially a witch, but this action also constitutes a profoundly ironic version of the Puritan covenant.[38] Faustus's gesture, his momentary imitation of Christ in this scene, is less self-sacrifice than self-investment in his ambitious but fatally delusional magical career.

Both the audacious and the delusional imitations of Christ certainly caught the attention of the later playwrights. The presence of Tamburlaine's sons in the earlier play evidently inspires the authors of *1 Henry VI* to build on or significantly revise an idealized masculinity with at least the potential of nurturing paternity. The grandiose heroics of Talbot and his son John lead, rhetorically, to Talbot's assertion, "If thou wilt fight, fight by thy father's side; / And, commendable proved, let's die in pride" (4.6.56–7). The heroics culminate, physically, in the presentation of John's corpse and Talbot's subsequent death from a broken heart. The evocation of "pride" here supports Reid's suggestion of Shakespeare's more positive configuration of that quality. Although Talbot calls his son "Icarus," Shakespeare refers to this mythological figure rarely, "only in *1 Henry VI* (twice) and once in … *3 Henry VI*," and "Talbot seems to be using him here as an example of filial devotion rather than an example of ambition to be shunned."[39] Thus this particular response in *1 Henry VI* may not after all ignore *Faustus*, since the rhetorical strategy seems a deliberate containment or significant revision of the quintessentially Faustian image of hubris.

What is most uncanny about Marlowe's very odd parody of the narrative of the Gospel of John in *Tamburlaine* is its curious anticipation of a compelling theological debate among postmodern scholars, the suggestion that the fourth gospel actually engages itself in a parody or critique of the "Gospel of Thomas," discovered at Nag Hammadi in 1945. Arguing that the latter text predates the former, Elaine Pagels suggests that John, if indeed he was the author of the gospel which bears his name, deliberately constructs Thomas in his narrative as a "particularly obtuse and faithless disciple" as a way of resisting an already "heretical" teaching embraced by a significant subset of early believers, "many of John's Christian contemporaries [who] revered Thomas as an extraordinary apostle, entrusted with Jesus' 'secret words'."[40] The teaching of Thomas, Pagels explains, essentially ignored the status of Jesus as second person of the Trinity, and his role as necessary Mediator, encouraging rather the belief in the divine presence in each individual. As such, this theological position clearly anticipated the Arian heresy of the fourth century: "Many Christians today who read the Gospel of Thomas assume at first that it is simply wrong, and deservedly called heretical. Yet what Christians have disparagingly called gnostic and heretical sometimes turn out to be forms of Christian teaching that are merely unfamiliar to us – unfamiliar precisely because of the active and successful opposition of Christians such as John."[41] It is an intriguing question whether heretical strains of thought through the centuries of the Common Era would have preserved any understanding, or an intimation, of the special status of the apostle Thomas, independent of the discovery at Nag Hammadi in the twentieth century. Also intriguing is the fact that the Gospel of John makes repeated reference to the "disciple whom Jesus loved," usually identified with the author himself, who appears to take precedence even over Peter, and who "leaned on Iesus bosome" (John 13:23) at the Last Supper. As briefly noted in chapter 1, Marlowe notoriously did claim, according to Richard Baines, that "St John the Evangelist was bedfellow to Christ and leaned always in his bosome, that he used him as the sinners of Sodoma."[42]

Regardless of the actual status of the disciple Thomas in the (underground) history of heretical thought, the "parody" of doubting Thomas in *Tamburlaine* casts the protagonist in the role of the resurrected Christ, and thus as an embodiment of some kind of "atonement," but the scene certainly raises challenges of interpretation. Is it in effect a parody of a parody, a sceptical take on a morally foundational tale of scepticism? Marlowe's own artistic intentions with respect to his creation – especially the perennial question of whether we are meant to blame or sympathize with Tamburlaine – remain vexing. Patrick Cheney returns to this question in his attempt to delineate Marlowe's response to Spenser. Relying on a supposition of Marlowe's ironic detachment from his hero, Cheney sees Tamburlaine's boastful transition from shepherd to conqueror as an implicit mockery of Spenser's transition from Virgilian pastoral to Virgilian epic: "In presenting Cosroe criticizing Tamburlaine as a 'devilish shepherd' with 'giantly presumption' who '*dare*[s] the force of angry Jupiter,' Marlowe is both implicating Spenser for his arrogant, aristocratic progression from pastoral to epic and making way for himself as a new counter-Virgilian artist."[43] This provocative suggestion of a secret sympathy with Tamburlaine's victims rather than with Tamburlaine nevertheless requires us to reconsider whether Spenser's *arrogance*, exactly, is the clear object of attack. Cheney argues that Cosroe's characterization of "giantly presumption" recalls Orgoglio from the first book of *The Faerie Queene,* a character whom critics, as observed above, identify with Spiritual Pride,[44] an interpretation which takes on particular significance in this context. The low-born Spenser may have crafted an epic poem about the challenges of self-fashioning by the upper classes and the nobility: "The generall end therefore of all the booke is to fashion a gentleman or noble person in vertuous and gentle discipline."[45] But it is difficult to believe that the processes of experience he depicts in his epic had no relevance to his own social aspirations, or for that matter to the aspirations of Raleigh, to whom this description was addressed; Raleigh was, as John Guy reminds us, not of the nobility but of distinctly lower social origins.[46] Moreover, especially if we can accept Kenneth Borris's thesis (see n. 32 above) that *The Faerie Queene* does not embody "Woodhouse's supposed disjunction between grace and nature," but rather a "cumulative development," it is surely crucial that the hero of book 1, the Legend of Holiness, appears initially, according to this same letter to Raleigh, as "a tall clownishe younge man."[47] Spenser's aristocratic "presumption," then, rests fundamentally, and rather paradoxically, on Protestant and Calvinist religious claims, which partly explains the critical difficulty in assigning him either to a monarchical or a more subversive social position.[48]

I suggest we consider not so much Spenser's *arrogance* as his *narcissism* as the subject of Marlowe's critique in *Tamburlaine*. Tamburlaine's resemblance either to a presumptuous poet or to the giant Orgoglio actually underlines his *failure* of manliness, of viable self-assertion, through an obsession with spiritual justification which emerges, gradually but irrevocably, as simply magical fantasy, theatrical but ultimately illusory bravado. Again, I am not suggesting a perfectly objective and anxiety-free critique on the part of Marlowe, with respect to the theologically motivated ambitions he reads in Spenser's work. The oft-quoted prayer by the Muslim Orcanes in part 2 of *Tamburlaine*, through which he expresses outrage over the perjury of his Christian "allies," offers a relevant example of theological conflict and uncertainty.

Orcanes first invokes a quasi-Arian deity – "He that sits on high and never sleeps / Nor in one place is circumscriptible, / But everywhere fills every continent / With strange infusion of His sacred vigour" (2.2.49–52) – a passage which sounds very much like Proctour's Arian heretic insisting on the limitless perfection of God. But the speech modulates into a prayer to Christ, in a kind of theological test-case, as "a perfect God / Worthy the worship of all faithful hearts" (56–7). Such tension speaks to confusions between Arian and Trinitarian theologies, and uncertainty of theological identifications, which create challenges with respect to masculine self-construction in Marlowe – and which may suggest similar challenges among early modern Protestants in general.

A likely more personal or peculiar tension between Marlowe's radicality and his anxiety lies behind that other notorious critical crux, the exact significance of Tamburlaine's final illness, apparently motivated by his burning of the Koran. I have speculated that Marlowe's "desire for the eradication of a Mediator, because of the burden of personal responsibility it introduced, would raise concomitant doubt and fear. Such doubt or fear manifests itself artistically as the retribution resulting from Tamburlaine's challenge to Mahomet. The primacy of the Son is reaffirmed ... Tamburlaine is not Christ, the all-controlling word, after all." Marlowe's portrayal of a Muslim praying to Christ perhaps reflects an Elizabethan failure to comprehend the Unitarian aspect of Islam; at any rate "Mahomet's supreme miracle was the revelation of the Koran, the divine word ... in a sense for Mahomet, as for Christ, the ontological gap between language and being is bridged through a direct contact with the Godhead."[49] Thus Tamburlaine's demise carries anxiety regarding atonement theology even in the midst of the hero's notably Arian assertions concerning "The God that sits in heaven ... For he is God alone, and none but he" (5.1.200–1).

In fact the collapsing binary identified at the beginning of this section between a fantasy of absolute control and an absolute loss of control – grounded in positive and negative conceptions of Calvinist predestination – may explain why the *Henry VI* plays allude to *Tamburlaine* and *Faustus* so indiscriminately. The hypermasculine wish fulfilment of *Tamburlaine* gives way in the middle scenes of *Faustus* to a rather desperate struggle for dominance between the magician and military figures somewhat closer to him, in terms of class, than the aristocrats he attempts to flatter and entertain. Such masculine competition, a cultural flashpoint for middle-class playwrights and audience members alike, may explain why the middle scenes of *Faustus* were the subject of elaborate expansion by later playwrights, where the appearance of the Knight at the court of the German Emperor in the A-text becomes three scenes involving Benvolio and company in the B-text. It is nevertheless striking upon reflection just how *adolescent* (from our perspective at least) such male competitiveness appears in both these plays, and how little it involves significant interaction with the opposite sex – Tamburlaine's seizure of Arabia's betrothed Zenocrate in part 1 notwithstanding. The most ludicrous example from *Tamburlaine* is probably the first scene in part 2, where Orcanes and Sigismond challenge each other in such ridiculous and overblown terms that the rather more sensible Gazellus must finally interrupt them: "We come from Turkey to confirm a league, / And not to dare each other to the field. / A friendly parley might become ye both" (1.1.115–17).

It is striking that the most Marlovian character in *1 Henry VI* is female: the controversial and contradictory figure of Joan mixes the fantastical aspiration of a warrior-magician with its inescapable denouement in the abject dependency of the witch. Here embodiment of the Faustian narcissistic dilemma also serves as a significant artistic exorcism, at the end of the play, of this psychological problem. While I treat Joan's role in more detail in *Magic and Masculinity*, her apparently deceptive energy and independence, which is dispersed by the revelation in act 5 of her demonic failure,[50] is a process sharply politicized in a manner that needs clarification here. The combination of Joan's linguistic manipulation and Faustian inflation is intriguingly suggested earlier in the play when she "bewitches" Burgundy to change political sides by asserting, "One drop of blood drawn from thy country's bosom / Should grieve thee more than streams of foreign gore" (3.3.54–5). By displacing theological with nationalistic concern, this secularized echo of Faustus's "See, see where Christ's blood streams in the firmament / One drop would save my soul" (A 5.2.78–9) suggests Joan's potential to appropriate Christ-like linguistic power – but also, through the final exposure of Joan as a witch, its ultimate inefficacy. Hence *1 Henry VI* contributes decisively to the effeminization of the radical Protestant psychological alternative, where masculine agency depends completely on divine grace, even while Joan's characterization is certainly no model of psychological cohesion or consistency.

The other crucial development towards the end of part 1 is the emergence "of a more subtle narcissism … that in part 2 begins to replace foolish magic with a more efficacious and insidious instrument of social disruption, the power of individual thought and words to shape and control, often unethically, social reality."[51] Such emergence signals, I contend, the definitive arrival of Shakespeare in the first tetralogy as dominant or controlling artistic agent, even as Margaret, who makes her first appearance in the same scene that Joan is captured, becomes the substitute "demonic" threat to English manliness. As the "magic" is now more metaphorical, the (hetero)erotic threat becomes more substantial.

Piety versus Virility

Unfortunately for his kingdom, the concomitant of Henry's piety appears to be his sexual incapacity, which largely vitiates the homosocial politics that his uncle Gloucester attempts to assert. Henry for religious reasons is initially receptive to the truce between France and England proposed via the Pope, the Emperor, and the Earl of Armagnac – "for I always thought / It was both impious and unnatural /

That such immanity [savagery] and bloody strife / Should reign among professors of one faith." But he callowly baulks at the suggestion of a political marriage: "Marriage, uncle! Alas, my years are young, / And fitter is my study and my books / Than wanton dalliance with a paramour" (part 1, 5.1.11–14, 21–3). It takes in effect a sexual surrogate, the unscrupulous Suffolk, to bring Henry to embrace matrimony in a much less politically desirable form to the penurious Margaret (rather than Armagnac's daughter). In fact, the beginning of part 2 clarifies that Margaret comes not with an impressive dowry but the *loss* of territory which Warwick equates with Christ's sacrifice: "And are the cities that I got with wounds / Delivered up again with peaceful words? / *Mort Dieu!*" (1.1.119–21).

Moreover, the rhetorical "temptation" offered by Suffolk to Henry at the end of part 1 smacks of magical delusion. As Henry responds:

> Your wondrous rare description, noble earl,
> Of beauteous Margaret hath astonished me.
>
> …
>
> So I am driven by breath of her renown
> Either to suffer shipwreck or arrive
> Where I may have fruition of her love. (5.5.1–9)

Significantly Suffolk's own initial infatuation with Margaret takes on Faustian overtones:

> O, stay! [*Aside.*] I have no power to let her pass;
> My hand would free her, but my heart says no.
> As plays the sun upon the glassy streams,
> Twinkling another counterfeited beam,
> So seems this gorgeous beauty to mine eyes. (5.3.60–4)

This speech's image of the sun reflected in a stream appears a subtle reworking of Faustus's famous apostrophe to Helen:

> Brighter art thou than flaming Jupiter
> When he appeared to hapless Semele,
> More lovely than the monarch of the sky [the sun god]
> In wanton Arethusa's azured arms [reflecting the sky];
> And none but thou shalt be my paramour. (5.1.106–10)

That the playwright intended this allusion is strengthened in part 2, where Shakespeare again alludes to *Faustus* in the context of Suffolk's passion for Margaret upon his banishment from England:

If I depart from thee, I cannot live,
And in thy sight to die, what were it else
But like a pleasant slumber in thy lap?
Here could I breathe my soul into the air,
As mild and gentle as the cradle babe
Dying with mother's dug between its lips –
Where, from thy sight, I should be raging mad
And cry out for thee to close up mine eyes,
To have thee with thy lips to stop my mouth.
So shouldst thou either turn [back] my flying soul,
Or I should breathe it so into thy body,
And then it lived in sweet Elysium. (3.2.388–99)

This speech contains significant overtones of Faustus's desperate and famous address to Helen of Troy: "Sweet Helen, make me immortal with a kiss. / Her lips suck forth my soul. See where it flies! / Come, Helen, come, give me my soul again ... for heaven be in these lips" (5.1.93–6).

Since Margaret is a woman rather than a devil in drag, Shakespeare implicitly downplays the homoeroticism of Marlowe. Nevertheless the first stage in this containment of homoeroticism involves a peculiar reconfiguration of Oedipal identifications; the man who in the previous play aspires to be a law unto himself (2.4.7–9) ultimately emerges, rather pathetically, the victim of his own narcissistic passions, passions strongly underwritten, apparently, by maternal longings.

The first tetralogy thus involves an interesting engagement with maternal and paternal identifications. Perhaps not surprisingly then, at moments in part 2 we return to the Virgilian context of *Dido Queen of Carthage* and proleptically of *Hamlet*. When the Duke of Gloucester, Protector of England, surrogate father to Henry, and one of the few ethical figures at court, is finally destroyed through the conspiracies of his enemies, the king collapses in a fit of piety – "O heavenly God" (3.2.37) – and, after a few feeble expressions of a desire to seek vengeance, surrenders in a masochistic adjuration to Suffolk: "Come, basilisk, / And kill the innocent gazer with thy sight; / For in the shade of death I shall find joy, / In life but double death, now Gloucester's dead" (52–5). Margaret narcissistically interprets this lamentation as a rejection of herself, although possibly she simply manipulates the emotional exchange to deflect attention away from her adulterous liaison with Suffolk:

Is all thy comfort shut in Gloucester's tomb?
Why, then, Dame Margaret was ne'er thy joy.

> Erect his statue and worship it,
> And make my image but an alehouse [a crudely painted] sign. (78–81)

The taunt significantly recalls Aeneas's prostration before the statue of Priam in Marlowe's *Dido*, desperate to internalize a paternal role model.

Margaret senses that her husband's lack of masculine identification renders him useless or at least undesirable as a lover, but she strives to dominate maternally even her successful or virile lover Suffolk, going so far as to incriminate his manliness when he fails to challenge his own banishment: "Fie, coward woman and softhearted wretch! / Hast thou not spirit to curse thine enemies?" (307–8). The Virgilian and Marlovian connections are reinforced when Margaret bitterly complains that, during her stormy voyage to England to meet her prospective husband,

> How often have I tempted Suffolk's tongue,
> The agent of thy [Henry's] foul inconstancy,
> To sit and witch me, as Ascanius did
> When he to madding Dido would unfold
> His father's acts commenced in burning Troy!
> Am I not witched like her, or thou not false like him? (114–19)

According to this analogy, Henry is false Aeneas – but not because of his devotion to imperial destiny, or theologically through his enslavement to his divine predestination, but because of his inchoate masculinity. Shakespeare thus insists on a more secular and humanist version of the Virgilian creation myth. Moreover, Margaret as Dido is victim not of Ascanius-Suffolk but in reality Cupid-Suffolk, if she knows the story correctly; if she *does*, she has in effect confessed her adultery with a boy-lover even as she berates her husband's ineffectuality. In Shakespeare's more secular version of the myth, agency and heroic status, as well as interesting moral ambiguity, are effectively transferred to the queen.

Although Henry in this scene suspects the truth, that Gloucester was murdered, he ineffectually fails to pursue his suspicions: "If my suspect be false, forgive me, God, / For judgment only doth belong to Thee" (3.2.139–40). Such weakness leads to a disturbing mixture of homo-erotic (rare in the early Shakespeare) and necrophilic longing:

> Fain would I go to chafe his [Gloucester's] paly [pale] lips
> With twenty thousand kisses, and to drain
> Upon his face an ocean of salt tears,
> To tell my love unto his dumb dear trunk
> And with my fingers feel his hand unfeeling. (141–5)

Clearly his uncle's paternal surrogacy has been rendered futile, and Henry has failed to internalize a necessary masculine self-object. When Gloucester's corpse is brought forth for a rather odd on-stage autopsy and the king invited to view the body, he laments:

> That is to see how deep my grave is made.
> For with his soul fled all my worldly solace;
> For seeing him I see my life in death. (150–2)

Yet the psychological cause is not entirely lost, for, in response to the king's self-effacing grief, the Earl of Warwick suddenly exclaims:

> As surely as my soul intends to live
> With that dread King that took our state upon Him
> To free us from His Father's wrathful curse,
> I do believe that violent hands were laid
> Upon the life of this thrice-famèd duke. (153–7)

While it contains a direct allusion to the Atonement, this speech constitutes in essence an early but significant expression in Shakespeare of the "secular Christ," an assertive or manly appropriation of divinity, or divine purpose, in the cause of justice and ultimately of social reform. It is perhaps not the first evocation in the play of this concept, for earlier York (of all people) has identified Gloucester as "the shepherd of the flock, / That virtuous prince, the good Duke Humphrey" (2.2.73–4). Here York ironically "prophesies" that his other political opponents, whom he now construes as cat's paws, must "snare" the good Duke in order to pave the way for his own ambitions. And indeed the prophecy comes true in act 3. As Warwick's examination of Gloucester's corpse confirms the murder, Suffolk (who in fact suborned the murderers) nervously challenges Warwick to identify the perpetrators. When Warwick does not scruple to implicate Suffolk, Margaret, and the Cardinal, Suffolk retaliates by accusing him of bastardy. The two men commit to a violent resolution, with Warwick asserting, rather like a fifth-act Hamlet, "I'll cope with thee / And do some service to Duke Humphrey's ghost" (230–1).

In spite of his weakness, the king does manage (prompted by the outraged Commons) to banish Suffolk; thereafter retribution for Gloucester's murder sets in quickly. The first instance seems potentially metaphysical, as the Cardinal, "raving and staring," is discovered, in his death-bed; his "entrance" thus ominously mirrors the presentation of Gloucester's corpse in the immediately preceding scene. Haunted

by eschatological terror, as well as apparently by visions of Gloucester's ghost, the mad Cardinal certainly earns Henry's pronouncement,
"Ah, what a sign it is of evil life, / Where death's approach is seen so
terrible" (3.3.5–6), and he dies with no gesture of hope or repentance.
Gloucester appears avenged, not only for his murder, but for the Cardinal's earlier, hypocritical accusation towards him:

> Thy heaven is on earth; thine eyes and thoughts
> Beat on a crown, the treasure of thy heart.
> Pernicious Protector, dangerous peer,
> That smooth'st it so with King and commonweal!

The charge had earned Gloucester's self-possessed retort:

> What, Cardinal, is your priesthood grown peremptory?
> *Tantaene animis caelestibus irae?*
> Churchmen so hot? Good uncle, hide such malice.
> With such holiness, can you do it? (2.1.19–26)

The Latin, "can there be such resentment in heavenly minds," ironically quotes Virgil's description of Juno's ire against the Trojans at the
beginning of the *Aeneid*, and thus the social position of spiritual dependency is again, in the tetralogy, associated with effeminization, and in
this case vindictiveness.

Masculinity and Aristocratic Privilege

The scene subsequent to the Cardinal's ignominious death, the notorious 4.1, extends this attack on unmanliness to aristocratic privilege in
general. Suffolk's focus on social position, echoed in his accusation of
Warwick's bastardy in 3.2, receives the ultimate come-uppance in his
violent death. While textually uncertain, the scene involves a *"fight at
sea"* where the ship carrying Suffolk and other gentlemen is intercepted
by "pirates," and lands on the Kentish coast. The playwright in fact
invents Suffolk's murderer, Walter Whitmore, as well as his fulfilment
of the prophecy, delivered by the spirit Asnath during the conjuration
sponsored by the Duchess of Gloucester, that the nobleman would die
"by water." A Lieutenant, called "Captain" at line 65 and line 107 but
not the captain of the ship, attempts to maintain order. Roger Warren
argues in the Oxford edition, "Perhaps Shakespeare changed the Captain to a Lieutenant (and added references to 'soldiers'?) to emphasize
their military, not merely piratical, nature, perhaps that they are some

of the 'ragged soldiers [sent] wounded home' [4.1.90], who have turned pirate. This would help to explain the sheer resentment, and consequent savagery, shown towards Suffolk during the scene."[52] To some extent, then, the scene represents the revenge of the lower classes on the selfishness and mismanagement of the aristocracy.

Whatever the exact nature of the intended depiction of social interaction in the scene, the interception by pirates, interestingly, may constitute Shakespeare's reflection upon a rather surprising source he again renders meaningful in *Hamlet*. Tom Rutter has argued that Hamlet's abduction by pirates in the later tragedy may echo a passage from the Protestant theologian Heinrich Bullinger, familiar to Elizabethan church-goers, which critiques the doctrine of Purgatory: "You shal finde other some contending that soules can not come into heauen, vnlesse they bee perfectlie purified with clensing fire, which they call purgatorie, as though they were intercepted by pyrates and robbers in the middest of their iourney, and cast into tormentes, vntill either they themselues make satisfaction, or other for them haue paide as it were the debt which they had else-where borrowed."[53] Rutter quotes a version of Bullinger's sermon published in 1587, and I suggest that image may have struck Shakespeare earlier in his career than during the composition of *Hamlet* around 1600. The interception of pirates as a psychological or spiritual equivalence to a sojourn in Purgatory comes to represent, for Shakespeare, not only purification or satisfaction of debt or sin, but the potential acquisition of spiritual *merit*, as suggested in the previous chapter. Even as early as the first tetralogy, Shakespeare is coming to associate the aristocracy with a kind of narcissism engendered through overly facile privilege or empowerment. Although frightened by the ominous implications of Walter or "Water," Suffolk at first, in the style of Tamburlaine, insists on the magical import of his own discourse, declaiming to the Lieutenant, "This hand of mine hath writ in thy behalf, / And therefore shall it charm thy riotous tongue" (4.1.63–4). While he might be assumed to continue the Tamburlainean vein of rhetoric as he exclaims, "O, that I were a god, to shoot forth thunder / Upon these paltry, servile, abject drudges" (104–5), the inflation here actually reflects more characteristically the Guise from *The Massacre at Paris*. Suffolk's subsequent desperate assertion, "It is impossible that I should die / By such a lowly vassal as thyself" (110–11), in fact parallels the dying Guise's utterance, "To die by peasants, what a grief is this!" (21.81).

Roger Warren observes that in the transition from act 3 to act 4 in *2 Henry VI* "the action broadens [beyond court intrigue] to involve the population at large, first with the murder of Suffolk in 4.1, and then in

Jack Cade's rebellion. These scenes are both a contrast and a mirror to those at court since, as Philip Brockbank says, 'the virulent ambition and hostility to law that characterized the barons ... equally characterize the workmen'."[54] Moral and political responsibility, or its failure, thus in effect extends to men throughout much of the social hierarchy. The notorious Cade initially emerges as a product of the Duke of York's machinations; the nobleman's first major move towards the crown is to "conjure up his surrogate"[55] in the form of Cade, before he leaves for Ireland – "This devil here shall be by substitute" (3.1.371) – but there is also a slight suggestion of erotic manipulation: "I have seduced a headstrong Kentishman, / John Cade of Ashford" (356–7). Even more than Suffolk, Shakespeare's Duke of York rhetorically resembles Marlowe's Duke of Guise. The parallels between York's major soliloquy and the speeches of the Guise are extensive:

> Now, York, or never, steel thy fearful thoughts
> And change misdoubt to resolution.
> Be that thou hop'st to be, or what thou art
> Resign to death; it is not worth th'enjoying.
> Let pale-faced fear keep with the mean-born man
> And find no harbor in a royal heart.
> Faster than springtime show'rs comes thought on thought,
> And not a thought but thinks on dignity.
> My brain, more busy than the laboring spider,
> Weaves tedious snares to trap mine enemies.
> ...
> I will stir up in England some black storm
> Shall blow ten thousand souls to heaven or hell;
> And this fell tempest shall not cease to rage
> Until the golden circuit on my head,
> Like to the glorious sun's transparent beams,
> Do calm the fury of this mad-bred flaw [tempest]. (2 *Henry VI* 3.1.331–54)

> Now, Guise, begins those deep-engender'd thoughts
> To burst abroad those never-dying flames
> Which cannot be extinguish'd but by blood.
> Oft have I levell'd, and at last have learn'd
> That peril is the chiefest way to happiness,
> And resolution honour's fairest aim.
> What glory is there in a common good
> That hangs for every peasant to achieve?
> ...
> For this [ambition], this head, this heart, this hand and sword,

Contrives, imagines, and fully executes
Matters of import, aim'd at by many,
Yet understood by none;
For this, hath heaven engender'd me of earth;
For this, this earth sustains my body's weight,
And with this weight I'll counterpoise a crown
Or with seditions weary all the world. (*Massacre* 2.31–56)

Moreover, York's admonition to himself in an earlier soliloquy – "Then York, be still awhile, till time to serve. / Watch thou and wake when others be asleep" (1.1.246–7) – very closely parallels the Guise's sentiment, in the above soliloquy, "For this, I wake, when others think I sleep; / For this, I wait, that scorns attendance [awaiting the directive of others] else" (2.45–6).

Both portraits of narcissistic excess apparently turn on the exposure of aristocratic self-indulgence and a failure of self-discipline, likely germane (as we observed earlier) to a proto-republican, middle-class project of social advancement. Such parallels obviously raise questions of who is imitating whom, questions perhaps rendered moot for those assuming the direct collaboration of Marlowe and Shakespeare. Yet I have been arguing that the first tetralogy attempts, artistically, something distinct from the monodrama of *Tamburlaine* and *Faustus*, as it is driven by something distinct in its theological and psychological focus. For the remainder of this chapter, I will offer a speculative chronology consistent with the critical assumptions I have been making. While intensifying his exploration of Machiavellian philosophical interests, indicated obviously through the prologue spoken by Machevil, Marlowe in *The Jew of Malta* begins to look at the process of self-fashioning through a more detailed social and cultural lens, with a more objectified consideration of ideological concern. Although I asserted its monodramatic structure at the outset, *The Jew* at least *begins* to move away from monodrama by introducing a crucial and more balanced – however controversially this opposition has been read by critics – ideological and psychological confrontation between Barabas and Ferneze. I assume these artistic developments still originate with Marlowe's own evolving psychological motives; indeed the peculiar intersection of homoerotic motive with incestuous longing for or control over a daughter (the latter noted briefly in the previous chapter) seems a Marlovian invention to which Shakespeare notably responds in *The Merchant of Venice*.

The Shakespearean Turn in the Late Marlowe

Nevertheless, three developments we have observed in this chapter – the increased possibilities for female agency, the ultimate circumvention rather than intensification of the psychological ramifications of a theology of grace, and finally the replacement of narcissistic aspiration via magical fantasy by a more subtle and more realistic depiction of narcissistic interpersonal reaction – are all attributable to the artistry of the first tetralogy and therefore likely originate primarily with Shakespeare. These developments constitute the prime influence on Marlowe's final two plays, *The Massacre at Paris* and *Edward II*. In these plays Marlowe and Shakespeare become, as it were, more sympathetically aligned, through an artistic effort to establish a more socially and psychologically viable form of self-fashioning. Shakespeare's Duke of York gave Marlowe the example of a ruthlessly ambitious nobleman whose political irresponsibility and its ramifications for various social classes can be indirectly critiqued, and ethically exposed, by the aspiring lower-class playwright. While the status of Guise as Catholic villain upheld the more propagandistic elements of Marlowe's portrayal of evidently Protestant sentiments in *The Massacre*, an incipient emphasis in both playwrights on coherent masculinity regardless of social status carries a political, potentially republican, import. In Marlowe this potential for the derivation of ethical manliness emerges even in spite of a more direct manifestation of radical sexual proclivity, through the characterization of the homosexual Henry III. The alliance between Navarre and Henry III – both intriguingly if uncertainly developed characters – in opposition to the Guise, and their simultaneous struggle for individuation, might explain the play's artistic failure: "Marlowe's muse has previously been most effectively inspired by the narcissistic fantasy of absolute control; since he now chooses to exorcise that fantasy, he experiences uncertain poetic inspiration and faces artistic difficulties that he does not resolve until turning to *Edward II*."[56]

Edward II, therefore somewhat paradoxically, represents Marlowe's development of Shakespeare's artistic influence at its fullest and most successful, while also thoroughly exploring a distinctly Marlovian theme or interest – homoeroticism – that Shakespeare initially eschews or resists, and that makes only a belated appearance in his work, under the continuing influence, again paradoxically, of Marlowe's psychological and culturally influence on *him*. While the final chapter will treat more closely the belatedness of homoeroticism in Shakespeare's plays, the structures of erotic desire in *Edward II* do in several ways echo erotic, albeit heteroerotic, relationships in the first tetralogy. The rather poisonous duplicity of Margaret in part 2 of *Henry VI*, most obviously perhaps in 3.2, where she attempts to defend her lover Suffolk to the king – "Why do you rate my lord of Suffolk thus? / Although the Duke was enemy to him, / Yet he most Christian-like laments his death" (56–8) – resembles, and likely influenced, Isabella's duplicitous claims as innocent and long-suffering queen in *Edward II*. Moreover, the banishment of Suffolk later in the same scene leads to the lamentation of the adulterous lovers, which finds an echo in the exchanges between Edward and Gaveston, when the latter is himself banished. Marlowe, I suggest, was attracted to an intriguing tension in the characterization of Margaret at this point. While Margaret's defence of Suffolk is hypocritical and devious – she ironically protests his innocence of a murder in which not only he but she is complicit – she nevertheless reveals the depth of her passion at the banishment of her lover:

> But wherefore grieve I at an hour's poor loss,
> Omitting Suffolk's exile, my soul's treasure?
> Why only, Suffolk, mourn I not for thee,
> And with the southern clouds contend in tears –
> Theirs for the earth's increase, mine for my sorrows. (3.2.381–5)

Despite the potentially narcissistic suggestion of a failure of true nurturance and emotional reciprocity in her choice of images, her pain seems genuine, as does Suffolk's when he asserts:

> 'Tis not the land I care for, wert thou thence.
> A wilderness is populous enough,
> So Suffolk had thy heavenly company;
> For where thou art, there is the world itself. (359–62)

Suffolk's language here anticipates not only Gaveston's initial assertion in *Edward II* of his passion for Edward, "Not that I love the city [London] or the men" (1.1.12), but Edward's reason for his deep obsession with Gaveston: "Because he loves me more than all the world" (1.4.77). Thus Marlowe displaces the political hypocrisy of Margaret onto Isabella, but maintains the "depth" or rather intensity of her romantic passion with Suffolk – albeit a primarily narcissistic passion – for his own homosexual king and lover.

Shakespeare had no need to demonstrate narcissistic relationships to Marlowe, for narcissism's typical binary of grandiosity and desperate dependency characterizes Marlowe's heroes, in one way or another, from the beginning. Yet what Shakespeare does catalyse in Marlowe's imagination is the working out of a narcissistic dynamic in romantic relationships contextualized by political conflict and struggle. The hypocrisy of the Machiavellian "actor" is clearly germane to *The Jew of Malta*, and the hero of that play notably destroys all the other characters who seek or engage in sexual activity, and who fatally come within his sphere of influence. Yet Barabas is also driven by unconscious erotic desires, specifically homoerotic ones,[57] which then surface decisively in *Massacre* through the portrayal of Henry III. Even more significantly, Marlowe also becomes influenced by Shakespeare's artistic exploration of "acting" as not simply Machiavellian manipulation but as the grounds of competent action and survival in the social world. Navarre in *The Massacre* shows some success in balancing his conflicting impulses, as between his aggression and his forbearance, which at times may even take on an aspect of viable spiritual faith. Such faith appears to become progressively less passive and naïve through the course of the play: "We must with resolute minds resolve to fight / In honour of our God and country's good" (16.10–11). Edward III in *Edward II* shows a similar potential for balancing active and passive impulses, although the exceptionally bleak and vicious social world portrayed in the play seems to render the spiritual potential within the characters mere echoes in a void. While Marlowe's early death prevented further artistic development along these lines, he clearly takes cues from the tensions within the characterizations of the second and third parts of *Henry VI* – tensions which potentially lead to greater psychological depth – in particular, as suggested above, the portrayal of Queen Margaret.

While in part 2 of *Henry VI* Margaret is remarkable for the extent of her duplicity and unethical manipulation, the queen emerges clearly in part 3 as a more admirable "masculine" figure, politically and martially; as Clifford pointedly advises the king, "I would Your Highness would depart the field, / The Queen hath best success when you are absent" (2.2.73–4). Margaret is admittedly allowed a moment of astonishing brutality in the scene in which she taunts York with the bloody napkin of his dead son Rutland, a scene memorable enough to Shakespeare's contemporary audiences to be alluded to as a kind of synecdoche of Shakespeare's budding art, in parodic form, in Robert Greene's – or perhaps Henry Chettle's – epistle "To those Gentlemen his Quondam acquaintance" in the notorious *Greenes Groatsworth of witte*.[58] It is not difficult to imagine why this scene had a powerful effect on an Elizabethan audience. Placed on a "molehill," crowned with paper, and taunted with "now looks he like a king" (1.4.96), York clearly experiences a mock crucifixion. Yet, as is so often the case, the nature of the satire, or the meaning of the parody in this manifestation of a secular Christ, is not easy to determine. Although York dies with spiritual emphasis – "Open Thy gate of mercy, gracious God! / My soul flies through these wounds to seek out Thee" (177–8) – his role is hardly spiritually consistent. During his capture, he boasts, "My ashes, as the phoenix, may bring forth / A bird that will revenge upon you all" (35–7), evoking an image often associated with Christ in the Renaissance to underline the divine destiny of his progeny. Yet the bird image is almost immediately ironized: as he is overpowered, Clifford mocks, "so strives the woodcock with the gin" (61). Clifford returns to bird imagery in his lecture to Henry two scenes later, concerning the king's disinheritance of his own son: "The smallest worm will turn, being trodden on, / And doves will peck in safeguard of their brood. / Ambitious York did level at thy crown" (2.2.17–19). Clifford clearly construes Henry's political irresponsibility as *unnatural*; and the degeneration of bird imagery from Phoenix to trapped woodcock and pecking dove thus figures York's "divine" ambition as wholly secular and worldly. But oddly York's prophecy is still substantiated in the play. His son King Edward "plays God" as he welcomes back his brother Clarence as prodigal son: "Now welcome more, and ten times more beloved, / Than if thou never hadst deserved our hate!" (5.1.103–4). And, ironically, Richard plays "Judas" (5.7.33) as he embraces his brother's royal family at the end of the play, but only after he hastens to London to "make a bloody supper in the Tower" (5.5.85), where the murder of Henry VI figures as a parodic communion.

Probably the most painful irony of York's crucifixion emerges from Margaret's brutality, her shockingly unfeminine behaviour as "She-wolf of France." However, despite her ruthlessness, Margaret at times in part 3 achieves a "manly" balance of military and rhetorical assertiveness that the whole tetralogy intimates as a kind of psychological ideal. This epitomizing contrasts greatly with Marlowe's development of female characters. While Marlowe's Isabella reflects Margaret's earlier duplicity and hypocrisy, this queen is not allowed to assume the political and military dominance of Shakespeare's. Isabella's most impressive and assertive political speech is rather ruthlessly cut off by her lover Mortimer: "Now madam, if you be a warrior, / Ye must not grow so passionate in speeches" (4.4.14–15). The two queens in fact are both faced with managing the problem of a weak and politically ineffective husband, although Isabella faces the additional challenge of Edward's homosexuality. To an extent they transfer the focus of their political hopes to their male offspring, driven by a sexual frustration that is only temporarily or partly mitigated by their respective lovers. But Marlowe denies the growth into effective and "manly" political agency to Isabella that Shakespeare grants Margaret.

The most interesting artistic coincidence between Shakespeare and Marlowe arises through the ramifications of a failure of masculine control. I believe that Charles Forker exaggerates, and in crucial ways may ultimately be critically mistaken, when he asserts that "What is perhaps more important than any of the hints, verbal or otherwise, that Marlowe may have taken from Shakespeare is the total difference of ethos and philosophic perspective that *Edward II* projects."[59] It is true that Henry VI continues to make pious if ineffectual and futile appeals to a spiritual power in part 3, while the metaphysical appeals and allusions in *Edward II* are more uncertain, nebulous and at times nightmarish; as for example the allusion to Lucifer through the name of Edward's murderer Lightborn. Yet it is not clear that Shakespeare makes any more persuasive a case for a "providential concept of historical process" in the first tetralogy,[60] although he could perhaps be said to gamely *play* with such an idea, an aspect to which I will return in the next chapter. Shakespeare clearly focuses more emphatically on the failure of the *transfer* of responsibility between generations, specifically between fathers and sons, so obviously highlighted symbolically in part 3, 2.5, where the king observes, "*Enter a Son that hath killed his father at one door [bearing in the dead body]*" and "*Enter at another door, a Father that hath killed his son, bearing of his son.*" The Son in this scene movingly echoes Christ's words of forgiveness on the cross – "Pardon me God, I knew not what I did" (69) – but this is clearly not a Christ-like utterance, rather an assertion of dire remorse over unintentionally tragic patricide. After listening to their respective lamentations, the king adds his own pathetically futile and self-effacing grief: "Woe above woe, grief more than common grief! / O, that my death would stay these ruthful deeds! / O, pity, pity, gentle heaven, pity!" (94–6). In Marlowe the failure of the transference or inheritance of power and responsibility is more narrowly focused on the three King Edwards: young Edward II's refusal to recognize his inheritance of kingly responsibility, or even to mourn his father, at the beginning of the play, as he writes to Gaveston, "My father is deceased; come, Gaveston, / And share the kingdom with thy dearest friend," and the careful resumption of responsibility, and the calculated, even possibly theatrical or factitious mourning, by Edward III at the end of the play.

Most crucially it is this careful distinction between "acting" – as hypocrisy, as misrepresentation, as self-serving manipulation – and "acting" as a necessary mode of responsible social action that Marlowe has gleaned from Shakespeare's example. The conclusion of my previous chapter suggested that such a crucial distinction – at the heart of the relationship between the two playwrights – is inherently downplayed or even rendered invisible by critical insistence on the "mere" performativity, and the denial of the deeper integrity of, the human self. Yet the two different tracks of theological concern which I have been tracing (initially via their contrasting responses to Spenser) clearly bring the playwrights to a similar, *existential* emphasis on the ethical and moral significance of human inwardness, where the further significance of "providence," if not absolutely irrelevant, pales by comparison in an analysis of psychological and political cause and effect.

Perhaps most striking of all is that it is Marlowe, and not Shakespeare, who focuses or clarifies this philosophical and moral emphasis through an image pattern that Shakespeare then amplifies and develops assiduously in *Richard III*. In what may be the play's most powerful lines, Edward II laments, during his imprisonment and imposed abdication at Killingworth Castle, "But what are kings when regiment is gone / But perfect shadows in a sunshine day?" (5.1.26–7). These lines appear to have struck a chord with late twentieth- and early twenty-first-century audiences, and in fact serve as part of the final voice-over at the end of Derek Jarman's film version of the play.[61] Perhaps they are now sensed as upholding the very vacuity of the human self that postmodernism repeatedly emphasizes, the seemingly endless reiteration that selves are void.[62] Yet it is more accurate, and more profound, to interpret them as surpassing the conscious understanding of Edward's own self-pity – as, in effect, a perfect expression of Edward's narcissism, his failure of tragic anagnorisis. The Marlovian (and Shakespearean) history play through this moment achieves a vision that true "kingliness," true integrity, resides not simply, and ultimately perhaps not at all, in "regiment," the external trappings of kingship; nor is the competency of any other social role invested simply in "externals" – be they material or indeed spiritual, in the form of a mediating Christ. True "kingliness" or integrity apparently resides in the aspiring nobleman – as primarily a mirror of middle-class ambition – who achieves responsible control over his physical being and social destiny, by in part managing to realize his own internalized, "spiritual" (moral and intellectual) resources.

The image of "shadows" does recur at earlier moments in Shakespeare's first tetralogy, although in limited and less ideologically crucial contexts. Part 1 of *Henry VI* contains two brief references. When the Countess of Auvergne attempts to entrap Talbot, he laughs off her plot: "No, no, I am but shadow of myself. / You are deceived. My substance is not here; / For what you see is but the smallest part / And least proportion of humanity" (2.3.51–4). His "substance" is the whole homosocial military network that upholds him, a significant part of which he proceeds to bring on stage by winding his horn. In 5.4 Alençon simply objects that King Henry's request for tribute reduces the Dauphin politically to a "shadow of himself" (133). Part 2 contains only one reference: Suffolk delivers up Margaret to the king's "most gracious hands, that are the substance / Of that great shadow I did represent" (1.1.14). In part 3 Margaret taunts the captured York, "Come, make him stand upon this molehill here, / That raught at mountains with outstretched arms / Yet parted but the shadow with his hand" (1.4.67–9); the image here suggests the emptiness of York's rapacious ambition. When the humiliated Warwick in 4.3, made a fool of diplomatically in France, switches his allegiance and helps restore Henry to the throne, he mocks his former ally King Edward's Tamburlainean claim that his mind "exceeds the compass of [Fortune's] wheel": "Then, for his mind [that is, in complete fantasy], be Edward England's king. / But Henry now shall wear the English crown / And be true king indeed, thou but a shadow" (47–50). King Henry subsequently and irresponsibly entrusts the kingdom to two (turncoat) protectors, Clarence and Warwick, since he wishes "to lead a private life" (4.6.42), again anticipating Edward II's desire to withdraw from political duty: "Make several kingdoms of this monarchy … So I may have some nook or corner left / To frolic with my dearest Gaveston" (1.4.70–3). Warwick reluctantly agrees, saying to Clarence, "We'll yoke together, like a double shadow / To Henry's body, and supply his place," although he immediately adds what seems a pointed criticism of Henry's irresponsibility: "I mean, in bearing weight of government / While he enjoys the honor and the ease" (4.6.49–52).

This veiled criticism comes closest to evoking the sense of moral and political failure in the "perfect shadows" that Marlowe puts in the mouth of the lamenting Edward; but Marlowe mentions, as well, the idea of sun or sunshine, and thus adds a significant metaphysical dimension to the image pattern. The significance of this image pattern should not be dismissed as simply a clichéd distinction between appearance and reality. That the binary of essence and reflection (or sign), substance and shadow (or form or performance) that Shakespeare, following this cue, subsequently develops so extensively in *Richard III* has an ultimately religious or spiritual significance for both playwrights is suggested by this later protagonist's somewhat surprising swearing by St. Paul; he is in fact the only character in Shakespeare to do so. The subsequent chapter will explore the political, psychological, and ideological ramifications of this development.

Chapter Four

The Shadow-King: Shakespeare's Development of Humanist History in *Richard III*, *Edward III*, and *King John*

Sun and Shadow in *Richard III*

As the end of the previous chapter claimed, Marlowe's image pattern in *Edward II*, "But what are kings when regiment is gone / But perfect shadows in a sunshine day," served as a key catalyst for Shakespeare's imagery in *Richard III*, partly through the addition of "sun" to the pattern of "shadows" that Shakespeare was only fitfully developing in the *Henry VI* plays. Such imagery is not without cultural precedence, and the sun image was traditionally associated with kingship, and, in English poetry, with Christhood. The image of the sun itself has special significance in *3 Henry VI* through the vision of the three suns in 2.1, which emblematizes the inheritance of masculine *virtus* and the loyalty underpinning homosocial bonds. Not yet aware of the brutal slaying of their father, the Duke of York, at the end of the previous act, his sons Edward and Richard wonder about his fate. Interrupting his account of the martial prowess of his father, Richard observes, "See how the morning opes her golden gates / And takes her farewell of the glorious sun!" For him the sight recalls simply the vitality of youthful and erotically charged masculinity: "How well resembles it the prime of youth, / Trimmed like a younker prancing to his love" (2.1.21–4). But immediately Edward exclaims, "Dazzle mine eyes, or do I see three suns?," to which Richard rejoins:

> Three glorious suns, each one a perfect sun,
> Not separated with the racking clouds,
> But severed in a pale clear-shining sky.
> See, see! They join, embrace, and seem to kiss,
> As if they vowed some league inviolable. (25–30)

For Edward it becomes a favourable omen that the three sons of York, "Each one already blazing by our meeds, / Should notwithstanding join our lights together / And overshine the earth as this the world" (36–8). But the apparent divinization of masculinity is quickly ironized, not just subsequently, where Richard's notorious soliloquy at 3.2.124–95 anticipates his murderous ambition in *Richard III*, but in his immediate comments here. To Edward's vow, "henceforward will I bear / Upon my target three fair-shining suns," Richard replies, ostensibly comically, "Nay, bear three daughters. By your leave I speak it, / You love the breeder better than the male" (2.1.39–42).

Richard's joke anticipates how (hetero)erotic interest can undermine the strength of homosocial bonds even as the abrasive humour seems to undercut the supposed sanctity, the metaphysical authenticity, of the "vision" of the three suns, which curiously Richard initially seems to emotionally embrace. The fourth play of the first tetralogy becomes an extended meditation on especially the latter feature, the potential validity, or simply the political and Machiavellian efficacy, of a providential view of history. The sexual meaning of *Richard III* becomes almost as ambiguous and obscure. Shakespeare's Henry VI had been in part a weak king because his futile piety fundamentally *excluded* viable erotic interest, opening his rule to the manipulations of Suffolk, Margaret, and others. Since Edward IV's excessive libido does, as Richard insinuates, create significant political problems even before the end of *3 Henry VI*, the "manliness" of true kingship would seem for Shakespeare, logically, to require a happy medium, a healthy if controlled (hetero)sexual interest. Shakespeare responds to but also decisively represses or contains the homoeroticism introduced by Marlowe, since *Edward II* suggests politically that excessive homoerotic interest, through its intense exacerbation of more traditional homosocial bonds, may play an even more disastrous role than excessive heteroerotic desire in failed masculine self-fashioning.

With Richard's career we arrive at another study of pathological behaviour, one arising, as both the soliloquy at *3 Henry VI* 3.2 and the opening soliloquy of *Richard III* suggest, in large part from thwarted erotic desire:

> Why, love foreswore me in my mother's womb;
> And, for I should not deal in her soft laws,
> She did corrupt frail nature with some bribe
>
> ...
>
> To disproportion me in every part,
> Like to a chaos, or an unlicked bear whelp

That carries no impression like the dam.
And am I then a man to be beloved? (*3 Henry VI* 3.2.153–63)

I, that am rudely stamped, and want love's majesty
To strut before a wanton ambling nymph;
…
Why, I, in this weak piping time of peace,
Have no delight to pass away the time,
Unless to see my shadow in the sun
And descant on mine own deformity.
And therefore, since I cannot prove a lover
To entertain these fair well-spoken days,
I am determinèd to play a villain. (*Richard III* 1.1.16–30)

For Janet Adelman the speech from *3 Henry VI* is so crucial that "in it we hear – I think for the first time in Shakespeare – the voice of a fully developed subjectivity, the characteristically Shakespearean illusion that a stage person has interior being, including motives that he himself does not fully understand." But she also significantly observes that what Richard speaks about "is the origin of his aggression in the problematic maternal body."[1] A connection between the maternal and the Marian influences of a Catholic upbringing may seem facile – and Adelman admittedly considers more general cultural conditions, such as withholding of breast-feeding and the vagaries and uncertainties of wet-nursing, which contributed to such anxieties. Yet the specific feature she observes, especially with respect to its generation of interiority, does not predominate in either Spenser or Marlowe.[2] The previous chapter observed a poetic world of deracinated heroes in Marlowe and Spenser, and this tendency appears to largely exclude both paternal *and* maternal presence.

Shakespeare's clearer focus on the maternal body may reflect a closer attention to the importance, in his work, of the role of physical "embodiment" in the development of human subjectivity. Interestingly, in the final line quoted above from the opening soliloquy of *Richard III*, "I am determinèd to play a villain," Shakespeare appears to equivocally present, perhaps even parody, ideas of determinism or predestination through Richard's Vice-like assertion of villainous agency. Twentieth-century (and later) readings of the play like to pose the question of the origins of Richard's pathology, opposing the assumed Elizabethan "essentialist" position of his deformity as a clear moral reflection of his evil character against a more sympathetic understanding that his psychopathology in fact *arises* from his physical limitations. As so often,

Shakespeare seems to have anticipated our modern and postmodern debates: the thematic core of the play emerges as the indeterminacy, the uncertainty of *signs* – even physical or natural "signs" – and the challenge of the correct reading of signs in human experience. In effect Shakespeare responds to Marlowe's own response to the *Henry VI* plays, in *Edward II*'s existential vision of humanist self-fashioning and human suffering, with a deeply ambiguous but fascinating exploration of the relation between human social performativity and moral speculation regarding human "essence."[3] In the process, the status of the "spiritual" takes on a more clearly psychological manifestation, without however becoming reducible to a merely material manifestation.

Richard III is certainly notable for its ambiguous rendering of the transcendental. Does the play support the Tudor myth of a vengeful divine agency fulfilling its vigorous expiation of the original (political) sin of the murder of Richard II, or are the cycles of revenge and retribution explainable purely on the level of human psychological tendencies, and the ways of secular politics? This is of course not a new critical question. It has often been asked, since Margaret's prophecies all seem to come true, does this guarantee her status as a divine prophetess? Antony Hammond notes in the 1981 Arden edition that "Margaret's curses come true, not because she utters them, but because in the circumstances their fulfilment is entirely probable."[4] A more recent analysis from the *Cambridge Companion to Shakespeare's History Plays*, however, suggests that, while Margaret invokes Heaven with a "diabolical spirit," "the fulfilment of her predictions ... gives [an] allegorical dimension to her role. Divine Justice or Providence is [therefore] seen to be at work."[5] Indeed, Richard as "scourge of God" is not in control of the final script, in spite of his brilliant performances, and once the (divine) chastisement of English society is finished, the scourge himself must be destroyed. Given the pressures of Tudor propaganda, and with a Tudor still sitting on the throne, the circumspect Shakespeare has obvious reasons for encouraging such an interpretation. This playwright had no need for Raleigh to point out to him that he who follows Truth too closely in the heels may get kicked in the teeth.

As already intimated, the interpretive ambiguity I have just briefly outlined may be considered the play's ideological point: the interrogative obfuscation of a "transcendental" signified through shifting signifiers. While I am personally sceptical about a Shakespeare who keenly perceived God's hand actively at work behind the scenes of human history, directly influencing effects beyond the consequences of individual human agency, this study contends that spiritual influences upon that very human agency were not to Shakespeare unimaginable. In *Richard III* there remains a specific theological component to Shakespeare's exploration of this theme of transcendent meaning, as witnessed by Richard's curious, and repeated, swearing by St. Paul. It is as if the playwright wants, or finds it necessary, to contextualize his first detailed exploration of human role playing as comprehensive self-fashioning with the Pauline and mystical assertion that, in reality, "[the human self is] dead, and [its] life is hid with Christ in God" (Colossians 3:3). That is, Richard's evocations of St. Paul should be read not simply as conscious hypocrisy, but as an unconscious intimation of his failure of spiritual and ethical substantiation. In fact, after his successful wooing of Anne, Richard gleefully elaborates on his initial pastime of watching his "shadow in the sun" (1.1.26) by asserting, "Shine out, fair sun, till I have bought a glass, / That I may see my shadow as I pass" (1.2.262–3). For an Elizabethan audience attuned to biblical texts, this elaboration would very likely recall St. Paul's famous meditation in 1 Corinthians: "For now we see through a glasse darkely" (13:12).

Marlowe's Posthumous Influence

Therefore a key image – the mirror – which Meredith Skura associates with Richard's paradoxical aggression and vulnerability as an *actor*, persistently carries a religious and Pauline significance.[6] The narcissistic dynamic is clearly signalled in *3 Henry VI*, where Richard's ambition, as Skura notes, echoes *Tamburlaine*:

> Father, do but think
> How sweet a thing it is to wear a crown,
> Within whose circuit is Elysium
> And all that poets feign of bliss and joy. (1.2.28–31)

This echo, however, occurs within a speech which begins by asserting not the Tamburlainean fantasy of absolute (poetic) control but the radically qualified power of human words and discourse: "An oath is of no moment, being not took / Before a true and lawful magistrate" (22–3). It is worth considering how far Richard's peculiar narcissism removes us from Marlovian fantasy. Indeed, as early as *1 Henry VI* the machinations of the Yorkist faction reveal a notable kind of politic "faith." In 2.5 the imprisoned and dying Mortimer warns Richard Plantagenet, "With silence, nephew, be thou politic. / Strong-fixèd is the house of Lancaster / And like a mountain, not to be removed" (101–3). Ironically, the house of Lancaster under the rule of Henry VI turns out to be exceptionally fragile. Nevertheless Mortimer's simile recalls, through inversion,

Jesus' description of faith the size of a mustard seed (Matthew 17:20), and Paul's description of the futility of such faith in the absence of love (1 Corinthians 13:1–2). This ambiguous reference powerfully foreshadows both the spectacularly successful aggression and the ultimate, and loveless, futility of Richard III's later manipulations.

Through such unconscious and ironic intimation of spiritual substantiation, Marlowe's influence remains I think decisive. In a general sense, Shakespeare in *Richard III* could be said to return to the monodramatic structure of the earlier Marlowe, as Richard, unlike Henry VI, completely dominates the action and plot development of this play. And the character of the protagonist, as hero-villain, so obviously parallels both Barabas from *The Jew of Malta* and the Guise from *The Massacre at Paris*, although the latter case again raises the question, as noted in the previous chapter, of who is imitating whom. In the famous soliloquy from *3 Henry VI* Richard muses:

> Why, then, I do but dream on sovereignty,
> Like one that stands upon a promontory
> And spies a far-off shore where he would tread.
> …
> And I – like one lost in a thorny wood,
> That rends the thorns and is rent with thorns,
> Seeking a way and straying from the way,
> Not knowing how to find the open air,
> But toiling desperately to find it out –
> Torment myself to catch the English crown;
> And from that torment I will free myself
> Or hew my way out with a bloody ax. (3.2.134–81)

The sense of the astonishing destructiveness of ambition is similarly if more crudely evoked in the Guise's assertion:

> That like I best that flies beyond my reach.
> Set me to scale the high Pyramides,
> And thereon set the diadem of France,
> I'll either rend it with my nails to naught
> Or mount the top with my aspiring wings,
> Although my downfall be the deepest hell. (2.39–44)

The ambiguity of the pronoun "it" in line 42 renders uncertain whether the Guise will actually destroy the thing, the crown, that he insatiably seeks. The purpose of the art here is not so much political analysis as it is a more general consideration of the nature of masculine ambition; a sense of the king as archetype of the male self again seems to predominate, even as the perverse self-destructiveness of the desire is emphasized.

Yet Shakespeare also emphasizes less conscious desires, and Marlowe's *Jew of Malta* once more serves as a crucial model. Consciously at first Richard gives no credence to deeper "spiritual" beliefs or intimations. He manipulates King Edward's susceptibility to such beliefs in order to imprison and to destroy his brother Clarence: "This day should Clarence closely be mewed up / About a prophecy, which says that G / Of Edward's heirs the murderer shall be" (*Richard III* 1.1.38–40). Clarence apparently shares Richard's incredulity:

> [Our brother] hearkens after prophecies and dreams,
> And from the crossrow plucks the letter G,
> And says a wizard told him that by G
> His issue disinherited should be;
> …
> These, as I learn, and suchlike toys as these
> Hath moved His Highness to commit me now. (1.1.54–61)

"Toys" may mean simply trifles, but in this context an allusion to Machevil's Prologue in *The Jew of Malta* seems likely: "I count religion but a childish toy, / And hold there is no sin but ignorance. / Birds of the air will tell of murders past? / I am ashamed to hear such fooleries!" (14–17). The prophecy in question, although for Clarence and Richard (at this point) a joke, ultimately is fulfilled, not through George, Duke of Clarence, but Richard, Duke of Gloucester. This further "toying" by Shakespeare sets the tone of the metaphysical references for the rest of the play, and possibly reinforces the significance of the above allusion to 1 Corinthians: "but when I became a man, I put away childish things" (13:11). Such rhetorical effects cannot be facilely dismissed as facetious. The "crossrow" that Clarence mentions refers to the cross which in the early modern period was prefixed to the alphabet; and Richard's description of himself as "rent with thorns" also recalls the crucifixion. Rather like the speaker in Herbert's "The Collar," the terms through which these characters dismiss the transcendent ironically confirm, or at least obliquely recall, its significance.

The Jew of Malta has a further influence on the text, in the sense of its evocation of less conscious erotic desires. In his ruthless ambition Richard, like Barabas, appears radically independent, and, like Marlowe's Jew, he disdains erotic bonds. He woos Anne, the widow of the previous

Prince of Wales, only for reasons of political expediency: "I'll have her, but I will not keep her long" (1.2.232). Unlike his brother Edward, he prefers the company of men. His connection to Buckingham, especially, seems noticeably fervent in its intensity. In response to Buckingham's encouraging and conspiratorial speech beginning, "My lord, whoever journeys to the Prince, / For God's sake let not us two stay at home," Richard replies, "My other self, my counsel's consistory, / My oracle, my prophet! My dear cousin, / I, as a child, will go by thy direction" (2.2.146–53). At this point in the text, which John Jowett describes as "a moment of unique and apparently unfeigned involvement with another person,"[7] it is difficult to discern whether the rhetoric is sincere, or simply a continuation of Richard's machinations and manipulations. The ambiguity is ultimately irresolvable, due primarily to the largely unconscious nature of the desire being expressed.

The exchange in fact directly echoes Barabas's address to the Turkish slave Ithamore after he has disowned his daughter Abigail in favour of his "adopted" son:

> Come near, my love, come near, thy master's life,
> My trusty servant, nay, my second self!
> For I have now no hope but even in thee,
> And on that hope my happiness is built. (3.4.14–17)

Jowett's commentary in the Oxford edition is instructive:

> Barabas and Richard use such hyperbole to weld together their alliances in crime. Both partnerships degenerate into rivalry that causes the accomplice to lose his life. The phrase "my other self" was proverbial for friendship, and indeed it had potential homoerotic implications to which Marlowe and perhaps Shakespeare respond. That Richard should engage in such mutuality might be puzzling, were it not that it complements his earlier narcissistic fantasy. Buckingham is indeed another self, taking on Richard's characteristics as a Protean actor.[8]

Jowett may underestimate the homoerotic and unconscious potential here. While there is evidence after the slave exits briefly that Barabas simply manipulates Ithamore – "Thus every villain ambles after wealth, / Although he ne'er be richer than in hope" (3.4.52–3) – the mistake of emotionally investing in and foolishly trusting a "friend not known but in distress" is repeated more glaringly near the end of the play with Ferneze – "Governor, I enlarge thee; live with me" (5.2.72, 91) – a passage which ironically echoes Marlowe's famous lyric of romantic invitation, "Come live with me and be my love." For these reasons this echo of Marlowe strikes me as one of the most pregnant in all of Shakespeare.

I am conscious in this study that, by focusing somewhat narrowly on one particular influence, I am necessarily filtering out a variety of possible influences – cultural, historical, personal, and literary (other than Marlowe) – on the greatest writer who ever lived. But because of this narrowness of focus, it strikes me as even more remarkable that Shakespeare would deliberately echo this passage from the work of one of his theatrical rivals, indeed a Marlovian passage that apparently did not reach print until long after the two playwrights' deaths. Since it involves in effect an acute understanding on Shakespeare's part of Marlowe's portrayal of largely unconscious desires, and since Adelman interestingly associates such portrayal as contributing to the illusion that stage personae possess interior being, it may therefore be possible to ascribe to Marlowe's influence on Shakespeare some role in the "invention of the human." This moment from *Richard III* represents a crucial moment of Marlovian influence on the playwright's conception of human emotions, as well as, paradoxically, a significant moment, at least at this point in Shakespeare's career, of containment or repression of homoerotic desire which Marlowe has brought to bear on the English stage.

In spite of its crucial evocation of the power, and the danger, of (unconscious) emotional needs, the earlier acts of *Richard III* more directly highlight the danger of a naïve or simplistic reading of signs and of human performances. Whatever the true nature of human essence, what really matters for much of the play, let us admit it, are the consequences of the role playing; what really determines the outcome of events is the use and misuse of signs and signifiers, and the characters' ability to read them accurately or inaccurately. Even the unconscious itself, with its deeper, potentially transcendental perceptions, can only communicate via signs, omens, portents, dreams. To take an example of a poor reader of the unconscious, Hastings is too obtuse to credit a series of such signs, which proves fatal for him:

> Woe, woe for England! Not a whit for me,
> For I, too fond, might have prevented this.
> Stanley did dream the boar did raze our helms,
> And I did scorn it and disdain to fly.
> Three times today my footcloth horse did stumble,
> And started, when he looked upon the Tower,
> As loath to bear me to the slaughterhouse. (3.4.80–6)

Clarence, "simple, plain Clarence" (1.1.118), may initially share this naïveté, but he becomes rather more sensitive to the issues welling up from his unconscious. In spite of the obvious symbolism of his dream in the Tower, with its suggestions of a guilty conscience, it takes the brutality of the murderers to make him realize the enmity of his brother Richard. If the howling ghosts in the Senecan underworld of Clarence's dream certainly emphasize his fear of divine vengeance, then it is particularly ironic that Shakespeare goes so far as to evoke a Eucharistic image when Clarence's murdered body is grotesquely imagined by his murderers to become a "sop" (1.4.159) in a butt of malmsey wine. If the stabbing by the First Murderer is not quite fatal, then Clarence, as his dream foretold, does indeed die by drowning: "Take that, and that! (*Stabs him.*) If all this will not do, / I'll drown you in the malmsey butt within" (272–3), says the killer before exiting with Clarence. The parallel between corpse and communion bread underlines the sacrilegious brutality, not to mention astonishing violation of personal faith, in Richard's fratricide, at the same time that the reduction of Clarence's body to a parodic Eucharistic fragment potentially ironizes the efficacy of atonement theology.

There are, moreover, curious echoes of the murder of Marlowe's Edward II in Clarence's death scene, although they are somewhat complicated by differences between copy texts: the First Quarto of 1597 (in Jowett's Oxford edition) and the First Folio (which Bevington employs). In the Quarto the Second Executioner says, "Come, shall we to this gear?" (1.4.140), which echoes Marlowe's Lightborn, "So now, must I about this gear; ne'er was there any / So finely handled as this king shall be" (5.5.38–9). Clarence's conversation with the Keeper (F), or with Brackenbury (Q), also echoes but significantly contrasts with the horrifying dialogue between Edward II and Lightborn. In the Quarto Clarence exclaims,

> O Brackenbury, I have done those things
> Which now bear evidence against my soul
> For Edward's sake, and see how he requites me.
> I pray thee, gentle keeper, stay by me.
> My soul is heavy, and I fain would sleep. (Jowett, 1.4.63–7)

Jowett suggests that "My soul is heavy" echoes "Christ's words expressing his sorrow and anticipation of death at Gethsemane (Matthew 27:38)." A Christ role is thus implicitly appropriated, not evoked in desperate dependency. The Folio adds the following four lines after "see how he requites me":

O God! If my deep prayers cannot appease thee,
But thou wilt be avenged on my misdeeds,
Yet execute thy wrath in me alone!
O, spare my guiltless wife and my poor children. (Bevington, 1.4.69–72)

In the Folio, Clarence says to the Keeper, "sit by me awhile," rather than "stay with me." In both versions the Keeper (or Brackenbury) responds, "I will my lord. God give Your Grace good rest." Clarence thus shows a deep sense of personal responsibility, both through a clear consciousness of guilt and a desire to spare his family, so that the effects of his crimes, unlike Original Sin, will not be transferred to his descendants; and the Keeper responds sympathetically, as comforter or almost indeed as Confessor.

Conversely the imprisoned Edward II displays not a recognition of past sins or errors, but a horrifying mixture of self-pity and terror. Tortured through sleep deprivation, he exclaims, "For not these ten days have these eyes' lids closed. / Now as I speak they fall, and yet with fear / Open again. O wherefore sits thou here?" To Lightborn's rejoinder, "If you mistrust me, I'll be gone, my lord," Edward responds, "No, no, for if thou mean'st to murder me, / Thou wilt return again, and therefore stay." He drifts momentarily off to sleep, quickly awakens, and repeats, "Yet stay, O stay a while." With mounting terror he finally insists, "therefore tell me, wherefore art thou come," earning Lightborn's suddenly brutal reply, "To rid thee of thy life" (5.5.93–106). The horror of this most terrifying death scene is intensified by Edward's desperate dependency, a narcissistic failure to ground his self-identification in any sense of personal responsibility for his suffering. Shakespeare's rewriting of the scene, with an apparent parody of Eucharistic imagery in Clarence's murder, is borne out through an attribution to the victim of a greater sense of "soul" or psychic depth, in spite of the resistance and fear that inescapably occur there as well.

Ironies of Historiography

Shakespeare evokes the Eucharist ironically again at the end of *Richard III*, when the supposedly saintly and divinely ordained Richmond proposes to take the sacrament to celebrate the union of the white and red roses, the Houses of York and Lancaster. Even the echo of colour in the roses, white for bread and red for wine, appears to reinforce the parallel between political and theological sanctification – at least if the audience has managed to forget the body of Clarence in the malmsey butt. Shakespeare subtly but daringly undercuts Richmond's spiritual status in the concluding scenes. For one thing, the gesture of taking the sacraments devolves almost immediately into a form of political coercion and intimidation:

> ... as we have ta'en the Sacrament,
> We will unite the white rose and the red.
> Smile heaven upon this fair conjunction,
> That long have frowned upon their enmity!
> What traitor hears me and says not amen? (5.5.18–22)

The refusal to "innocently" take part in the ritual, to say "amen," is tantamount to treason and carries the penalty of capital punishment. Moreover, Shakespeare fleetingly but rather astonishingly – especially considering his play's traditionally assumed relation to Tudor propaganda – includes the "unofficial view that Richmond owed his victory to a bribe."[9] On the eve of the Battle of Bosworth, Norfolk approaches Richard, shows him a paper, and states, "This found I on my tent this morning." Richard reads aloud, "'Jockey of Norfolk, be not so bold / For Dickon thy master is bought and sold'," but contemptuously dismisses the note as "A thing devisèd by the enemy" (5.3.303–6). Richmond would appear guilty either of attempted bribery or petty fear-mongering. And Richard's deservedly famous exclamation, "I think there be six Richmonds in the field; / Five have I slain today instead of him. / A horse! A horse! My kingdom for a horse!" (5.4.11–13), reveals one final rather disturbing aspect of Richmond's manipulation of signifiers, especially when we recall that this reference is Shakespeare's own invention. Richmond's calculating ruse to confuse his enemies and (duplicitously) increase his own chances for survival anticipates Shakespeare's ambiguous undermining of the regicide Henry IV's nobility at the Battle of Shrewsbury, where participation in the same ruse serves to emphasize his role as a counterfeit king in the second tetralogy. The six Richmonds in the field ironically suggest that Richmond, not Richard, has become a shadow-king, and Shakespeare through the foregoing references would seem to render the male achievement of the "sun" of Christhood all the more tentative.

It is tempting to speculate that the phonetic closeness of the two names, Richard and Richmond, appealed to Shakespeare, since two characters who are apparently diametrically opposed in a moral and theological sense are subtly revealed to be highly similar in their manipulation of roles and of the responses of others. Richard in a sense is justified when he refers to Richmond as "shallow" (5.3.219), interestingly in a speech which begins with his fifth and last adjuration to Paul.[10] Although in the context the epithet "shallow" seems mainly a slur against Richmond's martial inexperience or ineptitude, and, although we know Richard is doomed at Bosworth, it is difficult not to admire his courageous insistence that the sunless day that dawns may as easily be an ill omen for Richmond as for Richard: "For the selfsame heaven / That frowns on me looks sadly upon him" (5.3.286–7). Signs, including natural signs, are inherently ambiguous.

Significantly, nevertheless, the play stresses the very human need to fix signs and make them predictable or reliable. It is not just a need but a responsibility, as Marlowe had demonstrated: Mortimer's use of the ambiguously "unpointed" or unpunctuated Latin letter in *Edward II* 5.4, for example, to facilitate the murder of the king, underlines his political viciousness and lack of integrity. In *Richard III* Bosworth's gloomy day violates human prediction; Richard consults an almanac before retorting, "Then [the sun] disdains to shine, *for by the book* / He should have braved the east an hour ago" (5.3.278–9, my emphasis). The temptation to guarantee meaning and predict outcome through the written word emerges as a key humanist motif at the centre of the play, which contains a haunting exchange between the vulnerable boy-king Edward V and his uncle and Buckingham, concerning the historical status and virtuous stature of Julius Caesar. The topic is raised by the sighting of the Tower of London, supposedly built or at least begun by the Roman conqueror. In the context of English history the Tower is of course a negative or ominous *sign*, since so many political prisoners have perished there, and the boy-king recognizes the omen immediately: "I do not like the Tower, of any place" (3.1.68). He attempts to reinterpret the connotations of the image before him by asking Buckingham, "Did Julius Caesar build that place, my lord?" When answered that Caesar certainly began the edifice, Edward replies, "Is it upon record, or else reported / Successively from age to age he built it?," to which Buckingham replies, "Upon record." The prince then temporarily opts for a belief in a kind of transcendental signified:

> But say, my lord, it were not registered,
> Methinks the truth should live from age to age,
> As 'twere retailed to all posterity,
> Even to the general all-ending day. (75–8)

Although this prompts Richard's response in an aside, "So wise so young, they say, do never live long," it is rather tempting to attribute naïveté, not wisdom, to the prince's remark, or perhaps a desperate clutching at spiritual reality – and transcendental power (and punishment) – to offset his feelings of vulnerability and his premonition of death.

Yet Edward then continues in a more assertive, less naïve fashion when he seems to realize that "truth" cannot simply live, uncorrupted and unadulterated, in the hearts of successive generations of humankind:

> That Julius Caesar was a famous man;
> With what his valor did enrich his wit,
> His wit set down to make his valor live.
> Death makes no conquest of this conqueror,
> For now he lives in fame, though not in life. (84–8)

Here the boy-king recognizes the human, and humanist, need to "set down" or record the valour of such a "famous man"; in fact the very wit of the conqueror is responsible for making his fame to live after his own death. The positing of absolute, transcendental meaning is again qualified by the realization that the recording of truth, and in fact a high degree of personally inspired representation of inner worth, is absolutely essential for the continuing reception of belief – in honour or valour – in a social context. Edward follows this assertion with his own plans for personal fame: "An if I live until I be a man, / I'll win our ancient right in France again" (91–2). Presumably, had he lived he would have imitated Julius Caesar not only in valour but in the wit to "set it down."

More subversively, this idea of the necessity of recording historical "truth" is dramatically emphasized during the culminating tableau of Richmond and Richard on the eve of the Battle of Bosworth. Both actors give the identical command, "Give me some ink and paper" (5.3.23, 49). In Richmond's case the order is ostensibly to facilitate the drawing up of battle plans – "I'll draw the form and model of our battle" (24) – and we are perhaps to assume that Richard's motive is identical. Yet the parallel blocking between the two sides of the stage is surely meant by Shakespeare to symbolically indicate the general act of historiography – and personal and political representation – by these two military opponents whose encounter will determine English history. Richard writes, and falls asleep. Richmond prays to "Thou whose captain I account myself" (108), and then also falls asleep. What follows, of course, is the procession of the ghosts of Richard's victims, first cursing Richard and then blessing Richmond. But since the double gesture of writing immediately precedes their spectral appearances, the uncertain ontological status of the ghosts is thus connected to the act of discursive representation. We may regard the ghosts as projections of Richard's guilty conscience, as were the ghosts in Clarence's nightmare of the afterlife, although their communication with Richmond as well would suggest at least some kind of collective unconscious, some sharing of psychic and sociopolitical repercussions.

Consider again J. Dover Wilson's careful discussion of the ideological and theological problems posed by the Ghost in *Hamlet*, which emerges, "not from a mythical Tartarus, but from the place of departed spirits in which post-medieval England, despite a veneer of Protestantism, still believed at the end of the sixteenth century."[11] The "veneer" of Protestantism, if that is all it is, would necessitate, theoretically, the "real" appearance of ghosts as either (rarely) angels and (more commonly) devils; although the Protestant fold admittedly also included more credulous souls, such as Thomas Browne, and more sceptical ones, such as Reginald Scot. Perhaps in *Richard III* it is enough to pronounce the ghosts dramatically and theatrically effective, and, unlike *Hamlet*, nothing in the play encourages their status as specifically Catholic or purgatorial. But because their actuality is significantly challenged by the ideological context of the play, their simple cursing and blessing might be said to reflect, finally, the demonization and idealization in certain kinds of historical writing that earnestly if rather naïvely pre-cludes moral or political ambiguity and psychological complexity. As Harry Berger argues, "Considering the behavior in life of most of those ghosts, we're entitled to a certain skepticism about the Christian conscience they mediate. Such skepticism produces an odd if momentary effect: in spite of all we know, Richard appears in this episode to be the target of a conspiracy of bad faith."[12] The ghosts' appearance, in essence, suggests the kind of history that devolves too readily into political propaganda.

Rather than the moral or ethical climax of the play, the spectral procession (however theatrically compelling) is a pale echo of the far more ideologically effective discursive record of Richard's crimes, recited to him by Queen Elizabeth in act 4, a record that demolishes the shifting contexts of Richard's previously successful role playing and manipulation. Far more than the formerly formidable but now rather spectral Queen Margaret, Queen Elizabeth emerges as the play's most significant female character not only because she finally out-Richards Richard in duplicity and manipulation – pretending to acquiesce in his (incestuous) demand to marry her daughter – but because she establishes herself as the play's most effective historiographer.

Before ostensibly succumbing to his persuasions, she clearly and courageously inscribes in detail, and to Richard's face, the narrative of his perverse identity and corrupt self-fashioning, what she ironically terms "a story of [his] noble acts" (Jowett 4.4.256) or "a letter of [his] noble deeds" (Bevington 4.4.280). Her speeches expose not Richard's complete absence of a transcendental self or soul – impossible for any human to prove or disprove – but rather the complete vacuity of his necessarily relational self. What she proves is that there is nothing left for him to swear by, since he has violated every political or familial bond that he can now imagine; therefore all signifiers of kingly virtue are tainted:

> Thy George, profaned, hath lost his lordly honor;
> Thy Garter, blemished, pawned his knightly virtue;
> Thy crown, usurped, disgraced his kingly glory.
> If something thou wouldst swear to be believed,
> Swear then by something that thou hast not wronged. (369–73)

On the other hand, the "signifiers" of his viciousness are ubiquitous, and threaten into perpetuity:

> The children live whose fathers thou has slaughtered,
> Ungoverned youth, to wail it in their age;
> The parents live whose children thou hast butchered,
> Old barren plants, to wail it with their age.
> Swear not by time to come, for that thou hast
> Misused ere used, by times ill-used o'erpast. (391–6)

Queen Elizabeth cagily realizes our absolute dependency on signs to convey meaning and value, as well as our need to interpret them correctly or manipulate them effectively, which is why she finally feigns acquiescence to escape Richard's clutches.

Significantly, her emphasis on the necessity of signs, and the absence of proof of transcendental meaning, casts a peculiar shadow over the supposed political and spiritual resolutions of act 5, in particular the moral stature of Richmond, the man to whom Elizabeth ironically chooses to marry her daughter. It could be argued that the play wishes to justify the subtle Machiavellianism of the supposedly saintly Richmond, though it is very difficult to believe that Shakespeare simply holds up, as superior or preferable, *subtle* over *outrageous* hypocrisy. Rather, the play's intimation of the absolute necessity of signs and therefore of role playing in human interaction oddly works to rehabilitate Richard in the final act. It is true that, in his oration to his soldiers, Richard appeals mainly to the cultural construction of English manliness, as he warns about "a scum of Bretons" (5.3.317) who would rape English wives, whereas Richmond is his oration speaks more purely "in the name of God and all these rights" of peace and safety (263). Yet the taint of hypocrisy in the final analysis sits more heavily on the ostensibly purer speech. The direct rhetorical linkage of the six shadow Richmonds on the field of Bosworth to Richard's "A horse! A horse! My kingdom for a horse!" emphasizes not only Richard's greater courage but an astonishing willingness to begin the game all over again – to at least start from the lowest echelon of the aristocracy, a knight on horseback, and climb back up. In his next history play, *King John*, Shakespeare further transforms an exploration of the admittedly often treacherous capacity for role playing into a startling exposé of the uselessness of any "moral" position without individual agency and assertiveness to substantiate it in the context of pragmatic social interaction. *Richard III* thus accomplishes something I believe is central to Shakespeare's art: the text carries out a sceptical reading of a direct appeal to transcendental meaning even as it confirms that specific human behaviour and interaction can, and should, be related to, or evaluated in the *context* of, transcendent or "spiritual" values.

Titus Andronicus: A Senecan Interlude, with Ghosts of Kyd and Peele

Before turning to *King John*, however, I propose to first examine a history play, *Edward III*, that scholars have become increasingly willing to attribute, at least in part, to Shakespeare; and, before approaching this play, I will briefly consider what may well be a significant piece of the puzzle of Shakespeare's artistic development with respect to the religious critique I have been exploring. As mentioned in passing (see above, n. 3), Wells and Taylor recognize a probable artistic pause between the composition of *3 Henry VI* and *Richard III*, with the composition of *Titus Andronicus* in the interim possibly explaining "the tragic structure and Senecan detail" of the final play in the first tetralogy. Some Marlovian influence has been detected in *Titus* – Bevington observes that "Titus' killing of his son Mutius recalls *Tamburlaine Part II*, and Aaron's Vice-like boasting of wanton villainy recalls *The Jew of Malta*."[13] Yet the more thoroughly developed classical aspects and allusions that emerge at this moment in Shakespeare's career, as well as the extraordinarily violent revenge of *Titus*, speak perhaps more closely to the influence of Kyd's *The Spanish Tragedy*.[14] But the composition of *Titus* is now believed to have involved – somewhat confusingly – the hand of Peele: "The tragedy may be the reworking of an 'Ur-*Titus*' by

George Peele, as Jonathan Bate suggests, or a completion of a play for which Peele most likely wrote only the first act."[15] My argument here draws a distinction between playwrights who influenced Shakespeare – Marlowe and at this moment specifically Kyd – and those whose work Shakespeare felt compelled to actively rewrite – in this case Peele. In fact the final play considered in this chapter, *King John*, is now generally considered Shakespeare's major reworking of *The Troublesome Raigne of King John*, which recent scholarship has attributed to Peele with increasing confidence.[16]

I consider first the texts which sympathetically influenced Shakespeare. Kyd's *Spanish Tragedy* has notoriously given rise to contradictory readings, with some critics viewing Kyd as patriotically asserting England's political resistance to Spain's imperial dominance, and others seeing the playwright taking a dangerously subversive stance towards Kyd's own contemporary society. Such subversion carries a pronounced theological component. This subversive potential may be partly attributable to unconscious meaning; the apparently pious Kyd, who claimed to Sir John Puckering after the fallout from the Dutch Church Libel that he proposed to write a poem about St. Paul's conversion, actually produced a play which underlines the politically radical potential of Pauline theology.[17] Although he assumes a greater degree of conscious control on Shakespeare's part, Nicholas Moschovakis proposes a similar argument concerning *Titus*: "As though its pagan mores were not shocking enough," in this play Shakespeare "juxtaposes them with discordant reminders of the Christian cultural context that might be presumed to bound the audience's moral horizons."[18] Moschovakis makes a persuasive case for the anti-Christian thrust of the play. While both *The Spanish Tragedy* and *Titus* are centrally concerned with "the violent death of offspring," the actual motif of human sacrifice emerges pointedly only in *Titus*, a fact which earns Moschovakis's sardonic observation, "Quite apart from the relevance of sacrificial themes to contentious theological and liturgical questions, their use in *Titus* might cause some consternation to anyone who shares the Christian conception of Christ's passion as a sacrifice."[19] This distinction may suggest that Shakespeare rather than Kyd enters into a conscious critique of atonement theology; at the least the "deaths of Alarbus and Lavinia [for example] mark a trajectory of crime and expiation without redemption, the overarching design of which may be viewed as a parody of Christian history."[20]

While the death of Alarbus occurs in the first scene of *Titus*, often ascribed to Peele, Moschovakis's attribution of its more heterodox suggestions to Shakespeare can I think be maintained. While neither the theories of authorship concerning *Titus* nor the text itself are in my opinion exceptionally coherent, two other plays by Peele more clearly indicate a theological position which removes him to the margins of this study's concerns. Many commentators on *The Troublesome Raigne* have noted the anti-Catholic thrust of this text, which its most recent editor identifies as "Peele's strident anti-Catholicism."[21] Even more significantly, Mathew Martin in his edition of Peele's *David and Bathsheba* develops a compelling argument focusing on Peele's highly orthodox Protestantism: "The play's representation of David as poet, prophet, and, foremost, penitent explores the paradoxical political implications of one of the central problems of the Protestant Reformation, God's grace. Disturbingly, David's strength as God's anointed is not undermined but reinforced by his sinfulness."[22] We return in an important sense to Nandra Perry's consideration of Sidney's reading of the penitential David in *The Defense of Poetry*. In chapter 2, I asserted that such an interpretation carries the potential to relieve atonement theology of its tendency to short-circuit humanist self-fashioning, by broadening the possibilities for creative individualism. Yet in this case Peele's portrayal of David clarifies the inflexibility – and in effect the moral dead end – of the orthodox position: "No one, according to Protestant theology, not even David, can be worthy of or merit being ... elected by God and given His grace, whether that be the private grace of the individual believer or the political grace bestowed upon the divinely appointed ruler. Unlike Tamburlaine, Peele's David is obviously unworthy of his election, and the consequences of David's unworthiness are adultery, murder, and civil war."[23] While the fantastical triumphs of Marlowe's Tamburlaine admittedly indicate a "bloody, hypermasculine ethos," this hero's specifically erotic behaviour – carefully preserving Zenocrate's virginity to the end of part 1 – is actually superior to Peele's David. I suggest that Peele's pointed eradication of human merit appears the very thing Shakespeare resists, both within a (not altogether successful) rewriting or completion of *Titus* and then (as we shall see) in his revision of *The Troublesome Raigne*.

But patterns of Protestant self-justification with Marlowe and Kyd are intrinsically parodic and conflicted enough for Shakespeare to build on their implicit interrogation of orthodoxy. To return to parallels between *The Spanish Tragedy* and *Titus*, both these texts blend pagan and Christian references confusingly, but in a way that ultimately reduces the two competitive ideological systems to (often desperate and violent) acts of imagination on the part of the characters. They might therefore both represent a particularly dark manifestation of imaginative agency. Indeed, J.K. Barret has read *Titus* as a kind of cautionary tale, exposing the dangers of "Christian attempts to moralize Ovid's *Metamorphoses*." But if the play "exposes the disconnect between ... literal and metaphorical, letter and spirit that Ovidian moralisation breeds," I intuit a more radical critique of Christian orthodoxy than is suggested by an argument that the text "illustrate[s] the extent to which Ovid and Christianity don't mix."[24] A darker Christian potential also haunts *The Spanish Tragedy*. The fate of its characters, or at least one of them (Balthazar), is apparently fixed by Revenge at the beginning of *The Spanish Tragedy* – which may suggest that the play evokes, or possibly parodies, Calvinist predestination. If we accept the veracity of Kyd's uncomplicated devotion to Pauline theology in the letters to Puckering, and even more to the point if we recall his upbringing in the same Protestant milieu of late sixteenth-century London, even attendance at the same school that produced Spenser, we may wonder what prompted Kyd to develop, imaginatively, the more radical tendencies of Reformation theology. The violent artistic and seditious empowerment of Hieronimo at the play's conclusion suggests a theological response far removed from the socially deferential. Marlowe, with whom Kyd shared lodgings for a time, may certainly have influenced him, although I want for a moment to pursue other reasons for Shakespeare's specific interest in Kyd.

To do so I will focus on what I consider the most daring but compelling moment of Moschovakis's argument concerning *Titus*:

> Was Shakespeare giving form in *Titus* to opinions that we must classify as radical for their time? ... *Titus* presupposes the existence of an irenic standpoint from which the hope of compromise and reconciliation seems preferable to violent confrontation and even to the victory of any particular faction. Such a perspective would suggest an attitude more Erasmian than doctrinally protestant; anyone [in early modern England] who disapproved categorically of coercion, however, would be in this respect as radical as the most radical movements that emerged from the Reformation. At the same time, we must recognize that the latent radicalism of an irenic logic need not be mobilized in the cause of tolerance. It might instead be coordinated with a self-protective policy of Nicodemism, the outward dissimulation of conformity in contradiction to the dictates of one's private conscience.[25]

A policy of Nicodemism recalls, most interestingly, the influence of the Family of Love, although Moschovakis links the idea here simply to Shakespeare's characteristic circumspection: "Nowhere in his work does he unambiguously ally himself with a doctrine or a form of church government." But I wish to raise another feature of Familism which may be relevant to an aspect of both Kyd's and Shakespeare's art, the reduction of scriptural "truth" to allegory: "The allegorical or mystical interpretation of Scriptural events and prophecies was fundamental to [Hendrick] Niclaes' thought. Christ's death, burial and resurrection were not described as matters of literal truth, and it is actually impossible to determine whether H.N. accepted their historical reality."[26] Thus members of the sect "were said to believe that Christ and Antichrist were not real persons, heaven and hell not real places: all were states of mind."[27]

While the use of spiritual allegory can be related generally to the frequent literalization of metaphor in early modern drama – it is certainly frequent, almost ubiquitous, in Marlowe – a distinction regarding this feature can be made between the works of Marlowe and the works of Kyd and Shakespeare. A brief comparison of *Doctor Faustus*, *The Spanish Tragedy*, and *Titus Andronicus* may be illuminating. All three of these texts can be regarded as subversive of orthodox religious thought; all three invite sceptical interpretations of the divine frameworks posited in the dramatic action. Yet in *Faustus* there is a certain reversion of, one could even say attrition of, the sceptical impulse; for example in the famous exchange between Faustus and Mephistopheles: "'Come, I think hell's a fable.' / 'Ay, think so still, till experience change thy mind'" (A2.1.130–1). The language here might in fact be read as Marlowe's "toying" with Familist belief. Mephistopheles has earlier admittedly emphasized, in a sense, the *subjective* nature of hell, in answer to Faustus's question of how he has escaped that particular place:

> Why, this is hell, nor am I out of it.
> Think'st thou that I, who saw the face of God
> And tasted the eternal joys of heaven,
> Am not tormented with ten thousand hells
> In being deprived of everlasting bliss? (A1.3.78–82)

Nevertheless Faustus's final eschatological fate apparently confirms the literal reality of hell, even while the play leaves the efficacy, even potentially the reality, of the heavenly powers uncertain. Thus the play's particular form of scepticism can be said to participate, as recent criticism has reasonably emphasized, in an interrogation of Calvinism, and the doctrine of predestination. Yet ultimately the play contains, within the impulse of a more humane theology, the following core of orthodoxy: the nightmare of Faustus's experience coupled with his incipient humanity seems to beg the question of, or perhaps even ironically to assert subversively, the possibility of a more idealized, more loving concept of the deity.

In Kyd and Shakespeare the two protagonists seem increasingly obsessed with hell or the infernal world as a form of *madness*, as more clearly a *creation* of an excessive or twisted human desire for political or social control. When Lavinia first communicates the identity of her assailants by writing in the sand, Titus cries out – in a Latin quotation derived from Seneca – "Ruler of the mighty heavens, are you so slow to see and hear crimes?" (4.1.83–4). By the arrow-shooting scene, Titus has decided that Astraea, goddess of justice, has left the earth, and so he directs Publius and Sempronius to dig with mattock and spade down to Pluto's region and deliver a petition there (recalling Hieronimo's attempt to dig with his dagger in 3.12). Finally Titus exclaims, "sith there's no justice in earth nor hell, / We will solicit heaven and move the gods / To send down Justice for to wreak our wrongs" (4.3.49–51). He then directs his companions to shoot arrows up to various Roman gods; the men pretend to obey him, hoping to "feed his humor kindly" (29). Titus's madness is closely comparable to Hieronimo's. Their grief becomes so great that in their minds it reaches universal proportions; for them the world takes on – through a veritable theatrical demonstration of madness – the characteristics of their own subjective states. Titus claims:

> I am the sea. Hark how her sighs doth blow!
> She is the weeping welkin, I the earth.
> Then must the sea be movèd with her sighs,
> Then must my earth with her continual tears
> Become a deluge overflowed and drowned. (3.1.225–9)

Hieronimo believes his lamentations extend to the natural world in a similar way:

> Where shall I run to breathe abroad my woes,
> My woes whose weight hath wearied the earth?
> Or mine exclaims, that have surcharged the air
> With ceaseless plaints for my deceased son?
> The blustering winds, conspiring with my words,
> At my lament have moved the leafless trees,
> Disrobed the meadows of their flowered green,
> Made mountains marsh with spring-tides of my tears. (3.7.1–8)[28]

All this is more wish fulfilment than a reality – a narcissistic projection of a personal disorder so strong that it must find sympathy in the natural world.

I have not, however, included this brief consideration of *Titus* to make a case for a simply materialist or atheist reading of Kyd that inspires Shakespeare along similar ideological lines. The art of Kyd and Shakespeare does challenge more traditional religious and eschatological views by placing, despite the playwrights' social vision, a powerfully pagan emphasis on human embodiment and life within nature. Such an emphasis on the sanctity, if not the sanity, of the natural, is certainly present in Marlowe, and has been demonstrated most brilliantly in Edward Snow's analysis of *Doctor Faustus*.[29] But the theme receives I think more comprehensive development in Kyd and Shakespeare. *Titus* and *The Spanish Tragedy* explore the tragic results of traumatic injuries which unhinge the protagonists' usual modes of social identification within the generative processes of life, and invite vengeance at the presumed loss of "divine" justice.

Such exploration of control and embodiment can take on less tragic manifestations in dramatic art. According to Brian Vickers, Kyd and Shakespeare likely collaborated directly on the history play *Edward III*.[30] This play was probably written contemporaneously, or perhaps shortly after *Richard III* (Vickers speculates around 1593), and it effectively illustrates what I described in chapter 1 as a groping towards a kind of necessary Oedipalization of social structure in the theological tracts and heretical theological formulations of early modern England.

Humanist Kingship in *Edward III*

Edward III is slowly receiving recognition as part of the Shakespeare canon. In the second edition of *The Riverside Shakespeare* (1997), the editors include a full text of *Edward III*, although as an addendum and not as a component of their section of Shakespeare's "Histories." They nevertheless finally include it, as their Acknowledgments indicate, as "a history play now generally accepted as, at least in part, by Shakespeare, published here for the first time in a one-volume Works since the 1870s."[31] In his introduction to the play proper, J.J.M. Tobin asserts, "If Shakespeare had not written at least some of *Edward III*, most readers would argue that he certainly should have. All those plays about the politics of the reigns of Edward's descendants, from Richard II to Henry VIII, and (by implication) Elizabeth I and James I, cry out for some analogous dramatic treatment of the founding father and his rule." The "implications," especially concerning James I, are offered by Tobin as one good reason for the play's subsequent exclusion from the canon and the First Folio of 1623; the play's "bitterly satirical presentation of King David of Scotland" would have rendered it "politically incorrect in the extreme"[32] while James was still on the throne.

The play is certainly concerned with delineating a "founding father," as Tobin suggests, and the first half is clearly concerned with the fact that "King Edward, the conqueror of the French, must first be the conqueror of his own appetitive self." Complementing my general approach in this study, Tobin observes, "Self-mastery is a theme ubiquitous in the Shakespearean canon." The critic significantly adds, "the particular issue of illicit sexual desire on the part of a person with military or executive power occurs quite frequently."[33] In fact the "self-mastery" part of the play, in which King Edward overcomes his desire to seduce the Countess of Salisbury, has been the section of the text scholars are most anxious to assign to Shakespeare. Vickers's critical aim to attribute major portions of *Edward III* to Thomas Kyd interests me as a partial explanation of the apparent republican energies of this text, or perhaps what I will describe as simply the apparent aspirations of middle- or lower-class men which the text indirectly conveys, and which I find quite strongly paralleled in Kyd's *The Spanish Tragedy* through its middle-class tragic hero.[34] While Marlowe of course also offers Shakespeare examples of lower-class heroes, Faustus born of "parents base of stock" and the Scythian shepherd Tamburlaine, Kyd offers in *The Spanish Tragedy* a more carefully wrought social portrait of class conflict and tension.

In *Edward III* the passion of the king for the Countess of Salisbury, such an obvious test of his moral and sexual integrity, seems in some ways, almost comically at moments, to represent the struggles not of a medieval king but of a middle-class Renaissance humanist. He requests Lodwick, identified in the Dramatis Personae as simply the king's apparently classless "confidant," to bring him ink and paper and "walk and meditate alone" with him:

> This fellow is well read in poetry,
> And hath a lusty and persuasive spirit:
> I will acquaint him with my passion,
> Which he shall shadow with a veil of lawn,
> Through which the queen of beauty's queen shall see
> Herself the ground of my infirmity. (2.1.53–8)

In response to Lodwick's question, "[Write] I to a woman?," King Edward exclaims, "What beauty else could triumph [o'er] me, / Or who but women do our love lays greet? / What, thinkest thou I did bid thee praise a horse?" (95–8). Underneath the apparent comedy here, however, lie two fairly serious cultural corrections. Politically, Edward III clarifies that the romantic or sexual predilections which ruined his father's career, and which are presumably fairly fresh in the audience's recollection due to Marlowe's depiction of them in *Edward II*, are now virtually unthinkable. Moreover, the aura of humanist amity which temporarily seems to characterize the King Edward–Lodwick relationship seems productive strictly of a heteroerotic understanding between men and of a heterosexual literary creation. Edward proceeds to find fault with Lodwick's poetic efforts: the phrase "more fair and chaste" is objected to, since the king, bluntly, would rather have the countess "chas'd [pursued] than chaste [virginal]" (153); and he also refuses, unsurprisingly, the comparison "More bold in constancy than Judith was," since the "monstrous" line would necessitate the identification of Edward with Holofernes: "Put in the next [line] a sword," the king sarcastically interjects, "And I shall woo her to cut off my head" (167–71). Sounding even more like an aspiring scholar, Edward subsequently proposes to take over the task himself: "Love cannot sound well but in lovers' tongues. / Give me the pen and paper: I will write" (182–3).

Yet the actual composition is forestalled by the entrance of the Countess, who decisively rejects Edward's erotic invitation in terms that ideologically place an essentially true manliness above kingship or aristocratic status:

> But that your lips were sacred, my lord,
> You would profane the holy name of love.
>
> …
>
> In violating marriage' sacred law
> You break a greater honor than yourself.
> To be a king is of a younger house
> Than to be married: your progenitor,
> Sole-reigning Adam on the universe,
> By God was honor'd for a married man,
> But not by him anointed for a king. (2.1.249–66)

Although moved by both her beauty and her "words divine," Edward, still possessed by lust, quickly coerces, through the blind swearing of an oath, the Countess's father, the Earl of Warwick, to pressure his own daughter into the adulterous liaison. Left alone, the Earl exclaims bitterly, "O doting king! O detestable office!" (346), and sees the patriarchal duty to which he is perversely enforced as tantamount to a kind of incest: "How shall I enter in this graceless [errand]? / I must not call her child, for where's the father / That will in such a suit seduce his child?" (373–5). To his daughter he ostensibly argues, "What mighty men misdo they can amend" (394), but neither he nor the play believes this, and the Earl is delighted when his daughter categorically and courageously rejects the proposal. He rejoices:

> Why now thou speak'st as I would have thee speak,
> And mark how I unsay my words again:
> An honorable grave is more esteem'd
> Than the polluted closet of a king;
> The greater man, the greater is the thing,
> Be it good or bad, that he shall undertake. (430–5)

It is tempting to link such moral assertions to the politically radical potential of Protestant inwardness, the impetus behind so much republican thought in the early modern period. Warwick concludes his moralizing with three maxims, the first, "That poison shows worst in a golden cup," and the third an actual quotation from Sonnet 94, "Lilies that fester smell far worse than weeds" (449–51). Such a quotation may only indirectly encourage an attribution of *Edward III* to Shakespeare; but the homoerotic context of Sonnet 94 also intriguingly if only fleetingly suggests that the moral judgments underlined by the characters' attitudes at this moment in the play may ultimately apply both to heterosexual and homosexual motivation.

Even before King Edward is shamed into repentance by the spectacle of the Countess's willingness to die by her own hand rather than be dishonoured, he experiences a kind of moral essentialism related to physical embodiment when he views his son and reflects, "O how his mother's face, / Modell'd in his corrects my stray'd desire" (2.2.76–7). "I go to conquer kings," reasons Edward, "And shall I not then / Subdue myself" (98–9). Although lust makes one more stand in his soul – "Thy mother is but black, and thou [son, Edward the Black Prince], like her / Dost put it in my mind how foul she is" (108–9) – Edward manages to invert, finally, lust's dictum that "The sin is more to hack and hew poor men / Than to embrace in an unlawful bed / The register of all rarieties" (113–15). That is, he finally awakens from his "idle dream" of adulterous seduction (199). For postmodern readers the most depressing aspect of Edward's achievement of self-discipline is that it entails a tragic displacement of erotic desire into martial violence. But, as we have seen, such displacement repeatedly haunts Shakespeare's histories, and his tragedies.

In *Edward III* the impetus towards violence seems to carry republican, even revolutionary, energies as an apparently mitigating factor. The French dauphin significantly characterizes England as a place that harbours "malcontents, / Bloodthirsty and seditious Catilines, / Spendthrifts, and such as gape for nothing else / But changing and alteration of the state" (3.1.13–16). Edward's claim to the throne of France, like Henry V's in the later play, involves a challenge to the Salic law argument and is politically rather dubious, but the text of *Edward III* makes less of these uncomfortable political details. Edward refers to the French King John as "usurping King of France" (3.3.35); in return John calls Edward "A thievish pirate" (53), and taunts him with an "Exceeding store of treasure" and the challenge, "Let it be seen 'mongst other petty thefts, / How thou canst win this pillage manfully" (67–71). The English, however, rather opportunistically claim true manliness by accusing King John of being a bad father through his refusal to surrender the country; as Edward the Black Prince insists, "Ay, that approves thee, tyrant, what thou art: / No father, king, or shepherd of thy realm, / But one that tears her entrails with thy hands" (118–20).

The Secular Christ in *Edward III*

Prince Edward's equation of father, king, and shepherd may suggest the Christ-like status of the anointed king, but the relationship between King Edward and his heir soon takes on the distinctly Oedipal aura, in an even clearer manifestation than we observed in the previous chapter of the secular Christ. In preparation for battle, the king formally "dub[s]" the prince with "the type of chivalry," and with rhetoric that echoes his own recent moral accomplishment of repressing lust:

> Edward Plantagenet, in the name of God,
> As with this armor I impale [that is, enclose] thy breast,
> So be thy noble unrelenting heart
> Wall'd in with flint of matchless fortitude
> That never base affections enter there. (3.3.179–83)

Sending his son to the forefront of the battle, the king is soon informed by three of his noblemen of the prince's desperate position with respect to the French, but each time refuses to send succour. To the objection that the prince is "encompass'd with a world of odds," the king replies: "Then he will win a world of honor, too. / If he by valor can redeem him[self] thence; / If not, what remedy? We have more sons / Than one to comfort our declining age" (3.5.20–4). When Lord Audley objects, "'tis too much willfulness, / To let his blood be spilt that may be sav'd," the king reasons:

> Let Edward be deliver'd by our hands
> And still in danger he'll expect the like;
> But if himself himself redeem from thence,

> He will have vanquish'd, cheerful, death and fear,
> And ever after dread their force no more. (41–2, 48–52)

The Count of Artois, who has joined the English side, laments, "O would my life might ransom him from death!" (56), but this Christ-like sentiment contradicts the terms of the new secular Christ which the play offers.

The Prince of Wales in fact survives his military trial; he reappears triumphantly after his "winter's toil" (65) with the body of the King of Bohemia, but with no apparent bitterness towards his father, and is knighted by the king. Not only does his knighthood prove him "fit heir unto a king" (93), but King Edward oddly internalizes his son's achievement, as a recuperation of his own reputation, declaring, "Now, John of France, I hope / Thou knowest King Edward for no wantonness" (99–100). Even more oddly, the scene ends with the king asking the prince, "What picture's this" – pointing, editors surmise, to an emblem tacked to the corpse of the King of Bohemia – to which the son replies, "A pelican, my lord, / Wounding her bosom with her crooked beak, / That so her nest of young ones might be fed / With drops of blood that issue from her heart" (109–12). Although a common emblem of Christ in the Renaissance, the image here appears – attached to the body of a defeated king – deliberately ironic, since the son has redeemed not his fallen brethren through self-sacrifice, but in fact himself through violent assertion, and consequently his own flawed father.

The pattern of the Prince of Wales facing an apparently insuperable challenge and then almost miraculously overcoming it is repeated in the final sections of the play. Surrounded by French troops, the odds are so bad that this time the French can't resist sending taunting messages: the first from the French king advising that the prince and a hundred others "of name" sue on their knees for mercy; the second from the Duke of Normandy offering a "nimble-jointed jennet" on which the prince is invited to fly; the third from the second son of the French king, Prince Philip, offering the Prince of Wales a prayer book, since the prince's "hour of life / Entreats [him] that [he] meditate therein / And arm [his] soul for her long journey towards [heaven]" (4.4.69, 91, 106–8). Here religion is reduced to mockery; but the subsequent dialogue between Prince Edward and Lord Audley involves a courageous and dignified philosophical reflection on the inevitability of death. The prince commends Audley's reflections:

> Ah, good old man, a thousand thousand armors
> These words of thine have buckled on my back.
> Ah, what an idiot hast thou made of life,

To seek the thing it fears [that is, by bringing self-destruction on more
  quickly through desperation and fear];
…
Since for to live is but to seek to die,
And dying but beginning of new life …
Let come the hour when He that rules it will,
To live or die I hold indifferent. (150–62)

The end of this speech surely anticipates the more mature Hamlet near the
end of his tragedy, as he realizes calmly, "If it be now, 'tis not to come; if it
be not to come, it will be now … The readiness is all … Let be" (5.2.217–
22). But perhaps more intriguingly, the earlier part of the speech – "what
an idiot hast thou made of life" – also anticipates Macbeth's existential "It
is a tale / Told by an idiot" (5.5.26–7). As elsewhere in Shakespeare, the
actual reality of the metaphysical or transcendent remains significantly
ambiguous. In *Edward III* a prophecy about frightening fowl and flint-
stones which ostensibly favours the French eventually comes true in a
sense that perfectly fulfils English military ambitions. While ambiguity of
prophecy may also recall *Macbeth*, more directly this artistic and theatrical
teasing, this "playing with" the significance of prophecies and portents,
is very reminiscent of both the immediately previous *Richard III*, as we
have seen, and the subsequent *King John*. The prince's surprising triumph
allows him to rhetorically turn the tables on the French Prince Philip, but
the potentially "manly" mockery of religion remains the same: "Who
now[,] or you or I[,] have need to pray" (4.9.15), he taunts Philip.

What is perhaps most surprising in the play's denouement is the again
intensely republican fervour in the self-congratulations of Prince Edward
and Lord Audley, so relieved at their delivery from certain death. Prince
Edward exclaims to Audley, "If thou wilt drink the blood of captive kings,
/ Or that it were restorative, command / A [health] of kings' blood, and
I'll drink to thee," to which Audley replies, "Victorious prince – that
thou art so, behold / A Caesar's fame in king's captivity" (4.9.31–8). And
indeed, in the play's final scene, not only is the King of France led captive,
but an absolutely silent King David of Scotland is paraded as a prisoner
of the commoner John Copland, who took him in single fight and refuses
to surrender him even to King Edward's queen. Although at Copland's
entrance King Edward exclaims, "Is this the proud presumptuous esquire
of the north / That would not yield his prisoner to my queen," and asks
for explanation for his insubordination, Copland responds assertively:

No willful disobedience, mighty lord,
But my desert and public law at arms:
I took the king myself in single fight,

And, like a soldier, would be loth to lose
The least preeminence that I had won. (5.1.65–75) ·

Copland thus sounds remarkably like Horatio in *The Spanish Tragedy*, asserting a kind of middle-class enfranchisement through his rights to the prisoner Balthazar, whom he has captured in battle. Such apparent challenges to kingship and noble privilege by an assertive masculinity may be partly explained by the contributions of Kyd, since such emphatic recurrence is rather unusual for a history play (solely) by Shakespeare.

Nevertheless, the final reunion between King Edward and the Prince of Wales, while ostensibly royalist in its implications, contains a theological subversion which I contend is *not* at all atypical of Shakespeare's art. Edward welcomes his son in terms which clearly recall the parable of the prodigal son, thereby placing King Edward in the role of God the Father: "As things long lost, when they are found again, / So doth my son rejoice his father's heart" (5.1.187–8). Prince Edward responds in terms which strongly suggest a continuation of this analogy, and which assign to his own person the role of a martial and secular Christ:

Now, father, this petition Edward makes –
To Thee whose grace hath been his strongest shield,
That as Thy pleasure chose me for the man
To be the instrument to show Thy power,
So Thou wilt grant, that many princes more,
Bred and brought up within that little isle,
May still be famous for like victories! (216–22)

As David Womersley has argued, "the fact Edward triumphs through his son ... creates an audacious parallelism between the governance of England and of heaven."[35] Such an analogy in effect redefines a Christian paradigm in Oedipal and martial terms. But whether this redefinition involves an absolute triumph of the new secular vision remains in doubt, for Shakespeare, always notable for the ruthless multiplication of irony within his political vision, hints at future dissension and turmoil through the phrase "many princes." Historically Edward the Black Prince will predecease his father, and the prince's several brothers whom King Edward earlier relied upon to shore up the succession will in effect breed civil unrest,[36] since the grandson who inherits, Richard II, will tragically embody an ironically ineffectual secular Christ. And Shakespeare has effectively paved the way for his subsequent artistic endeavour, for he will soon delineate the fallout from this political failure in the second tetralogy.

King John and Spiritual Self-Determination

But before he does so, he writes another transitional history, *King John*, a play traditionally unpopular with critics and audiences, but politically one of Shakespeare's most fascinating works. The transition from *Richard III* through *Edward III* to *King John* reveals in fact a daring artistic and ideological development, and the latter play represents an experiment remarkable in its ramifications – which include political and psychological consequences so progressive that the playwright partially retreats from them again in the second tetralogy. The play has more recently, not surprisingly, received attention in light of current debates about Shakespeare's personal sympathy with either Protestant or Catholic religious positions. As Donna Hamilton observes, the play, "merely by virtue of its narrating an archetypal story of a king's struggle with the pope, situates itself in the midst of [anti-Catholic] discourse," yet Shakespeare has "eliminated from it the far more blatantly anti-catholic [sic] rhetoric of its presumed source play, the anonymous *Troublesome Raigne of King John.*"[37] John Klause in 2001 identified new sources for the play in the writings of Robert Southwell, the Elizabethan Catholic poet and martyr whose possible connections to Shakespeare have been elaborated upon by Richard Wilson and Alison Shell.[38] Klause's conclusion that "Shakespeare seems both consciously and unconsciously to have welcomed a Jesuit into his mind" may contradict Hamilton's reading that the play actually supports a radical Puritan, nonconformist position against the more obviously anti-Catholic bias of *The Troublesome Raigne*, a play ideologically underwritten by "the increasingly hierarchical and absolutist conformist platform" of Elizabethan church polity. I suggest that the playwright to an extent desaturates both religious platforms of their spirituality, insofar as such ideology compromises individual moral and rational agency, but without completely eradicating the "spiritual" significance of this evolving masculinity. In *King John* this striking emphasis on personal agency and masculinity finds expression through the character of the Bastard.

The object of much critical attention, the Bastard constitutes a most original development of the Vice figure in early modern drama. As Robert Weimann observes, "Faulconbridge is made faithfully to rehearse most of the attributes of the Vice, only to go beyond them ... He seeks to redeem the unbridled energy of the valiant performer on behalf of his arduous task in the building of, historically speaking, an anachronistic image of the nation-state."[39] While Shakespeare in *Richard III* sought to impose the more ritualized action of a morality play on the amoral political chaos of the *Henry VI* plays, the aggressive self-fashioning of the Vice-like Richard, as we have seen, threatened to overwhelm the pale cipher of the ideological saviour Richmond. In *King John* Shakespeare pushes the implications further. "Traditional" designations of right and wrong are systematically dismantled in the course of the plot, and the originally Vice-like Bastard grows into a peculiar kind of moral centre, elaborating upon the subversive potential of Shakespeare's portrayal of Richard III, although in a more distant and therefore safer historical context.

The first striking contradiction involving this characterization is the fact that King John in the play's opening scene defends the Bastard's rights to inheritance of his father's land, in opposition to old Sir Robert Faulconbridge's will, a move which is, as Robert Lane points out, "contrary to [the king's] own title, resting as it did on the will of Richard I."[40] In *The Troublesome Raigne* the younger son Robert is awarded the lands after the bastard Philip is repeatedly interrogated and finally confesses that his father was in fact Richard Coeur de Lion. In *King John*, on the other hand, Shakespeare "redirected the scene away from the issue of having to prove whether or not there has been adultery ... the issue that takes its place is whether a bastard can inherit, an issue which [is] settled in the affirmative."[41] The Shakespearean text, therefore, while echoing the nonconformist position which strove to limit the power of ecclesiastical courts over the matter of private thoughts, argues ultimately for the worthiness of the individual according to his or her virtuous character or action, regardless of social or sexual derivation. In terms of traditional codes of class privilege and legitimacy, the play appears highly unorthodox. That the Bastard *is* the offspring of Richard I might conceivably return us to an aristocratic bias in the play – the biological essentialism of royal blood – but Shakespeare's Bastard daringly relinquishes the Faulconbridge estate in order to accept service as a soldier to Queen Eleanor, and a knighthood from the king. He thus courageously forsakes material advantage for the opportunity of a fairly risky self-fashioning, replaying, voluntarily, the manly vigour of Richard III's desperate but heroic, "A horse! A horse! My kingdom for a horse!" The Bastard's speech to Queen Eleanor, "Who dares not stir by day must walk by night, / And have is have, however men do catch. / Near or far off, well won is still well shot, / And I am I, howe'er I was begot" (1.1.172–5), clearly echoes the contrast between "strong possession" and traditional "right," the terms which John and Eleanor earlier use to define the king's questionable claim to the throne.

Whether King John is ever quite strong *enough* in his possession of the crown emerges as one of the haunting ambiguities of the text. Morally he may possess too little virtue, or, conversely, too little masculine *virtus* or Machiavellian *virtù*. Shakespeare carefully and rather lovingly expands (3.3.19–69) the king's most shocking moral behaviour, subtly soliciting Hubert to kill Arthur, from what amounts to a single ambiguous line in *The Troublesome Raigne*.[42] King John's overall weakness ultimately seems more psychological than moral, and is connected, in Shakespeare's portrayal, to the presence of an unusually strong mother, Eleanor of Aquitaine, who dominates and directs him in various crucial asides, for example at 1.1.40–3 – "Your strong possession much more than your right, / Or else it must go wrong with you and me – / So much my conscience whispers in your ear" – or at 2.1.469–80, where she strongly advises her son to make up the match between Blanche of Spain and the French Dauphin. When the French invade England on the expectation of Arthur's murder, King John exclaims, "Where is my mother's care, / That such an army could be drawn in France / And she not hear of it" (4.2.117–19). Informed of her death, he rather pathetically sputters, "What, Mother dead?" (127), and, again, "My mother dead!" (182).

Shakespeare clearly expands this psychological pattern from one or two suggestions in *The Troublesome Raigne*. When Philip of France requests many English continental territories as part of Blanche's dowry, John asks Eleanor, "Mother what shall I doo? My brother got these lands / With much effusion of our English bloud" (part 1, 832–3). Yet he later announces his mother's death with more courageous acceptance and equanimity than Shakespeare's king (part 2, 226–8). Examining the ideological significance of Eleanor in Shakespeare's play, A.J. Piesse admits that she "is a political player who is ultimately powerless in the face of the male authority of the Church." Yet Piesse finds it significant, not only "that Pandulph persistently refers to Mother Church, the political, historical manifestation of religion easily superseding the localised, personal aspect of maternal power," but "that John's decision to return to Rome is made in almost the same breath that he learns of his mother's death."[43] In this sense of maternal dependency at least, John parallels the childlike Arthur, who, as a passive pawn of his mother Constance's ambitions, is portrayed as far more submissive, and less politic, than his counterpart in *The Troublesome Raigne* and the other historical sources; and he displays such weakness in the face of the fact that his "right" to the throne, according to primogeniture, is the clearest and least contestable.[44] Even Constance herself, although her grief and rage are powerfully conveyed, seems more emotionally self-indulgent and less self-possessed in Shakespeare, never showing the self-control she displays in *The Troublesome Raigne* – for example, in her advice to her son, "Goe in with me, reply not lovely boye, / We must obscure this mone with melodie, / Least worser wrack ensue our malecontent" (part 1, 901–3). Shakespeare, by this point in his career, apparently now takes artistic pains to emphasize a typically "feminine" psychological dependency and emotional excess.

In contrast to John and Arthur, the Bastard immediately distinguishes himself in terms of a highly independent and assertive manner and rhetorical style. Weimann, considering the passage at 1.1.172–5 ("well won is still well shot"), notes "the sexually charged praise for an accurate shot," and pronounces here the emergence of "the early modern dramatic male-gendered self."[45] This study has already recognized the construction, in often rather more inchoate forms, of a "dramatic male-gendered self" through a sometimes disturbing conflation of masculine self-assertion and martial masculinity. In the case of both Richard III and Edward III, such assertion involves a notable displacement of erotic desire. In the Bastard this masculine self is constituted through an intriguing and rather more controlled conflation of rhetorical and martial assertions – even as erotic interest (in spite of Weimann's sexual suggestion) seems in this character curiously suspended. Significantly, such suspension, or at least marginalization, of erotic interest will in fact characterize the entire second tetralogy.

Admittedly the Bastard's character, especially in the early stages of *King John*, seems unruly and is not without its misogynistic overtones, apparently consolidating Shakespeare's retreat from the potentially feminist elements in the first tetralogy. The Bastard excuses his mother's adultery with Richard Coeur de Lion with the comment, "He that perforce robs lions of their hearts / May easily win a woman's" (1.1.268–9). Later, when faced with "Black, fearful, comfortless, and horrible" tidings from Hubert, he replies, "Show me the very wound of this ill news. / I am no woman; I'll not swoon at it" (5.6.22–3). In spite of these less appealing elements, the Bastard's peculiar masculine robustness is dramatically attractive, particularly when contrasted with the darker and more violent misogyny displayed in *The Troublesome Raigne*'s Bastard, who threatens like "cursed *Nero*" to murder his mother unless she admits his paternity to him (part 1, 368–75), and who expresses some of the more notoriously anti-Catholic elements of the source play through his unpleasant sexual rapacity: "Now warres are done, I long to be at home / To dive into the Monkes and Abbots bags, / To make some sport among the smooth skin Nunnes" (part 1, 1129–31). Decidedly less narcissistic than his prototype, Shakespeare's Bastard demonstrates a self-cohesion which is, I think, rare in early modern theatre, where masculinity more often takes on the modes of desperate aggression or Machiavellian manipulation.

The Bastard's self-possession leads C.L. Barber and Richard Wheeler to contrast him, interestingly, with Hamlet: "unlike Hamlet, who spends most of the play not avenging his father's death ... Faulconbridge almost casually kills the murderer of his royal father in the third act, and then returns to the battlefield for more action. And unlike Hamlet, who feels sullied in his own person by his mother's adulterous union, the Bastard finds the source of his active strength in his mother's infidelity." These critics thus assert that for the Bastard "there is effortless, almost magical participation in the heroic manhood of the royal, lion-hearted, undramatized father he has never known."[46] This claim, however, leads us to one of the most intriguing contradictions in the text. The Bastard would seem to carry an almost mythological power of wish-fulfilment – he is, after all, "the play's most visibly unhistorical personage" – at the same time that he, contradictorily, embodies the mundane, the pragmatic, and initially the cynically worldly.[47]

Barber and Wheeler's designation of a "magical participation" is ill chosen, because the Bastard in fact eschews the magical invocations of his dramatic prototype in *The Troublesome Raigne*, who feels the need to curse the Austrian Duke even as he hunts him down: "And art thou gone, misfortune haunt thy steps, / And chill colde feare assaile thy times of rest. / *Morpheus* leave here thy silent Eban cave, / Besiedge his thoughts with dismall fantasies" (part 1, 656–9). When his mother inquires whether he has denied being a Faulconbridge, Shakespeare's Bastard cheerfully replies, "As faithfully as I deny the devil" (1.1.252), in a manner which anticipates Hotspur's impatient denunciation of Owen Glendower's claims to supernatural powers: "Tell truth and shame the devil" (*1 Henry IV* 3.1.56). The Bastard rather idealistically cuts himself free from a physically (and by inference psychologically) unprepossessing stepfather to embrace the potential nobility of Richard Coeur de Lion's genetic influence; but he quite pointedly rejects a magical belief in devils and spirits, implying that his achieved integrity will be independently controlled, not spiritually dependent. He again contrasts significantly, on this score, with his counterpart in *The Troublesome Raigne*, where the "notion of interrogating social and historical givens is so transgressive" that "the Faulconbridge character ... must envision an extraneous authority through the medium of divine inspiration," and finally admits his identity as Richard's bastard only by becoming "entranced in a sort of divine revelation."[48] Shakespeare's Bastard thus constitutes a "self-possession" that would seem the concomitant of "strong possession," an ideal which, as A.R. Braunmuller perceptively points out, is compromised elsewhere in the play by "a more sinister sense of 'possession'," in particular through characters that "imagine themselves possessed, by vision or some fearful emotion."[49]

Such self-possession would seem, for Shakespeare, to serve as the basis for a nascent secular morality, as psychological coherence paves the way for consistent ethical action. Even in his early, "unruly" stage, the Bastard reveals a moral sense of purpose, or at least a potential integrity in reserve. For example, he sardonically and satirically exclaims:

> ... this is worshipful society
> And fits the mounting spirit like myself,
> For he is but a bastard to the time
> That doth not smack of observation.
> And so am I – whether I smack or no,
> And not alone in habit and device,
> Exterior form, outward accoutrement,
> But from the inward motion – to deliver
> Sweet, sweet, sweet poison for the age's tooth;
> Which, though I will not practice to deceive,
> Yet, to avoid deceit, I mean to learn. (1.1.205–15)

Significantly the Bastard asserts that he will learn the ways of the world without radically embracing its methods. The "inward motion" may indicate the emergence of a socially viable, morally committed inwardness. When the Bastard later famously exclaims, "I am amazed, methinks, and lose my way / Among the thorns and dangers of this world" (4.3.140–1), his "recognition of his position within the wilderness of his time and of his vulnerability to its perils is accompanied," as David Womersley argues, "by an intensified awareness of the awfulness of living in a world without absolute values – a world stripped of life, right, and truth. The delinquency which he had earlier met with satire he now responds to with profound unease."[50]

Some commentators have claimed that this moment anticipates an absurdist one.[51] It is preferable, however, to see the emphasis on a necessary internalization, or rather inner assertion of ethical value, as the beginning of Shakespeare's accommodation of his secularizing impulses to his post-Reformation context, which has implications for Shakespeare's evocation of both Protestant and Catholic subject positions but also, I will argue, for possible sympathies with Familist belief. The Bastard is faced with the dilemma of having to create or fashion, individually, his own set of values vis-à-vis the corruption of the political world, according to the strength of his own inner self, his own inwardness. This project suggests the Protestant worshipper in the Lord's Supper, who, denied the magical efficacy of transubstantiation, must "read" the now purely symbolic images of bread and wine and apply them to a disciplined understanding of an inner renewal of spirit. We noted above the ironical undertones in the allusions to taking sacraments in *Richard III*. In *King John*, Lewis the Dauphin claims to have taken "the Sacrament" in order to "keep our faiths firm and inviolable" (5.2.6–7) to the English lords who have sworn to assist him against King John, even though they are luckily informed by Melun that the hypocritical "Dear amity and everlasting love" (5.4.20) promised by the Dauphin will be translated into an immediate beheading of the English noblemen should the French win the day.

Nevertheless this parallel to a Protestant reading of the Eucharist does not necessarily commit Shakespeare to a devoted and consistent Protestant political agenda throughout the play, and certainly does not embody the intensely partisan critique of Catholic religious hypocrisy in *The Troublesome Raigne*. There the playwright provides a much expanded version of a clandestine, hypocritical ("Under the cloke of holie Pilgrimage") meeting between the rebel English Lords and Lewes at the sacred "Shrine" of "sweet *S. Edmond* holy Saint in heaven" (part 2, 349–56). The idolatrous overtones of the meeting are further stressed by the elaborate oath-taking by all present "on the holie Altar" (431) of the shrine. When the French request to be given leave and the English withdraw, the Machiavellian nature of the former becomes evident: "Tis policie (my Lord) to bait our hookes / With merry smiles" (599–600). This complacent cynicism is followed by an almost laughably ironic moment, when Lewes swears before his countrymen "*On this same Altar*, and by heavens power" to behead all the English "traitors" once John is dispatched (609–14, my emphasis).

In Shakespeare it is *human* faith and trustworthiness, rather than specific doctrinal positions, that becomes crucial in such interaction. Ironically the political world of *King John* is characterized by the almost complete absence of such faith, a fact which raises the greatest moral and ethical problematic of the play and reverberates in the ambiguity of its theatrical and ideological resolution. Significantly the Bastard "does not buckle under the impact of [his] vision [of the thorns and dangers of this world]."[52] Perhaps surprisingly in that soliloquy he seems to have acquired a kind of transcendent faith: "The life, the right, and the truth of all this realm   /Is fled to heaven ... I'll to the King. / A thousand businesses are brief in hand, / And heaven itself doth frown upon the land" (4.3.144–59). As he has just bidden Hubert to bear away the body of Arthur, "this morsel of dead royalty," and as he has just prevented Hubert from being cut to pieces by the noblemen who assume him to be King John's henchman in the apparent murder, the Bastard's evocation of heaven seems not empty rhetoric, but a sincere attempt to preserve his allegiances and personal commitments while desperately searching for an understanding of a higher morality. The Bastard's newfound "religion" here is not a facile return to an older moral worldview, any more than Hamlet's realization or insistence that there is a "divinity that shapes our ends, / Rough-hew them how we will" reveals the fifth-act tragic hero as suddenly "an inhabitant of a much older cosmos, no more than the consenting instrument of God," as Catherine Belsey erroneously argues.[53] The struggle to achieve responsible agency is not abandoned in favour of an ideological relapse into an older worldview, but desperately requires, through its very assertions, a belief in a higher "meaning" to support the validity of its project.

The Limits of Rational and Irrational Individualism

If, as Womersley argues, *King John* eventually reasserts, in spite of the subversive nature of the Bastard's characterization, "the [apparently conservative] ideals of order and submission to monarchy," it does so in "an importantly qualified fashion," since "the Bastard adopts his final position of loyalty to the throne as the result of a conscious decision," and not, as Tudor propaganda insisted, through adherence to order and monarchy "unthinkingly as absolutes."[54] The Bastard's political choice is contingent on his own self-integration. Shakespeare's position might indeed be seen, politically, as an evocation of a kind of Protestant individualism and even Protestant rationalism. An interesting connection may be made here to Hamilton's reading of the play as sympathetic to the nonconformist position: "in *King John* ... the story is positioned so as to view the topic of church-state relations from the perspective of that law which was said to protect the liberties of the subject by placing limits on the king, in secular as well as in ecclesiastical matters." However, the positions of both Womersley and Hamilton may overemphasize Shakespeare's implication of the efficacy of reason as a political panacea. Hamilton's assertion that "all arguments grounding authority in possession and law continue to occur in speeches of the English king and virtually all arguments about a right that emanates from a power higher than a human power occur in the speeches of the foreigners and papists"[55] is not quite consistent either with the Bastard's growth, in spite of his scoffing at supernatural promptings, into "transcendental" belief that I have identified above, or with certain implications in the play's resolution.

The powers and limitations of reason, admittedly, emerge as one of the most crucial and complex issues of the play. Doubtless the power of reason underwrites the efficacy of moral agency in the play, and Hamilton is correct to perceive, in *King John*, a greater artistic emphasis on, or faith in, human reason, especially in contrast to the source. But the comparison in this case suggests that Shakespeare is governed not so much by a particular politico-religious position as by a politico-moral one. For while the play's positioning regarding, for example, the rights to individual privacy, and the interrogation of ecclesiastical court authority, may place him close to a nonconformist or "Puritan" position, in other significant ways *King John* seems to critique the "irrational" zeal of Puritan political justification. *The Troublesome Raigne* is after all dedicated to "Gentlemen Readers" who are commended for having "entertaind the Scythian Tamburlaine," and who are adjured to transfer their applause to a "warlike Christian" who endures "many a storme" for "Christs true faith." The fact that this supposed hero-king abjectly fails is attributed, in the prologue to part 2, to the "determinde Fate" of "heavens fixt time," so that John's "fatall tragedie" almost suggests a version of Calvinist predestination, although this certainly problematizes the Protestant position of the play's politics, which are thus mired in the revolutionary but theological thwarted impulses of the earlier Marlowe.

Most significant, however, is the play's extended presentation of supernatural phenomena and prophecy. *The Troublesome Raigne*'s Bastard first encounters Peter the Prophet while pillaging an abbey, and while he delivers the expected condemnation – "Sir, I know you will be a dissembling knave, that deludes the people with blinde prophecies" (part 1, 1308–9) – the playwright nevertheless chooses dramatically to present on the stage the "strange apparition" (1584) of the five moons, which even the Bastard in an "extasie" (1582) testifies to having already seen above John's head during the repeated coronation. In response John calls for the "Prophet of Pomfret," and, despite the king's own attempt to read the miraculous sign positively after a general political description from Peter, the prophet insists, on the basis of some "other knowledge" (1636), some mysterious supernatural source, that the king will be "dispossessed" before Ascension Day. The king angrily denounces Peter as a "Witch, hells damned secretarie" (1645), has him imprisoned, and threatens execution. Shakespeare in *King John* allows only one reference, as hearsay, to the astrological omen: "My lord, they say five moons were seen tonight ... Old men and beldams in the streets / Do prophesy upon it dangerously" (4.2.183–7). Peter of Pomfret makes only one brief appearance, and, when the Bastard paraphrases his prophecy concerning Ascension Day, the king has the presence of mind to propose that the prophet's imprisonment be concluded with his execution on that very day at noon. Of course the "prophecy" comes true, but only through John's abject political dependency on the Church's power, and his decision to surrender to Pandulph's demands in order to invalidate the invasion of the French. In Shakespeare the irony would appear less "cosmic," whereas *The Troublesome Raigne* has flirted, through its more sensational dramaturgy, with a supernatural soliciting not inconsistent with a Puritan emphasis on prophetic insight and spiritual enthusiasm, religious tendencies reflected, for example, in the career of William Hackett, a Puritan "prophet" who "claimed to have special gifts of clairvoyance and other miraculous powers, and acquired a considerable reputation as an exorcist and sorcerer" before he foolishly attempted a coup against the queen and was executed in 1591, the year *The Troublesome Raigne* was published.[56]

If a greater emphasis on the efficacy of human reason characterizes Shakespeare's treatment of social issues in *King John*, the playwright nevertheless concerns himself with the effects of religious belief on masculine self-fashioning in a manner not perfectly consistent with a proto-Protestant rationalism. John Klause has convincingly identified a "large pattern of ... correspondences" between Shakespeare's play and not only the poetry but the political writings of the Catholic priest and martyr Robert Southwell. Klause considers, in particular, *An Epistle of Comfort, to [Those] Restrayned in Durance for the Catholicke Fayth* (1587): "In this passionate attempt to offer persecuted English Catholics the most sternly principled of consolations (comforts that only heroes of faith could fully welcome), Southwell tries to sharpen their determination to resist, at whatever temporal cost, the encroachments of the heretical state-church upon their religious consciences."[57] We might here identify a possible parallel between the "Puritan" and the Catholic implications of a play-text which is concerned to justify the rights of individuals to maintain this "religious dimension of political choice" in their resistance to an ecclesiastical government, a "heretical state-church," attempting to prescribe, and proscribe, such commitments. Compare this with Hamilton's description of "James Morrice, the puritan lawyer and member of parliament who was taken into custody in 1593 for speaking in parliament against the powers exercised by the ecclesiastical courts," and who would, "in 1594, cite the story of John to show the similarities between John's struggle to keep the papists from usurping his prerogatives and the current struggle to halt the oppressive measures against nonconformists."[58] Yet the nature of such "commitments" varies significantly: the dedication described by the Jesuit Southwell embraces martyrdom, while the nonconformists insist on private worship and freedom of conscience within an increasingly secular state.

Some may wish to suggest that a Shakespeare "guardedly loyal to the Catholic faith," who attempts to distance himself and other moderate Catholics from the reckless and dangerous drive to martyrdom, shifted "responsibility for treason on to a demonised extreme."[59] Shakespeare's "welcoming a Jesuit into his mind" would thus occur on a somewhat ironic level. However, a closer examination of the playwright's sources in Southwell renders it less likely that Shakespeare subtly promotes a distinctly Catholic agenda, even a more "moderate" one, since the irony between this particular "source" and the play increases to an extent that a kind of ideological rupture takes place. This becomes especially evident when Klause focuses on an intriguing parallel between the Dauphin Lewis's acceptance of Blanche of Castile as a bride, and a passage from Southwell's poem *Saint Peters Complaint*. Lewis exclaims to his father King Philip:

> I do [accept her], my lord, and in her eyes I find
> A wonder, or a wondrous miracle,
> The shadow of myself formed in her eye,
> Which, being but a shadow of your son,
> Becomes a sun and makes your son a shadow. (2.1.497–501)

In *King John* Shakespeare develops the imagery involving eyes and seeing much more carefully than the author of *The Troublesome Raigne*, where it is limited to the scene involving the aborted blinding of Arthur, and the poetry in the above passage distinctly recalls Southwell's mystical praise of Christ's eyes:

> O living mirrours, seeing whom you shew,
> Which equall shaddows worthes with shadowed things:
> Ye make thinges nobler then in native hew,
> By being shap'd in those life giving springs.
> Much more my image in those eyes was grac'd,
> Then in my selfe.[60]

Yet such spiritual self-surrender to the beloved, whether a woman or Christ, is energetically resisted by the Bastard, who responds to Lewis's assertion, "I do protest I never loved myself / Till now infixèd I beheld myself / Drawn in the flattering table of her eye," with the outburst:

> Drawn in the flattering table of her eye!
> Hanged in the frowning wrinkle of her brow
> And quartered in her heart! He doth espy
> Himself love's traitor. This is pity now,
> That, hanged and drawn and quartered, there should be
> In such a love so vile a lout as he. (502–10)

Since Shakespeare has deleted the potential romantic interest between Faulconbridge and Blanche hinted at in *The Troublesome Raigne*, the objection here seems more philosophical than personal. The Bastard vigorously repudiates a mystical androgyny, a subjection to another that in his opinion vitiates manly agency and fortitude, and the imagery he employs here ironically alludes to Southwell's eventual execution, where the Catholic martyr was "infixèd" in a particularly horrible manner.

Such "fixing" recalls by contrast the play's recurring image of flowing and overflowing water, another image pattern that Shakespeare carefully and significantly elaborates from only a hint or two in the source play.[61] While sometimes alluding more negatively to the fickle turning of self-interest, what the Bastard terms Commodity – "this vile-drawing bias, / This sway of motion" (2.1.578–9) – such imagery nevertheless also figures more positively as the necessary force and assertion of individual value and moral commitment within a corruptible social context. King John, for example, attempts to both assert his right and also curtail further bloodshed between the English and the French when he proclaims:

> France, hast thou yet more blood to cast away?
> Say, shall the current of our right run on,
> Whose passage, vexed with thy impediment,
> Shall leave his native channel and o'erswell
> With course disturbed even thy confining shores,
> Unless thou let his silver water keep
> A peaceful progress to the ocean. (2.1.334–40)

While the king clearly implies his "strong possession" rather than his theoretical "right" here, the image evokes the idea of necessary action and masculine agency in the political arena, rather than ironized aggression and pride.

Familist Agency

This unusual use of morally inflected water imagery implies not self-relinquishment to Spirit through purification and baptism, but rather the committed agency of the spiritually focused individual. It implies the strength and efficacy of the individual will at the same time as it posits a certain ideological accommodation, with the avoidance of the fatal "inflexibility" of Catholic martyrdom. It may be traced, I suggest, to the founder of the Family of Love, Hendrick Niclaes, and "one of [his] best-known works," *Terra Pacis*, where the transformation through which the "individual believer became 'godded with god' … was presented as an extended allegory involving the believer's journey through a variety of troubled kingdoms and finally arriving at the land of peace."[62] In a close reading of this allegory, Douglas FitzHenry Jones notes that the ultimate destination of the believer is "symbolized by [an] unapproachable fortress, a structure with high stone walls setting the city of peace apart from the profane world."[63] Yet Niclaes complicates his allegory: "out of this City, there floweth an unsearchable or infinite deep River, with also a very tempestuous winde; in such sort that this River, with the same winde, gusheth vehemently forth, as with an exceeding violent, thorow-rushing stream; and breaketh out with such violent force, like burning heat and flames of fire, to the devouring of all Enemies of the same good City." The source of this "mighty strong River" is a "water-fountain within this good City … Out of this water-fountain … the children of Peace in this City, do learn all their wisdom; and fetch thereout all their Understanding and Knowledg."[64] While this moment in Niclaes's allegory possibly represents a revision of imagery from Psalm 46 – "Yet there is a River, whose streames shal make glad [the] Citie of God" – the constitution of divine wisdom within the believer radically rewrites the passive, mystical transcendence of the psalm ("Be stil and knowe that I am God"). Jones argues that, whereas "the fortress and its narrow gate called to mind the exclusivity of *Terra Pacis*, its separateness from the vicissitudes of material existence, the 'mighty river' or 'water fountain' implied an embrace of the world beyond the walls." Moreover, Niclaes later in *Terra Pacis* clarifies that "the spiritual understanding drawn from the fountain of God's infinite being altered the perspective of the faithful with regard to 'manly and natural things',"[65] presumably to enhance their survival and competence within the material world. We might compare here Janet Halley's provocative analysis of Niclaes's textual strategies: "In the relationship of text with practice, the referential ambiguity of Niclaes's language allows his followers to function as a community of the pure that nonetheless imitates, and traffics with, the corrupt world around it."[66] This project interestingly recalls the Bastard's aim to "deliver … sweet poison … Which, though I will not practice to deceive, / Yet to avoid deceit, I mean to learn."

Such imagery of moral but forceful self-assertion is almost immediately contrasted in *King John* with the description of what could be termed a (Spenserian) "fair hermaphrodite," the image employed by the Citizen of Angiers to suggest a marriage between Blanche of Spain, King John's niece, and the French Dauphin Lewis:

> He is the half part of a blessèd man,
> Left to be finishèd by such as she,
> And she a fair divided excellence,
> Whose fullness of perfection lies in him.
> O, two such silver currents, when they join,
> Do glorify the banks that bound them in;
> And two such shores to two such streams made one,
> Two such controlling bounds, shall you be, Kings,
> To these two princes, if you marry them. (2.1.438–46)

Yet not only, as we saw above, does the self-surrender, and the lack of self-completeness, of masculine subjectivity in such a hermaphroditic union undercut vigorous manliness, at least in the Bastard's view, but the Citizen's rhetoric comes close to casting not only Blanche but Lewis himself in the role of political pawn. Moreover, this marriage proposal, which the choric pronouncement of the Bastard ironizes so decisively, is very desperately suggested by the Citizen when both the English and the French kings, frustrated by Angier's refusal to back either one or the other, have agreed to mutually besiege the town.

I believe that the Citizen's offer constitutes an ideologically negative moment in the text, and must refute Robert Lane's argument that the Citizen's role highlights the "participation by the people in the selection of the monarch," the fact that "the voice of the subjects [was becoming] a salient element in the contest over succession." The historical development Lane identifies is significant for the ideological context of the play, but surely the point of the Citizen's role is that these particular subjects actually *surrender* the responsibility of choice on this crucial issue. Attempting to contain this very objection, Lane writes, "While the Citizen's demurral seems a refusal of political agency, its more salient effect is to expose the simplistically militaristic impulses of the kings."[67] This reading is predictable, underlining as it does the apparently self-defeating impulse of the kings to eradicate their own subjects or constituents, what in fact constitutes them as monarchs. But, again, the rhetoric of the Bastard is crucial in conveying the meaning of the scene when he asserts, "By heaven, these scroyles [scoundrels] of Angiers flout you, Kings, / And stand securely on their battlements / As in a theater, whence they gape and point / At your industrious scenes and acts of death" (2.1.373–6). That is, the citizens refuse to commit to a crucial political decision, opting instead for a safely voyeuristic engagement, one that carries absolutely no risk, until, of course both kings threaten to turn on the town.

"Without Contraries Is No Progression"

We need to make a special historical effort to regain an understanding of the importance of martial assertion to the construction of legitimate, even admirable masculinity in Shakespeare's age, and in Shakespeare's theatre. Nick de Somogyi notes that the "Siege of Angers in *King John* is at once formally symbolic and topically realistic. At the intersection between the two sit the Bastard's lines … 'By heaven,' his outburst begins, an oath that echoes the insistent pieties of the contending kings in the scene as a whole." Yet Shakespeare's "attention to realistic detail accompanies the Bastard's reproach to the citizens on their battlemented auditorium. Coningsby's report of the citizens of Rouen watching a skirmish from the 'bullwarks of the towne,' as if 'a tryumphe of sport,' rescues the episode in *King John* from any purely symbolic reading," since such "mockage" by the citizens "paradoxically confirms" the real sacrifices of military involvement. Moreover, it is interesting to note the cultural importance of fictional representations of soldiers, since, as Somogyi observes, part of the debate about the "perfect martialist" in Greene's *Euphues His Censure* reappears verbatim in the anonymous military pamphlet *A Myrrour for English Souldiers* in 1595.[68] Indeed, the idealizations in the *Myrrour* carry a distinctly poetic lustre, and the pamphlet seems a kind of later Renaissance, proto-bourgeois version of Castiglione's *The Courtier*.

One of the most interesting moments in the *Myrrour* is this startling assertion: "Than warre there is nothing more necessary: for the breach of friendship by dissention strengtheneth the powers of love in her new conjunction. Warre is the beautie of peace, the esteeme of all things, and the first finder out of vertue."[69] The almost mystical nature of the paradox is somewhat clarified by the statement that "Contention is honourable, chiefly where eyther religion or right is the ground thereof, yet ambitious warre is hateful." Conflict is unavoidable in life, but honourable if it involves service in a higher purpose, and not for private gain. The self-serving, self-protective "neutrality" of the citizens of Angiers is anything but honourable in the context of the play's action. Concerning the eventually unfavourable political outcome of the marriage proposal, Lane argues: "That the pragmatic character of [the Citizen's] proposal leaves matters potentially unstable because it does not resolve Arthur's claim is hardly the responsibility of the Citizens who acted … to spare themselves and their polity the destruction of war." Yet in this dramatic context, and especially in light of the Bastard's rhetoric, such a manoeuvre is clearly construed as, *contra* Lane, the result of "spineless passivity or indecision," not as "prudential adherence to a non-violent resolution," and does indeed lead to further political instability.[70]

There is a comparable scene later in the play (4.2) with King John's nobles standing uneasily at the repeated coronation, surreptitiously seeking some kind of confirmation concerning the king's murder of Arthur, an element original to Shakespeare, since in *The Troublesome Raigne* suspicions of Arthur's murder do not arise until Hubert enters after the coronation and the five-moon apparition to announce Arthur's (supposed) death. Regretting the expected news during the coronation celebration, Shakespeare's nobles are to an extent sympathetic and "moral," but also, concerning this issue at least, strikingly passive, since none of them, with the exception of Pembroke's rather belated request of Arthur's "enfranchisement" in this scene, has had the courage to directly challenge the king or offer Arthur sanctuary or protection. The fact that Shakespeare, more obviously and clearly than *The Troublesome Raigne*, alters history here, bringing Arthur back to England when actually he was, after King John failed to woo him away from his French allies, imprisoned in France, would seem to allow, at some point, for the lords' intervention. Yet they have chosen to simply wait instead for this other political shoe to drop. Pembroke's request in fact constitutes a distinctly obsequious, riskless rhetoric.

A.R. Braunmuller makes some related observations when he notes how Pembroke "portrays himself as the mere, almost the involuntary, instrument of a carefully vague 'these,' and his inverted syntax places justification before request, delaying the specific (and, he suspects, unwelcome) answer for five lines":

> Then I, as one that am the tongue of these
> To sound the purposes of all their hearts,
> Both for myself and them – but chief of all
> Your safety, for the which myself and them
> Bend their best studies – heartily request
> Th'enfranchisement of Arthur. (4.2.47–52)

Pembroke "neatly makes the move that smooths conflict into superficial, verbal unanimity":

> That the time's enemies may not have this
> To grace occasions, let it be our suit
> That you have bid us ask his liberty,
> Which for our goods we do no further ask
> Than whereupon our weal, on you depending,
> Counts it your weal he have his liberty. (61–6)

Nevertheless, for Braunmuller, "Pembroke's response is a masterly example of political language, stating the grounds of dispute, stating the price of its resolution, threatening rebellion if the dispute is not resolved, but phrased not as conflict but as agreement, not coercion, but request."[71] Since the noblemen fear the deed of Arthur's murder already done – "Indeed we feared his sickness was past cure" (86) – Pembroke's speech seems, to me, delivered not to effect the prince's enfranchisement but to absolve the nobles of any political responsibility, even as they proclaim their concern for the king and their "dependency" on his welfare.

Compare such rhetoric to Salisbury's later speech to the invading Dauphin, where the noblemen handily but dangerously switch their dependency (5.2.27–9), which ends in histrionic but (it is difficult not to make the accusation) hypocritical tears apparently designed to absolve the speaker of responsibility for the betrayal of the nation. Both these rhetorical performances fail the test of "manliness" in an assertive and consistent political commitment. Thus, while Pembroke's speech may appear in one light "a masterly example of political language," the crisis of authority and kingship in the play calls for language from the nobles with a sharper polemical edge, and for prompter political action. King John, ironically, berates Hubert subsequently for being one of the "slaves that take [kings'] humors for a warrant" (4.2.210) when he repents the supposed murder of Arthur. While this response underlines his own failure of responsibility and his abject dependency on the mirroring responses of his subjects, Shakespeare clearly emphasizes the importance of moral independence among subordinates, returning to the theme in *King Lear* through the contrast between the good servant Caius (Kent) and the obsequious Oswald.

The Ambiguous Triumph of Imaginative Agency

It is again left to the Bastard both preternaturally to suspect that the king needs the benefit of the doubt concerning the "murder" (although, ironically, the king is still guilty of intent, if not of Arthur's actual death) and also, even more surprisingly, rhetorically to refashion his king as the epitome of martial power and control: "warlike John … in his forehead sits / A bare-ribbed Death, whose office is this day / To feast upon whole thousands of the French" (5.2.176–9). Meanwhile the real king lies dying of a fever, which in Shakespeare ambiguously may, or may not, have anything to do with the monk who supposedly poisons him. In a crucial sense the Bastard shares his project with the Protestant historiographers who attempted to recuperate the reputation of this morally dubious historical figure. There is, of course, something subversive in such a project, demystifying the monarchy and empowering the heretofore socially marginalized male who dares to make such rhetorical reassessment.

The Bastard at times seems on the verge of successfully empowering the king. As John frets over his mother's death in act 4, he refuses any further "ill news." The Bastard offers an ironic form of manly counsel: "But if you be afeard to hear the worst, / Then let the worst unheard fall on your head." Recovering in the face of this warning, the king reasserts his ability to ride the tide of conflict, rather than be overwhelmed by it: "Bear with me cousin, for I was amazed / Under the tide; but now I breath again / Aloft the flood, and can give audience / To any tongue, speak it of what it will" (4.2.135–40). Perhaps the Bastard's most important speech occurs when he later attempts to hearten the king:

> But wherefore do you droop? Why look you sad?
> Be great in act, as you have been in thought.
> Let not the world see fear and sad distrust
> Govern the motion of a kingly eye.
> Be stirring as the time; be fire with fire;
> Threaten the threat'ner, and outface the brow
> Of bragging horror. So shall inferior eyes,
> That borrow their behaviors from the great,
> Grow great by your example and put on
> The dauntless spirit of resolution. (5.1.44–53)

How different is this speech from the advice the Bastard offers the king in *The Troublesome Raigne*: "Forgive the world and all your earthly foes, / And call on Christ, who is your latest friend" (part 2, 1072–3). There Faulconbridge sounds more like one of Faustus's scholar friends, feebly attempting to console him before his horrible demise. Shakespeare's Bastard in the above speech significantly reworks the play's recurring imagery of eyes and seeing: now the subject no longer loses himself in the gaze of a greater power, as we saw earlier in the Petrarchan and mystical rhetoric of Lewis and Southwell, but instead heroically internalizes the image of manly vigour, as a way of strengthening individual self-assertion in men of various classes.

In a sense we move from a pre-Oedipal dependence on the mirroring of an "omnipotent" or all-loving nurturer to a rather more Oedipal identification with the paternal "aggressor," or at least with a competent agent-in-the-world. Thus, in spite of Shakespeare's avoidance of the sensational and the magical, the artistic, psychological, and political processes involved here would seem to recognize, after all, the efficacy (in some form) of the irrational, the need for the mobilization of imaginative and emotional responses in the service of, yet again, the imaginative agency we first observed in chapter 2. As in the allegory of *Terra Pacis*, imagination is here enlisted to strengthen the spiritual course of masculine identification. The potential tragedy, for masculine self-fashioning, consists in this case of the precarious nature of King John as manly role model, although the energy of the Bastard himself provides the crucial (and subversive) recuperation in the face of the king's dissipating vitality. Braunmuller notes an intriguing passage from Holinshed, who complains, "But such was the malice of writers in times past, which they bare towards king Iohn, that whatsoeuer was doone in preiudice of him of his subiects, it was *still interpreted* to chance through his default, so as the blame still was imputed to him ... yet to thinke that he deserued the tenth part of the blame wherewith writers charged him, it might seeme a great lacke of aduised consideration in them that so should take it."[72] But this extension, this sharing of responsibility and blame, is also a remarkable appropriation of political power on the part of the individuals conducting the reevaluation, and on the part of the playwright writing this play. Braunmuller argues that "Shakespeare conceals his play's potential 'application' [to the politics of late Elizabethan England] and deflects the censor's gaze by creating a character whose ahistoricity guarantees him safe," but that, in the play's "particularly ambiguous" conclusion, "Characterization and plot have compelled the Bastard into military and de facto political command of England, authority he does not hold in Holinshed's text and never could have held ... in 1215–16."[73]

From the pen of what has seemed to many a politically conservative Shakespeare, the portrait of the socially marginalized Bastard – initially like Richard III a "Vice" figure of the self-made man, but one who reveals crucial military assertion, rhetorical skill, and moral growth during the course of the play – is going almost further in the accomplishment of competent masculinity than the playwright's own ideological worldview will tolerate. What is the (artistic) consequence? In the second tetralogy, after the interlude of a narcissistic king with a notable Christ complex, these characteristics are transferred back onto the clearly aristocratic Hal, even if here the absolute right to the English throne is still held in some doubt, and the moral growth seems to many readers a carefully calculated transformation. Interestingly, the re-embodiment of political power in Hal continues to render problematic the psychological need, and the artistic search, for a viable masculine role model: Hal's disturbing duplicity threatens to return us to the more Machiavellian, socially superficial Bastard of the earlier scenes. Moreover, twice in *2 Henry IV* – "[his] spirit lent a fire / Even to the dullest peasant in his camp" (1.1.112–13); "He was the mark and glass, copy and book / That fashioned others" (2.3.31–2) – Shakespeare identifies Hotspur, not Hal, as the (lamentably lost) inspiration for manliness in others, especially men of the lower classes, in spite of that character's unruly aggressiveness.

The imagery at the end of *King John* seems rather desperately to prepare for this shift from individualized, classless agency to a more conservative, hierarchical vision, as the vital flowing of the individual masculine spirit, the river of manly vigour, is subsumed in a variously vague imagery of some kind of greater "oceanic" power. The English noblemen vow to "Stoop low within those bounds we have o'erlooked / And calmly run on in obedience / Even to our ocean, to our great King John" (5.4.55–7); the invading French reinforcements are "cast away and sunk on Goodwin Sands" (5.5.13); and even the Bastard must admit to his dying king that "the best part of my power ... Were in the Washes all unwarily / Devourèd by the unexpected flood" (5.7.61–4). At this announcement the king immediately expires and his less tainted son Henry III ascends the throne, with the kingdom magically and conveniently evacuated of any effective opposition. Amid such magical resurgence, King John poignantly emerges as his own scapegoat king, with the universal and mythological significance of his desiccated and feverish body accompanied by his bitter exclamation, "none of you will bid the winter come / To thrust his icy fingers in my maw, / Nor let my kingdom's rivers take their course / Through my burned bosom ... Within me is a hell" (5.7.36–46).

Ironically with this Familist evocation of hell as a state of mind (and body), the genie of self-defining masculine vigour is put back in the bottle. Still, the implications of the Bastard's remarkable energy and potentially secular integrity are, ideologically and psychologically, highly significant. The potential power and responsibility of the newly secularized will manifests in both the English and in the French subject position within the play. Requested by Pandulph to "lie gently at the foot of peace" because of John's reconciliation with Rome, the Dauphin Lewis objects:

> must I back
> Because that John hath made his peace with Rome?
> Am I Rome's slave? What penny hath Rome borne,
> What men provided, what munition sent,
> To underprop this action? Is't not I
> That undergo this charge? (5.2.76, 95–100)

To Pandulph's objection, "You look but on the outside of this work," Lewis counters, "Outside or inside, I will not return" (109–10). Spiritual inwardness radically gives way to the secular motives of political power and personal ambition. Pandulph in this exchange certainly emerges as a character who "maintain[s] overconfidence about [his] vocal authority."[74] His language in fact reveals a kind of magical thinking ("It was my breath that blew this tempest up ... My tongue shall hush again this storm of war" [5.1.17–20]), which is decisively dismissed by the Dauphin's military determination. Yet Lewis's self-assertion is also closely linked to his sense of class privilege and social entitlement: "I am too highborn to be propertied, / To be a secondary at control, / Or useful servingman and instrument / To any sovereign state throughout the world" (5.2.79–82).

While Shakespeare does not emphasize Lewis's "Catholic" religious hypocrisy as extensively as the author of *The Troublesome Raigne*, the playwright daringly implicates the abuses of "Catholic" monarchy, and the interest *King John* shows in delineating a truly moral agency of masculine assertion finds its most memorable and significant expression through the socially radical, self-determining, proto-Protestant but also Familist-inflected position of the Bastard. It is principally this energetically independent figure who, through his respect for a higher "heavenly" purpose, potentially sanctifies the aspirations for greater autonomy of the increasingly politically engaged English commonalty, even while such aspirations are partly qualified in the succeeding history plays. With the wounded Melun's adjuration that the English nobles "welcome home again discarded faith" (5.4.12), the blurring of divine and human, political and personal faith underlines the complex significance of *King John* for the challenging project of masculine self-fashioning in the early modern period.

Chapter Five

The Containment of Marlovian Homoeroticism in the Later Shakespeare

Richard II: Compromised Christ, Displaced Original Sin

In all Renaissance drama, the tragic hero of *Richard II* would seem to offer the clearest example of a secular Christ. However, Richard only embodies or achieves this state in a fantastical and incompetent fashion. While this "anointed king" (3.2.55) identifies his political opponents as Judases and Pilates (4.1.171, 241) when they deliver him to his "sour cross" (242), it is difficult for many readers to ignore that the "hollow crown" through which and for which he suffers has been emptied out largely through his own "vain conceit" (3.2.160, 166). Thus tragic stature seems irrevocably compromised through a parody of masculine control. This exposure of specifically aristocratic incapacity may compensate for the imaginative agency apparently surrendered at the end of *King John*, where even the virile Bastard must await the magical resurgence of another anointed king. Yet largely through Marlowe's influence, *Richard II* raises but inadequately addresses a deeper challenge to masculine capacity that will continue to haunt Shakespeare to the end of his career.

In more recent critical literature *Richard II* has emerged as far more controversial than in the complacent approaches of earlier criticism. Since critical consensus has judged *The Troublesome Raigne of King John* (printed 1591) as a likely source of Shakespeare's *King John*, and not vice versa, the dating of the latter play around 1595–6 places it close to the time of composition of *Richard II*, and indeed recent commentary has been concerned to clarify the apparently close relation between these two texts. Peter Lake, for example, asserts that "In *King John* legitimacy is always already lost [due to John's displacement of the just claimant, Arthur], and the play is about what to do and how to act in its absence in order to get it back again. In *Richard II* the issue is what to do if the ultimate repository of legitimacy, the monarch, systematically destroys it." For Lake this difference in political situation "explains the very different stylistic and theatrical forms taken by the two plays. Where *King John* is antic, violent, full of action, conflict and noise, *Richard II* is stately, the verse formal and the action highly ritualised, at almost every stage adopting the forms of secularised liturgy that surrounds court life and kingly authority."[1]

Most careful readers, including especially anyone who has ever taught *Richard II*, realize that the first scene in the play is potentially very confusing. As Anthony Dawson and Paul Yachnin observe, "No one tells us that Bolingbroke's appeal against Mowbray for the murder of Gloucester is a proxy attack on the King. We are not told exactly what lies behind the controversy and we are not sure just who did what."[2] The second scene does underline that Richard "made the fault" and has "caused [Gloucester's] death" (1.2.5, 39), in the exchange between the Duchess of Gloucester and John of Gaunt. Here the duchess refers to the seven sons of Edward III as "seven vials of his sacred blood" (12), which Dawson and Yachnin identify as glass vessels "often associated in Christian iconography with sacred, restorative blood." However, Marlowe scholars like to point out that "vials" in the Bible are more often images of divine vengeance than divine grace,[3] an irony of allusion which I suggest has also not escaped Shakespeare. In light of the duchess's desire for vengeance for her husband's death, and her apparent outrage at the violation of the homosocial order, the darker suggestion in these "vials" is surely appropriate: "Ah, Gaunt, his blood was thine! That bed, that womb, / That metal, that self mold that fashioned thee, / *Made him a man*" (22–4, my emphasis). Gaunt declines his sister-in-law's call to vengeance, insisting that he cannot challenge "God's substitute, / His deputy anointed in His sight" (37–8), but this insistence on Richard's anointed, Christ-like status weakly answers, certainly does not successfully refute, the duchess's aristocratic (and proleptically Nietzschean) disdain: "That which in mean men we entitle patience / Is pale cold cowardice in noble breasts" (33–4). Echoing motifs we have observed in the first tetralogy, this moment emphasizes Shakespeare's continuing link between piety and emasculation.

Oddly the theological emphasis rather uneasily fills in for the obscurity of political motive. If the play's second scene ostensibly clarifies Richard's responsibility for Gloucester's murder, the actual reasons for the murder remain obscure, and nothing in the text (save his widow's vengeful promptings) serves to increase sympathy for a character we never see, or learn anything pertinent about. Perhaps the cynicism of this argument rings truer for postmodern audiences, although it would be naïve to assume that Elizabethan audiences were unacquainted with the necessity or expediency of political assassination – as we saw in the previous chapter, *King John* unsettles its audience with this very possibility. Because of *Richard II*'s vagueness of pragmatic detail, Gloucester's murder emerges, I suggest, as the peculiar and secular equivalent of Original Sin. Such a rhetorical effect is in fact heightened by Bolingbroke's assertion in the opening scene that Mowbray "did plot the Duke of Gloucester's death," and

> ... consequently, like a traitor coward,
> Sluiced out his innocent soul through streams of blood –
> Which blood, like sacrificing Abel's, cries
> Even from the tongueless caverns of the earth
> To me for justice and rough chastisement. (100–6)

Cain's murder of Abel is logically and "historically" but one remove from the sin of Adam and Eve. As we briefly observed in chapter 2, Heather Hirschfeld's reading of Original Sin in *Hamlet* hinges on just this transference.[4] Moreover, a fratricide – which clearly Richard more than Mowbray is guilty of – emblematizes all egregious violations of the homosocial order. Technically Richard is guilty of "avunculicide," and interestingly Bolingbroke's coded displacement of this crime into fratricide perfectly inverts Hamlet's symbolic portrayal in the "Mousetrap" of fratricide as uncle-killing ("one Lucianus, nephew to the king" [3.2.242]) in his attempt to ascertain the truth of the Ghost's claim to be murdered at the hands of Claudius. The suggestion of Original Sin, once removed, is repeated exactly at the end of *Richard II* when Bolingbroke as Henry IV, attempting to displace his own guilt of regicide onto Exton, exclaims, "With Cain go wander through the shades of night, / And never show thy head by day nor light" (5.6.43–4).

Shakespeare's theological analogies introduce other key inversions. Richard, a Christ figure, is the instigator of this Original Sin, not the instrument of Atonement. And Bolingbroke in his initial challenge to Mowbray presumptuously vows to answer the cries of the afflicted through his own personal aggression, thus becoming a militant Christ himself. But as generations of critics have observed, later consequences of this original (political) sin continue to haunt the conscience of Henry and his successor in the second tetralogy.

Such "haunting" raises intriguing questions regarding the Marlovian influence on Shakespeare. The aggressive Henry V, ironically the "mirror of all Christian kings" even as he skilfully navigates a rather uncertain succession arising from his father's usurpation of the throne, has often invited parallels to the potentially antinomian

Tamburlaine,[5] and his threats outside the walls of Harfleur also amplify violent details from *Dido Queen of Carthage,* as we noted in chapter 2. But Shakespeare's depiction of a weak king eventually subject to deposition and murder in *Richard II,* as an obvious reflection of Marlowe's narrative in *Edward II,* has always constituted a particularly controversial facet in discussions of Marlovian influence in Shakespeare. As Robert Logan observes, in spite of the obvious (superficial) parallels, critics have reached no consensus on the exact nature of the influence.[6] If Henry V constitutes Shakespeare's attempt to radically transform the narcissistic, hypermasculine nightmare of Tamburlaine into a viable (if still disturbing) embodiment of masculine aggression, Richard II is clearly his version of an opposing kind of narcissism: the tragic failure of masculine control within an originally unearned, gratuitous position of power. As we observed in chapter 3, this kind of (aristocratic) narcissism was clearly anticipated in the first tetralogy through the characterization of Suffolk in *2 Henry VI,* whose death throes closely parallel Marlowe's Guise. Shakespeare's return to this specific critique in *Richard II* makes the comparison with *King John* particularly compelling, since the suspension of erotic interest in the Bastard's otherwise "antic" career now takes on the weight of calculated evasiveness. *Richard II,* and its curious *moral* evasiveness vis-à-vis the Woodstock murder, reflects Shakespeare's struggle to come to terms, especially in an erotic sense, with a crucial artistic influence which brings about a traumatic interrogation of his own strategies of masculine self-fashioning and self-identification.

Richard II, Part One

Before pursuing these more "personal" aspects of influence, however, I will consider briefly the obscurity of historical reference at the beginning of *Richard II* to the question of the play's specific historical and artistic sources. Bradley Irish's "Writing Woodstock: The Prehistory of *Richard II* and Shakespeare's Dramatic Method" summarizes pertinent historical developments, observing that "Woodstock's death was not a discrete event but rather the culmination of a factional struggle that had gripped England for over a decade," so that Shakespeare feels compelled to write "Woodstock's prehistory into *Richard II*'s dramatic *unconscious*" (my emphasis). Yet Irish questionably asserts that "the prehistory of *Richard II* is ... not ... something that can be readily inferred through [the anonymous] *Thomas of Woodstock,*"[7] a potential "source" for Shakespeare's play that one recent edition subtitles *"or Richard the Second, Part One."* In fact the Revels editors, Peter Corbin and Douglas Sedge, argue plausibly that *Thomas of Woodstock* "is usually dated between 1591 and 1595 on the assumption that it was influenced by Shakespeare's *2 Henry VI* (dated by most scholars to 1590–91) and that in turn *Woodstock* influenced his *Richard II* (1595)."[8]

Irish does establish a complexity of historical readings over time that leaves this particular "prehistory," like Shakespeare's play, morally opaque: Richard II, grandson of Edward III, ascended the throne at the tender age of eleven in 1387, at which point three of uncles were still living: Gaunt, York, and Woodstock. Tensions between the noble party, eventually termed the Lords Appellant, and the king's favourites intensified during Richard's adolescence, leading (to make a long story short) to the Merciless Parliament, in which "the Lords Appellant orchestrated the eradication of the minions"; and then, a decade later, to an equally bloody retribution when the king turned the tables with his own Revenge Parliament, through which several key nobles were executed (including Woodstock) or banished. Two junior members of the Lords Appellant, Bolingbroke and Mowbray, "all the while, anxiously looked on as Richard took revenge on the senior lords, wondering if they would face a similar fate."[9] This ruthless cycle of revenge is variously interpreted in historical accounts – with various assignations of blame and culpability – while the narrative of *Woodstock* "is heavily biased against the king."[10] That Shakespeare was closely familiar with it, nevertheless, seems strongly indicated by the fact that his own play echoes *Woodstock* in crucial ways. As Corbin and Sedge point out, Richard's "damaging admission" in *Woodstock* – "And we his [Edward the Black Prince's] son, to ease our wanton youth, / Become a landlord to this warlike realm, / Rent out our kingdom like a pelting farm" (4.1.146–8) – is clearly echoed in Gaunt's lamentation in *Richard II* that England "Is now leased out – I die pronouncing it – / Like to a tenement or pelting farm" (2.1.59–60). Moreover, Gaunt further accuses Richard of being "Landlord of England" (2.1.113) – and this "charge that Richard is 'landlord' of England occurs five times in *Thomas of Woodstock* [including the above reference], though, significantly, not in Holinshed."[11]

But it is more than verbal echoes that make it difficult to entirely dismiss *Woodstock* while analysing Shakespeare's artistic motives in *Richard II*. Corbin and Sedge remark that "*Woodstock* has long been recognised as being remarkably critical of kingship among Elizabethan history plays ... Whilst the orthodox notion of adherence to the divine authority of the crown is repeatedly advocated by Woodstock himself, the tone of such avowals is increasingly desperate and the circumstances in which they are uttered make such policy appear progressively untenable."[12] This implicit challenge to "divine" authority manifests in the play largely through the actions and rhetoric of the nobility, much as in *Richard II*, where Bolingbroke is the key figure in the usurpation of the throne. On the other hand, *Woodstock* makes frequent references to the dissatisfied commons as allies of the nobility against the irresponsible king, unlike *Richard II*, where "Shakespeare tends to minimize the active role of the commons and to diminish almost altogether the place of the citizenry in the constitution of the state."[13] At moments *Woodstock* seems highly reminiscent of *Edward II* in its dramatic exposure of ambitious and unscrupulous lower-born flatterers – such as when Lancaster (Gaunt) exclaims to Woodstock, "Take open arms. Join with the vexèd commons / And hale [Richard's] minions from his wanton side. / Their heads cut off, the people's satisfied" (1.3.247–9).

However, *Woodstock* appears carefully to "correct" *Edward II* by portraying more responsible, less narcissistic and self-serving nobility, who in a sense respond almost democratically to the greater will of the nation, rather than (as often in Marlowe) their own petty self-interests. Interestingly, York in the opening scene of *Woodstock* refers almost comically to "our good brother Woodstock" as "Plain Thomas, for by th'rood so all men call him / For his plain dealing and his simple clothing … 'Let others jet in silk and gold', says he, / 'A coat of English frieze best pleaseth me'" (98–102). This echoes very closely Mortimer Junior's dismissal of Gaveston to his father in *Edward II*: "He wears a lord's revénue on his back, / And, Midas-like, he jets it in the court / With base outlandish cullions at his heels" (1.4.406–8). Also interestingly, these lines from *Edward II* echo *2 Henry VI*, where Margaret petulantly complains of Gloucester's wife, "She bears a duke's revenues on her back, / And in her heart she scorns our poverty" (1.3.80–1).

Thus whoever the playwright was,[14] *Woodstock* may profitably be considered as an important bridge, thematically and politically, between *Edward II* and *Richard II*. A key difference, nevertheless, between this famous pair of historical tragedies and *Woodstock* is that both Marlowe and Shakespeare tend to increase the sense of deracination and alienation from the patrilineal cycle that we first noted in chapter 3, especially with respect to the Spenserian context and the discussion of atonement theology and Original Sin. Edward II's failure to recognize his inheritance of kingly responsibility or to mourn his father as a prelude to his own psychological or moral growth, at the beginning of Marlowe's tragedy, compares with Richard's absence of paternal identification. In *Richard II* there is only one reference to Richard's father, by his youngest surviving brother York:

I am the last of noble Edward's sons,
Of whom thy father, Prince of Wales, was first.
In war was never lion raged more fierce,

> In peace was never gentle lamb more mild
> Than was that young and princely gentlemen.
> His face thou hast, for even so looked he,
> ...
> But when he frowned, it was against the French
> And not against his friends. (2.1.171–9)

Conversely, references to the Black Prince and the patrilineal succession are frequent in *Woodstock*, even by the king himself, and even when he confesses his own irresponsibility (as above) in his petulant determination to reduce England to a "pelting farm." The Richard of *Woodstock* in fact repeatedly swears by his father and grandfather:

> Beshrew the churls that makes my queen so sad.
> But by my grandsire Edward's kingly bones,
> My princely father's tomb, King Richard swears
> We'll make them weep these wrongs in bloody tears. (1.3.198–201)

Although his flatterers encourage their king to challenge the control of the nobles, especially the Protector Woodstock, they ironically do so by encouraging Richard to identify with stories of his grandfather and father. Richard decisively responds:

> Why should our proud Protector then presume
> And we not punish him whose treason's viler far
> Than ever was rebellious Mortimer's?
> Prithee, read on; examples such as these
> Will bring us to our kingly grandsire's spirit.
> ...
> A victory [by the Black Prince] most strange and admirable.
> Never was conquest got with such great odds.
> O princely Edward, had thy son such hap,
> Such fortune and success to follow him,
> His daring uncles and rebellious peers
> Durst not control and govern as they do.
> But these bright shining trophies shall awake me. (2.1.66–93)

While Shakespeare evidently knew the text of *Woodstock* well, he was careful not to reproduce such strong patriarchal identification on the part of the protagonist king, artistically determined instead to replicate the patrilineal alienation or isolation of *Edward II*.

From Patrilineal Breakdown to Homoeroticism

Significantly Shakespeare saves an emotionally close identification between father and son for the relationship between Gaunt and the future usurper Bolingbroke. Moreover, the highly positive portrayal of the eponymous hero of *Woodstock* has been plausibly compared to the highly idealized portrayal of Gaunt in *Richard II*: the anonymous playwright "has transformed the Duke of Gloucester, the 'man of high mind and stout stomach', the 'sore and a right severe man' of the chronicler, into ... a 'type of virtuous Englishry', much as Shakespeare transformed the Gaunt of Holinshed," who is in fact "a turbulent and self-seeking magnate," into "a father and patriot of grandiose stature, a prophet whose dying speech on England attracted the attention of the anthologist (for *England's Parnassus*) as early as 1600."[15] We observed the potential but futile search for a surrogate father through the characterization of that *other* Duke of Gloucester within the first tetralogy. It is as if in *Richard II* Shakespeare intentionally isolates his protagonist from such identifications, replicating perhaps more closely the "Protestant" aspects of Marlowe's traumatized response to Spenser's theology of grace, with its potential deracination of masculine identity from patrilineal social structure.

Richard II, as the foregoing discussion suggests, constitutes a decidedly problematic moment in Shakespeare's development. Lake, as noted at the outset, asserts the ritualistic quality of the play in comparison to the more robust action of *King John*. Why intensify the theological substructure at this point in the evolution of the histories? This question needs to be posed in tandem with another observation arising from the previous chapters. We noted in chapter 3 that the secular emphasis in the first tetralogy, and the eradication of the spiritual dependency – or the exposure of its inefficacy through the pious Henry VI – seems to increase the possibilities for female agency, in cooperation or competition with masculine assertion. But the thwarted erotic desire arguably at the root of Richard III's pathological villainy also begins in the Shakespeare canon what appears a misogynistic marginalization of female characters, so that in the second tetralogy they play a much diminished role, both politically and romantically. Moreover chapter 4 witnessed a crucial containment of the homoeroticism momentarily addressed in the Richard-Buckingham relationship. Where then do these observations lead us with one of the most notorious critical questions of *Richard II*, the presence or absence of a homoeroticism contingent upon this play's close textual relationship to *Edward II*?

The most direct, indeed the only direct, evocation of homoerotic desire occurs through the problematic accusations registered by Boling-broke immediately prior to the execution of Bushy and Green:

> Bushy and Green, I will not vex your souls –
> Since presently your souls must part your bodies
> – With too much urging your pernicious lives,
> For 'twere no charity; yet, to wash your blood
> From off my hands, here in the view of men
> I will unfold some causes of your deaths.
> You have misled a prince, a royal king,
> A happy gentleman in blood and lineaments,
> By you unhappied and disfigured clean.
> You have in manner with your sinful hours
> Made a divorce betwixt his queen and him,
> Broke the possession of a royal bed,
> And stained the beauty of a fair queen's cheeks
> With tears drawn from her eyes by your foul wrongs. (3.1.2–15)

This speech again carries a theological twist, whereby the militant Christ of the play's first scene now becomes a Pilate washing his hands of the taint of homoerotic dalliance that has infected his sovereign's relationships with flattering courtiers – a moral taint which oddly, he seems to fear, rebounds on himself through the act of ordering the execution. (Does Bolingbroke, like Pilate, have a guilty conscience already?) Nevertheless what is most surprising about this speech, as so many commentators have pointed out, is that nothing else in the play confirms this accusation.

For Paul Menzer this moment constitutes a clear example of "Mar-lowe's 'influence' lead[ing] Shakespeare into incoherence." Review-ing conflicting readings that debate the presumed fraudulence versus validity of Bolingbroke's charge – readings that agree on nothing other than Shakespeare's clear "borrowing" of implications and situations more accurately reflective of *Edward II* – Menzer concludes:

> this Marlovian import becomes a pea under the mattress that bruises the rest of the play, and *Richard II* shifts to accommodate this uncomfortable Edwardian import ... Ultimately, a critical habit that turns either to histori-cal or dramatic sources to explain this moment fails to fully contain it. The detail creates a "problem" without a solution ... In fact, the problem has no solution because Bolingbroke's charge *makes no sense*.[16]

Yet if the moment makes no sense with regard to Shakespeare's *conscious* artistic intentions, it serves at least as an invitation to consider unconscious motives at this point in the canon.

Here again the play's "unconscious" evocation of a prehistory, and the significance of *Woodstock*, proves illuminating. As if written directly under the influence of *Edward II*, *Woodstock* also, although not quite as awkwardly and uncomfortably, attempts to introduce the element of homoeroticism in Richard's behaviour. After Bagot informs the lawyer Tresilian that Richard intends to create him Lord Chief Justice of England, Greene advises him, "You must observe and fashion to the time / The habit of your laws" (1.2.38–9), the cadence and occasion of which are reminiscent of Spencer's advice to Baldock in *Edward II*, "You must be proud, bold, pleasant, resolute – / And now and then stab, as occasion serves" (2.1.42–3). Significantly Greene immediately adds, "The King is young, / Ay, and a little wanton – so perhaps are we" (39–40). Warned never to use his "laws" to punish his "benefactors," Tresilian exclaims, "How, sir, to punish you, the minions to the King, / The jewels of his heart, his dearest loves?" (42–3).

The suggestion of homoeroticism is stronger, in fact most explicit, in an exchange between Richard's queen, Anne of Bohemia, the Duchess of Gloucester (Woodstock's wife), and the Duchess of Ireland in 2.3. In response to Anne's anxious query, "Tell me, dear aunt, has Richard so forgot / The types of honour and nobility / So to disgrace his good and reverend uncles?," the Duchess of Gloucester asserts that they have been "all dismissèd from the council table, / Banished the court, and, / even before their faces, / Their offices bestowed on several grooms." The Duchess of Ireland then pointedly adds, "My husband Ireland, that unloving lord / – God pardon his amiss, he now is dead – / King Richard was the cause he left my bed," to which the queen abruptly asserts, "No more, good cousin" (10–13), in effect shutting down the one direct suggestion of sodomy on the part of the king. The rest of Anne's speech adds a crucial context which surprisingly but effectively contains the subversive sexual potential. She immediately continues, "Could I work the means, / He should not so disgrace his dearest friends … O riotous Richard, / A heavy blame is thine for this distress / That dost allow thy polling flatterers / To gild themselves with others' miseries" (13–26).

The queen then proceeds to reassure the Duchess of Gloucester:

> The sighs I vent are not mine own, dear aunt,
> I do not sorrow in mine own behalf,
> Nor now repent with peevish frowardness

> And wish I ne'er had seen this English shore,
> But think me happy in King Richard's love. (30–4)

This speech constitutes one of *Woodstock*'s clearest allusions to *Edward II*, since it essentially refutes Queen Isabella's lament in the face of Edward's continuing obsession with Gaveston:

> O miserable and distressèd queen!
> Would, when I left sweet France and was embarked,
> That charming Circe, walking on the waves,
> Had changed my shape, or at the marriage-day
> The cup of Hymen had been full of poison,
> Or with those arms that twined about my neck
> I had been stifled, and not lived to see
> The king my lord thus to abandon me. (1.4.170–7)

Woodstock's altruistic Queen Anne, much less narcissistically, asserts, "'Tis England's subjects' sorrow I sustain, / I fear they grudge against their sovereign," to which the Duchess of Ireland observes in response, "your virtuous charity, fair Queen, / So graciously hath won the commons' love / As only you have power to stay their rigour" (36–7, 43–4). Sir Cheney's observation upon this exchange is hardly surprising: "Why, there's one blessing yet, that England hath / A virtuous queen, although a wanton king" (61–2). And indeed when Anne dies, King Richard is reduced to extreme and violent grief – "all my earthly joys with her must die / And I am killed with cares eternally" (4.3.144–5) – which Corbin and Sedge suggest "seems designed to stimulate a measure of audience sympathy for the King,"[17] presumably not only because of his emotional pain but because of his renewed heteroerotic passion. The intense grief appears significantly underwritten by guilt – "O God, I fear even here begins our woe! / Her death's but chorus to some tragic scene" (149–50) – which again may curiously echo *Edward II*, when the panicking Isabella exclaims to Mortimer in the final scene, "Ay me, see where he [Edward III] comes, and they [the Lords] with him. / Now, Mortimer, begins our tragedy" (5.6.22–3).

Bolingbroke's accusation of sodomy in *Richard II* is certainly more awkward and less successfully contained, although it is possible to imagine ways that the playwright could have rendered it less so. In Shakespeare, Richard's relationship with his second wife Isabella is more distant. Unlike the assertive and altruistic Anne, Isabella is tentative and fragile, although she does finally express frustration over, even a kind of contempt for, her husband's lack of manliness:

> Hath Bolingbroke
> Deposed thine intellect? Hath he been in thy heart?
> The lion dying thrusteth forth his paw
> And wounds the earth, if nothing else, with rage
> To be o'erpowered; and wilt thou, pupil-like,
> Take the correction, mildly kiss the rod,
> And fawn on rage with base humility,
> Which art a lion and the king of beasts? (5.1.27–34)

The effect here, rhetorically, is rather like narcissism lecturing narcissism. While the greater emotional distance between Richard and Isabella might conceivably increase the possibility of sodomy in the context of the general action, such is not the effect of Shakespeare's portrayal, for in spite of the suggestions of irresponsibility and effeminacy, nothing in the text confirms the suggestion that Richard's courtiers have indulged in "sinful hours" that in fact have forced a "divorce" between the king and queen. How then do we do ultimately resolve Menzer's assertion that Bolingbroke's charge "makes no sense"?

The Sodomitical Unconscious

Another critic, taking a slightly different critical tack, also emphasizes the erotic, if still primarily unconscious potential of Richard's behaviour. Meredith Skura interestingly explores a kind of discontinuity or disjuncture in the text that emerges in the disjointed title of her article: "Marlowe's *Edward II*: Penetrating Language in Shakespeare's *Richard II*." As she suggests, "It may seem … that neither Edward's passion nor his violent death by penetration has any part in *Richard II*. Richard's trio of minions is unimportant and erotically neutral compared to Edward's Gaveston – it is hard to imagine Richard wishing to be 'another Bushy' or 'another Bagot', for example."[18] Nevertheless she mines the text of Shakespeare's play to demonstrate a buried emphasis on at least potential penetration.[19] Richard dismisses Queen Isabella in act 5 with the assertion, "I am sworn brother, sweet, / To grim Necessity, and he and I / Will keep a league till death" (5.1.20–2), so that "he imagines his own death as a transcendent brotherhood." Yet "[e]specially after his defeat, Richard sounds at times as if he were [masochistically] embracing *Bolingbroke* like his sworn brother Necessity – as if Bolingbroke's triumph over Richard was as erotically tinged as Lightbourne's triumph over Edward in Marlowe's play" (my emphasis). When the Groom informs Richard that Bolingbroke has ridden the usurped king's horse in his coronation procession, "Richard makes the horse into a symbol of fickle England" but then unfolds "a more personal and erotic metaphor":

> So proud that Bolingbroke was on his back!
> …
>
> Forgiveness, horse! Why do I rail on thee,
> Since thou, created to be awed by man,
> Wast born to bear? I was not made a horse,
> And yet I bear a burthen like an ass,
> Spur-galled and tired by jauncing Bolingbroke. (5.5.84–94)

Skura argues that "Shakespeare usually associates horses with hetero-sexual dominance,"[20] which is generally correct, but even details of this particular horse are significant. The Groom identifies the horse as the "roan Barbary" (78). The roan anticipates Hotspur's horse in *1 Henry IV*, which is certainly symbolic of his heterosexually assertive (if neverthe-less romantic) relationship with his wife Kate in 2.3.100–3 – "Come, wilt thou see me ride? / And when I am a-horseback, I will swear / I love thee infinitely." Even Hal gets the colour of the horse correct in the subsequent scene, although his parody of Hotspur and Kate totally misreads or misinterprets the genuine and moving affection between husband and wife.

Intriguingly, the name "Barbary" recurs in Shakespeare. It is the name of Desdemona's mother's maid, who died singing the willow song in *Othello*. Michael Neill remarks, "The name is strangely evocative in this play … since it recalls the 'Barbary Moors' of North Africa, and Iago's description of Othello as a 'Barbary horse' … and an 'erring barbar-ian'."[21] Even more strangely, the term appears in Hal's cruel teasing of Francis in *1 Henry IV*: "Why then your brown bastard is your only drink; for look you, Francis, your white canvas doublet will sully. In Barbary, sir, it cannot come to so much" (2.4.73–6). Some editors unsur-prisingly dismiss this as nonsense, but Bradley Tuggle has convincingly linked the passage to 1 Corinthians 14:11 – "Except I knowe then the power of the voyce, I shalbe vnto him that speaketh, a barbarian, and he that speaketh, shalbe a barbarian vnto me" – where Paul empha-sizes his preference for prophesying over speaking in tongues.[22] The horse's name thus evokes a complex of competing ideological and psy-chological imports. It seems to encapsulate concern for manly assertion as well as an awareness of the ways such assertion can override or nul-lify spiritual community. But it also suggests the way personal or social aggression can mitigate the limiting effects of an excessive or enervat-ing spiritual sensitivity, as Othello is perhaps rendered vulnerable not so much through pagan sexual energy as by Christian idealization of chastity and narcissistic dependency.

Skura's suggestion of a masochistic connection between Richard and Bolingbroke raises the (unconscious) possibility of eroticism not between the king and his friends and flatterers, but between the king and his arch-enemy. Her reading at this point resembles Debora Shuger's suggestion of a "zero-sum" game between Richard and Bolingbroke as paramount in Richard's, and perhaps especially Shakespeare's, imagination: "Richard's bucket sinks [during his sudden and virtually inexplicable abdication, in the face of Bolingbroke's rising bucket] not because it is laden with crimes but because his tears weigh it down. What interests Shakespeare is not Richard's demerits but his choking bitter anguish at ending up the loser."[23] Richard's line above, "Spur-galled and tired by jauncing Bolingbroke," suggests his anger at being finally *fucked* by Bolingbroke – primarily (consciously) in the metaphorical sense.[24] I suggest that the odd attenuation of the erotic significance accruing from Marlowe's *Edward II* which this chapter has been addressing may imply that for Shakespeare the idea of being *literally* penetrated by another man is ultimately *unimaginable* or *unthinkable*, at least consciously at this point in his career.

When Richard complains he "bear[s] a burthen like an ass," he evokes that most crucial of early modern mythological tropes, the story of Actaeon – wherein the image of the metamorphosed stag tends to emerge as asinine[25] – a key narrative for both Marlowe and Shakespeare, and one that evokes a combination of religious and sexual anxiety centring on male incapacity. Gaveston's envisaged masque at the beginning of *Edward II* – "One like Actaeon, peeping through the grove, / Shall by the angry goddess [a lovely boy in Dian's shape] be transformed" (1.1.60–7) – clearly constitutes a homoerotic version of this myth, even while it temporarily deflects (the "boy" does not directly threaten aggression) the horrifically "sodomitical" death that awaits Edward in the end. The spiritual implications of the Actaeon myth are clearly developed in Marlowe's *Doctor Faustus*, and Shakespeare deliberately echoes these in *The Comedy of Errors* and *A Midsummer Night's Dream*.[26] But if *Richard II* represents the beginnings of Shakespeare's exploration of a truly "tragic" Actaeon, the sexual component becomes increasingly problematic. It is difficult to deny the compulsion with which Shakespeare in his later career keeps returning to the possibility of homoerotic desire, keeps trying to finally address a way of coming to terms with it, or transmuting it, in his art.

In *Richard II* such "working through" appears not altogether successful. Although no one would deny the lyrical intensity, indeed brilliance, of the verse in *Richard II*, audiences over the years have expressed reservations concerning the tragic protagonist, despite the frequent assertion that he possesses the soul of a poet. Lois Potter admits that "Many critical studies of *Richard II*, and a surprising number of productions, start from [this] assumption: that Shakespeare wrote, and asked his leading actor to star in, a long play dominated by a character whose main effect on the audience was to be one of boredom, embarrassment, or at best contemptuous pity."[27] While one Marlowe critic has reasonably suggested that Edward II represents "Marlowe's most ambitious attempt to create a credible human being,"[28] Shakespeare in response to Marlowe's tragedy has created a protagonist who seems curiously *inauthentic* – or at least excessively detached, emotionally. It is almost as if Shakespeare, in attempting to mirror Marlowe's narcissistic king but anxious to repress or expunge the actual reality of homoerotic desire that Marlowe portrays, in effect *cauterizes* the necessary blood and guts, the very well-spring of Richard's emotions.

Shakespeare's mirroring of what I have termed above the deracination from patrilineal structures as a reflection of a more "Protestant" social dilemma may partly explain the emotional paucity or paralysis. It is significant that York, castigating Richard for illegally confiscating Gaunt's land and wealth at his death, defends Bolingbroke's inheritance with the exclamation, "Was not Gaunt just? And is not Harry true? / Did not the one deserve to have an heir? / Is not his heir a well-deserving son?" (2.1.192–4). The phrase "a well-deserving son" veritably encapsulates a position contrary to the Calvinist dismissal of human merit vis-à-vis the divine fatherhood of God, as we observed in chapter 3. Calvin in fact asserts that "God of his singular goodnesse aduaunceth men, to this so high a steppe [fatherhood]" only so that "they should acknowledge them selues to be so much more bound vnto him."[29] I would particularly emphasize the pathological implications of the theology here, since Calvin's idealization of the divine father, and emphasis on the abject dependency of human fathers, would seem to work *against* the development of a viable human fatherhood, which must exercise an independent and integrated authority, balancing love and responsibility, nurturance and correction.

The rather strange turn to a *private* religious concern, rather than his more characteristically public and self-pitying declaration of victimized Christhood, in Richard's soliloquies in 5.5 suggests Shakespeare's assertion of the anxious soul-searching of Protestant inwardness, a kind of microcosm of narcissism and uncertain self-identification:

> And these same thoughts people this little world,
> In humors like the people of this world,

For no thought is contented. The better sort,
As thoughts of things divine, are intermixed
With scruples and do set the word itself
Against the word, as thus, "Come little ones,"
And then again,
"It is as hard to come as for a camel
To thread the postern of a small needle's eye." (9–17)

The allusion to passages from the three synoptic gospels (Matthew 19:14, 24, Mark 10:14, 25, and Luke 18:16, 25) may be significant not just through their juxtaposition of faith/encouragement and doubt/ despair. Skura's exploration of imagery of penetration involves consideration of pins and brooches, probably most importantly the passage in 3.2 where Richard muses:

For within the hollow crown
That rounds the mortal temples of a king
Keeps Death his court, and there the antic [jester] sits,
Scoffing his state and grinning at his pomp,
Allowing him a breath, a little scene,
To monarchize, be feared, and kill with looks,
Infusing him with self and vain conceit,
As if this flesh which walls about our life
Were brass impregnable; and humored thus,
Comes at the last and with a little pin
Bores through his castle wall, and – farewell king! (160–70)

These two passages above in effect juxtapose the desperately dependent Christian soul itself, like Faustus swollen with self-conceit, trying to gain access, to "penetrate" the strait and narrow gate of the kingdom of heaven for protection and salvation, and the imagery of the masculinized, humanist self suddenly made aware of its vulnerability or penetrability.

In spite of the effectiveness of this rhetorical contrast, however, Shakespeare renders Richard's "trauma" less movingly than Marlowe conveys the final terror of Edward; as Skura must admit, "It may seem a long way from Lightbourne's spit to Richard's little pin."[30] Edward's passion for (especially) Gaveston may be notably narcissistic and certainly ill advised politically, but it is also intensely human. Richard's "passions," as they emerge belatedly in an oddly fractured manner, never extend beyond himself. Even Richard's striking Faustian allusion – "Was this face the face / That every day under his household roof / Did keep ten thousand men" (4.1.282–4) – surpasses Faustus in narcissism, as it hyperbolizes not a spectacular (if demonic) embodiment of idealized beauty but his own reflection in the mirror. Shakespeare's depiction of Richard II may recall critical judgments that are usually applied to Marlowe's Edward III at the end of *Edward II*; for example, Constance Kuriyama's assessment that "If the emergence of young Edward at the end of the play does not particularly inspire or reassure us, we can probably attribute our lack of enthusiasm to the fact that [his] triumph is theoretical, not something that Marlowe feels."[31] Indeed, the peculiar tension between emblematic representation and "realistic" psychological response that Marlowe deliberately seems to explore, in the secondary characters of *Edward II* in particular – and which may have influenced Shakespeare in the composition of *Richard II* – becomes more problematic when embodied within the play's tragic protagonist. With respect to his hero, Shakespeare does not achieve the startling paradox of Marlowe's art, where "the [sodomitically] 'emblematic' nature of Edward's death [actually] intensifies the horror."[32] Richard II seems almost at times a "theoretical" embodiment of narcissism in the political arena, translated into an emotionally stifled theological emblem.[33]

Shakespeare's king does perfectly demonstrate the narcissistic patterns of behaviour – culminating in the mirror episode of the abdication – that Peter Donaldson has noted in Marlowe's *Tamburlaine*, where the protagonist ultimately refuses to "engage with the risk of injury," preferring instead to desperately manipulate other characters to create "mirror[s] of a self that must desperately find its reflection everywhere rather than face its own emptiness."[34] Indeed, Richard's tendency either to prevent others from engaging in conflict and risk (his sudden cancellation of the combat between Bolingbroke and Mowbray) or to avoid engaging in conflict himself (his inexplicably sudden surrender to Bolingbroke in the deposition scene) may explain why the play has seemed to some dull in performance, even while he theoretically and precisely demonstrates a narcissistic behavioural pattern of avoidance of conflict. This feature of the play leads Dawson and Yachnin in the Oxford edition to their most interesting claim:

> … the centre of gravity of the play has to do with an historical action in which the onlookers in the playhouse are implicated. They are inheritors of a troubled legacy because the play places them as the beneficiaries of the violent transactions of their national history and because the arc of the action, which twice offers and then rescinds the pleasurable spectacle of violence (in the joust scene in 1.3 and before Flint Castle in 3.3), tends to make the audience wish for the assault that results in Richard's murder. The form of the play thus makes the audience a party to the regicide.[35]

I hesitate, however, to agree that this function or effect of the play was either wholly intentional on Shakespeare's part, or, more importantly, answers the artistic inadequacy, the actual problem of emotional identification I have been exploring. In addition to the aporia of a charge of homoerotic behaviour in a text which does nothing to substantiate it, there is also the odd aporia of a highly indulgent, effeminate, and passive king who nevertheless unscrupulously raises moneys for a war in Ireland, and then very surprisingly leaves England in order to actively *fight* such a war, like a quintessential medieval, manly, martial king. The anonymous playwright of *Thomas of Woodstock* does not force such an incredible contradiction of character upon his audience; and while Marlowe arguably does, once in his play, when Edward temporarily triumphs over his enemies, this victory is at least motivated by the fury Edward feels over the murder of his beloved Gaveston.

Shakespeare's indirect and ambivalent treatment of sodomitical desire recurs elsewhere, even relatively early in the canon. Like *Richard II*, *Venus and Adonis* (1593) presents sodomitical penetration in a far subtler fashion than Marlowe's *Edward II*. Goran Stanivukovic offers the most persuasive postmodern reading of this text, in an article that is interestingly torn, ideologically, between radical queer assertions and an ultimately conservative moral logic. Stanivukovic initially focuses on Adonis's death scene, at least as imagined by Venus. While Ovid's version had included the goring by the boar, Shakespeare turns the goring into a kiss:

> He ran upon the boar with his sharp spear,
> Who did not whet his teeth at him again,
> But by a kiss thought to persuade him there;
> > And, nuzzling in his flank, the loving swine
> > Sheathed unaware the tusk in his soft groin. (1112–16)

The tenderness of the gesture, as a possible projection of Venus's own desire for Adonis – and especially the fact that the penetration is performed by the boar "unaware," that is, unintentionally or unconsciously – does not finally prevent a persuasive conservative reading aimed primarily at the poem's dedicatee, the Earl of Southampton:

> Containment of sodomy, which denies procreation and in turn undermines marriage ... seems a good strategic move on the part of Shakespeare, who has just obtained patronage from a nobleman who refused a promising marriage arrangement. By insisting on the avoidance of Venus ... and by sending Adonis off in quest of masculinity, allegorized in the boar, Shakespeare captures ... some of the ambiguities of Southampton's private

life. The power of the poem's narrative to manipulate desire and exclude woman from the realm of erotic fulfilment establishes, through the act of reading, a homosocial union of Shakespeare with his … male readers. Yet Shakespeare's other eye, the one that often seems to look for finding ways of satisfying the normative moralism of the age, makes sure that Adonis's violent death appears threatening enough to aristocratic male readers who might find transgressive sexuality appealing. The eradication of the Adonis-sodomite at the end of the poem, therefore, suggests the final victory of normative moralism over illicit desire.[36]

Involvement with Southampton in the earlier 1590s may have led to a kind of hiatus, or even temporary and traumatic uncertainty, in Shakespeare's evolving masculine self-identification. Such uncertainty resulted in the mid-1590s in a unique engagement with Marlovian themes, as well as a deeply ambivalent response to class distinctions and indeed to aristocratic men, within *The Merchant of Venice*. This play combines theological themes with the portrayal of a thwarted, primarily unconscious, homoerotic desire, conveyed through the respectable (though soon to be archaic) codes of classical *amicitia* – interfused with late medieval concepts of sworn brotherhood – on the part of the titular character Antonio.[37] Shakespeare appears to be aware of the connection between these traditions at the time of the composition of *Richard II*, probably just a year or so earlier. We noted above, via Skura's analysis, Richard's assertion of a "sworn brother[hood]" with Necessity, which ultimately translates into his masochistic identification with Bolingbroke. But Richard is also capable of a less ironic, if rather pathetic, identification of this kind, as when he says to Aumerle:

> Or shall we play the wantons with our woes
> And make such pretty match with shedding tears?
> As thus, to drop them still upon one place,
> Till they have fretted us a pair of graves
> Within the earth; and therein laid – there lies
> Two kinsmen digged their graves with weeping eyes. (3.3.164–9)

This passage mirrors the tombs commemorating the linked loves and lives of various medieval brothers-in-arms.[38] Ironically, in Richard's case, neither Aumerle nor the king's other allies are inclined to encourage the moral paralysis of Richard's self-pitying ruminations in act 3. Similarly, in a psychological sense, Antonio's own Christ-like gesture of self-sacrifice for Bassanio seems underwritten by an attempt at a kind of masochistic, passive-aggressive manipulation of his beloved from beyond the grave: "You cannot better be employed, Bassanio, / Than to live still and write mine epitaph" (4.1.117–18). Antonio's fraught characterization still indicates the depth of Shakespeare's ambivalence, but contrasts with the rather lifeless tragic hero of *Richard II*, who offers Shakespeare a way of both interrogating gratuitous political power and emphasizing the crucial nature of personal or inner competence, while at the same time distancing himself from, and failing to transmute, the erotic indigestion of the Marlovian prototype.

Later Strategies of Containment: Familist Influence

After the tragedy of *Richard II*, the generic and erotic tone changes radically in the rest of the second tetralogy. The mode of *1 Henry IV* is predominantly comic, with a surprising darkening of mood in part 2. The figure of Hal emerges as the most crucial component in a process which Harry Berger has provocatively described as "the familiar story of disenchantment in which religious attitudes towards history and politics give way to secular and humanistic attitudes," becoming "crossed by the no less familiar story of the Protestant reenchantment that intensifies both the intimacy and the vividness of the spiritual warfare which transpires in the subject's dialogue with himself and God."[39] The implications of the religious reenchantment become most evident in the final play of the tetralogy. In *Henry V* the king, struggling to refute Williams's assertion that "if the cause be not good the King himself hath a heavy reckoning to make" (4.1.134–5), attempts to displace political into spiritual responsibility: "Every subject's duty is the King's; but every subject's soul is his own" (176–7). Yet he ends the scene with a special appeal to the "God of battles," both for his soldiers, and for his own guilty association with his father's crime. Artistically, the justification of aristocratic privilege (in the face of dubious legitimacy) seems ironically accompanied by a compromised moral independence – both in a strictly humanist sense, because of the attempted displacement, and in a "transcendental" sense, through the guilty appeal to the Godhead.

The ultimate triumph of Hal's politico-religious self-fashioning involves the banishment, at the end of the previous play, of its more subversively Protestant – in fact Puritan – shadow in the form of Falstaff. While Hal's pronouncement, "I know thee not, old man," constitutes a well-known allusion to Paul's admonition to cast off the old man, or carnal self, in favour of the new man, reborn of the spirit,[40] the knight's unruliness in the two parts of *Henry IV* represents not just the Pauline "old man" or carnal self but the "grotesque Puritan" figure under interrogation in late sixteenth-century England, as Kristen Poole's crucial reading has helped us understand.[41] Intriguingly, however, the allusion may signify not just Pauline but, more radically, Familist doctrine. When Hendrik Niclaes signed his works with his initials "H.N.," "Some believed that he was claiming to be Homo Novus, or a new-made man, one who lived without sin."[42] Thus *Henry IV* may emerge not exactly as a postmodern "allegory of the characters' psychosocial lives" – the kind of reading, as chapter 1 noted, that Timothy Rosendale objects to – but as an exploration of an alternative religious view in the late sixteenth century.

Indeed, Falstaff's parodic "resurrection" near the end of *1 Henry IV* suggests not a parody of Christ's resurrection so much as a bogus version of the Familist imitation of Christ that was to be undergone by all true believers, within the course of their own lives. Recall Etherington's assertion, "he that doth believe it is possible to keep all the ten commandments hath the right faith in Christ and they that do attain to the perfect keeping of them are risen from the dead, according to scriptures, and as holiness is Christ and the son of God, so sin is Antichrist and the son of the devil."[43] Thus Hal's identification of Falstaff as "that old white-bearded Satan" (2.4.458) may be less (comic) demonization than (seriocomic) indictment of his failure of mature self-fashioning. Certainly, patterns of regeneration are not always necessarily heterodox: an orthodox worldview may also address the participation of the faithful in spiritual rebirth and resurrection. Yet the "allegories" in the second tetralogy very often seem highly resistant to orthodox readings. Consider Hal's evocation of a virtually "Antichrist" stance – taking on Hotspur's (martial) glory while he washes away his own personal shame:

> I will redeem all this on Percy's head
> And in the closing of some glorious day
> Be bold to tell you that I am your son,
> When I will wear a garment all of blood
> And stain my favors in a bloody mask,
> Which, washed away, shall scour my shame with it. (*1 Henry IV* 3.2.132–7)

This stance – besides embodying the pride and self-interest which in Familist doctrine would constitute an Antichrist state – virtually cancels Hal's later, Christ-like offer to engage in single combat with Hotspur to save casualties on either side of the conflict. Religious readings of Hal's transformation – which sometimes implicitly recognize Hal's Nicodemism or duplicity – consistently have trouble avoiding their more heterodox implications. For example, Beatrice Groves offers an interesting link between Hal's role playing, perhaps rather euphemistically described as "masked virtue," to Christ's deception of Satan during the harrowing of Hell, through the Son of God's "concealment of his true nature." But Groves is forced to conclude that Hal succeeds as a king because "the illusion of divinity is part of his masterful manipulation of appearance, not the result of his [genuinely] Christian kingship."[44] Moreover, Hal's remark concerning Falstaff's "Satanic" persona highlights the dangerously tempting but incompetent paternal surrogacy that Falstaff (evident in the phallic implications of his name) offers in the play.

The very process of Hal's self-fashioning is worth further consideration in light of Familist doctrine. As in the previous chapter, Niclaes's *Terra Pacis* may again be relevant to Hal's aim to learn – like the Bastard in *King John* – the ways of the world without embracing its corruption. Douglas Jones observes that Niclaes "ask[s] his reader to 'consider well of the strange States of the wildernessed Lands and People' – the anomie just outside the fortified walls of *Terra Pacis*," where individuals are "crushed under the weight of their own unprofitable labor. Becoming 'bewitched' by the products of their hands, they soon slid[e] comfortably into idolatry." Niclaes offers a long list of pastimes beginning with "playing Tables, Draft-boards, Chess-boards, Cards and Mummeries and Masks, for to delight the idle people with such foolish vanity." Jones pointedly observes that the "litany of images, textures, and sounds is reminiscent of … the Bankside activities of Shakespeare's London."[45] The passage indeed evokes Hal's disdain for the "unyoked humor of [his companions'] idleness" and their "playing holidays" (*1 Henry IV* 1.2.190, 198). But it also evokes Henry IV's lingering (and potent) fears on his deathbed that Hal's lawless reign will ruin England:

> Harry the Fifth is crowned. Up, Vanity!
> Down, royal state! All you sage counselors, hence!
> …
> O my poor kingdom, sick with civil blows!
> When that my care could not withhold thy riots,
> What wilt thou do when riot is thy care?
> O, thou wilt be a wilderness again,
> Peopled with wolves, thy old inhabitants. (*2 Henry IV* 4.5.119–37)

Niclaes not only repeatedly refers to the "wildernessed" lands – admittedly a common biblical motif – in *Terra Pacis* but also observes that outside the City of Peace "there is nothing but death, misery and calamity; for without the same are the Inchanters, the Dogs and Wolves, and all

wilde beasts ... all undiscreetness and unrighteousness."[46] Wolves also
recur (less frequently) in the Bible, where they most famously signify
rather a threat to the true flock of believers (Matthew 7:15, Acts 20:29)
than an existential condition of sin.

The irony of Henry IV's final words, after reconciling with Hal, also
suggests a Familist paradox. When the king learns that the "lodging where [he] first did swoon" is named Jerusalem, he surprisingly
rejoices:

> Laud be to God! Even there my life must end.
> It hath been prophesied to me many years
> I should not die but in Jerusalem,
> Which vainly I supposed the Holy Land.
> But bear me to that chamber; there I'll lie.
> In that Jerusalem shall Henry die. (4.5.235–40)

Shakespeare alters Holinshed by having the king directly request to be
returned to this chamber, as a form of self-fulfilling prophecy. For Shakespeare, apparently, the agency is all. Beatrice Groves as well notices this
change from Holinshed, in a more recent essay than the harrowing of
Hell discussion: "Shakespeare has changed a natural question ('Where
am I?') into an unnatural one ('Where was I when I was first taken ill?');
it is the price he is willing to pay in order to give his king agency over
his place of death."[47] Interestingly, in her struggle with Niclaes's apocalyptic language, Janet Halley cannot resolve the following conundrum:
"either history is desubstantiated, into an allegory for spiritual reality,
or the person of HN actually *is* the New Jerusalem." The tainted and
self-tortured Henry is clearly no apocalyptic Christ. Yet his political
resurgence in *Richard II* does recall the water imagery from *King John*,
and may also suggest (perhaps more ironically) the committed agency
of the spiritually focused individual, with its Familist origins in *Terra
Pacis* that we observed in chapter 4. As Scroop informs Richard:

> Like an unseasonable stormy day,
> Which makes the silver rivers drown their shores
> As if the world were all dissolved to tears,
> So high above his limits swells the rage
> Of Bolingbroke, covering your fearful land
> With hard bright steel and hearts harder than steel. (3.2.106–11)

Recall Douglas Jones's argument that the "mighty river" of *Terra Pacis*
implies courageous acceptance of the world beyond the walls of the

City of Peace, and of the vicissitudes of material existence. Henry's celebratory language and his embracement of transcendent death at the end of *2 Henry IV* again suggests this recurring contradiction in Familist discourse, as described by Halley: "the spiritualist's transcendence of the material world into a realm of neoplatonic unity collides with an assertion that the divine order is materially embodied in this earth."[48]

Through a similar heightening of material reality, Groves argues that Henry's projected journey to Jerusalem "creates a unifying trope for the entire Henriad." Henry's death in the Jerusalem Chamber is not simply deeply ironic, a "symbolic failure" of the crusading impulse, "since early modern biblical interpretation, which foregrounded the typological importance of the present time, had begun to identify London with the new Jerusalem."[49] Groves does not here consider Familist influence; indeed much of her argument hinges on Barbara Lewalski's influential argument that "reformed exegesis" encouraged English Protestants to perceive biblical history not merely "as exemplary to them but as actually recapitulated in their lives."[50] Yet the Henry-Hal relationship in the second tetralogy – although it involves notable estrangement – does not exactly reflect the patrilineal alienation typical of Calvinism. Moreover, Shakespeare's politicization of biblical "allegories" complicates and I think ironizes parts of Groves's reading which seem overly sanguine or optimistic, such as her assertion that "the fallen Eden of *Richard II* becomes the victorious homecoming of *Henry V*."[51]

Certainly, Hal more skilfully than his father at least *appears* to avoid the taint of political corruption. While the complex process of his education over the two parts of *Henry IV* constitutes a huge critical question I cannot do justice to here, I will briefly appeal to Sherman Hawkins's argument that the confident soliloquy at the end of 1.2 in part 1 may mislead us to assume Hal has the trick of "learning instantly." Despite Hal's assertion, "I know you all," his self-mastery emerges only gradually through his ideological and psychological engagement with (especially) Falstaff, Hotspur, and King Henry. Hawkins interestingly reads these three figures as corresponding, respectively, to "the Platonic parts of the soul, the appetitive, the spirited, and the rational," as expressed in the *Republic*. Civil war in the *Henry IV* plays stands in for the psychomachia within Hal's soul: "England is … divided against itself, and its mirror is Prince Hal."[52] Such compartmentalizing, and the challenge of interpreting Hal's internalization of idealized aspects of his masculine role models, leads logically to various psychoanalytic speculations which may be expected to employ classical sources and paradigms more than Christian ones. Yet this apparent Oedipalization of identity and social structure – adumbrated, as chapter 1 argued, in the writings of Perkins and Gifford – emerges decisively in the hierarchies of identification that Hendrik Niclaes presents in *Terra Pacis*, where moral and spiritual growth is unimaginable outside carefully controlled, and carefully navigated, homosocial networks:

> Therefore must the traveller keep a diligent watch in the said grace of the Lord, and in the obedience to the Requiring of the same foregoing service; and so constantly follow after ... the service of love, according to the counsel of the wise or elders in the same, for otherwise he becometh hindered and deceived upon the way ... For that cause the traveller (in the youngness of his understanding) must (in the beginning when the wisdom groweth first in him) have his proceeding forward according to the counsel of his elder in the Family of Love, who hath obediently performed the requiring of the gracious Word and his service, and so is grown up therein unto the old age of the godly understanding of the gracious Word of the Lord, and well exercised in the passing over the way to the good life and land of the Living, to the end that he may likewise (to the overcoming of all foolishness and seducing that meeteth him) attaine to the old age of the manly wisdom without harm, and so go into the good land of the upright Wise, and Understanding ones.[53]

Admittedly this description offers a simplified version of identification and obedience in comparison with Hal's cagey and complex engagement with his morally problematic masculine others. Moreover, there is an interesting confusion of terms, whereby in the Pauline context the "old man" signifies the carnal self, whereas in Familist discourse "old age" often – as in the above example – implies a spiritually mature state. Shakespeare clearly evokes the Pauline sense in Hal's rejection of Falstaff: "I know thee not, old man." Yet the playwright may also address this significant confusion between youth and age in 1.2 of *2 Henry IV*, where the Lord Chief Justice is rather astonished to hear the aged Falstaff dismiss him with the assertion, "You that are old consider not the capacities of us that are young" (172–3). Even the most persuasive consideration of the Pauline context of the *Henry IV* plays evokes this compelling youth-age paradox in its conclusion: "Such ... mockery of expectations is seen in the rejection of Falstaff, which we have been led to anticipate from the very start, but which we actually witness with a feeling of regret, for in banishing the old man, as in burying his father, Hal has also cast off his youth."[54]

Janet Halley, who notes the "rigid hierarchy of elders" within the Family of Love, certainly recognizes the evasiveness and obscurity of Niclaes's language and his metaphors.[55] I regret the paucity of sociological detail within Familist writings, and I am not suggesting an unproblematically singular influence – unqualified by revision or irony – of the Family of Love on texts such as *King John* and the second tetralogy.[56] But I do assert (again) that this sect offered Shakespeare and other early modern writers a potent example of the internalization of spiritual understanding conflated with an insistence on individual maturation and self-control that rendered it more influential and less marginal than critics have previously assumed. Theologically I suspect its greatest attraction was also what most outraged English Puritan writers. As Jones reminds us, the Puritan John Knewstub "believed that, by imposing particularities on the [scriptural] text, the Familists had committed the most dangerous of all exegetical sins: denying the truth of the atonement."[57] This denial constitutes its core "unspeakable" sin, which may speak to Halley's recognition of "the heretics' importance to *the development of orthodoxy itself*." Halley considers how "the hermeneutic problem posed to orthodox contemporaries by Familist Nicodemism" complicates, but also becomes a necessary component of, the present historical inquiry.[58] I further suggest that the determinant of the calculated silences and evasions of Familist discourse was more fundamentally the practicality or pragmatism of the early modern social experience, a fact evident (and not infrequently attractive) to contemporaries outside the sect. Indeed, the religiously inflected "allegories" of Shakespearean characters' "psychosocial lives," to reiterate the point above, seem distinctly removed from an orthodox Protestant, or at least Calvinist, position.

The Persistence of Sodomitical Desire

What the vagueness of spiritual allegory in Familist discourse apparently does not offer Shakespeare is a meaningfully "pragmatic" exploration of specifically erotic temptation. The *Henry IV* plays, like *Richard II*, continue a significant displacement of such themes, but in a different key. While Falstaff is, in a psychoanalytic sense, so infantile that it is just possible, especially for readers who never get to part 2, to credit his own assertion concerning a wholly disinterested sexuality – "that [I am], saving your reverence, a whoremaster, that I utterly deny" (*1 Henry IV* 2.4.464–5) – Heather Findlay has indeed "inspire[d] a little healthy suspicion" about the nature of Falstaff's "tastes when it comes to pleasures of the flesh."[59] Findlay relies on the familiar cultural link of pederasty and pedagogy,[60] and the competitive and reciprocal "tutoring" between Falstaff and Hal (among other textual details) over the two parts of *Henry IV*, to make her case for a sodomitical subtext, arguing that we need to consider "the development of early modes of capitalist economy, the dominance of relatively secularized schools in Renaissance England[,] and the 'trundling-in' of 'woman' as man's sexual other in his epistemological relation to truth." With respect to capitalism, Findlay notes that "Falstaff represents the symbolic territory of the district of Eastcheap, a bustling commercial area which has buying and selling built into its name." With respect to "secularized schools," Findlay notes that "the sodomitical aura surrounding Falstaff is intensified by comparisons of Falstaff and Hal to classical figures in the great pedagogical, and often pederastic, chain beginning with Socrates and ending with Alexander the Great."[61] Hence Hal's description of Falstaff as "misleader of youth" in *1 Henry IV* (2.4.457) would carry a significant insinuation for the more sophisticated Elizabethan audience members.

The most pointed evidence of sexual malfeasance, however, arises in part 2. There the much abused Mistress Quickly asserts, presumably metaphorically, "take heed of [Falstaff]! He stabbed me in mine own house, most beastly, in good faith. 'A cares not what mischief he does; if his weapon be out, he will foin like any devil; he will spare neither man, woman, nor child" (2.1.13–17), suggesting Falstaff's unpleasantly eclectic sexual tastes. The Lord Chief Justice directly accuses Falstaff of abusing Quickly both financially and sexually: "You have … practiced upon the easy-yielding spirit of this woman and made her serve your uses both in purse and in person" (2.1.112–14). As Falstaff dallies with Doll Tearsheet in 2.4, the disguised Poins says to the disguised Hal, "Let's beat him before his whore" (256), suggesting that Falstaff is a veritable whoremaster after all. The specifically sodomitical suggestions in part 2 create a rather disturbing subtext. In 5.3 Falstaff, echoing the Chief Justice's language above, observes that Justice Shallow's boy Davy "serves you for good uses. He is your servingman and your husband" (10–11). Slightly later in the same scene Davy exclaims, "I hope to see London once ere I die," to which Bardolph rather creepily responds, "An I might see you there, Davy!" Shallow assures Bardolph, "The knave will stick by thee," to which Bardolph rejoins, "And I'll stick by him, sir" (60–8). Beatrice Groves's treatment of the Jerusalem motif in the second tetralogy perhaps unwittingly casts light on the darker implications in this exchange. Acknowledging Davy's "wistful" desire to see London before he dies, Groves observes, "The classic pilgrim-longing to see Jerusalem once before death had been recently, if rather profanely, used in a similarly comic manner in Thomas Nashe's *Choise of Valentines* (c. 1592), where the lover's premature ejaculation is described as 'to dye ere it hath seene Ierusalem'. Shallow's provincial servant casts London as Jerusalem: the devoutly desired but almost mythically unreachable urban space."[62] The context in Shakespeare, however, suggests an eventual urban encounter for Davy less "devoutly" to be wished.

It is likely that a critical methodology more acutely focused than mine on theatrical practice could see in this scene a veiled allusion to boy actors as objects of sodomitical seduction on the part of the adult actors – a practice whose possibility seems, historically, extremely likely. Shakespeare's deeper involvement in the theatrical profession would here suggest a competing source of homoerotic expression or influence, in contradistinction to the literary-Marlovian one I have been emphasizing. Nevertheless, my conviction that recent criticism has underestimated what Stanivukovic terms "Shakespeare's other eye" – the "one that often seems to look for finding ways of satisfying the normative moralism of the age" – leaves me reluctant to read this particular allusiveness, especially in terms of Elizabethan audience response, as comic accommodation. In the exchange between Bardolph, Davy, and Shallow, Bardolph refers to sharing with Davy a "pottle-pot," a two-quart container of ale. Earlier in the play Poins aggressively exclaims to Bardolph, "Wherefore blush you now? What a maidenly man-at-arms are you become! Isn't such a matter to get a pottle-pot's maidenhead?" (2.2.72–4). The Page or boy whom Hal has obtained for Falstaff's service then daringly makes a joke at Bardolph's expense, earning Hal's commendation, although Poins poignantly adds, "O, that this blossom could be kept from cankers!" (88). Although the image of blossoms nipped by frost recurs within the play in various rhetorical contexts, in the present instance Poins's line suggests premature sexual deflowering; it is difficult not to suspect "pottle-pot" as a code word in Shakespeare's lexicon for sodomitical predation.

Clearly the tension between natural and unnatural imagery is important in *2 Henry IV*. Just prior to the entrance of Bardolph and the Page in 2.2, Hal asks Poins why the prince's expression of grief for his sick father would be perceived as hypocrisy, earning Poins's response, "Why, because you have been so lewd and so much engraffed to Falstaff" (58–9). This is one of the references which allows Vin Nardizzi to construct a queer reading of Hal's career, in which "Figures of plant grafting ... yoke together the seemingly antithetical discourses of marital procreation and sodomy."[63] The textual moment that apparently clinches this subversive overlapping between marital and sodomitical coupling is King Henry's exchange with Burgundy, after he has wooed the French princess Catherine at the end of *Henry V*. Burgundy offers the salacious advice, "for maids, well summered and warm kept, are like flies at Bartholomew-tide: blind, though they have eyes, and then they will endure handling, which before would not abide looking on."

King Henry replies, "This moral ties me over to time and a hot summer; and so shall I catch the fly, your cousin, in the latter end, and she must be blind too" (5.2.308–15). While Nardizzi's reading of his evidence is often compelling, I am not ultimately convinced that such imagery suggests sodomitical exchanges between Falstaff and Hal – the reading becomes less persuasive when Nardizzi explicitly tries to do so. Findlay's identification of a deliberate confusion of a more symbolically sexual exchange between these principal friends seems a more plausible historical interpretation.

Falstaff near the end of 2 *Henry IV*, in spite of anxieties he has periodically expressed over Hal's loyalty, is certainly convinced that his ship has now come in: "Master Shallow! I know the young King is sick for me. Let us take any man's horses; the laws of England are at my commandment. Blessed are they that have been my friends, and woe to my Lord Chief Justice!" (5.3.137–41). What Falstaff clearly underestimates is the extent to which the Law of the Father has now come home to roost. Findlay observes that Falstaff, as he greets the new King Henry in his coronation procession, "casts himself as Henry's Ganymede":[64] "My King! My Jove! I speak to thee, my heart" (5.5.47). Conversely, however, Falstaff three lines earlier also casts himself in the role of Jove in the same relationship: "God save thee, my sweet boy" (43). This deconstruction of the riddle concerning "who's on top" continues in the same scene, where Hal calls Falstaff "The tutor and the feeder of my riots" (62), but has now clearly assumed the upper hand.

Falstaff has ironically expressed contempt for Justice Shallow in 2 *Henry IV* due to his "vice of lying" (3.2.302), when, as he well knows himself, he has ably earned Hal's description as "father of lies" in part 1. Chapter 1 noted one of Falstaff's more egregious lies: his exclamation in 1 *Henry IV*, "*ecce signum* [behold the sign]," pointing to his sword "hacked like a handsaw" as evidence of his valour during the Gadshill robbery (2.4.166–7). While undeniably a comic moment, such misrepresentation carries increasingly serious implications in the later action. The point for Shakespeare seems not finally the "genuineness" of role playing, of self-representation. Even at his best or most earnest, as in his dealings with his dying father over the business of the borrowed crown, the actual authenticity of Hal's performances is always somewhat in doubt. The point is that Hal takes almost absolute responsibility for the *consequences* of his various roles and performances – that is, up until (arguably) he apparently disperses or displaces moral responsibility for battle casualties in his response to Williams in *Henry V* (4.1). This is almost exactly the conclusion we reached with respect to *Richard III*: whatever these texts say about the reality of human or of divine essence, which is clearly *not* dismissed as illusory or irrelevant, what really matters are the consequences of role playing. Such consequences arise not just through manipulation or deception. What really determines the outcome of events is the use and misuse of signs and signifiers – especially through the avoidance or assumption of real risk – and the characters' ability to read them accurately or inaccurately. The connection between Falstaff's purely specious performance of valour at Gadshill and the Eucharist emerges as, in effect, an oblique but daring critique of the Christian doctrine of Atonement, which enervates pragmatic masculine self-assertion and autonomy. Falstaff may wittily, paradoxically "prove" the essence of Hal's royalty as divinely endorsed by sophistically asserting that, like the lion, he instinctively recognized the "true prince," but it is rather the actual, pragmatic performances of Hal which ultimately establishes his sovereignty.

This "mirror of all Christian kings" certainly remains haunted by his father's act of regicide on the eve of the Battle of Agincourt. Yet whether "Hal appears different in kind from all other (male) subjects,"[65] or rather emerges instead as some kind of archetype of the new masculinity in nascent capitalist culture, are critical questions beyond the scope of this study. What does seem clear is that, because Hal's intimacy with Falstaff becomes indirectly invested with a sodomitical aura, it must be decisively rejected or contained in the *Henry IV* plays. Because of this decisive containment of sodomitical desire, the Marlovian influence in the latter part of the second tetralogy actually appears quite weak. With the sodomitical threat to manliness so effectively contained through the imminent banishment of Falstaff, the fantasy of absolute control that underwrites homoerotic desire in Marlowe's *Tamburlaine* is now rendered completely laughable, as in Pistol's notorious speech:

> These be good humors, indeed! Shall packhorses
> And hollow pampered jades of Asia,
> Which cannot go but thirty mile a day,
> Compare with Caesars and with cannibals,
> And Trojan Greeks? (*2 Henry IV* 2.4.162–6)

As most readers recognize, this speech by a cowardly rogue clearly parodies, in fact renders fatuous, Tamburlaine's literalization as the Scourge of God and his savage mockery and torture of his captive kings in part 2 (4.3.1–2): "Holla, ye pampered jades of Asia! / What, can ye draw but twenty miles a day?"

In her exploration of connections between pederasty and pedagogy, Findlay makes another important series of observations concerning the containment of homoeroticism that Shakespeare temporarily achieves in the second tetralogy. Since the "Renaissance witnessed the domination of the educational system over the Church as the privileged ideological state apparatus for the rising middle class," the episodes of direct homoerotic desire from classical literature, as in Virgil and Ovid, emerged "not as allegories for aspects of the divine," as they had been in the Middle Ages, but simply as formal exercises for imitation: "the form of artistic appreciation which Marlowe's education instilled in him constituted the possibility of his seeing homosexual desire in texts previously regarded as allegories for divine love," as in, for example, Ovid's account of the rape of Ganymede. But for Shakespeare the sexual politics take a decisive turn. Findlay appeals to Joel Fineman's argument that "Shakespeare, in his sonnets, 'invents, which is to say comes upon, the only subjectivity that [historically] survives.'" The result is a surprisingly conservative reaction that, until comparatively recently in Western culture, has rather darkly influenced our own response to human sexuality:

> According to Fineman, Shakespeare comes upon this essentially heterogeneous conception of subject and the subject's desire in the sonnets to the dark lady, and contrasts this subject to the one he develops in his sequence to the young man. Thus the invention of poetic subjectivity depends on the subject's distance from (again in Fineman's words) "a tradition of erotic homogeneity" ... and its approach toward alienated, misogynistic and heterosexual desire.[66]

Such a development, however, remains problematic and in crucial ways psychologically incoherent. Fineman's assertion, and Findlay's use of it in the context of the containment of a sodomitical Falstaff, echoes David Coleman's striking observation in *Drama and the Sacraments in Sixteenth-Century England* that "For Shakespeare as much as for Foucault, confession of truth is almost always the truth of sex; and the tradition of late medieval and early modern Christianity means that Shakespearean notions of sex are always inflected with an anxiety about sin. It is in this complex way that one can say that sexual sin, for Shakespeare, creates the subject."[67]

Developing (Homo)erotic Idealizations

I suspect, moreover, a possible connection between this process and the suggestion of a necessary (and potentially homoerotic) self-recognition implied when Adonis says to Venus, "Fair queen ... if any love you owe me, / Measure my strangeness with my unripe years; / Before I know myself, seek not to know me" (523–5). This response may imply a need to overcome a pre-Oedipal dependence on the maternal, not a popular reading at present in postmodern critical discourse. As Stanivukovic admits, the passage suggests "that the politics of sexuality constructs sodomy not only as a rhetorical ambivalence but also as a psychological (developmental) ambivalence. Adonis is on his way to masculinity but is not there yet"; nevertheless "the argument against her seduction is undone in his *love* for the boar hunt."[68] It is probably significant that the eroticized version of Adonis's death occurs only in Venus's imagination of the consummation; the queen of sexual desire must see this union in sexual terms. Adonis's hunt for the boar may not be so much a sign of male yearning for sexual union with another man as it is an attempt at identification with male aggression; as Stanivukovic observes, the "cultural tradition – heraldic representations, emblems, painting, and literature – of the boar's symbolism links this animal with virility and masculine power."[69]

Although the poem predates the plays considered in this chapter, it will be helpful to consider *Venus and Adonis* further, in terms of Venus's symbolic or psychological significance in the poem. She in fact represents an overwhelming maternal power and presence: when she anxiously runs in search of Adonis on the morning he is killed, Shakespeare states that she is "Like a milch doe, whose swelling dugs do ache, / Hasting to feed her fawn hid in some brake" (875–6). Thus Adonis's rejection of her is not so much a homoerotic rejection of heterosexual love as it is an attempt to break free from a narcissistic dependence on a maternal figure. The poem, however, ultimately portrays a tragic failure of masculine self-assertion, for when Venus perceives the triumphant boar, it has a "frothy mouth, bepainted all with red, / Like milk and blood being mingled both together" (901–2), as if it has become, in a sense, the murderous counterpart of her overwhelming maternal concern for Adonis. Venus is left to *imagine* the homoerotic nature of the consummation between the boar and Adonis, and ironically adds, "Had I been toothed like him, I must confess, / With kissing him I should have killed him first" (1117–18). It is interesting that, in the complex allegorical readings that have traditionally accompanied the Venus and Adonis myth, Adonis is identified with beauty and with *nature* in its unfallen state. The youth is finally metamorphosed into a purple and white flower, the anemone, which Venus cradles in her breast – "Here was thy father's bed, here in my breast" (1183), she says to the flower – but while his natural being continues at this unconscious, infantile level, the individuated masculine form has definitely perished.

As briefly speculated in chapter 4 at the beginning of the discussion of *Richard III*, Shakespeare's greater focus on maternal presence and the role of physical embodiment may possibly be related to Marian aspects of his Catholic background. Here again a contrast between Shakespeare and the more Protestant writers Spenser and Marlowe suggests itself. Stanivukovic calls attention to the apotheosis of the passion of Venus and Adonis in the Garden of Adonis episode from *The Faerie Queene*, book 3, canto 6: "In stanza 48 ... Spenser tells us that after Venus has 'firmly emprisoned' in a cave the castrating boar who threatened Adonis, Adonis continues to 'liue [...] in eternall bliss, / Ioying his goddesse, and of her enioyed.' Yet this heteroerotic bliss is immediately interrupted in stanza 49, where Spenser represents the dalliance of Adonis and the idle Cupid."[70] Stanza 49 certainly does present a "sexual mystery," in which Cupid, after

> ... he hath with spoiles and cruelty
> Ransackt the world, and in the wofull harts
> Of many wretches set his triumphes hye,
> Thither resorts, and laying his sad darts
> Aside, with faire *Adonis* playes his wanton parts.

And the sexual mystery undeniably does carry a further suggestion of "erotic transgression." As with my earlier discussion of the creation myth in book 2 of *The Faerie Queene*, I confess again my own belief that the contradictions in Spenser's allegory at times multiply to the point of incoherence.

Yet one identifiable pattern in Spenser's depiction of early modern sexuality is worth pointing out. There is an odd congruence, as in this culminating description of the Garden of Adonis, between the purely physical or pagan expression of sexual desire and a Protestant, perhaps even Puritan, self-idealization, and this congruence manifests peculiarly but repeatedly in homoerotic affect, so that Spenser portrays a recurring conflation of spiritual idealization and homoerotic attraction. Another example occurs in book 1, after a troop of fauns and satyrs saves Una, the one true (Protestant) faith, from the would-be rapist Sans Loy. Una subsequently falls under the gaze of the wood-god Sylvanus, who is overwhelmed with her unearthly beauty, but who then surprisingly compares her directly with a pagan male beloved:

> By vew of her he ginneth to revive
> His ancient love, and dearest *Cyparisse*,
> And calles to mind his pourtraiture alive,
> How faire he was, and yet not faire to this,
> And how he slew with glauncing dart amisse

A gentle Hynd, the which the lovely boy
Did love as life, above all worldly blisse;
For griefe whereof the lad n'ould after joy,
But pynd away in anguish and selfe-wil[le]d annoy. (1.6.17)

The conflation in question appears as well in Marlowe. In *Tamburlaine*, Marlowe employs quasi-religious terminology to express idealized longings between the protagonist and his male allies, since "the Neoplatonic frame for this [romantic] surrender allows Marlowe to evade the possibility of sexual involvement" which he had perhaps not yet come consciously to accept.[71] Admittedly in the early Marlowe the conflation of religious and sexual desire is already subject to parodic interrogation. Although the notorious induction of *Dido* – where a sodomitical Jupiter fondles Ganymede as a catamite – may on one level attempt to parody or explode such idealizations, the more educated audience members would also recognize that this mythical tableau "was [commonly] interpreted also in neo-Platonic terms as the *mens humana*, beloved by ... the Supreme being ... and abducted to heaven by means of an eagle to a state of enraptured contemplation."[72]

At stake here in Marlowe is the fantasy of absolute control. Like the spiritualized version of the Ganymede myth, the Sylvanus passage from Spenser obliquely conveys a premature, narcissistic longing for immortality and an inability to accept change and death (and interestingly foreshadows the Puritan Marvell's nymph complaining for the death of her fawn). This psychological dilemma, I suggest again, may be a particularly Protestant one, arising from the doctrine of *sola fide*, a faith available only through the grace of God. The masculine individual attempts to deflect this radical spiritual dependency of Reformation theology by appropriating his own spiritual justification – incorporating the divine "other" into the self – and by deflecting a corresponding sexual insecurity through various displacements, often, as in *Tamburlaine*, hypermasculine ones. In book 1 of *The Faerie Queene* the homoerotic longing, or nostalgia, appears relatively unthreatening – Sylvanus is a pagan god, after all – and the other fauns and satyrs misread Una's holiness, attempting to make her "th'Image of Idolatryes" (6.19). Her vulnerability eventually requires her deliverance at the end of book 1 through the manly trials of the Redcrosse Knight, even though his final defeat of the dragon is only effected through the sacramental intervention of the Well and the Tree of Life, that is, the gracious (Protestant) sacraments of baptism and the Eucharist. But even in the Sylvanus episode, Una needs to be delivered by the hypermasculine Satyrane, who apparently suggests the importance of a manly control of, and interaction with, Nature in the fallen world, and who figures prominently in the later books, where (following Woodhouse) Spenser concentrates on the order of Nature rather than the order of Grace.

Satyrane may therefore imply an "Adonis" who actually succeeds in first establishing his "manliness" in the natural world before undergoing whatever trials of sexual or religious self-surrender may be his fate; his characterization, like so many others in the subsequent books of *The Faerie Queene*, speaks to recurring concerns with muscular Christianity in later centuries of Western culture. Shakespeare's own "Protestant reenchantment" in the second tetralogy involves an arguably hypermasculine character whose famous identification with the Earl of Essex in the prologue to act 5 of *Henry V* – "the General of our gracious Empress" (30) – involves in effect a subsumption or displacement of the potential threat to the playwright's masculinity embodied, for Shakespeare, in Essex's follower and close friend the Earl of Southampton. Perhaps just as significant in *Henry V* is the prologue to act 1:

> O, for a Muse of fire, that would ascend
> The brightest heaven of invention!
> …
> Then should the warlike Harry, like himself,
> Assume the port of Mars; and at his heels,
> Leashed in like hounds, should famine, sword and fire
> Crouch for employment.

While Gary Taylor identifies Mars with the leashed hounds a traditional personification of war,[73] this image carries further significance. Not without irony, like so much else in this play, the passage proclaims Henry as the opposite of the spiritually compromised Actaeon, as an anti-Actaeon, who rather than being consumed or dismembered by his passions, ruthlessly (and frighteningly) *controls* them. The militant Harry in fact indirectly compensates for the undertones of Actaeon in Adonis, whom Venus first comforts with the imagery of protection – "I'll be a park, and thou shalt be my deer … No dog shall rouse thee, though a thousand bark" (231, 240) – but then later warns him, when he remains adamant to hunt the boar, with the story of Wat the hare, terrified by the hounds closing in on him (679–707).

In general, the Choric pronouncements in *Henry V* carry theologically subversive potential. When the Chorus at the beginning of act 3 adjures the audience to "Work, work your thoughts, and therein see a siege" (25), we are reminded that the apparent "sacrament whose real power lay in the minds of the spectators," as Jeffrey Knapp puts it, appeals not so much to "grace" as to human imaginative *work*, a most intriguing instance of imaginative agency. The final Chorus, delivered rather ironically in the form of an English sonnet, asserts, "with rough and all-unable pen / Our bending author hath pursued the story, / In little room confining mighty men" (1–3). Joel Altman has very intriguingly argued that through the Chorus's appearances in *Henry V*, "[a]mplication has become agon," where the audience "finds itself inducted into combat duty against the beckoning shadow on the stage, a strangely appealing master-mistress who invites ravishment." Again, the shadow of sodomy has not been dispelled: "the sonneteer returning at the end of *Henry V* as a master disabler who is himself disabled – the 'bending author' who 'with rough and all-unable pen' has managed to confine mighty men, 'Mangling by starts the full course of their glory' (5.Epi.1–4) – figures in small the reciprocal economy that drives the play as a whole."[74] Despite the trope of humility, "In [a] little room" recalls Marlowe's "Infinite riches in a little room" from *The Jew of Malta* (1.1.37), an allusion carrying implicit praise, and which itself is a blasphemous parody of the womb of the pregnant Virgin Mary. To this audacious appropriation of creative power, Shakespeare adds a last subversive touch, a reference to the successor, "Henry the Sixth, in infant bands, crowned king" (9). Although the playwright doesn't quite dare translate to biblical terms, "infant bands" means "swaddling clothes." Among all the other ironies which circulate here, the reference suggests the political inefficacy of the Christ-like but overly pious Henry VI.

The high level of irony, indeed the arguably increasing density of irony across the second tetralogy, makes a final evaluation of Shakespeare's appropriation of Protestant and other heretical doctrine in the second tetralogy difficult. On one level the ambivalent relationship of Hal to his father Henry IV echoes patterns of emotional expression and reader response that, as chapter 1 noted, Debora Shuger traces in the Calvinist passion narratives: "[These narratives] depict Christ's relation to [the] Father as an unstable compound of dependence, self-assertion, obedience, and subversion ... Christ is simultaneously child, champion, dutiful son, and aggressor ... [and] ends up, as most oedipal sons do, becoming *like* his Father."[75] Yet, despite the intimations of regicidal intent that haunt Hal's rhetoric and behaviour, even as he attempts to reassure his father of his love and support, his conduct as king ultimately upholds the patrilineal succession and hierarchy, especially through the rejection of his surrogate father Falstaff and a commendation of the Law in the figure of the Lord Chief Justice.

This theological process in the *Henry IV* plays, as we have seen, parallels the more conservative or restrained Protestant ideological reaction we observed in George Gifford's Oedipal identifications in his writings against the Donatists or Brownists, which anticipated the Family of Love's resistance to the infantilizing potential of a theology of grace. Like *Richard II*, where the marginalized patrilineal social structure of Gaunt and Bolingbroke nevertheless emphasizes the validity of human merit (and masculine competition), the theological implications of the *Henry IV* plays seem also to resist the doctrine of predestination, which is consistent with Familist writers who implied "that predestination led to licentious living."[76] Not surprisingly, the irresponsibility and self-indulgence of Falstaff are, comically but disturbingly, particularly associated with this doctrine: "Poins! Now we shall know if Gadshill have set a match. O, if men were to be saved by merit, what hole in hell were hot enough for him?" (*1 Henry IV* 1.2.104–6).

Some of Hal's admittedly opaque witticisms, especially in *2 Henry IV*, also hint at this theological critique, by subtly confirming human agency and responsibility. For example, he insults Poins: "the rest of the low countries have made a shift to eat up thy holland [fine linen]. And God knows whether those that bawl out the ruins of thy linen [presumably Poins's bastards begotten in the stews, wrapped in his cast-off shirts as swaddling clothes] shall inherit His kingdom. But the midwives say the children are not in the fault, whereupon the world increases and kindreds [families] are mightily strengthened" (2.2.21–6). The apparently witty denial of Original Sin places moral responsibility squarely on the actions of the present father. As this moment forms a prelude to Hal's insistence on his real concern for his sick father in spite of his refusal of a hypocritical show of mourning, his essential commitment to the patrilineal order, in the face of the vagaries of role playing, becomes evident. Ultimately all these connections between psychoanalytic and theological structures carry an erotic significance. Thus Hal's rejection of Falstaff, "I know thee not, old man," implies not just a social and moral rejection of a former undisciplined, carnally minded friend, but the termination of any previous erotic "knowing," as Heather Findlay implies, in the new sexual economy of heterogeneity. And the rejection of Falstaff immediately following the knight's appeal to Hal as "my sweet boy" and "my Jove" also effectively contains this potent but dangerously unstable evocation of the Ganymede myth.

**The Containment of Sodomy in *As You Like It*
and *Hero and Leander***

Yet this containment of sodomy is certainly not the end of the story. The Ganymede figure returns, profoundly, in *As You Like It*, via the disguise

Rosalind adopts in the Forest of Arden. *As You Like It*, written probably in 1599, shortly after *Henry V*, represents a key text in any discussion of Marlowe's influence on Shakespeare, since Phoebe's exclamation, "Dead shepherd, now I find thy saw of might, / 'Who ever loved that loved not at first sight'" (3.5.81–2), constitutes, as we observed at the beginning of chapter 2, the only occasion where Shakespeare directly acknowledges and quotes the work of a contemporary author. Shakespeare calls Marlowe "Dead shepherd" presumably because he is the author of the pastoral lyric "The Passionate Shepherd to His Love," and also because *As You Like It* embodies Shakespeare's most comprehensive treatment of the pastoral mode. Not surprisingly Marlowe is again on Shakespeare's mind in 1599 after the appearance that year of *The Passionate Pilgrim by W. Shakespeare*, an edition of poems containing some five by Shakespeare (including two of the sonnets), padded out with fifteen other poems, including a version of "The Passionate Shepherd." This false attribution of one of the most famous lyrics of the age to himself may have surprised Shakespeare, but he had already acknowledged its currency, as James Shapiro observes, by having a character from *The Merry Wives of Windsor* (ca. 1597–8) deliver "a slightly garbled version [of the poem] in [a] thick Welsh accent … [while] nervously waiting to fight a duel."[77] Evidently anxious tests of masculinity made Shakespeare think of Marlowe.

There are further reasons for the resurrection of Marlowe (now dead six years) in Shakespeare's imagination at this point. Marlowe's *Hero and Leander*, from which Phoebe quotes, appeared the previous year, 1598, divided into sestiads in its second edition and completed by George Chapman. Also in June 1599, a week after the Bishop of London and the Archbishop of Canterbury had ordered the burning of the second print run of John Hayward's *The History of Henry the Fourth*, a "much larger conflagration" took place when a dozen other titles were confiscated and burned, including Marlowe's translation of Ovid's *Elegies*.[78] To explain the significance of these literary "events," Charles Nicholl goes back two years to the publication in 1597 of Thomas Beard's *The Theatre of God's Judgements*. In a chapter entitled "Of Epicures and Atheists," Beard designates Marlowe's death by stabbing as a "manifest sign of God's judgement":

It so fell out that in London streets, as he purposed to stab one whom he [owed] a grudge with his dagger, the other party perceiving, so avoided the stroke that withal catching hold of his wrist, he stabbed his own dagger into his own head, in such sort that notwithstanding all the means of surgery that could be wrought, he shortly after died thereof.

Beard's book was followed one year later by Francis Meres's *Palladis Tamia*, a miscellany or "wit's treasury" of quotations, reflections, and literary gossip. While Meres refers readers to Beard's account of Marlowe's death, he also offers a version of his own, which, as Nicholl observes, adds a new dimension to the story: "As the poet Lycophron was shot to death by a certain rival of his, so Christopher Marlowe was stabbed to death by a bawdy serving-man, a rival of his in his lewd love." This account conflicts with the official report of the coroner's inquest, which claims that Marlowe became involved in a quarrel over the "recknynge," "'the sum of pence owed' for the day's food and drink,"[79] and was killed by one of the men he had spent the day with, Ingram Frizer, who was judged at the inquest to be acting in self-defence. Thus Meres's tale of "lewd love" may be the first account to add the theme of homoeroticism to the circumstances of Marlowe's death, although certainly not to his life and general reputation, as the Baines Note attests.

Nicholl suggests that Shakespeare in *As You Like It* is thinking specifically of Meres's account of Marlowe's lewd love, which the surviving playwright seeks implicitly to refute in Rosalind's melancholy and cynical speech prompted by Orlando's romantic idealism:

> The poor world is almost six thousand years old, and in all this time there was not any man died in his own person, [that is to say], in a love cause. Troilus had his brains dashed out with a Grecian club, yet he did what he could to die before, and he is one of the patterns of love. Leander, he would have lived many a fair year though Hero had turned nun, if it had not been for a hot midsummer night; for, good youth, he went but forth to wash him in the Hellespont and being take with the cramp was drowned; and the foolish chroniclers of that age found it was – Hero of Sestos. But these are all lies. Men have died from time to time, and worms have eaten them, but not for love. (4.1.89–102)

The allusion to the Hero and Leander myth a year after the publication of the epyllion certainly contributes to the network of Marlowe references, and the implication is, Nicholl argues, that Marlowe died, but not for love, lewd or otherwise. That is, the moral or salacious accounts of Marlowe's death are "all lies."

As You Like It contains still other allusions to Marlowe's death and work. Touchstone in his bantering with the ignorant Audrey asserts that "When a man's verses cannot be understood, nor a man's good wit seconded with the forward child, understanding, it strikes a man more dead than a great reckoning in a little room" (3.3.10–13). For many scholars this passage not only constitutes a clear allusion to the coroner's inquest with its reference to the reckoning, but again also recalls the famous line from Marlowe's *Jew of Malta*, "Infinite riches in a little room." In fact the Marlovian ramifications continue; in the same scene Touchstone says to Audrey, "I am here with thee and thy goats, as the most capricious poet, honest Ovid, was among the Goths [pronounced 'goats' by Elizabethans]" (5–7). "Capricious," which literally means goatlike, suggests "lecherous," and lecherous Ovid recalls Marlowe's translations of Ovid's "wanton" *Elegies*, burned in the Bishops' Ban. Having made this connection, it remains for Nicholl to provide a bawdy interpretation of the very bawdy Touchstone's phrase "more dead than a great reckoning in a little room":

> "Dead" meaning detumescent is part of a subterranean literary imagery [familiar to all readers of early modern literature] in which "spirit" means semen, and "death" means ejaculation … "Room", rather less subtly, is the vagina. [Nicholl offers an example from *The Massacre at Paris*.] Touchstone's "great reckoning in a little room" can therefore be read to mean an ejaculation. The overall meaning of the lines would be that the poor reception of a poet's work ["When a man's verses cannot be understood"] is more dismal to him than post-coital *tristesse*.[80]

"Room" as vagina possibly extends or displaces the uterine allusion to the pregnant Virgin Mary in Marlowe; and Ovid's *Elegies* are definitely heteroerotic poems. Nevertheless I believe Nicholl goes slightly awry not only in his final emphasis on critical reception as the key to Touchstone's riddle, but also in his elision of the homoerotic nature of both Marlowe's creative output and Shakespeare's conscious awareness of this Marlovian legacy. *As You Like It* represents a decisive moment in Shakespeare's containment of this legacy or influence, a containment which, although in part a eulogistic celebration, also carries an ironic suggestion of the tragic limitations of Marlowe's discursive explorations of Renaissance homoeroticism.

Let us consider briefly Marlowe's *Hero and Leander*, and speculate about Shakespeare's response to it. Although the brevity of the present discussion cannot begin to do justice to the claim, the work itself is astonishingly accomplished; it is difficult to refute Patrick Cheney's suggestion that this poem, rather than *Doctor Faustus*, is Marlowe's masterpiece.[81] Shakespeare must have perceived its greatness. Moreover, while it depicts a consummation of heterosexual desire, it simultaneously evokes homoerotic desire in daringly direct ways, poetically and emotionally; far more direct than the fleeting suggestion of (symbolic) sodomy in *Venus and Adonis*. It does so both through the contrast between the initial descriptions of the two young protagonists (with clearly a keener sexual interest in the male), and in the later Neptune episode. As Jim Ellis observes, "Marlowe was, like the other young poets who wrote epyllia, educated and ambitious, [but] also more seriously invested in shocking or challenging orthodoxy than were either Shakespeare or the young men at the Inns of Court ... Marlowe's poem differs from [other epyllia] by openly displaying the homoerotic desire that informs all of these poems, at the level of both story and narration."[82] In fact the general thesis of Ellis's study is worth considering here, for it is one of the more significant postmodern treatments of early modern sexuality to date. Its main title, *Sexuality and Citizenship*, emphasizes the transformation of male subjectivity at a crucial historical moment through an idiosyncratic literary form specific to the 1590s: "the epyllion invents, through its reinterpretation of Ovidian mythical narratives, a new version of heterosexuality ... The epyllion, like the epic, works to establish the basis of community or nation; unlike the epic, its primary concern is the [more pragmatic] psychology of national belonging as opposed to the ideal subject of nationhood (the epic hero)."[83]

Ellis's discussion of Marlowe's and Shakespeare's narrative poems replicates some of the same ideological ambivalence observed in Stanivukovic's treatment of *Venus and Adonis*. For example, there are some curious logical turns when Ellis considers an earlier critic's treatment of the "phallic potential" of the boar, and of Adonis's engagement with it:

> "Shakespeare's Boar is ugly and destructive, and, by extension, the phallic energy he embodies may be ungentle, violent, and even painful, but it is also clearly necessary and productive." Necessary for and productive of what? Heterosexuality? Phallic masculinity? I do not want to suggest that these are not conclusions one can draw from the poem: indeed, part of [my] argument ... is that epyllia work to install precisely that version of phallic masculinity ... We must, however, be careful not to confuse the imperatives or norms of a particular cultural order with universal prescriptions. In other words, Shakespeare's poem might be participating in the inauguration of a new mode of phallic masculinity, a shift in the dominant fiction, rather than simply showing how Adonis falls short of a timeless masculine ideal.[84]

The obvious, perhaps too obvious, answer to the question, "necessary for and productive of what," is *procreation*. Stanivukovic, and Ellis elsewhere in his discussion, are prepared to acknowledge the sterility of sodomy. The inauguration of a new mode of masculinity at this historical moment, when the harshness of medieval proscription is being qualified by a greater breadth of "classical" expression, is not completely gratuitous or oppressive – although we certainly want now to revise it – and it is not just aristocratic men like Southampton who must at least be warned to carefully (re)consider "transgressive sexuality."

The otherwise clear line of argument Ellis employs becomes obfuscated or refracted by his theoretical consideration of Lacan and Žižek in this chapter, which like so much theoretical abstraction overestimates the power of language and discourse, at the expense of philosophically and morally coming to terms with the reality of the human body, and the role of human agency with respect to it. Postmodern criticism in general might take more care in its assertions of "compulsory heterosexuality." The phrase is most persuasive in the context of *essentialist* assumptions which the current critical consensus purports to loathe, as an identification of the enormous suffering arising from the imposition of a sexual function on individuals ultimately incapable of adopting it, or of maintaining it constructively for any length of time. It is not clear to me what happens to the political impetus behind a "queer" critical agenda when the existence of such persons, at any point in history, is elided; it is also not clear to me how extensively queer theory benefits gay people outside the academy. But it *is* clear that no one can ultimately profit from the denial of the (timeless) necessity of heterosexuality per se, or the suggestion that it, *in itself*, somehow constitutes a tyrannical mode of social oppression.

Nevertheless Ellis's conclusions regarding *Hero and Leander* are profound, since the key problematic of "phallic masculinity" remains, in fact is highlighted, in Marlowe's exploration of human sexuality. The psychological movement of the poem involves Leander's transformation "from the sexually ambiguous youth who was the object of everyone's desire" – via "his rejection of Neptune, [and] his apparently violent seduction of Hero" – into "a man, a desiring subject." This process involves the rejection of narcissistic, Petrarchan constructions of sexual response in favour of a more aggressive Ovidian sexual agency, which tragically involves disturbingly darker impulses. Ellis observes the famously "brutal image" – "Even as a bird, which in our hands we wring, / Forth plungeth, and oft flutters with her wing, / She trembling strove" (2.289–91) – on the heels of observing John Leonard's suggestion that "it now seems that Hero's resistance is precisely what is stimulating Leander's desire."[85] This passage immediately follows what may be the poem's most notable, equally brutal, couplet: "Love is not full of pity (as men say) / But deaf and cruel where he means to prey" (287–8).

What is perhaps most intriguing about this moment is that the passage temporarily suspends or simplifies, through an apparently unambiguous moral denunciation, the pattern of almost unrelenting *paradox* which characterizes the rest of the poem. Even the brutality of Leander's seduction apparently leads, disturbingly, to *Hero*'s increasing pleasure in a process (the narrative suggests) that is intensely creative: "She trembling strove; this strife of hers (like that / Which made the world) another world begat / Of unknown joy" (291–3). Ellis observes the further disconcerting paradox that, through her seduction, Hero "seems more alive than ever before ... She is now no longer ... a triumph of art over nature, or the flesh made sign ... Marlowe has transformed an image into a person,"[86] so that Ovidian lust leads finally, ironically, to a kind of humanization. Appallingly, however, this transformation comes at the cost of her experiencing violation and exposure; evidently the female must pay the price for the heterosexualization of the male.

Besides exposing Hero, the poem thus exposes, through its unusual explicitness, "the homoerotic basis of Renaissance humanism, and the violence implicit in the emergent heterosexuality."[87] But we should hesitate before assuming the poem indicates that heterosexuality itself depends on this dynamic of violence, or must manifest violently. In fact the poem ultimately expresses the violent potential of *desire*, not the inherent violence of any form of sexuality. I have much sympathy with the socially progressive motives with which Claude Summers begins his analysis of *Hero and Leander*: "Marlowe's project of destabilisation may be seen most clearly in his treatment of homosexuality, [which he represents] more frequently and more variously than any other figure of his day. A writer deeply immersed in both religion and classics, he characteristically reflects in his work the tension between Christian culture's condemnation and classical culture's acceptance of homoerotics."[88] Summers here echoes Heather Findley's observation concerning Marlowe's humanist education, and how it facilitated his perception of homoeroticism as transcending simple allegories of divine love; clearly the classical contexts of *Hero and Leander* largely enable its more celebratory moments of homoerotic desire. Conversely, however, the classical worldview also in effect intensifies the poem's darker moments, for a Christian morality would presumably disallow or invalidate the reflection, "Love is not full of pity (as men say) / But deaf and cruel where he means to prey."

While that passage directly mirrors the aggression of Leander's seduction of Hero, the poem's homoerotic passion further highlights emotional and moral paradoxes. In fact the text appears to contradict itself when – after Neptune has called back the mace with which he would have injured Leander, and the youth appears to pity the god's self-inflicted injury – the narrator declares:

> In gentle breasts
> Relenting thoughts, remorse and pity rests.
> And who have hard hearts and obdurate minds,
> But vicious, harebrained, and illit'rate hinds?
> The god, seeing him with pity to be movèd,
> Thereon concluded that he was belovèd.
> (Love is too full of faith, too credulous,
> With folly and false hope deluding us.) (2.215–22)

Here love is associated not with cruelty and selfish desire but pity, tenderness, civilized affect. Such tenderness is admittedly qualified. Leander's colour, we are told, "went and came, *as if he rued*" (214, my emphasis) Neptune's suffering; it may be that he only blanches and blenches at the sight of blood. Neptune appears to be sensitively "full of faith," but only perhaps because he (narcissistically) believes now he is beloved. He *has* attempted to cruelly injure Leander when his tale of homoerotic love (a version of Narcissus?) was ignored by Leander, although the god *did* recall the mace before it reached its intended target, "for love made him repent" (210).

Neptune's self-injury at this moment recalls Tamburlaine's self-inflicted wound in the doubting Thomas parody; both the sea god and the shepherd-turned-world-conqueror become oddly Christ-like in these acts of self-sacrifice; in both cases apparent "omnipotence" seems *almost* capable of suffering. In *Hero and Leander* Marlowe associates this tenderer aspect of love with homoeroticism, even though murderous aggression, as Neptune briefly indicates, can just as easily arise from such desire. The passage thus evokes the quintessential instability of morality in Marlowe.

In spite of – or perhaps, through the ultimate paradox, *because of* – Marlowe's cruel exposure of a dark will to power within sexual desire, the poem nevertheless achieves this humanization of romantic passion. Ellis makes a relevant observation: "this desire for the youth is not played out through a goddess [as in *Venus and Adonis*], but rather more clearly located in adult admirers, foremost among them the narrator, whose disingenuous claim about his inability to blazon forth the loves of men comes in the middle of one of the most homoerotic passages in English poetry."[89] It might in fact be Marlowe's willingness to extend the *humanity* of homoerotic desire that distinguishes him from Shakespeare at this point. Although Robert Logan "guess[es]" that probably neither of these artists was aware of the other's poem when they wrote their epyllia,[90] there is at least one textual hint in *Venus and Adonis* that may suggest Shakespeare was responding directly to Marlowe's poem, in the passage wherein Venus temporarily, if ultimately futilely, seems to overcome Adonis's resistance:

> Hot, faint, and weary with her hard embracing,
> *Like a wild bird being tamed with too much handling,*
> Or as the fleet-foot roe that's tired of chasing,
> Or like the forward infant stilled with dandling,
> > He now obeys, and now no more resisteth,
> > While she takes all she can, not all she listeth. (559–64)

The italicized line echoes Marlowe's "brutal image" of the fluttering bird wrung in human hands. Shakespeare demonstrates that a darker will to power in human experience characterizes female as much as male desire, rendering the actual possession of a phallus irrelevant to this particular dynamic of cruelty and control. Yet Shakespeare's works in general ultimately thwart the "divine" as well as the human possibility of homoerotic desire, a tendency emblematized in the canon by Portia preventing the Christ-like sacrifice of Antonio for Bassanio in *The Merchant of Venice*, even as she appears to magically reestablish his mercantile credentials.

While Neptune in *Hero and Leander* raises Leander to the surface – recognizing his humanity after mistaking him for Ganymede – Shakespeare in *As You Like It* turns the Ganymede image into a veritable symbol of the containment or elision of homoeroticism. In the process the text encapsulates some vexing tensions between hetero- and homoerotic modes of desire. Mario DiGangi observes how the "explicit naming of mythological figures in the play, along with the representation of banishment, familial discord, and homoerotic desire, evokes a tale familiar to Shakespeare and his contemporaries: Jupiter's replacement of Hebe with Ganymede, a move that angers Juno and alienates her from the marriage bed."[91] An influential classical dictionary of the time relates that one day when Hebe "chaunsed to fall, and disclosed further of hir neather partes, then comlinesse woulde have to be shewen, Jupiter, to the great displeasure of his wyfe Juno, removed hir from that office, and appointed *Ganymedes* to serve hym at his cuppe."[92] What is the connection between this rather misogynistic myth and Rosalind's performance as Ganymede? An answer that involves an inversion of values: by temporarily encouraging a kind of homoerotic flirtation between Ganymede and Orlando, she tests his devotion but also cures him of excessive romantic idealism – the narcissistic tendency to indulge in "immortal longings." He does finally reject the homoerotic Ganymede for the real heterosexual Rosalind because, as he asserts, he "can live no longer live by thinking" (5.2.49); that is, idealism must be tempered by an acceptance of physical reality, but, characteristically in Shakespeare, the physical is heterosexually realized. We potentially return, disturbingly, to the reading of homosexuality as the product of arrested development.

Yet the line "I can live no longer by thinking," one of the most powerful in Shakespeare, takes on other meanings in a text that also asserts – ironically from the mouth of the arch-materialist Touchstone – that the "truest poetry is the most feigning" (3.3.17). Emotionally such suggestions cut in exactly the opposite direction, morally or "ideally," from the insistence on the acceptance of physical (that is, heterosexual) reality. The contrast between the excessively idealistic and Petrarchan Orlando and the excessively earthy Rosalind curiously shifts during the play's action. Orlando carefully tends Duke Senior in the forest (does he pragmatically guess the real identity of Ganymede?), while the very physical passion for the half-naked wrestler Orlando that drives Rosalind morphs into the most intense kind of romantic idealism – "O coz, coz, coz, my pretty little coz, that thou didst know how many fathom deep I am in love" (4.1.197–8) – an idealism I would identify as the most persuasive romantic experience in the play, probably even in Shakespeare.

At the same time the play includes other "cures" for homoerotic affect. As frequently observed, Celia's initial affection for her cousin Rosalind is distinctly homoerotic, as her rhetoric consciously and unconsciously indicates. But in the Forest of Arden Celia, renamed Aliena, becomes a stranger to her own desires; excluded from intimacy with Rosalind by the latter's obsession with Orlando, Aliena falls conveniently in love with Orlando's evil elder brother Oliver, whose nature is suddenly converted by Orlando's self-sacrificing (but masculinized) rescue of his brother from a female lion and a female serpent. Thus homoerotic desire is effectively displaced through a series of quasi-religious and politically troubling symbolizations, so that Celia, restored to the "heavenly" meaning of her name, can settle down in heterosexual marriage. A further example is the shepherdess Phoebe, the one who actually quotes Marlowe's "who ever loved that loved not at first sight," and who, as DiGangi ingeniously points out, has "Hebe" inscribed in her own name. Phoebe's admiring blazon of effeminate Ganymede's parts – parts which seem distinctly feminine, although she believes Ganymede to be a young man – is exposed as an erotic dead end when Ganymede "resolves" the romantic issues by finally discovering herself as Rosalind.

What may, however, deserve more critical attention is the possibly homoerotic character of the former libertine and continuing bachelor Jaques. For James Shapiro this character is "something of an enigma. He has a significant presence in the play ... but no effect on it. He changes nothing, fails to persuade or reform anyone. Mostly, he likes to watch." Shapiro suggests that he represents, or rather embodies, Shakespeare's first significant attempt at satire: "Jaques's obsession with purging society helps explain the name Shakespeare gives him – pronounced like 'jakes,' the Elizabethan word for privy or water closet."[93] Jaques's character certainly contains a striking conflation of cynicism and idealism, and thus emotionally encapsulates the entire thematic spectrum of the play, which also perhaps explains his interestingly ambivalent attraction to and repulsion for Touchstone, his alter ego but also his scapegoat for the uncontrolled sexual response that, Duke Senior claims, characterized Jaques's own youth (2.7.64–9).

Intriguingly, Robert Schwartz has not implausibly linked the enigmatic Jaques, and other oddities of the play, to Familist doctrine and its controversial reception in the late sixteenth century.[94] Duke Senior's accusation of Jaques's libertine past may evoke, as we observed in chapter 1, the *mis*conception of Familists as devoted to licentiousness: "In general, as George Mosse writing about Puritan [and other religious] radicalism tells us, 'libertinage ... had meant, in the sixteenth century, those who were filled with the "Holy Spirit" and thus thought themselves free from any ecclesiastical discipline'." The key characteristic of Jaques would then be moral growth: in spite of their "alleged doctrinal aversion to marriage ... we know Familists did in fact marry and moreover were pretty orthodox on this point." Jaques's particular interest in Touchstone "grows ... from the fact that he sees his own past [presumably scandalously exaggerated by Duke Senior] in Touchstone, and in fact catches the Fool in his affair with Audrey on the verge of making the same mistake in abusing license under the guise of religiousness (rejecting the orthodox rituals of the church as antinomians were thought to have done)." Schwartz's reading apparently confuses the question of whether Duke Senior stands within or without (true) Familist assumptions; nevertheless he compellingly suggests that Duke Senior's ambiguous assertion, "Here feel we not the penalty of Adam," directly reflects the "fundamental Familist belief that [humankind], regenerated in nature by spiritual awakening, was free from the effects of original sin."[95] As we shall see, the duke's assertion anticipates *The Winter's Tale* in its radical humanist claim to moral independence from

Original Sin, which at the same time intersects oddly with a barely repressed homoerotic dynamic – as if Shakespeare cannot stifle the tendency for his theological radicality to become linked with subversive erotic desire.

Whatever the ideological foundation of his characterization, Jaques's final withdrawal to a hermitage, and keen interest in the converted Duke Frederick, reveal the fate of those who expect either too much or too little from the body's pleasures, which are sanctified finally only by the imaginative conjuration of the god of heterosexual marriage, Hymen. Although not as thoroughly theologized as the Christ-like, if narcissistically driven, Antonio in *The Merchant of Venice*, Jaques's final marginalization from the world of heterosexual marriage resembles the Antonio of *Twelfth Night*, whose climactic exclamation to Sebastian, "How have you made division of yourself" (5.1.222), potentially alludes to controversial claims regarding the inability of Christ's body – at least according to Protestant doctrine – to exist simultaneously in heaven and on earth.[96] Those who do not conform to "natural" modes of sexuality, the passage symbolically suggests, reveal a failure to balance the spirit and the flesh.

Probably the most surprising containment of homoeroticism in *As You Like It*, and the tendency of Rosalind's "magic" to uphold a normative and seemingly compulsory heterosexuality, occurs when the boy who plays Rosalind speaks the epilogue:

> My way is to conjure you, and I'll begin with the women. I charge you, O women, for the love you bear to men, to like as much of this play as please you; and I charge you, O men, for the love you bear to women – as I perceive by your simpering, none of you hates them – that between you and the women the play may please. If I were a woman I would kiss as many of you as had beards that pleased me, complexions that liked me, and breaths that I defied not.

That crucial "if" at the beginning of the final sentence quoted logically contains or denies the homoerotic potential of boy actors in the theatre, a reputation that certainly surrounded them, in early modern anti-theatrical tracts. Through this direct exposure of the actual illusion-making process of early modern theatre, in particular with regards to the portrayal of gender roles, the epilogue constitutes a rather startling moment where Shakespeare deliberately restricts the possibilities of potentially more varied sexual response, especially in light of the fact that the pastoral mode which he develops most fully in *As You Like It* would have been recognized by his humanist-trained audience members as a characteristically "homoerotic space" through many of its classical precursors.[97]

While much of pastoral literature is indeed elegiac, the containment of homoeroticism in *As You Like It* nevertheless represents I think a particularly melancholy limitation of what I have termed in this study Shakespeare's imaginative agency, the virtually "magical" mobilization of (the artist's and the audience's) irrational and emotional responses ultimately to effect significant psychological and social transformations. Through much of the play, the erotic potential of the classical Ganymede is constrained and distorted by a partly Christianized Ganymede. When "Ganymede" claims, "I have, since I was three years old, conversed with a magician, most profound in his art, and yet not damnable" (5.2.58–60), this figure recalls his/her reference to "an old religious uncle of mine [who] taught me to speak" (3.2.336–7) and anticipates Orlando's assertion, "[This boy] hath been tutored in the rudiments / Of many desperate studies by his uncle, / Whom he reports to be a great magician" (5.4.30–2). The hint of classical, pederastic pedagogy becomes overwhelmed by the sense of sacred knowledge. Religious undertones in this play are ubiquitous; even the pagan god of marriage Hymen speaks of "atonement": "Then is there mirth in heaven / When earthly things made even / Atone together" (5.4.107–9).

Significantly, again, the requisite balance between flesh and spirit seems only achieved in a heterosexual sense: while the erotic Ganymede disappears into the loving (and self-surrendering) bride Rosalind, the spiritual or transcendent Ganymede seems displaced or subsumed by Rosalind's "convertite" uncle Frederick, soon to be joined (spiritually) with Jaques. When we reconsider moments in *King John* and *Hamlet* where we have observed this phenomenon of imaginative agency – and the playwright who has completed *As You Like It* stands just on the verge of composing his most famous play – such "transformations" for Shakespeare appear peculiarly committed to identifications which tragically exclude, or occlude, homoerotic self-realization.

Returning, finally, to the significance of Touchstone's riddle: in the humane but conservative worldview of Shakespeare's plays, a great reckoning in a little room may finally suggest not, or not just, post-coital *tristesse* over poor poetic reception but an "expense of spirit in a waste of shame" offering no procreative possibilities, Shakespeare perhaps making a more direct allusion to Marlowe's evocation of sodomitical desire than Charles Nicholl argues.[98] Shakespeare laments, but ironically simultaneously asserts, that the termination of one's creative output and its limited social and cultural reception parallel the failure to inscribe one's masculine identity in the discourses of "nature." While

As You Like It is shot through with the melancholy of unfulfilled homo-erotic desire, and while it contains the greatest density of allusion to Marlowe's work, Shakespeare there refrains from extending the path of humane possibility for homosexuality that Marlowe more daringly if implicitly proposes, even while Shakespeare is careful to humanize patterns of heterosexuality that Marlowe more darkly depicts.

Conclusion: Shakespearean Resolutions

It is of course a literary cliché to observe that, when engaging in a critical exploration of Shakespeare, one never feels one has reached the end of the discussion. I repeat here a reservation I expressed directly in chapter 4, that by focusing narrowly on one particular influence I am necessarily filtering out a variety of possible influences – cultural, historical, personal, and literary (other than Marlowe) – on the greatest writer who ever lived.[1] With respect to specifically erotic influence, a critical embracement of queer theory might indeed have alleviated my anxiety over the perceived naïveté of a narrower focus on Marlowe, since recent practitioners of such theory not infrequently assume "queering … to be an act of reading."[2] Presumably such reading could be construed not just on the part of postmodern readers but, in this case, on the part of Shakespeare himself, responding to Marlowe's work. Yet the reader of the present study will understand – from various assertions I have made – the impossibility of my adopting such a theoretical position. With respect to sexuality and the etiology of desire I sense something more deeply personal is at stake, for Shakespeare as he reads Marlowe, and for Marlowe as he composes his own remarkable works. In general my own intuitions as a reader sense something more is at stake for three playwrights of the period in particular: Marlowe, Shakespeare, and Chapman, with the possible addition of Kyd.[3] It may be that my own reading and study have not been extensive enough to consider other possible candidates. It may also be that the homoeroticism so intriguingly highlighted in early modern literature really does represent a kind of universal temptation, as Alan Bray famously argued, to which all men are subject.[4] Queer theory, especially as applied to early modern texts, has its roots in this historical claim.

Queer theorists, it is worth observing, sometimes make strikingly transhistorical claims, for example when Stanivukovic asserts that Shakespeare's sonnets exercise "the threat of desire to the autonomy of self and creation."[5] As we read the works of the past, "desire" comes in both familiar and unfamiliar forms, but it is perhaps the theological identifications that now require from us the greater effort of reconstruction. Interestingly, Stanivukovic in the essay from which I have just quoted attempts to link Marlowe and Shakespeare through the possible echo of the motto on the putative Corpus Christi portrait of Marlowe – "Quod me nutrit me destruit" – in line 12 of Sonnet 73: "Consumed with that which it was nourished by." It is not in fact true that "No biographer of either Marlowe or Shakespeare has speculated about the connection between [the playwrights] through the connection between the sonnet and the portrait"; A.D. Wraight did just that in her 1965 study *In Search of Christopher Marlowe*, long before the advent of queer theory.[6] Nevertheless a direct connection or influence is not in this case easy to establish, as Stanivukovic demonstrates. Perhaps his most interesting observation is that "a similar motto appears in Latin in Geoffrey Whitney's *A Choice of Emblemes* (1586) … [where] it reads 'Qui me alit me extinguit' ('Who feeds me extinguishes me'). The subscription below the image of a burning torch turned upside down … compares the reward of spiritual love ('The godlie loue, doth louers croune with fame') with the unsettling effect of carnal love ('louers lewde doe vainlie languishe still')."[7] This emblem and motto, as Wraight also observes, recur in act 2 of *Pericles*. What is significant about the rather ironic implication of the visual emblem here is that love as either salvific or self-destructive ultimately entails a *loss* of self, actually a form of self-consumption. Desire, whether sexual or spiritual, indeed threatens the autonomy of the self. Even as the early modern imagination explored the greater variety of sexual response reflected in classical poetic precedents, the (re-)invention or consolidation of a "phallic masculinity," especially on the part of ambitious, socially mobile men from the lower classes, seems historically unsurprising – if still fraught with anxiety and uncertainty in the face of Christian religious scruples.

For Shakespeare such invention was a complex process extending through much of the canon. In the second tetralogy the "Protestant re-enchantment" demonstrated by Hal ultimately evokes a remarkable degree of self-mastery, and yet this achievement comes at the cost (in the opinion of many readers) of almost any genuine emotionality. While the degree of responsibility demonstrated by Hal is thoroughly admirable, the difficulty remains of identifying or isolating any *desire* that he deeply experiences – other than the very attainment of political and emotional control through which he achieves personal dominance. Shakespeare's great tragic period appears to stand as a testament to the need for further and deeper artistic and psychological explorations of self-fashioning. As chapter 2 suggested, in *Hamlet* Shakespeare revisits the challenges to masculine self-formation posed by the Protestant, indeed more specifically Calvinist theology of his age, in a moment where he crucially recalls Marlowe's *Dido Queen of Carthage*, a text which serves as a catalyst for the development of Shakespeare's renegotiation of the feminine, paradoxically through its demonstration of a lack of integrated masculinity. A surprisingly traumatized masculinity characterizes the remaining great tragedies, where the male heroes seem less "heroic" agents than paragons of narcissism. The meaning of the tragedies of course represents such an enormous critical question in Shakespeare studies that even a brief survey would seem futile; I have elsewhere explored more specifically the effects of Calvinist doctrine on Shakespeare's characterization of these predominantly narcissistic tragic protagonists.[8] Future critical inquiry may focus fruitfully on other intersections of theological and sexual identifications and desires within the plays, specifically Shakespeare's sometimes strikingly daring reworking of Christian myth.

The Secular Christ in *Antony and Cleopatra*

I would like to conclude by briefly considering two later Shakespeare plays that seem crucial to, indeed paradigmatic of, this process. The first is another Shakespearean text that is often discussed in terms of Marlovian influence: *Antony and Cleopatra* as a response to, again, *Dido Queen of Carthage*. Robert Logan suggests that in this case "both the specific and general influences on *Antony and Cleopatra* have more to do with dramatic technique than ideas and attitudes, and, with a freshly invented fusion of different kinds of language – a throwback to the fusion of epic, hyperbolic, idealizing language with which Marlowe clearly intended to awe his audiences."[9] This observation in effect echoes J.B. Steane's memorable argument from the 1960s that "above all *Dido* suggests *Antony and Cleopatra*. Here it is not so much a matter of local similarities or general resemblances of plot but essentially of a similar 'feel' in the substance of the poetry."[10] Moreover, Logan bolsters his reading by considering Janet Adelman's reading that "both playwrights allow their lovers to posit the value of love largely through the assertive power of a highly metaphoric language."[11] It is indeed extraordinary that Shakespeare's most profound dramatic exploration of romantic love returns us to Marlowe's early play, which Shakespeare clearly had taken to heart.

Nevertheless, *Antony and Cleopatra* like *Dido* portrays the tragic failure of romantic love, and in a way that, if it has not (as in critical discussions of *Dido*) invited the suggestion of outright burlesque or parody, certainly has raised the necessity of addressing the odd blend of comic and tragic affect – the very quality that has set *Antony and Cleopatra* apart from the other "great" Shakespearean tragedies. I suggest that this quality can be partly understood by acknowledging the very *subversiveness* of the theological subtext of the play. Shakespeare is no longer simply interrogating the effects of Protestant and Calvinist theological assumptions on masculine self-formation, as he was in *Hamlet*, *Othello*, *King Lear*, and *Macbeth*. He has in one sense transcended the anxious exploration of the nature of Nature that compelled the earlier plays. Sexuality, and desire itself, now emerge unstigmatized. The tragedy remains that the masculine hero Antony cannot control such desire; but the consolation manifests in the inhumanity of the alternative: the shrewdly scheming, Machiavellian Caesar. As early as *A Midsummer Night's Dream*, and possibly *The Comedy of Errors*, Shakespeare's plays promote a binary between Apollonian rational control and the chaotic energy of the irrational Dionysian; this dichotomy first emerges in tension with, and gradually supersedes, the Christian distinction between good and evil, or divine and satanic, partly because the question of masculine self-coherence remains so completely vexed, in fact irresolvable, in the context of such distinctions. As chapter 5 suggested, Marlowe's development of the Actaeon myth in *Doctor Faustus* probably laid the imaginative groundwork for this ideological transformation.

The imagery of *Antony and Cleopatra* implicitly but repeatedly stresses the need for a balance between these two ontological states. That Cleopatra so fully embodies the Dionysian – completely beyond the reach of Apollonian "control" – means this tragedy I think misses the feminist potential of the final romances. Michael Neill in the Oxford edition offers the following crucial observation: "In the case of Cleopatra, as John Bayley has demonstrated, a host of small omissions and changes in emphasis serve to diminish the political seriousness of a queen whom Plutarch shows as Antonius's colleague in government, reducing her to an archetype of feminine frivolity and wilfulness, the perfect antithesis to Caesar and his single-minded obsession with power."[12] However else we interpret this play, the tension between the Dionysian Cleopatra and the Apollonian Caesar, and the tragic hero Antony's failure to integrate these two qualities in his own self-fashioning, inescapably constitutes its central thematic significance.

The more compelling critical questions then become, what would such a synthesis ideally look like, psychologically and politically, for Antony, and why does Shakespeare couch Antony's failure in the form of a kind of parody of the life of Christ?

And indeed he rather surprisingly does just that. This feature is rendered admirably clear and comprehensive in Hannibal Hamlin's treatment of the play under the chapter subtitle "Creative Anachronism." The militarily and politically ascendant Caesar announces in 4.6, "The time of universal peace is near" (5). For early modern audiences this announcement "would have had an additional resonance from the Gospel of Luke, in which the angels sing to the shepherds, 'Glorie be to God in the high heavens, and peace in earth, and towards men good will' (Luke 2:14)." Other Renaissance writers, such as Milton in the Nativity Ode, noted or implied that "the Roman and Christian [periods of peace] coincided, since Luke's Jesus was born in the reign of Augustus Caesar (Luke 2:1)"; in fact the "tradition of aligning the *Pax Romana* and the *Pax Christi* goes back at least as far as the medieval interpretation of Virgil's fourth eclogue, only slightly modified by Renaissance humanists, according to which Virgil prophesied the return of the 'Virgin' and the birth of a child 'by whom the Age of Iron gives way to the Golden Age'."[13] Yet Shakespeare ironizes the allusion intriguingly. Immediately subsequent to Caesar's talk of "bear[ing] the olive freely," a messenger announces the arrival of Antony into the field, to which Caesar replies, "Go charge Agrippa / Plant those that have revolted [that is, come over to Caesar's side] in the van [front lines], / That Antony may seem to spend his fury / Upon himself" (8–11). So much for human charity – or fidelity, or loyalty – all those "transcendent" virtues that Shakespeare's work repeatedly upholds, in spite of his theological heterodoxy. While Neill suggests that "Caesar's order turns the battle into an enactment of Anthony's self-division,"[14] it reflects more emphatically Caesar's brutally ruthless cynicism and manipulation. While Augustus, as Hamlin indicates, may be culturally associated with Christ by Renaissance historiographers and mythographers, Shakespeare's Caesar is more an Antichrist. If this scene anticipates the death or sacrifice of Christ, then it is a *humanist* Christ, and Antony is the man.

While the play's allusions to Herod are relevant to this creation of a secular Christ, they are also certainly more opaque. Charmian says to the Soothsayer, "Let me be married to three kings in a forenoon and widow them all. Let me [miraculously] have a child at fifty, to whom Herod of Jewry may do homage" (1.2.27–30). Later when Alexas tells Cleopatra, "Herod of Jewry dare not look upon you / But when you are well pleased," Cleopatra replies, "That Herod's head / I'll have; but how, when Antony is gone, / Through whom I might command it?" (3.3.3–6). The potential confusion of Herod the Great and his son Herod Antipas is less remarkable than the potential conflation of Herod and John the Baptist, not to mention Charmian and the Virgin Mary. Shakespeare plays a near-blasphemous game by conflating stories related to the Nativity with the sense of the unimpeded power of female sexuality, although Cleopatra's remark possibly suggests deference to Antony's authority, or at least a pretence of such deference.

The play's astonishing elevation of sexual desire and attraction emerges in the opening scene, where, in response to Cleopatra's "I'll set a bourn how far to be beloved," Antony replies, "Then must thou needs find out new heaven, new earth" (16–17), a daring echo of Revelation. When Antony experiences his brief martial recovery after the disaster of Actium, Cleopatra addresses him as "Lord of lords" (4.8.16); as Hamlin observes, this phrase, coupled with Antony's desire that his sons may be "kings of kings" (3.6.13), furthers the Christ allusion. Hamlin also observes that, "Like Christ … Antony is betrayed by a follower who loves him, Enobarbus … He does not commit suicide like Judas, but his weird death does seem somehow self-willed."[15] Moreover, "Enobarbus abandons Antony after 'one other gaudy night,' recalling previous, more dissolute feasts like that on Pompey's barge, but also suggesting a kind of last supper" involving a kind of "conviviality" which reinforces "why Antony's men love him."[16]

In fact the great love and devotion that Antony inspires among his men indicates a potential misreading by Neill in the Oxford edition. Neill believes that 3.1 constitutes a clear mirror of Plutarch's assertion that "Antonius (like Octavius Caesar) enjoyed greater military success through his subordinates than in his own person."[17] Yet Ventidius declines Sillius's invitation for further conquest with the words, "Better to leave undone than by our deed / Acquire too high a fame when him we serve's away" (14–15). Deference and respect limit the ambition of Antony's followers, to the extent that respect emerges as true love and devotion: "I'll humbly signify what in his name, / That magical word of war, we have effected" (31–2). Neill more accurately emphasizes Shakespeare's significant revision of Plutarch when, with the fall of Lepidus, the playwright "deliberately plays down the machiavellism of his historical original" by "suppressing Anthony's involvement."[18] That is, Shakespeare consistently humanizes Antony to heighten his moral and emotional differences from Caesar, who inspires affection in no one.

While Hamlin offers other highly persuasive examples of biblical analogy, I would like to focus on what Antony as secular or humanist

Christ suggests about the nature of his tragic failure to integrate the disparate aspects of his character. While he inspires deep love among his men, in particular Enobarbus, his tragedy clearly arises from his love for Cleopatra, which essentially ruins and unmans him. Numerous commentators have noted the gender inversion in the play, as in the oft-cited passage:

> That time – O times! –
> I laughed him out of patience; and that night
> I laughed him into patience. And the next morn,
> Ere the ninth hour, I drunk him to his bed,
> Then put my tires and mantles on him,
> Whilst I wore his sword Philippan. (2.5.18–23)

The cross-dressing and Cleopatra's appropriation of Antony's sword signify the ultimate defeat of "phallic masculinity" – ludicrously echoed later in the play when the self-wounded, half-dead Antony must be hauled up by the women to the top of the monument, because a self-protective Cleopatra "dare[s] not" descend. Since the Gospels indicate that Jesus died at "the ninth hour," the passage also signifies Antony's loss of masculinity as his "crucifixion." Antony's "sword Philippan" was named after his victory over Brutus and Cassius at Philippi. Perhaps Shakespeare here recalls the moment from *Julius Caesar* where Brutus, having dealt Julius Caesar his death-blow, exclaims, "Stoop, Romans, stoop, / And let us bathe our hands in Caesar's blood / Up to the elbows and besmear our swords" (3.1.106–8), a "ritual performance" which becomes a kind of "inversion of the normal rituals associated with blood-guilt."[19]

Whatever the significance of its complex and at times seemingly parodic web of theological allusions, for postmodern readers the ultimate meaning of *Antony and Cleopatra* must lie between the idealized neoclassical essentialism of Dryden's *All for Love* and Plutarch's clear moral denunciation of Antony: "the horse of the minde as Plato termeth it, that is so hard of rayne (I mean the unreyned lust of concupiscence) did put out of Antonius heade, all honest and commendable thoughtes."[20] As Ronald Horton observes, "Critical sentiment generally finds inadequate Plutarch's explanation of Antony's behavior ... Yet the play does attend to moral consequence."[21] I would like to focus on one specific scene in order to contemplate an integrated balance of Apollonian and Dionysian within Antony's character, as Shakespeare might have imagined it, before Cleopatra's rhetorical, and fantastical, apotheosis of her lover's character in act 5, wherein he ideally emerges as both a "sun and moon," achieving such a resolution only after his death. In 1.3 Antony, at the news of Fulvia's death, for once successfully separates himself from Cleopatra in order to return to Rome, in spite of her interruptions, mind-games, and ironic taunts. One taunt is nevertheless highly significant:

> O most false love!
> Where be the sacred vials thou shouldst fill
> With sorrowful water?
> Now I see, I see,
> In Fulvia's death how mine received shall be. (62–5)

The vials refer to lachrymatory vessels to hold the tears of the grieving, but this study has already observed the potentially ironic use of "vials," which in biblical contexts signify destructive more often than salvific agents. The image may thus suggest, beyond Cleopatra's conscious intention, that romantic passion, however "sacred," leads more emphatically to self-destruction than to spiritual fulfilment or self-confirmation. I pause over the image since it significantly colours my reading of Antony's response, one of the most crucial passages in the play:

> Quarrel no more, but be prepared to know
> The purposes I bear, which are or cease
> As you shall give th' advice. By the fire
> That quickens Nilus' slime, I go from hence
> Thy soldier, servant, making peace or war
> As thou affects. (66–71)

The speech represents Antony's most integrated, emotionally viable response to Cleopatra. He must leave her, but not because he fails to love her; he goes as her "soldier-servant" (the reading of the Folio text). Neill suggests that the term means "warrior-lover and obedient subordinate; *servant* here means both chivalric lover and feudal vassal." The term thus balances phallic masculinity (masculine ego) and responsible duty and service (transcendence of egotism), as well as Ovidian sexual vitality and Petrarchan devotion.

Even more significant than "soldier-servant" is Antony's swearing "By the fire / That quickens Nilus' slime." The image in effect conflates the higher, Apollonian elements (fire, air) with the lower Dionysian elements (water, earth). Every commentator I have consulted offers a version of Neill's explanation: the passage indicates the "sun which brings life to the Nile mud; Anthony is thinking not merely of agricultural fertility, but of the process whereby scarabs, serpents, and crocodiles were supposed to hatch spontaneously from the Nile mud through the action of the sun."[22] Such generation, I do not contest, is the dominant meaning of this passage; it certainly receives support from Gabriel Egan's observations that "In his favourite classical text, Ovid's *Metamorphoses*, Shakespeare found the following account: 'So when the seven-mouthed Nile has receded from the drenched fields and has returned again to its former bed, and the fresh slime has been heated by the sun's rays, farmers as they turn over the lumps of earth find many animate things'."[23] This reading ultimately underlines the play's sympathies towards a Dionysian fertility or "overflowing" in the face of Apollonian containment; the overflowing Nile was the very reason for Egypt's remarkable fertility, and Egypt was a key source of the Roman Empire's grain production.[24]

I nevertheless want to suggest a secondary reading, a kind of subtext or "shadow reading," which implies a more negative aspect to this lack of containment. Through a potential ambivalence of the image, "By the fire / That quickens Nilus' slime," Shakespeare may also have been thinking of Egyptian brick-making from the Nile silt, so that the fire would represent not metaphorically the sun, but literally the kiln fire needed to "quicken" or kindle the bricks in order to harden them. It is difficult to ascertain what Shakespeare would have known about the history of Egyptian brick-making. It was not until the Roman period that the bricks were actually baked in a kiln; before that innovation, they were simply dried in the sun, and consequently were subject to dissolution if exposed to too much moisture. There is one contemporary text, a version of Plutarch in fact, which emphasizes, through metaphorical use, the early modern familiarity with the advantages of kiln-baking. Philemon Holland's 1603 translation of Plutarch's *Morals*[25] contains a chapter "Of Fortune," which asserts through a series of pragmatic examples the efficacy and indeed necessity of human agency and skill in the face of the external vagaries of fortune:

> Shall we say then that the greatest and most principall things that are, even those that be most materiall and necessarie for mans felicitie, use not wisedome, nor participate one whit with providence and the judgement of reason? There is no man so blockish and voide of understanding, that after he hath tempered clay and water together, lets it alone and goeth his way when he hath so done, looking that of the[ir] own accord, or by fortune there will be bricks or tiles made thereof: neither is any one such a sot, as when he hath bought wool & leather, sits him downe & praies unto fortune, that thereof he may have garments or shooes.[26]

It may be objected that "quicken" meaning "to animate" rather than "to kindle" is the likelier reading of the passage in question, thus excluding the dual interpretation I am suggesting. Yet, intriguingly, when Shakespeare does refer to bricks directly, he seems to conflate these two very actions. In *2 Henry VI*, Cade claims his father to be a lost son of the Earl of March, son of the Duke of York, who eventually became a bricklayer, and sired Cade. In the face of Stafford's unsurprising incredulity, Cade's companion Dick insists on the story's veracity, with Smith adding, "Sir, he made a chimney in my father's house, and the bricks are alive at this day to testify it" (4.2.143–4). In spite of the rebels' ignorance and brutality, Cade's followers associate artisanal skill with not just workmanlike competence but creative vitality.

If we accept my "secondary" reading, then the passage "By the fire / That quickens Nilus' slime" does not just evoke Antony's identification with Dionysian fertility as the participatory agent of his vitality but also emphasizes his necessary *capacity to contain* – to carry or uphold – such vital energy. The image of the lachrymatory vial in Cleopatra's immediately preceding speech strengthens this reading, even with its darker suggestion. Shakespeare may indeed be conscious here of New Testament passages employing imagery of the devout soul as a "fit vessel" of the spirit. The pseudo-Pauline 2 Timothy 2:21 reads, "If anie man therefore purge him self from these [dishonourable qualities], he shalbe a vessel vnto honour, sanctified, and mete for the Lord, and prepared vnto euerie good worke"; the subsequent verse clarifies the main quality to purge or avoid: "the lustes of youth." Interestingly, a genuinely Pauline passage more emphatically suggests predestination, downplaying human self-discipline: "But, o man, who art thou which pleadest against God? shal the thing formed say to him that formed it, Why hast thou made me thus? Hathe not the potter power of the claie to make of the same lompe one vessel to honour, and another vnto dishonour?" (Romans 9:20–1). Paul sounds somewhat more conciliatory and encouraging in 2 Corinthians 4: "For God that commanded the light to shine out of darkenes, is he which hathe shined in our hearts, to giue the light of the knowledge of the glorie of God in the face of Iesus Christ. But we haue this treasure in earthen vessels, that the excellence of that power might be of God and not of vs" (6–7). Crucially, however, Shakespeare rewrites the theological significance: Antony as secular Christ is his own "sun" or "fire," and must discipline his own passion and vitality.

Shakespeare at least twice in his work uses "vessel" as an image of an emotionally overwrought character. In *Julius Caesar*, Clitus observes Brutus before his suicide and comments, "Now is that noble vessel full of grief, / That runs over even at his eyes" (5.5.13–14). In *The Winter's*

Tale, Antigonus relates his dream, or nightmare, involving the ghost of Hermione – "I never saw a vessel of like sorrow / So filled and so becoming" (3.3.20–1) – before her eyes become rather horrifyingly "two spouts." The playwright also includes, twice in the tragedies, the image of the cistern, which for the Elizabethans would most likely be constructed of stone or brick. In both cases the image implies a lack of emotional containment, and a failure of political responsibility. When the terrified Messenger announcing news of Antony's marriage exclaims to the queen, "Should I lie, madam?," Cleopatra responds, "O, I would thou didst, / So half my Egypt were submerged and made / A cistern for scaled snakes!" (2.5.95–7). In *Macbeth*, when the fugitive Malcolm tests Macduff in England, the prince asserts, "But there's no bottom, none, / In my voluptuousness. Your wives, your daughters, / Your matrons, and your maides could not fill up / The cistern of my lust" (4.3.61–4).

Antony *potentially* demonstrates the necessary containment of such passion. Perhaps even more significant than Antony's swearing by Nilus's slime in 1.3 is the manner in which the scene ends. Finally containing her own jealousy and fear, Cleopatra concludes:

> But sir, forgive me,
> Since my becomings kill me when they do not
> Eye well to you. Your honor calls you hence;
> Therefore be deaf to my unpitied folly,
> And all the gods go with you! (96–100)

Antony responds:

> Let us go. Come;
> Our separation so abides and flies
> That thou, residing here, goes yet with me,
> And I, hence fleeting, here remain with thee. (102–5)

Through the paradox of movement and stasis and the verbal construction "fleeting," this passage constitutes, I contend, the most profound echo of *Dido Queen of Carthage*. After dissuading her lover Aeneas from his first attempt at departure, Dido uneasily surveys his naval equipment and expresses her continuing distrust:

> Are these the sails that in despite of me
> Pack'd with the winds to bear Aeneas hence?
> I'll hang ye in the chamber where I lie.

> Drive, if you can, my house to Italy:
> I'll set the casement open that the winds
> May enter in and once again conspire
> Against the life of me, poor Carthage Queen;
> But, though he go, he stays in Carthage still,
> And let rich Carthage fleet upon the seas,
> So I may have Aeneas in mine arms. (4.4.126–35)

Shakespeare answers a description of narcissistic control and desperation from Marlowe with a brief speech that embodies, simultaneously, both deep love and the exercise of personal responsibility and self-control. As in *Hamlet*, Antony's speech at the conclusion of 1.3 again reveals Shakespeare responding to Marlowe's first play to effect a transformation of narcissism.

Admittedly Antony fails, emotionally and intellectually, to maintain such integration of character, but this tragedy profoundly confirms the depth of his human love, even in the face of the play's sometimes darkly comic ironies. In spite of the disaster of Actium, and the fiasco of Antony's failure at a cleanly and properly "manly" Roman suicide, his self-injury can I think be considered an echo of both Tamburlaine's self-mutilation and Neptune's self-wounding in *Hero and Leander*. But now the "parody" of Christhood is more clearly a celebration of humanity, rather than an interrogation of the limits of theological orthodoxy, or of human fantasies of omnipotence. *Antony and Cleopatra* conjoins two profound personalities, one (Antony) who transcends his narcissism, and one (Cleopatra) who, movingly, does not. Artistically, therefore, the masculine search for psychic wholeness through the integration with the feminine continues in the final tragicomic romances.

Natural Grace and the Limits of the Imagination in *The Winter's Tale*

I will consider finally one text which again, like *Antony and Cleopatra*, apparently challenges Christian constructions of human suffering to an almost blasphemous degree, or at the very least still responds deeply to Marlowe's interrogation of a theology of grace. In *Antony and Cleopatra* the agency which Cleopatra accords Antony after his death – another interesting if highly idealized example of imaginative agency in Shakespeare – is sufficiently potent to allow her, via Antony's ghost, to dismiss Caesar (of all people) as a victim of Actaeon-like dismemberment or dissolution – "O, couldst thou speak, / That I might hear thee call great Caesar ass / Unpolicied!" (5.2.306–8). And she manages to assert such "transcendental humanism"[27] in spite of Caesar's material triumph. But in *The Winter's Tale* the initial challenge to a theology of grace is now no longer made in favour of a humanist agency but in terms of actual human *desire*:

> We were as twinned lambs that did frisk i' the sun
> And bleat the one at th' other. What we changed
> Was innocence for innocence; we knew not
> The doctrine of ill-doing, nor dreamed
> That any did. Had we pursued that life,
> And our weak spirits ne'er been higher reared
> With stronger blood, we should have answered heaven
> Boldly "Not guilty," the imposition cleared
> Hereditary ours. (1.2.67–75)

There is perhaps no single more important text, ideologically, in the Shakespeare canon, since in *The Winter's Tale* the playwright daringly redefines the relation between Nature and Grace. Theologically, he renders grace not as divine fiat but as the ultimate result of the human acceptance, and imaginative transformation, of the natural. Original Sin is clearly represented in Polixenes' speech above not only as sexual, but crucially, in spite of a radical dismissal of Calvinist depravity, as a human misinterpretation of the sexual. Leontes' and Polixenes' sexual past, and their homoerotic friendship, carries with it a sense of narcissistic idealism – "weak spirits" suggesting the vulnerability of a visionary but as yet inchoate selfhood – which resists the demonic associations of female sexuality and the necessity of the "stronger blood" of sexual maturity. When Polixenes implies that their male, edenic innocence ("to be boy eternal" [65]) necessarily predated the "tripp[ing]" (76) or falling into heterosexual attraction, Hermione responds, "Grace to boot! / Of this make no conclusion, lest you say / Your queen and I are devils" (80–2).

Such a misinterpretation of the sexual returns us to the troubling issue of Shakespeare's potentially Oedipal configurations inviting readings in which homoeroticism suggests "a psychological (developmental) ambivalence," as Stanivukovic noted in Adonis, a young man "on his way to masculinity" but not there yet. The demonization of female sexuality, and/or the demonization of male heterosexual attraction for women, is certainly a problem to be addressed – both an early modern problem, as Hermione's amused but concerned response indicates, and a problem for later historical periods, including our own, with its narcissistic tendency to decry all forms of "phallic masculinity."

Nevertheless one critical advantage of an emphasis on the homoerotic nature of the friendship between Polixenes and Leontes is that it clarifies the otherwise strange eruption of Leontes' jealousy. The first critic to suggest such a reading was J.I.M. Stewart:

> An early fixation of his affections upon his friend, long dormant, is reawakened in Leontes – though without being brought to conscious focus – by that friend's actual presence for the first time since their "twyn'd" boyhood. An unconscious conflict ensues and the issue is behaviour having as its object the violent repudiation of the newly reactivated homosexual component in this character. In other words, Leontes projects upon his wife the desires he has to repudiate in himself.[28]

Thus Leontes' passion is certainly irrational, since unconsciously motivated, but not completely gratuitous or inexplicable: it is I suggest quite *natural*, indeed essential. After sixteen years of the most intense, character-changing suffering, the king's homoerotic feelings apparently remain intact, what they always were; at first sight of Florizell, Leontes states with astonishing honesty:

> Your mother was most true to wedlock, Prince,   ·
> For she did print your royal father off,
> Conceiving you. Were I but twenty-one,
> Your father's image is so hit in you,
> His very air, that I should call you brother,
> As I did him, and speak of something wildly
> By us performed before. (5.1.124–30)

This speech, however, also raises a disturbing subtext: Leontes emphasizes his desire to call Florizell "brother," as he did Polixenes, in fact from the very beginning of the play; while it may evoke, again, the idea of *amicitia* through "sworn brotherhood," the homoeroticism also carries, symbolically, a taint of incest.[29]

Stephen Guy-Bray, in a compelling reading of *The Winter's Tale*, observes in a note, after citing J.I.M. Stewart's seminal discussion of the homoerotic dynamic, the "most famous" psychoanalytic readings of the play: Murray Schwartz's two articles, "Leontes' Jealousy in *The Winter's Tale*" and its continuation, "*The Winter's Tale*: Loss and Transformation."[30] While profound, these discussions are also, for the reader, intimidating owing to their length and complexity. Indeed, Schwartz's opening critical manoeuvre is to tentatively accept Stewart's Freudian hypothesis, but to warn that "the focus of Leontes' rage cannot be accounted for if we assume that Hermione is merely a surrogate for himself in relation to Polixenes. Freud's formula ... closes off rather than opens up a consideration of jealousy in the play as a whole." Consequently Schwartz approvingly cites C.L. Barber's exploration of "a deeper fabric of motives" which considers a child's Oedipal interactions with both mother and father, involving "a loss of relation to the crucial man as to the crucial woman, crucial in the sense that they are those in whom is invested the core of love which has its root in childhood and is the ground of piety toward the larger powers of life which we encounter first through the parents."[31]

A critical appeal to "the ground of piety toward the larger powers of life" poses a problem, ideologically, for postmodern criticism – and for anyone (including myself) anxious to preserve a society in which a plurality or even absence of religious beliefs is allowed to coexist. Nevertheless in this study, which began with the assertion of the need to acknowledge the groping towards a kind of necessary Oedipalization of social structure in the theological tracts and heretical formulations of early modern England, I don't think we can, or should, easily dismiss the parallels between Oedipal and Christian narratives that Shakespeare's works apparently suggest. It seems to me likely that some version of psychoanalytic familial identification will continue to haunt Shakespearean criticism, even as we understandably seek to transform the family. In human experience these identifications run deep, very deep. Even Aristotle, denizen of the thoroughly androcentric and homosocially oriented culture of ancient Greece, appeals in the *Poetics* to the most powerful, apparently transhistorical emotions catalysed by the violation of "family values":

> Let us determine, then, which kinds of happening are felt by the spectator to be fearful, and which pitiable. Now such acts are necessarily the work of persons who are near and dear (close blood kin) to one another, or enemies, or neither. But when an enemy attacks an enemy there is nothing pathetic about either the intention or the deed, except in the actual pain suffered by the victim; nor when the act is done by "neutrals"; but when the tragic acts come within the limits of close blood relationship, as when brother kills or intends to kill brother or do something else of that kind to him, or son to father or mother to son or son to mother – those are the situations one should look for.[32]

I must introduce my own necessary qualification of Aristotle's position: my intent in recognizing the power of such identifications certainly does not involve denying "contentment" to those outside more traditional family structures. The kind of maturation that interests me encourages responsible interaction and dedication between individuated, self-aware individuals of whatever cultural or sexual persuasion who express deep emotional commitment to each other. Critical attempts to deny possible contentment through the "remedy" of romantic love, and the social structures for which it provides a foundation,[33] seem to me either a political displacement of another kind of narcissism, or an evocation of a world that disbelieves entirely in the responsibilities and rewards of human love.

Let me return to the unshaken presence of homoerotic desire at the end of *The Winter's Tale*. Guy-Bray asserts a further manifestation that has escaped previous commentators. When the arrival of Prince Florizel and his princess is announced at Leontes' court in act 5, Paulina states:

> Had our prince
> Jewel of children, seen this hour, he had paired
> Well with this lord. There was not full a month
> Between their births. (5.1.116–19)

Guy-Bray comments:

The reference to Mamillius emphasizes the all-important substitution of a girl for a boy that will finally take place [at the Sicilian court] when Perdita enters, and the reference to the closeness in birth of the two sons emphasizes their similarity, as opposed to the all-important difference between male and female in the union of Perdita and Florizel. Nevertheless, the passage still testifies to the possibility that things might have worked out differently. If we are to consider the boys as twins, then we have to recall that Polixenes and Leontes were originally "twinned lambs." And while Paulina may use "pair[e]d" simply to denote a similarity, the word cannot be stripped of its erotic charge.

The speculation that "things might have worked out differently" is perhaps a postmodern projection, yet the homoerotic presence is certainly daringly preserved in the play, at least by Leontes' desire for Polixenes. Guy-Bray adds, poignantly, "Connected in this case not by their births but by their Latinate names, Mamillius and Florizel are the couple whose story Shakespeare cannot tell, even in a narrative categorized as a winter's tale."[34]

These names suggest further crucial sameness and difference. Stephen Orgel suggests that the name Florizel, and the dramatic situation, "appear to come from the popular Spanish romance *Amadis de Grecia* (first published 1535), a continuation of the Amadis of Gaul story, in which Don Florisel is a prince disguised as a shepherd wooing a shepherdess who is in reality a princess."[35] Unless this tale is radically undercut by a homoerotic subtext, the source of the name presumably suggests a generic transformation from classical, homoerotic pastoral to a Renaissance heteroerotic romance. Florizel does mention the goddess Flora in his first speech, associating his own name with natural beauty, in the manner of Adonis. Florizel is, in my opinion, the most persuasively heterosexual of all of Shakespeare's masculine lovers. He is "Apollonian" only in the sense of his own moving identification with "Golden Apollo" (4.4.30). In a play which has now dispensed entirely with the binary of reason versus passion, he represents higher irrationality (good dreams, deep love, faith) in opposition to, or in answer to, the lower irrationality of Leontes' destructive madness (bad dreams, uncontrolled passion, jealousy).

Mamillius's name clearly evokes a tragedy of narcissism, the maternal dependence that he manfully (for a young boy) attempts to resist, but fails to transcend, in a sense dying through a displacement of his mother's trauma. He playfully but significantly resists the coddling of his mother's ladies-in-waiting at the beginning of 2.1 – "[you] speak to me as if / I were a baby still" (5–6), and eventually answers his mother's request for a tale: "A sad tale's best for winter [the necessary integration of potentially tragic process]. I have one / Of sprites and goblins … There was a man [what he needs to become] … Dwelt by a churchyard [evoking inhibiting theological dependencies]. I will tell it softly." Just as his mother invites him to tell it "in mine ear [underlining a final intimacy, but failure of individuation]," all hell breaks loose with the entrance of Leontes: "How blest am I / In my just censure, in my true opinion" (25–37). In a final painful metamorphosis, the whole rest of the play in a sense becomes the "winter's tale" that Mamillius begins to tell; as he fails to transcend his own narrative, the play memorializes his own tragic attempt at imaginative agency.

Leontes' "blest" encapsulates the familiar etymological conflation in English poetry of salvific and destructive agency.[36] The recuperation of feminine nature in the play, and the undoing of the demonization of (hetero)sexuality, is largely due to the agency of Paulina, ironically so named as a reflection of St. Paul, in perhaps Shakespeare's most pointed interrogation of Reformation theology. At the play's resolution, Paulina "require[s]" Leontes, "You do awake your faith" (5.3.95), a faith not in arbitrary divine agency but in human suffering as meaningful and ultimately restorative, and in art itself as the means to render human, and natural, process understandable in such terms. Paulina – inverting Pauline doctrine – thus restores Leontes to the body of this life, rather than delivering him from the body of this death. The grace finally realized in Paulina's (literally artful) gallery and chapel is pronounced by Leontes to be a magic or an art coequal with Nature, as "Lawful as eating" (111). The statue of the supposedly dead Hermione, imminently leading to a female resurrection, serves as a final dismissal of male narcissism, the tendency either to demonize or excessively idealize women – to obscure their own personhood or subjectivity. The ageing of Hermione's image encompasses the alterations of time, even as it "pierc[es]" Leontes' soul (34) and "conjure[s]" his past evils in his remembrance (40).

Such "piercing" in fact allows Huston Diehl to make an interesting case for Paulina's role as a parallel to, rather than an inversion of, St. Paul's. The statue's magic is "not the magic of the Roman Catholic icon, with the power to heal, protect, grant desires, or save, but rather a very different kind of magic … reminding the viewer of his own impurity."[37] Thus Paulina's statue "functions as a visual rebuke," with links to her earlier, rhetorical rebukes to Leontes, which Diehl finds characteristically Pauline. However, the necessary additional parallel Diehl is forced to draw between Paulina's or Shakespeare's manipulation of words and spectacles, and Paul's (or the Protestant preacher's) attempts at conversion of sinners, seems to me to render Leontes' receptiveness "to the possibility of grace"[38] quite problematic in a theological sense.[39] The king does not undergo a Pauline transformation from carnal "old man" to transcendent "new man" (Ephesians 4:22–4), so much as he accepts a renewed commitment to his physical and sexual connections as husband and father, and to a rather poignant acceptance of the now more pressing limitations of his remaining time in the world: "Hastily lead away" (5.3.155). The poignancy is increased by the fact that in act 5 Leontes still expresses, still virtually embodies, homoerotic desire, as already observed. The fact that Hermione embraces him after descending from the pedestal implies a renewal of their conjugal connection, but significantly she never directly addresses him, or anyone else, other than her daughter Perdita. And most astonishingly Leontes finally imposes a marriage on Paulina and his counsellor Camillo. But he is another character whose devotion to Leontes – in their final reunion "They seemed almost, with staring on one another, to tear the cases of their eyes … They looked as they had heard of a world ransomed, or one destroyed" (5.2.12–16) – definitely borders on the homoerotic, again intensified in a quasi-spiritual sense. For me Leontes' action is inexplicable, except to admit critically that, in the profound joy that characterizes the conclusion of the play, Shakespeare is willing to include, even to sadistically *invite*, this one painful flash of what is undeniably a startling cruel containment.

Such cruelty oddly accentuates the son-in-law Florizel's heteroerotic triumph, possibly in compensation for the narcissistic dissolution of the original son Mamillius. While Polixenes' nostalgic description of the two original royal sons as "twinned lambs" clearly recalls one of the central images in Christian iconography of a sacrificial innocence, Florizel significantly appears at the sheep-shearing festival as a *shepherd* or master whose willingness to sacrifice every material advantage through his essential passion for Perdita paradoxically ensures his ultimate elevation in the social hierarchy of the play. The resolution is not gratuitous – even if it seems to depend on a series of chance events, and is thus partly identifiable as a product of a higher "grace" – but arises from Florizel's own depth of feeling, and ability to take risks. We find the theatrical art or magic of the late Shakespeare not in the service of theological orthodoxy, but in the encouragement of the acceptance of individual responsibility for both rational and irrational responses in personal and social relationships. The aristocratic context of *The Winter's Tale* may ironically carry, or encourage, a covert expression of wish fulfilment for the lower-class members of its Jacobean audience by emphasizing Florizel's essential virtue in the face of the trials of time and fortune: "Why look you [Perdita] so upon me? / I am but sorry, not afeard; delayed, / But nothing altered. What I was, I am" (4.4.464–7).[40] In fact, as Florizel is a prince masquerading (earnestly and lovingly) as a shepherd, there may be an echo in his final sentence here of Jesus' audacious claim, "Before Abraham was, I am."

To return one last time to the question of Marlowe's influence, I take up the conclusion to my second chapter. There I considered Aeneas's crucial exclamation in *Dido Queen of Carthage*, when he re-encounters the woods where he first landed destitute upon Carthage's shores, "O, how these irksome labours now delight / And overjoy my thoughts with their escape! / Who would not undergo all kind of toil / To be well stor'd with such a winter's tale?" (3.3.56–9). I characterized this speech as the infantilization of a necessary reconstitution of experience, a reduction of the process of maturation to a child's fantasy, a delight in storytelling. And yet I recognized its potential to represent a truly disciplined working through of the challenging processes of experience, and suggested that Shakespeare keenly perceived this potential, the power of human imaginative production to facilitate a more practical and socially responsible self-fashioning. In early modern English "a winter's tale" suggested a fantastic or fabulous story, "especially a ghost story."[41] Mamillius before his tragic death is about to tell a tale of sprites and ghosts. The question of whether Shakespeare's play contains a "real" ghost might lead to a reconsideration of the plausibility of Hermione's death and resurrection, and of her visionary appearance before the unfortunate Antigonus. As the phrase was proverbial, there is no direct proof that Shakespeare in writing *The Winter's Tale* was deliberately responding to Aeneas's speech, although he is clearly still responding to *Dido* in *Antony and Cleopatra*, only about three or four years before. But there is another piece of evidence to suggest that Shakespeare, circa 1610, has remained haunted by Marlowe's ghost.

A decade earlier, in 1600, Thomas Thorpe published Marlowe's translation of Lucan's *Pharsalia*, with a dedication to his "fellow-publisher and 'true friend'" Edward Blount: "Blount, I purpose to be blunt with you, and out of my dullness to encounter you with a dedication in the memory of that pure elemental wit, Christopher Marlow, whose ghost or genius is to be seen walk in the Churchyard in at the least three or four sheets." According to Charles Nicholl, Thorpe is referring to the "sudden printed effusion of Marlowe's work. His 'ghost' (his poetry) walks in the 'churchyard' (the bookmart in St Paul's) in different 'sheets' (the various editions of *Hero*, with a pun on winding-sheets and sheets of paper). In this more humorous vein, Thorpe conveys the sense of Marlowe's continued *presence*,"[42] a presence that lingered, I suggest, to the end of Shakespeare's writing career. Nicholl interestingly identifies Blount as "a voice in Marlowe's favour at a time when other voices were dragging his name through the mud."[43] Shakespeare would not have failed to purchase, and to revisit, any publication of Marlowe's work, and the respectful and affectionate exchange between Thorpe and Blount in the dedication would have caught Shakespeare's attention – as well as, perhaps, the potential intimacy of the phrase "encounter you." Even the metonymic reference to the bookmart in St. Paul's as the "churchyard"[44] finds an echo in Mamillius's aborted tale, and would likely have appealed to Shakespeare as an evocation of the humanist production of literature that was both his life's work and Marlowe's – symbolically and significantly in the face of the theological constraints both of them worked through in their poetry and plays. While Prospero's exclamation "I'll drown my books" as an echo of Faustus's "I'll burn my books" is often cited as Shakespeare's valedictory acknowledgment of Marlowe's influence, I suggest the complex presence of Marlowe's ghost through the entirety of *The Winter's Tale* – as a tragicomic extension of Mamillius's precluded story – stands as Shakespeare's most profound parting reflection on their artistic relationship.

Notes

Introduction: Marlowe, Shakespeare, and Religious Toleration

1 Logan, *Shakespeare's Marlowe*, 1, 120.

2 Ibid., 7.

3 Bloom, *The Anxiety of Influence*, 2nd ed., xxi.

4 Ibid., xx.

5 Kuriyama, *Christopher Marlowe*, 71. Kuriyama's suggestion doesn't quite explain why Marlowe seems to have enjoyed a somewhat special status within the secret service, first when the Privy Council intervened to guarantee that he be awarded the MA from Cambridge in 1587, amid rumours concerning his illicit or treasonous activities (which might relate to employment more serious than mere letter carrying), or later in 1592, when, having been arrested for coining money, a capital offence, in Flushing, he escaped serious punishment and was at liberty shortly afterward (for an effective summary, see Charles Nicholl's entry on Marlowe in the *Oxford Dictionary of Nation Biography*). But then again, why, upon his arrest for coining, should Marlowe have to explain that he knew powerful men like Northumberland and Strange, "if … he was a government agent?," as J.A. Downie inquires ("Marlowe: Facts and Fictions," 22). Possibly the interrogator in this case, Robert Sidney, had not been informed of the "special status" conferred on Marlowe by, say, Burghley? Speculations about Marlowe's espionage invariably go round in circles such as these.

6 As Meredith Skura argues in *Shakespeare the Actor and the Purposes of Playing*.

7 Kuriyama, *Christopher Marlowe*, 118.

8 Riggs, *The World of Christopher Marlowe*, 70. Jane Stevenson, in a review of Riggs, questions his assertion that "there were no more Cardinal Wolseys in early modern England": "But Marlowe's contemporary, George Abbot,

was precisely equivalent: a poor clothworker's son from Guildford who ended up as Archbishop of Canterbury" (http://www.theguardian .com/books/2004/apr/18/ biography.christophermarlowe). Marlowe's heterodoxy may have been as crucial as his lower-class status in determining his lack of advancement.

9 Assumptions concerning Marlowe's emotionally and physically volatile nature have not gone unquestioned. In "Was Marlowe a Violent Man?," Rosalind Barber offers a noteworthy interrogation for at least two reasons. Readers may wonder if legal records themselves in effect tend to exaggerate the assertive nature of especially lower-class figures in history who have not left extensive traces of other kinds. I have at times wondered, for example, about the accuracy of William Urry's assessment of Marlowe's father John as "a noisy, self-assertive, improvident fellow" (quoted approvingly by Kuriyama, *Christopher Marlowe*, 18). In addition, Barber's analysis perhaps does not question Marlowe's violent temper so much as it stresses the unremarkable or commonplace nature of what we now (sensitized by critiques of "toxic masculinity") may consider shocking aggression on the part of early modern men in general. In this sense the essay offers a useful corrective of historical perspective. But I also find one crucial turn in Barber's argument logically vulnerable: "Marlowe's posthumous reputation as a violent man by personal testimony begins and ends with Thomas Kyd, who in two letters to Sir John Puckering … calls him 'intemperate & of a cruel hart' and then accuses him of 'rashness in attempting sudden privy injuries to men'" (55). Like other commentators, Barber notes that Kyd here writes under extreme duress, and in the knowledge that Marlowe is already dead. But she also notes that Kyd's main rhetorical motive is, as he states, "to clear myself of being thought an Atheist." With such a purpose in mind, why does Kyd not then concentrate solely on what he can report of Marlowe's heresies? The inclusion of observations attesting to Marlowe's violent nature would seem, in a sense, beside the point, and – especially in an age where masculine aggression was apparently quite common – a rather potent and credible expansion of context by a witness who knew Marlowe well.

10 Riggs, *The World of Christopher Marlowe*, 4.

11 Bloom, *The Anxiety of Influence*, xxviii.

12 Debora Shuger, *The Renaissance Bible*, 4.

13 Although "cultural materialism" is often viewed as emerging (within literary studies) in tandem with new historicism in the 1980s, it is difficult to see the former as in any way eclipsed. As David Hawkes observes, "A majority of today's literary critics take the basic assumptions of materialism for granted, although their application of these tenets varies

considerably. 'Cultural materialism' … continues to thrive within literary studies" ("Against Materialism in Literary Theory," 244).

14 I confess to a personal interest in the anti-Trinitarianism that emerges so decisively in early modern culture. As Nigel Smith observes, "it represented the revival of an ancient idea that had been demonized as heresy in the early church, a demonization reaffirmed by the Reformation churches … Anti-Trinitarianism was more pervasive and spread more diversely in Europe and in England than any other single unorthodox view. It was seemingly everywhere and came from every quarter" ("'And if God was one of us'," 160]. While such ubiquity has begun to receive increasing attention from scholars of the later Renaissance, this heresy's earlier manifestations in the sixteenth century remain I believe under-examined.

15 Consider a seminal expression of this tendency: in identifying praxis, the "single most important concept of material analysis," Jonathan Dollimore writes, "It is a concept which severs the connection between individuality and man, between subjectivity and the human condition. Consequently it rejects the 'tragic' belief in a human essence which by its own nature as well as its relation to the universal order of things, must inevitably suffer" (*Radical Tragedy*, 157).

16 A significant, more recent case in point emerges in Charles Taylor's critique of Foucault: "I already have raised the question of whether or not Foucault really does away with freedom … There are all sorts of ways in which power can be inscribed in a situation in which both dominators and dominated are caught up … But power needs targets. Something must be imposed on someone if there is to be domination. Perhaps that person also is helping to impose it on himself, but then there must be an element of fraud, illusion, false pretenses involved in this. Otherwise it is not clear that the imposition is in any sense an exercise of domination" ("Foucault on Freedom and Truth," 172).

17 An emphasis on Christian morality ironically seems at times the source of psychological inefficacy, as well as unpragmatic evasiveness, in orthodox positions. For example, in *Spiritual Discourse and the Meaning of Persons*, Patrick Grant argues that "The injunction of the Great Commandment [to love your neighbour as yourself] is effected through transfiguration – the mutual and simultaneous liberation, that is, of one's self and of the other, in which the transformative power of personal agency is disclosed" (9–10). Throughout this study, focused (as are my own interests) on personhood within Western spiritual traditions, I search with some frustration for a sufficient emphasis on the *establishment* of personal agency before the achievement of its "transformative power"; that is, the book's argument is not just underwritten but potentially undermined through its recurring

appeal to mystical self-surrender or self-transcendence. Without rigorous self-integration, an obsession with self-transcendence remains, I suspect, often gratuitous or fantastical. I include this response to clarify that my own work challenges the assumptions of subjective "inadequacy" on the part of both cultural materialists, on the one hand, and theologically orthodox critics, on the other. Such a project appears to me increasingly pressing at this cultural moment.

18 Benson, *Heterodox Shakespeare*, 139, quoting Shell, *Shakespeare and Religion*, 235.
19 Knapp, *Shakespeare's Tribe*, 120.

1. Theological Contexts: Grace, Individualism, and Agency

 1 Jackson and Marotti, "The Turn to Religion in Early Modern Studies," 182.
 2 Beckwith, "Stephen Greenblatt's *Hamlet* and the Forms of Oblivion," 262.
 3 Cox, "Was Shakespeare a Christian, and If So, What Kind of Christian Was He?," 544.
 4 Kastan, *A Will to Believe*, 4, 10.
 5 Ibid., 35–6.
 6 Lupton, "Paul Shakespeare," 214, 216.
 7 Kneidel, *Rethinking the Turn to Religion*, 8.
 8 Lupton, "Paul Shakespeare," 232, 218.
 9 Stephen Westerholm, *Israel's Law and the Church's Faith*, 3.
10 Unless otherwise indicated, all biblical quotations are from the Geneva Bible (facsimile of the 1560 edition).
11 Armstrong, *A History of God*, 87.
12 Wilson, *Jesus*, 256.
13 Hirschfeld, *The End of Satisfaction*, 73. Elaine Pagels partly exonerates Paul as instigator of the doctrine of Original Sin, arguing that Augustine misread the Greek text of Romans 5:12: "'Through one man … sin entered the world, and through sin, death; and thus death came upon all men, *in that* … all sinned.'" Mistakenly Augustine "insisted that it meant that 'death came upon all men, *in whom* [that is, in Adam] all sinned'" (*Adam, Eve, and the Serpent*, 109). For me, the subtle linguistic argument does not cancel the fact of Paul's claim that Christ "died for our sins," as the only available remedy.
14 Wilson, *Jesus*, 38.
15 Pagels, *Adam, Eve, and the Serpent*, xxiii–xxiv.
16 Žižek, *The Fragile Absolute*, 2.
17 Shuger, "The Reformation of Penance," 557, quoting Dennis Taylor, "Introduction: Shakespeare and the Reformation," 1, 14, 8–9, 14–15.
18 Shuger, "The Reformation of Penance," 558.
19 Ibid., 558, 561.

20 Simpson, "The Reformation of Scholarship," 260.
21 Simpson, *Permanent Revolution*, 1, 9, 9–10.
22 Hirschfeld, *The End of Satisfaction*, 33, 93.
23 Rosendale, *Theology and Agency in Early Modern Literature*, 9.
24 Mathew Martin claims that Marlowe's tragedies are all "trauma narratives," and reminds us that "trauma" is "derived from the Greek word for wound" (*Tragedy and Trauma in the Plays of Christopher Marlowe*, 1]. While Martin pursues his exploration of Marlowe under the Lacanian assumption of "the subject traumatized by the call of the Other" (19), I posit rather a subject gradually encouraged by various others through a sometimes "traumatic" process of maturation.
25 Cefalu, *The Johannine Renaissance in Early Modern English Literature and Theology*, 322.
26 Baines Note quoted from Constance Kuriyama, *Christopher Marlowe*, 219–22.
27 All quotations of Shakespeare in this study are from *The Complete Works of Shakespeare*, 4th edition, ed. David Bevington (New York: Longman, 1997). Quotations of Marlowe are from the following editions: *The Complete Poems and Translations*, ed. Stephen Orgel (New York: Penguin, 2007); *Dido Queen of Carthage* and *The Massacre at Paris*, ed. H.J. Oliver (Cambridge, MA: Harvard University Press, 1968); *Doctor Faustus A- and B-texts (1604, 1616)*, ed. David Bevington and Eric Rasmussen (Manchester: Manchester University Press, 1993); *Edward the Second*, ed. Charles R. Forker (Manchester: Manchester University Press, 1994); *The Jew of Malta*, ed. N.W. Bawcutt (Manchester: Manchester University Press, 1978); *Tamburlaine the Great*, ed. J.S. Cunningham and Eithne Henson (Manchester: Manchester University Press, 1998).
28 Mark Albert Johnston, review of Zysk, *Shadow and Substance*, 277.
29 Roberts, "Marlowe and the Metaphysics of Magicians," 60–1.
30 Zysk, *Shadow and Substance*, chapter 4: "Father Faustus? Confection and Conjuration in *Everyman* and *Doctor Faustus*."
31 Greenblatt, *Renaissance Self-Fashioning*, 210.
32 See my discussion of *The Jew of Malta* in *The Irony of Identity*, 146–53.
33 Purvis F. Boyette, "Wanton Humour and Wanton Poets," 47.
34 Deats, "Myth and Metamorphosis in *Edward II*," 311.
35 Charles R. Forker, Introduction to *Edward the Second*, 99.
36 Hirschfeld, *The End of Satisfaction*, 73.
37 See chapter 2 of *The End of Satisfaction*, "The Satisfactions of Hell: *Doctor Faustus* and the Descensus Tradition."
38 Cummings, *Literary Culture of the Reformation*, 171.
39 Diarmaid MacCulloch, *The Reformation*, 665–6.
40 Cummings, *Literary Culture of the Reformation*, 12.

41 Ibid., 14.

42 Ibid., 29, 52–3.

43 Jennifer Waldron has challenged a traditional critical distinction between a Catholic liturgy of embodiment and the anti-materialist tendencies of Protestantism, by emphasizing the importance of the body in Protestant worship. Yet she significantly argues that "the 'lawful magic' or 'counter-magic' governing the body in this period ... worked from the top downward, with divine agency operating in various ways on the material world." Therefore, historically, antitheatrical charges "drew on the similarities between the lively and natural sacraments of the Protestant church and ... the 'lively and unnatural' phenomenology of the public theatres. Instead of suiting their actions to the Word of God, players suited them to human scripts. And instead of being 'moved by the livelie worke of God' ... theatergoers witnessed a living, somatic art form with origins in the idolatrous human imagination" (*Reformations of the Body*, 60, 73–4). My approach argues for a more heretical thrust in the drama of the period, positing a greater validity to creations of the human imagination, as a *necessary* faculty, not a constantly qualified or corrected one.

44 MacCulloch, *The Reformation*, 96.

45 Cummings, *Literary Culture of the Reformation*, 246, 249–50.

46 Ibid., 257, 256, 258.

47 Pinciss, "Marlowe's Cambridge Years and the Writing of *Doctor Faustus*," 252.

48 Breward, Introduction to *The Work of William Perkins*, 15, 24–5.

49 Cummings, *Literary Culture of the Reformation*, 260.

50 Breward, Introduction to *The Works of William Perkins*, 39.

51 Perkins, *A Treatise of Mans Imaginations*, 459–61, 477.

52 Cummings, *Literary Culture of the Reformation*, 260–1.

53 Tyacke, *Anti-Calvinists*, 246.

54 Like Pinciss, Lars Engle appeals to Arminianism in an attempt to resolve key contradictions in Marlowe's most famous play. He asserts that we must carefully distinguish between Doctor Faustus and *Doctor Faustus*. After observing other significant interrogations of Calvinist predestination during the 1580s and 1590s – including writings by Jacobus Arminius and Samuel Harsnett – Engle concludes, "Marlowe thought through these alternatives, and his Faustus exemplifies someone who is lost among them and who chooses, in effect, to make something creative and temporarily powerful out of the 'curse God and die' option." Although the play portrays "a Calvinist atheist attempting to be a resolute epicurean in an emerging Arminian dispensation," we can still comfortably argue "that Marlowe exemplifies Renaissance individualism and prefigures modern selfhood" ("Marlowe and the Self," 209). While I concur with the final

assertion, I see Faustus psychologically driven by more than epicureanism, and Marlowe driven by something more radical than Arminianism – in fact by Arianism, which I take up in the following section.

55 The best introduction to this incident is still Arthur Freeman, "Marlowe, Kyd, and the Dutch Church Libel."

56 Kuriyama, *Christopher Marlowe*, 217; citing John Bakeless, *The Tragicall History of Christopher Marlowe*.

57 Proctour, *The Fal of the Late Arrian*, sig. C3r, B4v, D2r, J8r–J8v.

58 Ibid., sig. P2r–P2v, P4v.

59 Ibid., sig. P6r. See Elaine Pagels, *Beyond Belief*, 171–81, for a discussion of the rise of the original Arian heresy and the response of the early church at the time of the Council of Nicaea.

60 Proctour, *Fal of the Late Arrian*, sig. R5r–R5v, S3v–S4r.

61 Ibid., sig. D2v–D3v.

62 Riggs, *The World of Christopher Marlowe*, 37, 42.

63 Roy Kendall cites one of the more well-known early modern claims for Marlowe's "atheism": the "Remembraunces of wordes & matter against Ric Cholmeley" by an "unknown informer" states "That he [Cholmeley] saieth & verely beleveth that one Marlowe is able to showe more sounde reasons for Atheisme then any devine in Englande is able to geve to prove devinitie & that Marloe tolde him that hee hath read the Atheist lecture to Sir walter Raliegh & others" (*Christopher Marlowe and Richard Baines*, 244). While early twentieth-century scholarship may have rather fancifully embroidered such suggestions into now discredited speculations regarding a "School of Night," it is interesting to consider possible ideological connections between Raleigh and Marlowe, with respect to their parallel Arian interests. See my *The Irony of Identity*, 30.

64 As when Stephen Greenblatt describes the Renaissance as a time when "it became increasingly possible to turn away from a preoccupation with ... immaterial causes and to focus instead on things of this world" (*The Swerve*, 9–10).

65 Hawkes, "Against Materialism in Literary Theory," 238.

66 Perkins, *A Warning Against The Idolatrie of the last times*, in *The Workes of That Famous and Worthy Minister of Christ ... William Perkins*, 1:673, 673, 675.

67 Shuger, *Habits of Thought in the English Renaissance*, 11.

68 Shuger, *The Renaissance Bible*, 7, 90, 100, 107, 122.

69 Gifford, *A short treatise against the Donatists of England, whome we call Brownists*, sig. A2r–A2v.

70 Ibid., sig. A3r, E2v.

71 Ibid., sig. G3r.

72 Ibid., sig. I4r, I4v.

73 Ibid., sig. L3r.

74 Ibid., sig. K1v.

75 Gifford, *A Plaine Declaration that our Brownists be full Donatists, by comparing them together from point to point out of the writings of Augustine*, sig. I1r.

76 Gifford, *A short treatise against the Donatists*, sig. O2v.

77 Ibid., sig. P2r–P2v.

78 Gifford, *A Treatise of True Fortitude*, sig. B1r–B1v.

79 Ibid., sig. B7r–B7v.

80 Grant, *The Transformation of Sin*, 4–5.

81 McCabe, *Incest, Drama and Nature's Law 1550–1700*, 21.

82 Bacon, *The Wisedome of the Ancients*, 151–3.

83 Shuger, *The Renaissance Bible*, 190.

84 Shuger, *Habits of Thought in the English Renaissance*, 9–10.

85 When I read Richard Webster's *Why Freud Was Wrong*, I find that the often quite compelling argument has, logically, the exact opposite effect of the rhetorically intended one. From a scientific perspective, Freud's methods were of course sometimes highly dubious. The accusation here is that he behaved more like a messianic founder of a new faith than a discoverer of scientific truth; the former is indeed closer to an accurate description, since he so often explored aspects of experience that obviously cannot be scientifically measured or controlled, but are nevertheless crucial to an understanding of the human predicament. As the author of a world-altering mythology, Freud is truly a religious writer. It is hard to think of any individual thinker since Augustine who has more profoundly affected the course of Western history and the way we conceive of ourselves as human beings, with the possible exception of Darwin, who was a scientist in the sense which Freud clearly was not.

86 Shuger, *The Renaissance Bible*, 110–11.

87 I am in this discussion offering a very careful and narrow reading of the evidence for Marlowe's radical theological beliefs. While Roy Kendall's *Christopher Marlowe and Richard Baines* is highly speculative and often labyrinthine in its arguments, it contains much of interest to readers who wish to trace the course of heretical thought in the latter sixteenth century. Most intriguing from the perspective of this study is Kendall's observation that "Four years after Marlowe's death Thomas Beard, Oliver Cromwell's schoolmaster at Huntingdon, wrote [in *The Theatre of Gods Judgements*] that '*Marlin* [marginal note: *Marlow*] ... not only in word blasphemed the trinitie, but also (as it is credibly reported) wrote books against it" (184–5). As Kendall indicates, rumours of such a book or books seem to persist in subsequent years.

88 Honan, *Christopher Marlowe*, 79–81.

89 Graham, Introduction to *Shakespeare and Religious Change*, 2.

90 As I argue in my review of Richard Wilson's *Secret Shakespeare*. Another point I would like to reiterate is my acceptance of the "Spiritual Testament" linking Shakespeare's father John to a secret but staunch Catholicism. I am thus in agreement with Patrick Collinson's response to Colin Burrow's assumption, expressed in the course of the latter's review of Greenblatt's *Will in the World*, that the document discovered in the roof space of John Shakespeare's house in Henley Street in 1757 is "too good to be true": "Sammy Schoenbaum, who provided most of the facts, had his own reservations as to the value of the Borromeo text as evidence of John Shakespeare's Catholicism. I am not so cautious." Commentators will continue to speculate on the nature of Shakespeare's mature religious views; resistance to the idea of his upbringing within a committed Catholic family appears to me a more questionable scholarly prejudice.

91 McAdam, *Magic and Masculinity*, 129–30.

92 Poole, *Radical Religion from Shakespeare to Milton*, chapter 3: "Lewd Conversations: The Perversions of the Family of Love."

93 Marsh, *The Family of Love in English Society, 1550–1630*, 201, 203.

94 Carter, "The Family of Love and Its Enemies," 654, 653.

95 David Loewenstein, for example, describes the sect as "a mystical religious fellowship that provoked strong fears despite their small membership" (*Treacherous Faith*, 176). The gist of Loewenstein's argument nevertheless is that the Family's troubling doctrines were heterodox enough to threaten not only Elizabethan theologians but later Jacobean writers as well, including King James himself.

96 Wootton, "John Donne's Religion of Love," 32. See also Janet Halley's compelling discussion, "Heresy, Orthodoxy, and the Politics of Religious Discourse," which opens with the assertion, "The Family of Love was an important radical spiritualist movement of sixteenth-century Europe and England. Jan van Dorsten calls the Family of Love the 'most controversial and probably the most influential' of the 'unofficial churches' of London."

97 Wootton, "Reginald Scot/Abraham Fleming/The Family of Love."

98 Lake, *The Boxmaker's Revenge*.

99 I find particularly dubious, for example, Wootton's attempt to argue that no "extraordinary sociological insight was necessary to enable Scot to explain witchcraft accusations in terms of a breakdown in charity between neighbours" ("Reginald Scot/Abraham Fleming," 133–4), since his moral sense was clearly guided by the Familist insistence on "the knot of unitie and concord." Fascinating and admirable as Family of Love doctrine is, the sect can hardly have held a monopoly on the insistence of Christian charity in the communities of sixteenth-century England.

100 Ibid., 132.

101 Harsnett's influence on *King Lear* has long been recognized. I discuss such sceptical influences in detail in *Magic and Masculinity*.

102 Anglo, "Reginald Scot's *Discoverie of Witchcraft*, 126–7.

103 Scot, *The discoverie of witchcraft*, 539.

104 Wootton, "Reginald Scot/Abraham Fleming," 122.

105 Healy, *Shakespeare, Alchemy and the Creative Imagination*, 202–3.

106 Marsh, *The Family of Love in English Society*, 23.

107 Ibid., 23–4 (emphasis in original).

108 Wootton, "Reginald Scot/Abraham Fleming," 129.

109 Marsh, *The Family of Love in English Society*, 75.

110 Lake, *The Boxmaker's Revenge*, 110.

111 Carter, "The Family of Love and Its Enemies," 663.

112 Healy, *Shakespeare, Alchemy and the Creative Imagination*, 204; Hamilton, *The Family of Love*, 142.

113 Quoted in Marsh, *The Family of Love in English Society*, 20.

114 Marsh, *The Family of Love in English Society*, 33.

115 Knewstub, *A Confutation of monstrous and horrible heresies, taught by H.N. and embraced of a number, who call themselves the Familie of Love*, sig. 2r, 19v, 26v, 35r.

116 Lasch, *The Minimal Self*, 20.

117 Healy, *Shakespeare, Alchemy and the Creative Imagination*, 209–10.

118 Freud, *Civilization and Its Discontents*, 72–3.

119 McAlindon, *Shakespeare's Tragic Cosmos*, 4–12.

2. *Dido Queen of Carthage, Hamlet,* and the Transformation of Narcissism

1 This traditional assumption has been challenged by Martin Wiggins, who sees *Dido* not as a product of the latter end of Marlowe's university career, but as initially written for the Children of the Royal Chapel: "*Dido* also seems to belong in the London period, and specifically in its first half, before the city's boy companies collapsed in 1590" ("Marlowe's Chronology and Canon," 8).

2 Shepard and Powell, Introduction to *Fantasies of Troy*, 1, 3.

3 Carscallen, "How Troy Came to Spenser," in *Fantasies of Troy*, 15.

4 On this question the essay by J.R. Mulryne and Stephen Fender, "Marlowe and the 'Comic Distance'," is still highly pertinent and still frequently cited.

5 Crowley, "Arms and the Boy," 408–10.

6 Ibid., 428–30; citing Bowers, "Hysterics, High Camp, and *Dido Queene of Carthage*," 98.

7 Mathew Martin also sees a Calvinist connection, asserting that *Dido* "explores an experience analogous to the experience Calvin … claimed

to be at the heart of Christian faith: responding to God's call without mediation" (1), but proceeds to mount a Derridean analysis, arguing that "Calvin would not have completely agreed with Derrida's description of faith" ("Pious Aeneas, False Aeneas," 1, 3).

8 See my *The Irony of Identity*, 67–8, for a discussion of the ambiguity of the wall imagery in the play.

9 Crowley, "Arms and the Boy," 429.

10 Shuger, *Habits of Thought in the English Renaissance*, 223, n. 20. Shuger cites a "recent study in cross-cultural psychology [which] seems to corroborate the existence of maternal qualities in Christian symbolizations of the father and God."

11 Interestingly, Shuger in *Habits of Thought* observes that "Even Calvin's *Institutes*, a work not known for its sentimental warmth, consistently associates fathers with pity and nurturing care" (222), but this position is not quite consistent with her reading of "the contrast between the harsh patriarch and the desolate child" in the English Calvinist passion narratives in *The Renaissance Bible*, 111. It is an interesting historical question whether forms of English Calvinism promoted by Perkins and his contemporaries were fundamental in the progressive "hardening" of the patriarchal role in subsequent societies, at least those influenced by these particular developments in Calvinist theology.

12 Dawson, "Priamus Is Dead: Memorial Repetition in Marlowe and Shakespeare," 75.

13 Nevertheless M.L. Stapleton's *Marlowe's Ovid* certainly deserves mention here, especially in its treatment of the "humorous amorality" of Barabas, who "embodies the Ovidian persona with whom his creator was the most intimately acquainted, the glib, delusional, and self-aggrandizing young lover in the *Amores* whose hundreds of lines he translated into English" (205).

14 Crowley, "Arms and the Boy," 436.

15 Wells, *Shakespeare on Masculinity*, 207, 2.

16 See, for example, my review of Alan Shepard's *Marlowe's Soldiers*.

17 Black, "Hamlet Hears Marlowe," 18–19.

18 Mathew Martin's reading suggests this potential is effectively contained: "Virgil's Aeneas turns trauma into a moral exemplum that substantiates rather than ruptures ethics and provides a continuity between past and present fully in keeping with the epic's ... teleological perspective" ("Pious Aeneas, False Aeneas," 11).

19 McAdam, *The Irony of Identity*, 49–57.

20 Dawson, "Priamus Is Dead," 73.

21 Perhaps not surprisingly, I have much sympathy with Avi Erlich's challenge to Freud's Oedipal reading of *Hamlet*: "Hamlet has a highly specific conflict

deriving not so much from his desire to have killed his father but rather from his *lack* of a strong father" (*Hamlet's Absent Father*, 23).

22 Quoted in R. Chris Hassel, "Frustrated Communion in *The Merchant of Venice*," 23.

23 Shuger, *The Renaissance Bible*, 107, quoting Calvin.

24 Black, "Hamlet Hears Marlowe," 20.

25 Ibid., 23–4, 21.

26 As in Robert Logan's *Shakespeare's Marlowe*. Logan observes that "If Marlowe is interested in capturing the intense power of Dido's love, Shakespeare is interested in conveying the elusive sources of Cleopatra's ability to captivate" (172).

27 The title page of the 1594 edition of the play states that it was acted by the Children of Her Majesty's Chapel. The production of *Dido* at Shakespeare's Globe Theatre in 2003, directed by Tim Carroll, rather fittingly set the action in a children's playground, which not only suggested that the human actors were playthings of the God but more importantly emphasized the narcissistic motivations of the tragic heroes themselves.

28 Black, "Hamlet Hears Marlowe," 25.

29 See my description, *The Irony of Identity*, 50.

30 Black, "Hamlet Hears Marlowe," 25.

31 Wilson, "'The words of Mercury'," 51.

32 Wilson's emphasis on the "aesthetic" might suggest parallels between the term I have chosen, "imaginative agency," and the "instrumental aesthetics" that Genevieve Guenther employs in her reading of Renaissance texts concerned with magical expression: "Rewriting the Renaissance commonplace that literature should teach and delight, [key Renaissance] texts suggest that literature teaches *by delighting*: that literary pleasure itself produces ... normative ethical and social effects in readers and spectators. Taking my cue from Sidney – who writes that poetry is an 'instrumental cause' of virtue, 'the ending end of earthly learning' – I adopted the phrase *instrumental aesthetics* to identify this theory of efficacious beauty and the poetic and theatrical practices it motivated." One of Guenther's first critical moves is to observe that "Sidney sounds almost exactly like Cornelius Agrippa" (*Magical Imaginations*, 4). The term "imaginative agency" suggests that this concept can apply more broadly to literature not directly concerned with magical processes; moreover, my concept ultimately implies, I think, a greater degree of voluntary agency.

33 Bloom, *The Anatomy of Influence*, 48–9.

34 *King John* seems to me a significant artistic expression or development of this principle, as chapter 4 will explore.

35 All quotations are from Virgil, *Aeneid*, trans. Robert Fitzgerald (New York: Vintage Books, 1984).

36 Lewis, *The Allegory of Love*. Interestingly, Virgil is one of the figures to whom Lewis imagines we would now have trouble explaining the doctrine of romantic love as an ennobling passion (3). In spite of the surprising depth of passion experienced between Aeneas and the shade of Creusa, she is conveniently evacuated from the plot of the *Aeneid* to make way for the purely dynastic connection with the cypher Lavinia in Italy.

37 This idea is in essence the *raison d'être* of Renaissance dramatic art. Anne Barton offers a succinct formulation in her discussion of Ben Jonson: "Playing shapes reality, not because it is an agent of deceit and imposture … but because it is a way of uncovering and articulating hidden emotional truths" (*Ben Jonson, Dramatist*, 226).

38 Hiscock, "'What's Hecuba to him …'," 163, 170.

39 Nietzsche, quoted in the introduction to *The Victorian Novel*, ed. Harold Bloom (New York: Chelsea House, 2004), 8.

40 According to Courtney Bailey Parker, this textual moment – as an allusion to "Christ's command to the disciples at the Last Supper" – has "produced a maelstrom of arguments surrounding Eucharistic themes in *Hamlet*," and her brief article offers a helpful survey of significant recent treatments ("'Remember Me'").

41 Dover Wilson, *What Happens in Hamlet*, 86.

42 Greenblatt, *Hamlet in Purgatory*, 45.

43 Ibid., 44.

44 Martin, "The Family of Love in England," 105.

45 Greenblatt, *Hamlet in Purgatory*, 66.

46 Shuger, *The Renaissance Bible*, 110–11.

47 Calvin quoted in Shuger, *The Renaissance Bible*, 107.

48 Gillies, "The Question of Original Sin in *Hamlet*," 397.

49 Hirschfeld, "Hamlet's 'First Corse'," 424, 436.

50 Ibid., 446.

51 Gillies, "The Question of Original Sin in *Hamlet*," 398.

52 Perry, "*Imitatio* and Identity," 375.

53 Ibid., 401–2.

54 Ibid., 402.

55 Dover Wilson, *What Happens in Hamlet*, 57, 58.

56 Pollard, "What's Hecuba to Shakespeare?," 1061, 1063.

57 See my *The Irony of Identity*, 154.

58 Pollard, "What's Hecuba to Shakespeare?," 1063, 1066.

59 Ibid., 1075.

60 Ibid., 1065.

61 Ibid., 1087–8.

62 Mathew Martin also at least anticipates this idea when he argues that the actor playing Aeneas in 2.2 "seeks to translate trauma's emotive force into

a community of empathetic witnesses who along with him rail against Hecuba's misfortune" ("*Translatio* and Trauma," 319–20).

63 Sweetnam, "*Hamlet* and the Reformation of the Eucharist," 20–1.

64 That consideration is certainly not insignificant, and unsurprisingly highlighted in Hieronimo's famous and self-conflicted "*Vindicta mihi!*" soliloquy within *The Spanish Tragedy* (3.13).

65 Pollard, "What's Hecuba to Shakespeare?," 1087, 1085.

66 Relationships frequently considered in this light include Lear-Cordelia, Prospero-Miranda, and Pericles-Marina. Perhaps more unusually, Robert Darcy considers the potential for at least symbolic incest between Shylock and Jessica, and Portia and her dead father, in "Freeing Daughters on Open Markets." Here again the portrayal of quasi-incestuous passion between Barabas and Abigail in *The Jew of Malta* – particularly in the balcony scene (2.1) where Abigail restores her father's riches – may have served as a model.

67 Adelman, *Suffocating Mothers*, 10.

68 Bowers, "Hysterics, High Camp, and *Dido Queene of Carthage*," 105.

69 In my reading experience, the most natural and persuasive (as opposed to factitious or ambivalent) heterosexual passion in Shakespeare is expressed by female for male characters: for example, Juliet for Romeo, and Rosalind for Orlando.

70 The viability of political self-fashioning may carry in this case progressive, even revolutionary tendencies of early modern masculinity, the germ of which Shakespeare perceives in Marlowe. Patrick Cheney observes that "At the end of *Dido*, when the queen prophesies the 'revenge' of Hannibal against Rome, Marlowe re-routes republican discourse, using the anti-imperial general to critique not simply the imperial Virgil but also imperial England (with its myth of Roman origin) and finally Elizabethan England's Virgilian epicist, Spenser" (*Marlowe's Republican Authorship*, 96).

71 Potter, "Shakespeare, Marlowe, and the Fortunes of Catharsis," 295.

72 Potter, "Marlowe's *Dido* and the Staging of Catharsis," and "Ekphrastic Catharsis."

73 Potter, "Shakespeare, Marlowe, and the Fortunes of Catharsis," 288.

74 Sinfield, "Hamlet's Special Providence," 97.

75 Kerrigan, *Hamlet's Perfection*, 144–5.

76 Ibid., 150.

3. Marlowe and Shakespeare's Early Histories: The Attenuation of Grace

1 McAdam, *Magic and Masculinity in Early Modern English Drama*, 97.

2 Freebury-Jones, "Those Who Think Marlowe Co-Wrote Plays with Shakespeare May Kyd Themselves." Gary Taylor and his colleagues at

the *New Oxford Shakespeare* have fostered an important school of critics celebrating Shakespeare's entrance into "the era of Big Data" (Taylor, qtd. in Daniel Pollack-Pelzner, "The Radical Argument of the New Oxford Shakespeare"). This school argues not only for Marlowe's co-authorship of the *Henry VI* plays but also for Shakespeare's part-authorship of *Arden of Faversham*. These developments have led to a notably acrimonious debate between the Taylor and the Brian Vickers camps of early modern authorship attribution studies. See my review of Rory Loughnane and Andrew J. Powers, eds., *Early Shakespeare, 1588–1594*, a collection in which Taylor provides a significant concluding discussion. I offer here a somewhat less neutral stance concerning questions of Marlowe's co-authorship and other attribution arguments: in my opinion, subsequent articles by (especially) Freebury-Jones cast serious doubts on some of the claims of the Taylor school, as well as offering convincing evidence for enlarging the Kyd canon to include *Arden*. Regarding Marlowe's co-authorship in the first tetralogy, readers may consult Freebury-Jones, "Exploring Co-Authorship in *2 Henry VI*," and "Did Shakespeare Really Co-Write *2 Henry VI* with Marlowe." Regarding the increasing recognition of Kyd's influence and importance within the development of early modern drama, see "Kyd and Shakespeare" and "The Diminution of Thomas Kyd." Freebury-Jones has also co-authored an important article with Marcus Dahl that offers a somewhat broader critique of some of the more doubtful aspects of current computerized textual analysis: "The Limitations of Microattribution." Freebury-Jones and Dahl ultimately favour "Albert Yang, Chung-Kang Peng, and Ary L. Goldberger's conclusion, based on word rank order and frequency analysis, that 'the authorship of these early Shakespeare [history] plays cannot be attributed to Marlowe, but at the same time, support the hypothesis that Marlowe did have an important influence on Shakespeare's works during this formative phase of his career'" (479–83). This seems a reasonable claim on which to settle. Nevertheless, I am hopeful that my argument in this chapter can accommodate or absorb readers of various persuasions regarding specific authorship. Clearly in these plays the artistic projects of Marlowe and Shakespeare are closely related and to some extent intertwined.

3 Forker, Introduction to *Edward the Second*, 17.

4 Freebury-Jones asserts, "There is firm evidence that Shakespeare added scenes to *Henry VI Part One*, which was originally written by Thomas Nashe and Thomas Kyd for Lord Strange's Men in order to, as E.K. Chambers put it in 1930, 'exploit an earlier theme which had been successful' with Shakespeare's audiences." Freebury-Jones enlists readings by both Martin Wiggins and Brian Vickers in support of this claim

("Did Shakespeare Really Co-Write 2 *Henry VI* with Marlowe," 138). My own scepticism admittedly at times extends indiscriminately to the competing camps of attribution scholars, and I wonder why Shakespeare's surviving colleagues did not scruple to include a play in the First Folio which contained, apparently, only a few scenes by the late playwright, unless Shakespeare's revisions really were extensive. Gary Taylor has attempted to dismiss this reservation: "We might normally go so far as to claim that Shakespeare had the *main* hand [in plays included in the First Folio]: this premise might explain both the exclusion of *Pericles* and *The Two Noble Kinsmen* and the inclusion of *All is True, Timon of Athens*, and *Macbeth*. But the 'Henry VI' plays do not constitute a 'normal' case" ('Shakespeare and Others," 147). I also seem to represent a critical school of one in my lingering impression that the beginning of 2 *Henry VI* seems a very odd and awkward moment in this particular story to begin what was originally a two-part play by Shakespeare, which then (according to the argument) encouraged the later composition of Nashe and Kyd's play.

5 I continue to believe, for reasons offered in *The Irony of Identity* (see p. 266, n.1), that *The Massacre* preceded *Edward II* and served in a sense as an inspiration for it.

6 For a helpful summary about the general consensus that *Dido* predates *Tamburlaine*, including a consideration of critical challenges to this chronology, see Ruth Lunney, "*Dido, Queen of Carthage*," 15–16. In *The Irony of Identity* I offered a psychological rationale for this direct artistic link, "Tamburlaine [as] a compensatory figure for the weak and uncertain Aeneas" with confirmation in object-relations psychoanalysis: "the movement from *Dido* to *Tamburlaine* reflects an 'important rule [Heinz] Kohut draws attention to: 'When [potentially] higher forms of adaptation fail, then the grandiose self emerges'" (73).

7 Greenblatt, *Renaissance Self-Fashioning*, 212–13.

8 See my discussion "Calvinism and the Problematic of Character in *The Revenger's Tragedy*."

9 Streete, *Protestantism and Drama in Early Modern England*, 213.

10 C.L. Barber and Richard P. Wheeler, *The Whole Journey*, 1–3.

11 Ibid., 8–9.

12 Van Es, *Shakespeare in Company*, 21–2, 23.

13 Knapp, *Shakespeare's Tribe*, 121.

14 Reid, "Spenser and Shakespeare," 108–9.

15 For a major exploration of this theme, see Patrick Cheney, *Marlowe's Counterfeit Profession*.

16 Taylor, "Forms of Opposition," 310.

17 Patterson, *Reading Holinshed's* Chronicles, xii–xiii.

18 Gatti, *The Renaissance Drama of Knowledge*, 15.

19 Lethbridge, "Introduction," 15.

20 Miller, "Temperance, Interpretation, and 'the bodie of this death'," 376.

21 Romany and Lindsey, eds., *Christopher Marlowe: The Complete Plays*, 570.

22 Oliver, ed., *Dido Queen of Carthage*, 32–3.

23 Miller, "Temperance, Interpretation, and 'the bodie of this death'," 377–8.

24 Ibid., 378.

25 Spenser, *The Faerie Queene*, ed. A.C. Hamilton (London: Longman, 1977).

26 Miller, "Pauline Allegory," 380.

27 Ibid., 379.

28 Hamilton, ed., *The Faerie Queene*, 180.

29 See Oliver's edition, 29–30.

30 MacFaul, *Problem Fathers in Shakespeare and Renaissance Drama*, 14.

31 MacFaul, *Poetry and Paternity in Renaissance England*, 98–9.

32 Kenneth Borris has opposed the critical tendency to insist on a sharp ideological distinction between the orders of grace and nature, and the experiences of books 1 and 2 of *The Faerie Queene*, by reading Alma's Castle in book 2 as not just a portrayal of "the natural body" but of "the mystical body" as well. Nevertheless this reading still appears to me to replicate the Pauline problem: "Maleger's forces continue to threaten Alma's household, as befits the unremitting spiritual warfare attributed even to renovated human nature during life, as in Romans 7:22–24" ("Flesh, Spirit, and the Glorified Body," 32–3). Borris also briefly considers how "Spenser's notions of the body's potential for sanctity seem to produce his own Protestant erotics" (43) in the description of Amoret in the Temple of Venus, towards the end of book 4. While Marlowe is generally assumed to have read the first three books of Spenser's epic in manuscript during the late 1580s, it is perhaps more problematic to assume when, or if, he read books 4 to 6, not published until three years after his death. As MacFaul observes, "The 1590 *Faerie Queene*, until [the hermaphroditic union of Scudamour and Amoret in the final, cancelled stanzas] is rather sexless" (*Poetry and Paternity*, 115).

33 Debora Shuger, "'Gums of Glutinous Heat' and the Stream of Consciousness," 6.

34 Miller, "Temperance, Interpretation, and 'the bodie of this death'," 382.

35 Ibid., 385.

36 See Vivien Thomas and William Tydeman, eds., *Christopher Marlowe*, 69–70.

37 John Blanpied sees in the awkward stichomythic exchange between Talbot and his son an incongruous potential for comedy: "By the logic of metatheater, Talbot is 'entrapped' because he is trappable – that is, because he embodies the static and exhausted order" ("'Art and Baleful Sorcery'," 222).

38 For a broader discussion of this irony, see my *Magic and Masculinity*, 52–5.

39 Michael Taylor, ed., *Henry VI Part One*, 213, n. 55.

40 Pagels, *Beyond Belief*, 70.

41 Ibid., 73.

42 Marlowe, if he made this claim, clearly echoes the language of John 13:23, whose erotic suggestiveness does seem ironically confirmed by the rather anxiously corrective gloss in the Geneva Bible: "Their facio[n] was not to sit at table, but hauing their shoes of, and cusshions vnder their elbowes, leaned on their sides, as it were half lying." Marlowe was not the only heretic in history to reputedly make such a claim. Another example is Francesco Calcagno (1528–1550), a Franciscan friar executed for blasphemy and sodomy under the Venetian Inquisition.

43 Cheney, *Marlowe's Counterfeit Profession*, 125.

44 The logic of this identification, although not unanimous among scholars, is for me persuasive, as Spenser intends at this point in book 1 a contrast with Lucifera, or carnal pride.

45 "A Letter of the Authors to Sir Walter Raleigh," in *The Faerie Queene*, ed. Hamilton, 737.

46 Guy, *Elizabeth*, 60–4.

47 "A Letter … to Sir Walter Raleigh," 738.

48 Cheney's distinction between an "imperial" Spenser and a "subversive" Marlowe leads him into a complex engagement with Richard Helgerson's argument in *Forms of Nationhood* that both Spenser and Marlowe actually engage in "an involuntary (and sometimes not so involuntary) lèse-majesté" against monarchical control (Cheney, *Marlowe's Counterfeit Profession*, 19, citing Helgerson, *Forms of Nationhood*).

49 McAdam, *The Irony of Identity*, 104–7.

50 See McAdam, *Magic and Masculinity*, 104–8.

51 Ibid., 119.

52 Warren, "Textual Introduction," *Henry VI Part Two*, 92.

53 Rutter, "*Hamlet*, Pirates, and Purgatory," 125–6.

54 Warren, "Introduction," *Henry VI Part Two*, 50, quoting Brockbank, "Shakespeare: His Histories, English and Roman," in *English Drama to 1710*, ed. C. Ricks, Sphere History, 3 (London: Sphere Books, 1971), 172.

55 John Blanpied, *Time and the Artist in Shakespeare's English Histories*, 56.

56 McAdam, *The Irony of Identity*, 175–6.

57 See my discussion, "The Failure of Carnal Identity," in *The Irony of Identity*.

58 See John Jowett, "Johannes Factotum."

59 Forker, Introduction to *Edward the Second*, 34.

60 The terms within Forker's judgment regarding true religious significance could in fact be reversed. As James Shapiro argues, "In veering away from a drama of national and political concerns, Marlowe retains … a sense of the sacredness of kingship, one that Shakespeare's plays deconstruct so effectively. This very sacredness, however, intensifies the

power of the destructive impulses: the echo of Edward's horrid scream at Kenilworth lasts long after the production ends" (*Rival Playwrights*, 95, citing Philip Edwards, *Threshold of a Nation* [Cambridge: Cambridge University Press, 1979], 54–65).

61 *Edward II*, dir. Derek Jarman (British Screen and BBC Films, 1992). To these lines Jarman's voice-over adds, "I know not; but of this am I assured, / That death ends all, and I can die but once" (5.1.151–2), and finally, "Come, death, and with thy fingers close my eyes, / Or if I live, let me forget myself" (110–11), as if death and self-dissolution are all that remain to be desired.

62 As in Katharine Eisaman Maus, *Inwardness and Theater in the English Renaissance*, 28. See my review article, "Renaissance Inwardness and Current Critical Practice," for a general resistance to this assumption, via an appeal to object-relations psychoanalysis.

4. The Shadow-King: Shakespeare's Development of Humanist History in *Richard III, Edward III,* and *King John*

1 Adelman, *Suffocating Mothers*, 1–2.

2 See Joanne Craig, "'All Flesh Doth Frailtie Breed',' " for an interesting and succinct introduction to problematic mothers in Spenser. Craig observes, "For all Spenser's interest in the female and the feminine, not least the royal reader to whom *The Faerie Queene* is addressed, the poem reveals deep anxiety about women's sexuality. This anxiety manifests itself in a series of threatening figures that are simultaneously mothers, mistresses, and queens, and, as if in response to those figures, in a series of fantasies of origin that struggle unsuccessfully to minimize or *even altogether to exclude* the contamination of maternity" (16, my emphasis).

3 My argument in favour of a significant "break" between the first three and the last play of the first tetralogy receives some support from Stanley Wells and Gary Taylor, who observe, "Critics have always agreed that the play post-dates *Contention* and *Richard Duke of York* [2 and 3 *Henry VI*]; as Mincoff astutely argued, the remarkable difference in dramatic power and stylistic control between *Richard Duke of York* and *Richard III* suggests that the latter did not immediately follow completion of the former. In particular, Mincoff suggested that the tragic structure and Senecan detail of *Richard III* owed much to Shakespeare's composition of *Titus* in the interim" (*William Shakespeare: A Textual Companion*, 115). I will briefly take up the possible significance of *Titus* later in this chapter.

4 Hammond, ed., *King Richard III*, 110.

5 Marie-Hélène Besnault and Michel Bitot, "Historical Legacy and Fiction," 118.

6 Skura, *Shakespeare the Actor and the Purposes of Playing*, 64–73.

7 John Jowett, Introduction to *Richard III*, 28.

8 Ibid., 28–9.

9 See Jowett, ed., *Richard III*, 350, n. 34.

10 Although one in which Paul is finally referred to as "the Apostle" rather than as "Saint." Does Shakespeare wish finally to emphasize Paul's apostolic career rather than his mediating role as saint?

11 Dover Wilson, *What Happens in Hamlet*, 56.

12 Berger, "Conscience and Complicity in *Richard III*," 415.

13 Bevington, *Complete Works of Shakespeare*, 938.

14 Lukas Erne speaks persuasively about the Kydian influence on Shakespeare in general: "[Shakespeare's] second tragedy, *Romeo and Juliet*, did what only Kyd's *Soliman and Perseda* among extant plays had done before on the public stage, namely to place a conflict of love at the centre of a tragedy [although this claim rather undercuts the potentially 'tragic' status of Marlowe's *Edward II*]. His third tragedy, *Julius Caesar*, covers the same period of Roman history as Kyd's *Cornelia*, and Shakespeare's Brutus may well owe something to Kyd's. Finally, the chief source of Shakespeare's fourth tragedy, *Hamlet*, is undoubtedly Kyd's work of the same name" (*Beyond* The Spanish Tragedy, 5).

15 Farah Karim-Cooper, "Introduction," 1.

16 The identification of the playwright as George Peele is carefully argued in Charles R. Forker's Revels edition of the play.

17 This argument is expanded in my discussion *"The Spanish Tragedy* and the Politico-Religious Unconscious."

18 Moschovakis, "'Irreligious Piety' and Christian History," 461.

19 Ibid., 468, 467.

20 Ibid., 469.

21 Forker, ed., *The troublesome reign of John, King of England*, 9.

22 Mathew Martin, Introduction to George Peele, *David and Bathsheba* (Manchester: Manchester University Press, 2018), 47.

23 Ibid., 16.

24 Barret, "Chained Allusions, Patterned Futures, and the Dangers of Interpretation in *Titus Andronicus*," 454, 477–8.

25 Moschovakis, "'Irreligious Piety'," 484.

26 Christopher Marsh, *The Family of Love in English Society, 1550–1630*, 22–3.

27 Christopher Hill, *Milton and the English Revolution*, 75.

28 Kyd, *The Spanish Tragedy*, ed. Philip Edwards (London: Methuen, 1959).

29 See Snow, "*Doctor Faustus* and the Ends of Desire."

30 Vickers, "The Two Authors of *Edward III*." Albert C. Yang has recently employed an "information categorization method" which supports this joint attribution to Kyd and Shakespeare ("Validating the Enlarged Kyd Canon").

31 "Acknowledgements for the Second Edition," *The Riverside Shakespeare*, vii. All quotations of *Edward III* are from this edition.

32 J.J.M. Tobin, in ibid., 1732.

33 Ibid., 1733.

34 Both playwrights' interest in Edward III may in fact have been piqued by Holinshed. As Annabel Patterson observes, "If one were to rely on Holinshed alone, one would assume that parliamentary sessions in the reign of Edward III were exclusively focused on taxation." But the narrative of taxation in this case highlights the successful resistance of the Commons to "evill guidance by evill officers" around the king. The successful resolution of the conflict "applies the practice of negotiation established by Magna Carta to a broader fiscal sphere, where access to the country's tax revenues can be traded in return for the resolution of grievances; and it also ... identifies the Commons as the source of initial resistance, whose language, as Holinshed reports it, was far from deferential" (*Reading Holinshed's* Chronicles, 111–12).

35 Womersley, *Divinity and State*, 145.

36 As Tom MacFaul observes, in *Problem Fathers in Shakespeare and Renaissance Drama*, 67.

37 Hamilton, *Shakespeare and the Politics of Protestant England*, 31.

38 Klause, "New Sources for Shakespeare's *King John*," 426; Wilson, *Secret Shakespeare*; Shell, "Why Didn't Shakespeare Write Religious Verse?"

39 Weimann, "Mingling Vice and 'Worthiness' in *King John*," 111.

40 Lane, "'The sequence of posterity'," 467.

41 Hamilton, *Shakespeare and the Politics of Protestant England*, 39.

42 There John says to Hubert, "*Hubert* keepe him [Arthur] safe, / For on his life doth hang thy Soveraignes crowne, / But in his death consists thy Soveraignes blisse" (part 1, 1119–21). All quotations of *The Troublesome Raigne* are from Geoffrey Bullough, ed., *Narrative and Dramatic Sources of Shakespeare*.

43 Piesse, "*King John*: Changing Perspectives," 134.

44 See Lane, "'The sequence of posterity'," 470.

45 Weimann, "Mingling Vice and 'Worthiness'," 128–9.

46 Barber and Wheeler, *The Whole Journey*, 240, 241.

47 Bevington, *Complete Works of Shakespeare*, 684.

48 Piesse, "*King John*: Changing Perspectives," 130–1.

49 Braunmuller, Introduction to *King John*, 50–1.

50 Womersley, "The Politics of Shakespeare's *King John*," 509.

51 Deborah Curren-Aquino argues that contradictory and unheroic elements "make the play very much at home in a century that has known existentialism and the absurd, and moved from the order of new criticism to the indeterminacy of deconstruction." "Introduction: *King John* Resurgent," 14.

52 Womersley, "The Politics of Shakespeare's *King John*," 510.
53 Belsey, *The Subject of Tragedy*, 42.
54 Womersley, "The Politics of Shakespeare's *King John*," 514.
55 Hamilton, *Shakespeare and the Politics of Protestant England*, 42–3.
56 See Alexandra Walsham, "William Hackett."
57 Klause, "New Sources for Shakespeare's *King John*," 407–8.
58 Hamilton, *Shakespeare and the Politics of Protestant England*, 32.
59 Stephen Greenblatt's description, on the back blurb of Wilson, *Secret Shakespeare*; and Wilson, *Secret Shakespeare*, 198.
60 Quoted in Klause, "New Sources for Shakespeare's *King John*," 405.
61 *The Troublesome Raigne* contains two references to an overwhelming flood, versions of which Shakespeare retains: when the Bastard admits that "our troupes … Passing the Washes with our carriages, / The impartiall tyde deadly and inexorable … swallowed up the most of all our men" (part 2, 831–5); and when the Messenger informs the French army that all their reinforcements from France were lost "on the Goodwin sands" (part 2, 962).
62 Christopher Marsh, *The Family of Love in English Society*, 20.
63 Jones, "A Straying Collective," 90.
64 Niclaes, *Terra pacis a true testification of the spiritual land of peace, or the heavenly city of Jerusalem*, 107–9. *Terra Pacis* was available in an English translation as early as 1575.
65 Jones, "A Straying Collective," 92–3; Niclaes, *Terra Pacis*, 167.
66 Halley, "Heresy, Orthodoxy, and the Politics of Religious Discourse," 310.
67 Lane, "'The sequence of posterity'," 478.
68 Nick de Somogyi, *Shakespeare's Theatre of War*, 103–4, 6.
69 Anonymous, *A Myrrour for English Souldiers*, sig. E2r.
70 Lane, "'The sequence of posterity'," 481, 480.
71 Braunmuller, Introduction to *King John*, 41–3.
72 Braunmuller, "*King John* and Historiography," 321.
73 Ibid., 314.
74 Gina Bloom, "Words Made of Breath," 140.

5. The Containment of Marlovian Homoeroticism in the Later Shakespeare

1 Lake, *How Shakespeare Put Politics on the Stage*, 245–6. The suggestion that the incontestably legitimate Richard "systematically destroys" his own legitimacy raises a striking aporia in the text, or at least in the critical commentary on it. Lake must, early in his commentary on the play, take significant issue with the argument of another notably perceptive critic: his assertion that the play "is very careful to demonstrate with almost

forensic clarity just how and why Richard is guilty of tyranny" (238) carries a footnote clarifying how he finds himself "entirely at odds with Debora Shuger's claim that while other Elizabethan renditions of the reign concentrate on the details of 'Richard's misgovernment', in Shakespeare's account 'the question … is left hopelessly murky'" (Shuger, "'In a Christian Climate'," 40–1). This remarkable disagreement between a first-rate historian and a first-rate critic may arguably be resolved in favour of Lake, after a careful sifting of the relevant textual evidence; but I want nevertheless to explore the curious evasiveness of the dramatic presentation that Shakespeare offers here, which I think Shuger's reading highlights.

2 Dawson and Yachnin, Introduction to *Richard II*, 37.

3 Bevington and Rasmussen, for example, comment on the Old Man's speech in *Doctor Faustus* A-text, at 5.1.55: "Although Revelation v.8 speaks of 'golden vials full of odours, which are the prayers of saints', most images of vials in that apocalyptic book are instruments of divine vengeance," and offer nine examples (*Doctor Faustus A- and B-texts*, 188).

4 Hirschfeld, "Hamlet's 'First Corse'."

5 For a survey of such response, see chapter 6 of Logan's *Shakespeare's Marlowe*.

6 Logan, *Shakespeare's Marlowe*, 83.

7 Irish, "Writing Woodstock," 132, 134.

8 Corbin and Sedge, Introduction to *Thomas of Woodstock, or Richard the Second, Part One*, 4.

9 Irish, "Writing Woodstock," 136, 137.

10 Peter Ure, Introduction to *King Richard II*, xxxv.

11 Corbin and Sedge, Introduction to *Woodstock*, 7. Ure makes a good case for *Woodstock* as predating *Richard II*: "It is of course more likely that Shakespeare remembered the word because it is repeated so often in the other play than that the author of *Woodstock* expanded the single reference in *Richard II* into so abundant a treatment in his own work" (xxxviii).

12 Corbin and Sedge, Introduction to *Woodstock*, 37.

13 Dawson and Yachnin, Introduction to *Richard II*, 26.

14 Michael Egan successfully refutes Macdonald P. Jackson's attribution of the play to Samuel Rowley, but does not make a persuasive case for his own attribution to Shakespeare (see "Did Samuel Rowley Write *Thomas of Woodstock?*"). I do not feel the play stylistically recalls any of the early 1590s playwrights (Marlowe, Kyd, Peele, Shakespeare) talented enough to have written this fairly accomplished text. It does, nevertheless, contain deeply persistent, genuinely felt Catholic references that suggest either a Catholic playwright or one sympathetic to that theological position – and it does so in spite of its anti-monarchical, anti-absolutist subtext, which is perhaps subtly aimed at the contemporary Protestant monarchy.

15 Ure, Introduction to *King Richard II*, xxxvi, xxxiv.
16 Menzer, "c.f. Marlowe," 118, 126.
17 Corbin and Sedge, Introduction to *Woodstock*, 156.
18 Skura, "Marlowe's *Edward II*," 47.
19 It is admittedly necessary at this critical juncture to defend Skura's overriding assumption that Marlowe in *Edward II* is certainly interested in the "touch of men's bodies" in a sodomitical sense. The debate has largely centred on the actual staging of Edward's death. As Simon Shepherd argues, "that spit, as Stephen Orgel so sensibly points out, is a critical fantasy ... 'we want the murder to be precisely what Marlowe refuses to make it ... the mirror of Edward's unspeakable vice'" (Shepherd, "A Bit of Ruff," 114; quoting Orgel, *Impersonations*, 48). In a recent contribution to this debate, Christopher Shirley asserts, "The indeterminacy of Edward's murder, signaled by a lack of stage direction describing it, invades the rest of the play, thus demonstrating sodomy's supplementarity as a categorical descriptor and an epistemological construct" ("Sodomy and Stage Directions in Christopher Marlowe's *Edward(s) II*," 283), an argument in which the contested critical point perhaps threatens to dissolve in jargon. On this point I defend what Shirley describes as the most editorially extreme decision of Charles Forker's, who "offers an almost pornographically detailed solution" (Shirley, "Sodomy and Stage Directions," 280) in the stage direction he inserts in the Revels edition. While editors may seem irresponsible to assume that "everyone knows" how Edward died, Elizabethan historiographers comment carefully on the horrific nature of the murder, not just Holinshed – to which Marlowe's play clearly alludes at 5.5.30–3 ("get me a spit, and let it be red hot ... What else? A table and a featherbed") – but also in Richard Grafton's *Chronicle at large and mere History of the affayres of Englande* (1569), as Forker points out (63–5). Moreover, as I observed in *The Irony of Identity*, Julia Briggs has commented "on the 'striking parallels' developed in a 'notorious' Catholic League pamphlet by Jean Boucher entitled *Histoire tragique et mémorable de Pierre de Gaveston*, published in July 1588. Boucher in his preface 'makes explicit' the analogy between Gaveston and Epernoun, both corrupters of kings, and warns Henry III of Edward's fate, who died impaled upon 'une brouche rouge de feu' ... It seems likely that the parallel drawn by Boucher prompted Marlowe, for his subsequent [and last] dramatic endeavor, to turn to Holinshed in order to investigate the details of Edward's reign" (McAdam, *The Irony of Identity*, 266, n. 1; quoting Briggs, "Marlowe's *Masssacre at Paris*," 264). Scholars often comment on Marlowe's unusual choice of the unpromising nature of the reign of Edward II for his history play; surely homoerotic interest played a key role in this decision. Moreover, the horrifically emblematic nature of Edward's death

is consistent with not only Marlowe's penchant for the literalization of metaphor in his work but also his imaginative concern with the reification of Christian morality. It is not "we" but Marlowe who wanted Edward's murder to mirror his "unspeakable vice," although he anticipated postmodern reception in asserting an irony so powerful that it inverts the moral significance which gives rise to it.

20 Skura, "Marlowe's *Edward II*," 47, 49, 50.

21 Neill, ed., *Othello, the Moor of Venice*, 357, n. 24.

22 Tuggle, "'Barbary' in *Henry IV, Part 1*."

23 Shuger, "'In a Christian Climate'," 42.

24 The observation of Jeffrey Masten upon consideration of a series of entries from Florio's Italian-English *A Worlde of Wordes* is relevant here: "The hierarchical, transitive quality of the verb *fuck* is obviously enough still with us (erased though it is by the *OED*'s glossing of it as to 'have sexual intercourse with [a person]'), and it is echoed in the usage of the now-obsolete (but etymologically hazy) terms *jape, sard,* and *swive*" (*Queer Philologies*, 103–4).

25 See Leonard Barkan, "Diana and Actaeon."

26 As I have traced in *Magic and Masculinity*, especially chapter 2, "Puritan Magic in *Doctor Faustus*," and chapter 4, "Shakespeare's Comic Actaeon and the Turn to Tragedy."

27 Potter, "The Antic Disposition of Richard II," 33.

28 Constance Kuriyama, *Hammer or Anvil*, 181.

29 Quoted in Adrian Streete, *Protestantism and Drama in Early Modern England*, 213.

30 Skura, "Marlowe's *Edward II*," 51.

31 Kuriyama, *Hammer or Anvil*, 208–9.

32 McAdam, *The Irony of Identity*, 217.

33 Admittedly what I call "emotionally stifled" can prove fodder for postmodern theoretical approaches. Donovan Sherman's "'What more remains?'" through its very title suggests an approach related to mine, but comes close to virtually embodying every critical tendency I have been contesting in this study. Sherman employs Pauline theology to trace the paradoxical process whereby "Richard exposes a form of grace inherent to a well-executed failure of performance" (47). The argument does, however, lead to a striking admission when it contrasts Richard's behaviour with the "more … resolutely representative logic … emblematized … by Bolingbroke. On the surface, the suggestion that compulsively irrelevant processes articulate anything radical is absurd, since as a result of this irrelevance the very notions of space and time must become unstitched from their roles in ensuring a knowable future" (35–6).

34 Donaldson, "Conflict and Coherence," 46.

35 Dawson and Yachnin, Introduction to *Richard II*, 36–7.

36 Stanivukovic, "'Kissing the Boar'," 103.
37 I explore more fully both the influence of Marlowe on Shakespeare in this case and the intersection of the religious and sexual themes in Shakespeare's controversial play in two articles: "*The Jew of Malta* and *The Merchant of Venice*" and "Eucharistic Love in *The Merchant of Venice*." I begin the latter essay with a consideration of Alan Bray's treatment of the tradition of sworn brotherhood in late medieval society, in which "the mass provided a familiar culmination for the creation of ritual 'brothers,' a ritual complete in their taking Holy Communion together" (*The Friend*, 25).
38 These are also explored in Bray's *The Friend*. See previous note.
39 Berger, "On the Continuity of the *Henriad*," 229, 231.
40 The most helpful discussion remains D.J. Palmer, "Casting Off the Old Man."
41 Poole, "Saints Alive! Falstaff, Martin Marprelate, and the Staging of Puritanism"; later revised as a chapter in *Radical Religion from Shakespeare to Milton*.
42 Christopher Carter, "The Family of Love and Its Enemies," 654.
43 Quoted in Peter Lake, *The Boxmaker's Revenge*, 110.
44 Groves, "Hal as Self-Styled Redeemer," 240, 245, 248.
45 Jones, "A Straying Collective," 91; Niclaes, *Terra Pacis*, 31.
46 Niclaes, *Terra Pacis*, 122.
47 Groves, "England's Jerusalem in Shakespeare's Henriad," 99.
48 Halley, "Heresy, Orthodoxy, and the Politics of Religious Discourse," 309.
49 Groves, "England's Jerusalem," 88, 87, 88.
50 Ibid., 92; quoting Barbara Lewalski, *Protestant Poetics and the Seventeenth-Century Religious Lyric*, 131–2.
51 Groves, "England's Jerusalem," 90.
52 Hawkins, "Virtue and Kingship in Shakespeare's *Henry IV*," 324–5.
53 Niclaes, *Terra Pacis*, 38–9, 40–1.
54 Palmer, "Casting Off the Old Man," 283.
55 Halley, "Heresy, Orthodoxy, and the Politics of Religious Discourse," 305, 307.
56 I must also admit an incongruity between the spiritual masculinity of the Family of Love and the often martial masculinity of Shakespeare's history plays. As Halley relates, a Familist sect in Surrey "did prohibite bearing of weapons, but at the length perceiuing them selues to be noted and marked for the same, they haue allowed the bearing of staues." One contemporary critic of this sect "objected that Niclaes's ... pacifist utopia placed in question the magistrate's right to the sword and, with it, all magistracy." Halley argues: "Obliged to resume bearing weapons, the Familists double the possible meanings of the act – it can now mean either submission to or protest against a weaponed prince – and thus render it illegible, meaningless in the sheer surplus of meaning" ("Heresy, Orthodoxy, and the Politics of Religious Discourse," 319–20). To excuse this incongruity of pacifist and military expression, it is tempting to return to the suggestion

in chapter 2 that the martial masculinity within Shakespeare's plays constitutes, on some level, a form of "imaginative agency," a largely symbolic realization of necessary masculine assertiveness.

57 Jones, "A Straying Collective," 144.

58 Halley, "Heresy, Orthodoxy, and the Politics of Religious Discourse," 306.

59 Findlay, "Renaissance Pederasty and Pedagogy," 229.

60 Although its origins lie in classical Greece, complex manifestations of this link in the early modern period are explored by Alan Stewart in chapter 3 of *Close Readers: Humanism and Sodomy in Early Modern England*. This application of a classical paradigm complicates traditional, and psychoanalytic, readings of the second tetralogy focusing on father-son relationships with more recent concerns to delineate classical friendships between men of approximately equal status. A comprehensive treatment of the tradition of *amicitia*, Laurie Shannon's *Sovereign Amity* explores the political and sociological ramifications of the idealized union between two friends in the Renaissance as constituting a "private sovereignty." This argument is relevant here since it takes up the monarch not merely as a metaphor for friendship; Shannon observes how an actual monarch's commitment to *amicitia* can lead to the scandal of *mignonnerie* – dependency on minions – if he fails to subordinate his desires to the good of the realm. In Shannon's simultaneous consideration of Marlowe's *Edward II* and Shakespeare's *Henriad*, this potential "scandal" seems ultimately contained, since the latter work functions as an ideological and psychological reversal of the former, with its depiction of the fatal lack of mutual discipline between Edward and Gaveston (159). Nevertheless, Shannon says surprisingly little about homoeroticism in her treatment of the *Henriad* as a reversal of *Edward II*.

61 Findlay, "Renaissance Pederasty and Pedagogy," 229, 230.

62 Groves, "England's Jerusalem," 95.

63 Nardizzi, "Grafted to Falstaff and Compounded with Catherine," 151.

64 Findlay, "Renaissance Pederasty and Pedagogy," 231.

65 Shannon, *Sovereign Amity*, 168.

66 Findlay, "Renaissance Pederasty and Pedagogy," 233–4; quoting Fineman, *Shakespeare's Perjured Eye* (Berkeley: University of California Press, 1987), 2, 21.

67 Coleman, *Drama and the Sacraments in Sixteenth-Century England*, 119.

68 Stanivukovic, "'Kissing the Boar'," 99.

69 Ibid., 91.

70 Ibid., 88.

71 McAdam, *The Irony of Identity*, 89–90.

72 Brian Gibbons, "Unstable Proteus," 45–6.

73 Taylor, ed., *Henry V*, 91–2, nn. 6–8.

74 Altman, "'Vile Participation'," 19–20.

75 Shuger, *The Renaissance Bible*, 110–11.

76 See Christopher Marsh, *The Family of Love in English Society*, 59. The particular assertion here is certainly not limited to proponents of the Family of Love. In *Magic and Masculinity* (213–14) I considered the interesting treatise with the running title "Puritanisme the Mother, Sinne the Daughter, or A treatise, wherein is demonstrated from Twenty severall Doctrines and Positions of *Puritanisme*; That the *Fayth* and *Religion* of the *Puritans*, doth forcibly induce its Professours to the perpetrating of sinne, and doth warrant the committing of the same" (STC 4264). Although it was published in 1633, in response to the discovery in London in 1632 of a "Society of certaine Sodomites," I argued that the author of the main tract, "B.C.," was likely the Catholic convert Benjamin Carrier (1566–1614), an almost exact contemporary of Shakespeare's. One of Carrier's most notable claims in this treatise is to accuse some of the major figures of the Reformation, such as Beza and Calvin, of sodomy; this linkage is reflected in Shakespeare's association of Falstaff, originally named after the Lollard (and therefore proto-Puritan) martyr Oldcastle, with the image of the "grotesque Puritan" identified by Poole.

77 Shapiro, *A Year in the Life of Shakespeare*, 197.

78 Ibid., 136.

79 Nicholl, *The Reckoning*, 65–7, 17.

80 Ibid., 75–6.

81 Cheney, "'The Passionate Shepherd to His Love' and *Hero and Leander*," 164.

82 Ellis, *Sexuality and Citizenship*, 94–5.

83 Ibid., 4, 7.

84 Ibid., 89–90; quoting William Sheidley, "'Unless It Be a Boar': Love and Wisdom in Shakespeare's *Venus and Adonis*," *Modern Language Quarterly* 35 (1974): 14.

85 Ellis, *Sexuality and Citizenship*, 105, 104; citing Leonard, "Marlowe's Doric Muse," 64–5.

86 Ellis, *Sexuality and Citizenship*, 105.

87 Ibid., 108.

88 Claude J. Summers, "*Hero and Leander*," 134.

89 Ellis, *Sexuality and Citizenship*, 99.

90 Logan, *Shakespeare's Marlowe*, 56.

91 DiGangi, "Queering the Shakespearean Family," 271.

92 Quoted in ibid., 272.

93 Shapiro, *A Year in the Life of Shakespeare*, 219.

94 Schwartz, "Rosalynde among the Familists."

95 Ibid., 71, 73, 74, 73.

96 See Paul Dean, "'Nothing that is so is so'," 282–3.

97 See Stephen Guy-Bray, *Homoerotic Space*, especially 12–18.

98 This idea has also occurred to Stanivukovic. See "Beyond Sodomy," 58.

Conclusion: Shakespearean Resolutions

1 For example, Jim Ellis's configuration of the epyllion as a genre instigating, as part of a cultural movement, the metamorphosis of sexuality across a range of early modern male writers certainly implies a broader context for this inauguration of "phallic" masculinity and a containment of the homoerotic affect to which humanist explorations of classical texts had given rise, or (perhaps more accurately) facilitated.

2 See Stanivukovic, "Beyond Sodomy," 42–3.

3 Even a critic whose queer theoretical credentials are as impeccable as Jeffrey Masten's seems at times to drift back towards a more essentialist position; for example, when he discusses Marlowe: "I think, in this modern cultural context, that it has been *strategically* useful and indeed intellectually productive for scholarship and pedagogy to experience the generative irritant of at least one playwright from this period who has seemed *in some sense* to cohere with a modern conception of 'homosexuality.'" Another example, although perhaps not as obviously, arises when he discusses Kyd: "'All excellent thinges are rare,' declares the marginal gloss on this sentence in the 1577 translation [of Cicero's *De Amicitia*], and in this context, Kyd's rare love or familiar friendship with Marlowe [from whom he desperately but duplicitously, it is implied, tries to distance himself in the letters to Puckering] begins to look not only rare (unusual) but also rare (valuable, excellent)" – this from a man whose "circle of relations … seems to have been largely extrafamilial" and who "has already admitted to consorting with Marlowe" (*Queer Philologies*, 151–2, 90, 96, 92, emphasis in original).

4 Bray, *Homosexuality in Renaissance England*: "To talk of an individual in this period as being or not being 'a homosexual' is an anachronism and ruinously misleading. The temptation to debauchery, from which homosexuality was not clearly distinguished, was accepted as part of the common lot, be it never so abhorred" (16–17).

5 Stanivukovic, "Beyond Sodomy," 57–8.

6 Wraight, *In Search of Christopher Marlowe*, 66–8.

7 Stanivukovic, "Beyond Sodomy," 54, 49.

8 Especially in chapters 5 and 6 of *Magic and Masculinity in Early Modern English Drama*, "Magic and Nature in the Later Shakespeare," and "*Macbeth* and the Jacobean Witchcraft Plays."

9 Logan, *Shakespeare's Marlowe*, 171.

10 Steane, *Marlowe*, 59.

11 Adelman, *The Common Liar*, 77.

12 Neill, Introduction to *Anthony and Cleopatra*, 13; quoting John Bayley, *Shakespeare and Tragedy* (London, 1981), chapter 5, "Determined Things: The Case of the Caesars."

13 Hamlin, *The Bible in Shakespeare*, 214–15.

14 Neill, ed., *Anthony and Cleopatra*, 271.

15 Hamlin, *The Bible in Shakespeare*, 222–3.

16 Ibid., 223.

17 Neill, ed., *Anthony and Cleopatra*, 219, n. 3.1.

18 Ibid., 231, nn. 17–18.

19 See Harold Fisch, *The Biblical Presence in Shakespeare, Milton, and Blake*, chapter 1 "*Julius Caesar*: Stones or Men?," 3–34.

20 Plutarch, "The Life of Marcus Antonius," 283.

21 Horton, "The Seven Deadly Sins and Shakespeare's Jacobean Tragedies," 249.

22 Neill, ed., *Anthony and Cleopatra*, 166, nn. 68–9.

23 Egan, *Green Shakespeare*, 111.

24 As Bruce Bartlett observes, "The reason why Egypt retained its special economic system and was not allowed to share in the general economic freedom of the Roman Empire is that it was the main source of Rome's grain supply. Maintenance of this supply was critical to Rome's survival, especially due to the policy of distributing free grain (later bread) to all Rome's citizens which began in 58 B.C." ("How Excessive Government Killed Ancient Rome," 289).

25 There may be further reasons for the playwright noting this translation other than an interest in Plutarch. Katherine Duncan-Jones identifies Holland as the "Most prolific and talented" of the three Warwickshire writers (in addition to Shakespeare) mentioned in Thomas Fuller's *History of the Worthies of England* (*Ungentle Shakespeare*, 4–5).

26 Plutarch, *The philosophie, commonlie called, the morals written by the learned philosopher Plutarch of Chaeronea*, trans. Holland, 232.

27 The phrase G. Wilson Knight applies to his central discussion of *Antony and Cleopatra* in *The Imperial Theme* (London: Methuen, 1931).

28 Stewart, *Character and Motive in Shakespeare*, 35.

29 Such a possibility, admittedly problematic in the face of my reading of the pure "naturalness" of homoerotic desire, certainly recurs elsewhere in Shakespeare; in the romances, repeatedly. I touch on this recurrence in "Magic and Gender in Late Shakespeare," 249–54. Richard McCabe's *Incest, Drama and Nature's Law 1550–1700* contains an interesting chapter on Shakespeare which concludes, "The tragic Shakespearean family, unlike its ancient analogues, meets its fate in the conflicting forces of its own emotional bonding rather than the operation of hostile gods. Activating the fragile faultlines of those relationships, the recurrent problem of incestuous desire threatens the foundations of the entire social edifice" (189–90).

30 Guy-Bray, *Homoerotic Space*, 245, n. 42.

31 Schwartz, "Leontes' Jealousy in *The Winter's Tale*," 252–3; quoting C.L. Barber, "'Thou that begett'st him that did thee beget'," 65.

32 Aristotle, "The Poetics," 102.

33 As in, for example, Catherine Belsey's *Shakespeare and the Loss of Eden*.

34 Guy-Bray, *Homoerotic Space*, 215.

35 Orgel, ed., *The Winter's Tale*, 160, n. 22.

36 "Blest" originates in an Old English verb meaning to "mark or consecrate with blood," suggesting a necessary sacrifice.

37 Diehl, "'Does not the stone rebuke me?'," 81.

38 Ibid., 82.

39 Schwartz's complex reading in *"The Winter's Tale*: Loss and Transformation" perhaps offers a clue to the ironic nature of Paulina's Pauline status. She initially "assumes the role of the maternal superego" (147). Her first attempts to rebuke Leontes fail, since she "is imagined to contain precisely that aspect of feminine power Leontes sought to eject magically in the image of the spider [2.1.39–45], the power to render him passive and to overwhelm him psychically … To accept Paulina's truth would be to equate himself with his feminine issue, to contradict his masculine ego. But … Leontes must be 're-created' before he can accept so radical re-definition of himself" (149–50).

40 In another treatment of Shakespearean sexual politics, Guy-Bray argues that the plays "present heterosexuality as something that is made up, rather than as something that is an essence or as something that the characters naturally do." *The Winter's Tale, Twelfth Night*, and especially *The Two Gentlemen of Verona* demonstrate that "heterosexuality is clearly culture rather than nature, and it takes a great deal of work." While Guy-Bray and I would probably agree on the "naturalness" of homoerotic desire, a fully integrated subjectivity involves much more than a recognition of desire. For decades now I have been arguing that something that "takes a great deal of work" cannot be invalidated or categorically dismissed as a tyrannical construct on those grounds alone. At any rate, this claim appears to contradict Guy-Bray's later assertion, "If masculinity is not inherent but rather something that can be put on like a garment" – a not uncommon claim in postmodern discourse, but one (in this formulation at least) rendered highly questionable or problematic almost everywhere in early modern literature – "then heterosexuality and homosexuality themselves cannot be stable categories" ("Shakespeare and the Invention of the Heterosexual," para. 5, 19). The instability of either heterosexuality or homosexuality does not arise I think from the facility of their imposition.

41 Ernest Schanzer, ed., *The Winter's Tale* (Harmondsworth: Penguin, 1969), 7.

42 Nicholl, *The Reckoning*, 70.

43 Ibid., 69.

44 András Kiséry has added some interesting observations concerning Thorpe's dedication to Blount. Kiséry identifies the bookmart in St. Paul's as the "bookshop at the sign of the Black Bear," which "occupied what before the Reformation had been the charnel house of the cathedral," a fact which lingered in London's cultural memory until well into the seventeenth century ("Companionate Publishing, Literary Publics, and the Wit of Epyllia," 170). In the same collection, Sarah Wall-Randell, building on Kiséry's observations, notes the appropriateness of situating "Thorpe's invocation of Marlowe's ghost … within an awareness of the many uneasy [pre-Reformation] spirits to whom those dispersed bones belonged, who might be wandering among the bookshops of the churchyard in 1600 without a resting place" ("Marlowe's Lucan," 13). But Kiséry also notes that Thorpe "announces an act of necromancy, raising this *Lucan* 'in the circle of [Blount's] Patronage'" (170). Kiséry relates this image to the men's professional and commercial connections; but I suggest that the "close intimacy between Thorpe and Blount" (171) that he observes carries (further) erotic potential. The act of necromancy in the dedication seems a homoerotic version of a recurring magical-erotic motif in early modern literature, as when Mercutio taunts Romeo, "'Twould anger him / To raise a spirit in his mistress' circle / Of some strange nature, letting it there stand / Till she had laid it and conjur'd it down" (2.1.24–7). Since Thorpe, as Wall-Randell reminds us, "would later become the publisher of Shakespeare's *Sonnets*" (12) in 1609, there emerges another reason for Shakespeare's musing, or brooding, on Marlowe shortly before the composition of *The Winter's Tale*.

Bibliography

Adelman, Janet. *The Common Liar: An Essay on "Antony and Cleopatra."* New Haven: Yale University Press, 1973.

– *Suffocating Mothers: Fantasies of Maternal Origin in Shakespeare's Plays, Hamlet to The Tempest.* New York: Routledge, 1992.

Altman, Joel B. "'Vile Participation': The Amplification of Violence in the Theater of *Henry V.*" *Shakespeare Quarterly* 4 (1991): 1–32.

Anglo, Sydney. "Reginald Scot's *Discoverie of Witchcraft*: Scepticism and Sadduceeism." In *The Damned Art: Essays in Literature and Witchcraft*, edited by Sydney Anglo, 106–39. London: Routledge and Kegan Paul, 1977.

Anonymous. *A Myrrour for English Souldiers.* London: Nicholas Ling, 1595. STC 10418.

Anonymous. *Thomas Woodstock, or Richard the Second Part One.* Edited by Peter Corbin and Douglas Sedge. Manchester: Manchester University Press, 2002.

Anonymous. "The Troublesome Raigne of King John." In *Narrative and Dramatic Sources of Shakespeare*, edited by Geoffrey Bullough. Vol. 4. London: Routledge and Kegan Paul, 1962.

Aristotle. "The Poetics." In *The Harcourt Brace Anthology of Drama*, 2nd ed., edited by W.B. Worthen. Fort Worth: Harcourt Brace 1996.

Armstrong, Karen. *A History of God: The 4000-Year Quest of Judaism, Christianity, and Islam.* New York: Knopf, 1993.

Bacon, Francis. *The Wisdome of the Ancients.* Translated by Arthur Gorges. London: John Bill, 1617. STC 1130.

Bakeless, John. *The Tragicall History of Christopher Marlowe.* Cambridge, MA: Harvard University Press, 1942.

Barber, C.L. "'Thou that begett'st him that did thee beget': Transformation in *Pericles* and *The Winter's Tale.*" *Shakespeare Survey* 22 (1969): 59–67.

Barber, C.L., and Richard P. Wheeler. *The Whole Journey: Shakespeare's Power of Development.* Berkeley: University of California Press, 1986.

Barber, Rosalind. "Was Marlowe a Violent Man?" In *Christopher Marlowe the Craftsman: Lives, Stage, and Page*, edited by Sarah K. Scott and M.L. Stapleton, 47–59. Farnham and Burlington: Ashgate, 2010.

Barkan, Leonard. "Diana and Actaeon: The Myth as Synthesis." *English Literary Renaissance* 10 (1980): 317–59.

Barrett, J.K. "Chained Allusions, Patterned Futures, and the Dangers of Interpretation in *Titus Andronicus*." *English Literary Renaissance* 44 (2014): 452–85.

Bartlett, Bruce. "How Excessive Government Killed Ancient Rome." *Cato Journal* 14 (1994): 287–303.

Barton, Anne. *Ben Jonson, Dramatist*. Cambridge: Cambridge University Press, 1984.

Bayley, John. *Shakespeare and Tragedy*. London: Routledge, 1981.

Beckwith, Sarah. "Stephen Greenblatt's *Hamlet* and the Forms of Oblivion." *Journal of Medieval and Early Modern Studies* 33 (2003): 261–80.

Belsey, Catherine. *Shakespeare and the Loss of Eden: Construction of Family Values in Early Modern Culture*. New Brunswick, NJ: Rutgers University Press, 1999.

– *The Subject of Tragedy: Identity and Difference in Renaissance Drama*. London: Methuen, 1985.

Benson, Sean. *Heterodox Shakespeare*. Madison: Fairleigh Dickinson University Press, 2017.

Berger, Harry. "Conscience and Complicity in *Richard III*." In *Richard III: Norton Critical Edition*, edited by Thomas Cartelli, 400–17. New York: Norton, 2009.

– "On the Continuity of the *Henriad*." In *Shakespeare Left and Right*, edited by Ivo Kamps, 225–40. New York: Routledge, 1991.

Besnault, Marie-Hélène, and Michel Bitot. "Historical Legacy and Fiction: The Poetical Reinvention of King Richard III." In *The Cambridge Companion to Shakespeare's History Plays*, edited by Michael Hattaway, 106–25. Cambridge: Cambridge University Press, 2002.

Black, James. "Hamlet Hears Marlowe; Shakespeare Reads Virgil." *Renaissance and Reformation* 18, no. 4 (1994): 17–28.

Blanpied, John. "'Art and Baleful Sorcery': The Counterconsciousness of *Henry VI, Part I*." *Studies in English Literature* 15 (1975): 213–27.

– *Time and the Artist in Shakespeare's English Histories*. Newark: University of Delaware Press, 1983.

Bloom, Gina. "Words Made of Breath: Gender and Vocal Agency in *King John*." *Shakespeare Studies* 33 (2005): 125–55.

Bloom, Harold. *The Anatomy of Influence: Literature as a Way of Life*. New Haven: Yale University Press, 2011.

– *The Anxiety of Influence*. 2nd ed. New York: Oxford University Press, 1997.

– *Shakespeare: The Invention of the Human*. New York: Riverhead Books, 1998.

Borris, Kenneth. "Flesh, Spirit, and the Glorified Body: Spenser's Anthropomorphic Houses of Pride, Holiness, and Temperance." *Spenser Studies* 15 (2001): 17–52.

Bowers, Rick. "Hysterics, High Camp, and *Dido Queene of Carthage*." In *Marlowe's Empery: Expanding His Critical Contexts*, edited by Sara Munson Deats and Robert A. Logan, 95–106. Newark: University of Delaware Press, 2002.

Boyette, Purvis F. "Wanton Humour and Wanton Poets: Homosexuality in Marlowe's *Edward II*." *Tulane Studies in English* 22 (1977): 33–50.

Braunmuller, A.R. "*King John* and Historiography." *English Literary History* 55 (1988): 309–32.

Bray, Alan. *The Friend*. Chicago: University of Chicago Press, 2003.

– *Homosexuality in Renaissance England*. London: Gay Men's Press, 1982.

Briggs, Julia. "Marlowe's *Massacre at Paris*: A Reconsideration." *Review of English Studies* 34 (1983): 257–78.

Bullough, Geoffrey, ed. *Narrative and Dramatic Sources of Shakespeare*, vol. 4. London: Routledge and Kegan Paul, 1962.

Burrow, Colin. "Who Wouldn't Buy It?" Review of Stephen Greenblatt, *Will in the World*. *London Review of Books* 27, no. 2 (20 January 2005).

Carrier, Benjamin. *Puritanisme the Mother, Sinne the Daughter*. [St. Omer: English College Press], 1633. STC 4264.

Carscallen, James. "How Troy Came to Spenser." In *Fantasies of Troy: Classical Tales and the Social Imaginary in Medieval and Early Modern Europe*, edited by Alan Shepard and Stephen D. Powell, 15–38. Toronto: Centre for Reformation and Renaissance Studies, 2004.

Carter, Christopher. "The Family of Love and Its Enemies." *Sixteenth Century Journal* 37 (2006): 651–72.

Cefalu, Paul. *The Johannine Renaissance in Early Modern English Literature and Theology*. Oxford: Oxford University Press, 2017.

Cheney, Patrick. *Marlowe's Counterfeit Profession: Ovid, Spenser, Counter-Nationhood*. Toronto: University of Toronto Press, 1997.

– *Marlowe's Republican Authorship: Lucan, Liberty, and the Sublime*. Basingstoke and New York: Palgrave Macmillan, 2009.

– "'The Passionate Shepherd to His Love' and *Hero and Leander*." In *Christopher Marlowe at 450*, edited by Sara Munson Deats and Robert A. Logan, 163–99. Farnham: Ashgate, 2015.

Coleman, David. *Drama and the Sacraments in Sixteenth-Century England: Indelible Characters*. Basingstoke: Palgrave Macmillan, 2007.

Collinson, Patrick. Letter in response to Colin Burrow's "Who Wouldn't Buy It?". *London Review of Books* 27, no. 3 (3 February 2005).

Coolidge, John S. *The Pauline Renaissance in England: Puritanism and the Bible*. Oxford: Clarendon Press, 1970.

Cox, John D. "Was Shakespeare a Christian, and If So, What Kind of Christian Was He?" *Christianity and Literature* 55 (2006): 539–66.

Craig, Joanne. "'All Flesh Doth Frailtie Breed': Mothers and Children in *The Faerie Queene*." *Texas Studies in Literature and Language* 42 (2000): 16–32.

Crowley, Timothy D. "Arms and the Boy: Marlowe's Aeneas and the Parody of Imitation in *Dido, Queen of Carthage*." *English Literary Renaissance* 38 (2008): 408–38.

Cummings, Brian. *Literary Culture of the Reformation: Grammar and Grace*. Oxford: Oxford University Press, 2002.

Curren-Aquino, Deborah. "Introduction: *King John* Resurgent." In *King John: New Perspectives*, edited by Deborah Curren-Aquino, 11–26. Newark: University of Delaware Press, 1989.

Darcy, Robert. "Freeing Daughters on Open Markets: The Incest Clause in *The Merchant of Venice*." In *Money and the Age of Shakespeare: Essays in New Economic Criticism*, edited by Linda Woodbridge, 189–200. New York: Palgrave Macmillan, 2003.

Dawson, Anthony B. "Priamus Is Dead: Memorial Repetition in Marlowe and Shakespeare." In *Shakespeare, Memory, and Performance*, edited by Peter Holland, 63–84. Cambridge: Cambridge University Press, 2006.

Dean, Paul. "'Nothing that is so is so': *Twelfth Night* and Transubstantiation." *Literature & Theology* 17 (2003): 281–97.

Deats, Sara Munson. "Myth and Metamorphosis in Marlowe's *Edward II*." *Texas Studies in Literature and Language* 22 (1980): 304–21.

De Somogyi, Nick. *Shakespeare's Theatre of War*. Aldershot: Ashgate, 1998.

Diehl, Huston. "'Does not the stone rebuke me?': The Pauline Rebuke and Paulina's Lawful Magic in *The Winter's Tale*." In *Shakespeare and the Cultures of Performance*, edited by Paul Yachnin and Patricia Badir, 69–82. Aldershot: Ashgate, 2008.

DiGangi, Mario. "Queering the Shakespearean Family." *Shakespeare Quarterly* 47 (1996): 269–90.

Dollimore, Jonathan. *Radical Tragedy: Religion, Ideology, and Power in the Drama of Shakespeare and His Contemporaries*. Chicago: University of Chicago Press, 1984.

Donaldson, Peter S. "Conflict and Coherence: Narcissism and Tragic Structure in Marlowe." In *Narcissism and the Text: Studies in Literature and the Psychology of Self*, edited by Lynne Layton and Barbara Ann Schapiro, 36–63. New York: New York University Press, 1986.

Downie, J.A. "Marlowe: Facts and Fictions." In *Constructing Christopher Marlowe*, edited by J.A. Downie and J.T. Parnell, 13–29. Cambridge: Cambridge University Press, 2000.

Duncan-Jones, Katherine. *Ungentle Shakespeare: Scenes from His Life*. London: Arden Shakespeare, 2001.

Egan, Gabriel. *Green Shakespeare: From Ecopolitics to Ecocriticism*. London: Routledge, 2006.

Egan, Michael. "Did Samuel Rowley Write *Thomas of Woodstock*?" *The Oxfordian* 10 (2007): 1–20.

Ellis, Jim. *Sexuality and Citizenship: Metamorphosis in Elizabethan Erotic Verse*. Toronto: University of Toronto Press, 2003.

Engle, Lars. "Marlowe and the Self." In *Christopher Marlowe in Context*, edited by Emily C. Bartels and Emma Smith, 202–11. Cambridge: Cambridge University Press, 2013.

Erlich, Avi. *Hamlet's Absent Father*. Princeton: Princeton University Press, 1977.

Erne, Lukas. *Beyond* The Spanish Tragedy: *A Study of the Works of Thomas Kyd*. Manchester: Manchester University Press, 2001.

Findlay, Heather. "Renaissance Pederasty and Pedagogy: The 'Case' of Shakespeare's Falstaff." *Yale Journal of Criticism* 3 (1989): 229–38.

Fisch, Harold. *The Biblical Presence in Shakespeare, Milton and Blake: A Comparative Study*. Oxford: Clarendon Press, 1999.

Freebury-Jones, Darren. "Did Shakespeare Really Co-Write *2 Henry VI* with Marlowe?" *ANQ: A Quarterly Journal of Short Articles, Notes, and Reviews* 30, no. 3 (2017): 137–41.

– "The Diminution of Thomas Kyd." *Journal of Early Modern Studies* no. 8 (2019): 251–77.

– "Exploring Co-Authorship in *2 Henry VI*." *Journal of Early Modern Studies* no. 5 (2016): 201–16.

– "Kyd and Shakespeare: Authorship versus Influence." *Authorship* 6, no. 1 (2017): 1–24.

– "Those Who Think Marlowe Co-Wrote Plays with Shakespeare May Kyd Themselves." *The Independent*, 25 October 2016. www.indpendent.co.uk /arts/those-who-think-marlowe- cowrote-plays-with-shakespeare-may -kyd-themselves-a7379961.html.

Freebury-Jones, Darren, and Marcus Dahl. "The Limitations of Microattribution." *Texas Studies in Literature and Language* 60 (2018): 467–95.

Freeman, Arthur. "Marlowe, Kyd, and the Dutch Church Libel." *English Literary Renaissance* 3 (1973): 44–52.

Freud, Sigmund. *Civilization and Its Discontents*. Translated by James Strachey. New York: Norton, 1961.

Gatti, Hilary. *The Renaissance Drama of Knowledge: Giordano Bruno in England*. London: Routledge, 1989.

Geneva Bible. A facsimile of the 1560 edition. Introduction by Lloyd E. Berry. Madison: University of Wisconsin Press, 1969.

Gibbons, Brian. "Unstable Proteus: Marlowe's *The Tragedy of Dido Queen of Carthage*." In *Christopher Marlowe: Mermaid Critical Commentaries*, edited by Brian Morris, 25–46. London: Ernest Benn, 1968.

Gifford, George. *A Plaine Declaration that our Brownists be full Donatists, by comparing them together from point to point out of the writings of Augustine*. London: Toby Cooke, 1590. STC 11862.

– *A short treatise against the Donatists of England, whome we call Brownists*. London: Toby Cooke, 1590. STC 11869.

– *A Treatise of True Fortitude*. London: John Hardie, 1594. STC 11870.

Gillies, John. "The Question of Original Sin in *Hamlet*." *Shakespeare Quarterly* 64 (2013): 396–424.

Graham, Kenneth J.E. Introduction to *Shakespeare and Religious Change*, edited by Kenneth J.E. Graham and Philip D. Collington, 1–13. Basingstoke and New York: Palgrave Macmillan, 2009.

Grant, Patrick. *Spiritual Discourse and the Meaning of Persons*. New York: St. Martin's Press, 1994.

– *The Transformation of Sin: Studies in Donne, Herbert, Vaughan, and Traherne*. Montreal and Kingston: McGill-Queen's University Press; Amherst: University of Massachusetts Press, 1974.

Greenblatt, Stephen. *Hamlet in Purgatory*. Princeton: Princeton University Press, 2001.

– *Renaissance Self-Fashioning: From More to Shakespeare*. Chicago: University of Chicago Press, 1980.

– *The Swerve: How the World Became Modern*. New York: Norton, 2011.

Groves, Beatrice. "England's Jerusalem in Shakespeare's Henriad." In *The Bible on the Shakespearean Stage: Cultures of Interpretation in Reformation England*, edited by Thomas Fulton and Kristen Poole, 87–102. Cambridge: Cambridge University Press, 2018.

– "Hal as Self-Styled Redeemer: The Harrowing of Hell in *Henry IV Part 1*." *Shakespeare Survey* 57 (2004): 236–48.

Guenther, Genevieve. *Magical Imaginations: Instrumental Aesthetics in the English Renaissance*. Toronto: University of Toronto Press, 2012.

Guy, John. *Elizabeth: The Forgotten Years*. New York: Viking, 2016.

Guy-Bray, Stephen. *Homoerotic Space: The Poetics of Loss in Renaissance Literature*. Toronto: University of Toronto Press, 2002.

– "Shakespeare and the Invention of the Heterosexual." *Early Modern Literary Studies*, special issue 16 (2007).

Halley, Janet. "Heresy, Orthodoxy, and the Politics of Religious Discourse: The Case of the English Family of Love." In *Representing the English Renaissance*, edited by Stephen Greenblatt, 303–25. Berkeley: University of California Press, 1988.

Hamilton, Alastair. *The Family of Love*. Cambridge: James Clarke, 1981.

Hamilton, Donna. *Shakespeare and the Politics of Protestant England*. Lexington: University Press of Kentucky, 1992.

Hamlin, Hannibal. *The Bible in Shakespeare*. Oxford: Oxford University Press, 2013.

Hassel, R. Chris. "Frustrated Communion in *The Merchant of Venice*." *Cithara: Essays in the Judaeo-Christian Tradition* 13, no. 2 (1974): 19–33.

Hawkes, David. "Against Materialism in Literary Theory." In *The Return of Theory in Early Modern Studies: Tarrying with the Subjunctive*, edited by Paul Cefalu and Bryan Reynolds, 237–57. New York: Palgrave Macmillan, 2011.

Hawkins, Sherman. "Virtue and Kingship in Shakespeare's *Henry IV*." *English Literary Renaissance* 5 (1975): 313–43.

Healy, Margaret. *Shakespeare, Alchemy and the Creative Imagination: The Sonnets and a Lover's Complaint*. Cambridge: Cambridge University Press, 2011.

Helgerson, Richard. *Forms of Nationhood: The Elizabethan Writing of England*. Chicago: University of Chicago Press, 1992.

Hill, Christopher. *Milton and the English Revolution*. London: Faber and Faber, 1977.

Hirschfeld, Heather. *The End of Satisfaction: Drama and Repentance in the Age of Shakespeare*. Ithaca: Cornell University Press, 2014.

– "Hamlet's 'First Corse': Repetition, Trauma, and the Displacement of Redemptive Typology." *Shakespeare Quarterly* 54.4 (2003): 424–48.

Hiscock, Andrew. "'What's Hecuba to him …': Trojan Heroes and Rhetorical Selves in Shakespeare's *Hamlet*." In *Fantasies of Troy: Classical Tales and the Social Imaginary in Medieval and Early Modern Europe*, edited by Alan Shepard and Stephen D. Powell, 161–75. Toronto: Centre for Reformation and Renaissance Studies, 2004.

Honan, Park. *Christopher Marlowe: Poet and Spy*. Oxford: Oxford University Press, 2005.

– *Shakespeare: A Life*. Oxford: Oxford University Press, 1998.

Horton, Ronald. "The Seven Deadly Sins and Shakespeare's Jacobean Tragedies." In *Shakespeare and Spenser: Attractive Opposites*, edited by J.B. Lethbridge, 242–58. Manchester: Manchester University Press, 2008.

Irish, Bradley. "Writing Woodstock: The Prehistory of *Richard II* and Shakespeare's Dramatic Method." *Renaissance Drama* n.s. 41 (2013): 131–49.

Jackson, Ken, and Arthur F. Marotti. "The Turn to Religion in Early Modern Studies." *Criticism* 46 (2004): 167–90.

Johnston, Mark Albert. Review of Jay Zysk, *Shadow and Substance: Eucharistic Controversy and English Drama across the Reformation Divide*. *Renaissance and Reformation* 41 (2018): 277–80.

Jones, Douglas FitzHenry. "A Straying Collective: Familism and the Establishment of Orthodox Belief in Sixteenth-Century England." PhD thesis, University of Iowa, 2011. http://ir.uiowa.edu/etd/994.

Jowett, John. "Johannes Factotum: Henry Chettle and *Greene's Groatsworth of Wit*." *Papers of the Bibliographical Society of America* 87 (1993): 453–86.

Karim-Cooper, Farah. "Introduction." In *Titus Andronicus: The State of Play*, edited by Farah Karim-Cooper, 1–11. London and New York: Bloomsbury, 2019.

Kastan, David Scott. *A Will to Believe: Shakespeare and Religion*. Oxford: Oxford University Press, 2014.

Kendall, Roy. *Christopher Marlowe and Richard Baines: Journeys through the Elizabethan Underground*. Madison: Fairleigh Dickinson University Press, 2003.

Kerrigan, William. *Hamlet's Perfection*. Baltimore: Johns Hopkins University Press, 1994.

Kiséry, András. "Companionate Publishing, Literary Publics, and the Wit of Epyllia: The Early Success of *Hero and Leander*." In *Christopher Marlowe, Theatrical Commerce, and the Book Trade*, edited by Kirk Melnikoff and Roslyn Knutson, 165–81. Cambridge: Cambridge University Press, 2018.

Klause, John. "New Sources for Shakespeare's *King John*: The Writings of Robert Southwell." *Studies in Philology* 98 (2001): 401–27.

Knapp, Jeffrey. *Shakespeare's Tribe: Church, Nation, and Theater in Renaissance England*. Chicago: University of Chicago Press, 2002.

Kneidel, Gregory. *Rethinking the Turn to Religion in Early Modern Literature: The Poetics of All Believers*. Basingstoke and New York: Palgrave Macmillan, 2008.

Knewstub, John. *A Confutation of monstrous and horrible heresies, taught by H.N. and embraced of a number, who call themselves the Familie of Love*. London: Thomas Dawson for Richard Sergier, 1579. STC 15040.

Kuriyama, Constance Brown. *Christopher Marlowe: A Renaissance Life*. Ithaca: Cornell University Press, 2002.

– *Hammer or Anvil: Psychological Patterns in Christopher Marlowe's Plays*. New Brunswick, NJ: Rutgers University Press, 1980.

Lake, Peter. *The Boxmaker's Revenge*. Manchester: Manchester University Press, 2000.

– *How Shakespeare Put Politics on the Stage: Power and Succession in the History Plays*. New Haven: Yale University Press, 2016.

Lane, Robert. "'The sequence of posterity': Shakespeare's *King John* and the Succession Controversy." *Studies in Philology* 92 (1995): 460–81.

Lasch, Christopher. *The Minimal Self: Psychic Survival in Troubled Times*. New York: Norton, 1984.

Lethbridge, J.B. "Introduction: Spenser, Marlowe, Shakespeare: Methodological Investigations." In *Shakespeare and Spenser: Attractive Opposites*, edited by J.B. Lethbridge, 1–53. Manchester: Manchester University Press, 2011.

Leonard, John. "Marlowe's Doric Muse: Lust and Aggression in *Hero and Leander*." *English Literary Renaissance* 30 (2000): 55–76.

Lewalski, Barbara. *Protestant Poetics and the Seventeenth-Century Religious Lyric*. Princeton: Princeton University Press, 1979.

Lewis, C.S. *The Allegory of Love: A Study in Medieval Tradition*. Oxford: Oxford University Press, 1936.

Loewenstein, David. *Treacherous Faith: The Specter of Heresy in Early Modern English Literature and Culture*. Oxford: Oxford University Press, 2013.

Logan, Robert A. *Shakespeare's Marlowe: The Influence of Christopher Marlowe on Shakespeare's Artistry*. Aldershot and Burlington: Ashgate, 2007.

Lunney, Ruth. "*Dido, Queen of Carthage*." In *Christopher Marlowe at 450*, edited by Sara Munson Deats and Robert A. Logan, 13–49. Farnham: Ashgate, 2015.

Lupton, Julia Reinhard. "Paul Shakespeare: Exegetical Exercises." In *Religion and Drama in Early Modern England: The Performance of Religion on the Renaissance Stage*, edited by Jane Hwang Degenhardt and Elizabeth Williamson, 209–32. Farnham and Burlington: Ashgate, 2011.

MacCulloch, Diarmaid. *The Reformation*. New York: Viking, 2003.

MacFaul, Tom. *Poetry and Paternity in Renaissance England: Sidney, Spenser, Shakespeare, Donne and Jonson*. Cambridge: Cambridge University Press, 2010.

– *Problem Fathers in Shakespeare and Renaissance Drama*. Cambridge: Cambridge University Press, 2012.

Marlowe, Christopher. *Christopher Marlowe: The Complete Plays*. Edited by Frank Romany and Robert Lindsey. London: Penguin, 2003.

– *The Complete Poems and Translations*. Edited by Stephen Orgel. Harmondsworth: Penguin, 2007.

– *Dido Queen of Carthage* and *The Massacre at Paris*. Edited by H.J. Oliver. Cambridge: Harvard University Press, 1968.

– *Doctor Faustus A- and B-texts (1604, 1616)*. Edited by David Bevington and Eric Rasmussen. Manchester: Manchester University Press, 1993.

– *Edward the Second*. Edited by Charles R. Forker. Manchester: Manchester University Press, 1994.

– *The Jew of Malta*. Edited by N.W. Bawcutt. Manchester: Manchester University Press, 1978.

– *Tamburlaine the Great*. Edited by J.S. Cunningham and Eithne Henson. Manchester: Manchester University Press, 1998.

Marsh, Christopher. *The Family of Love in English Society, 1550–1630*. Cambridge: Cambridge University Press, 1994.

Martin, Lynnewood F. "The Family of Love in England: Conforming Millenarians." *Sixteenth Century Journal* 3 (1972): 99–108.

Martin, Mathew. "Pious Aeneas, False Aeneas: Marlowe's *Dido Queen of Carthage* and the Gift of Death." *Early Modern Literary Studies* 16, no. 1 (2012).

– *Tragedy and Trauma in the Plays of Christopher Marlowe*. Farnham: Ashgate, 2015.

– "*Translatio* and Trauma: *Oedipus*, *Hamlet*, and Marlowe's *Dido Queen of Carthage*." *Lit: Literature Interpretation Theory* 23 (2012): 305–25.

Masten, Jeffrey. *Queer Philologies: Sex, Language, and Affect in Shakespeare's Time*. Philadelphia: University of Pennsylvania Press, 2016.

Maus, Katharine Eisaman. *Inwardness and Theater in the English Renaissance*. Chicago: University of Chicago Press, 1995.

McAdam, Ian. "Calvinism and the Problematic of Character in *The Revenger's Tragedy*." In *The Revenger's Tragedy: The State of Play*, edited by Gretchen Minton, 85–109. London: Bloomsbury, 2018.

– "Eucharistic Love in *The Merchant of Venice*." *Renaissance and Reformation* 38 (2015): 83–116.

– *The Irony of Identity: Self and Imagination in the Drama of Christopher Marlowe.* Newark: University of Delaware Press, 1999.
– "*The Jew of Malta* and *The Merchant of Venice*: A Reconsideration of Influence." In *The Jew of Malta: A Critical Reader*, edited by Robert A. Logan, 107–27. London: Bloomsbury, 2013.
– "Magic and Gender in Late Shakespeare." In *Late Shakespeare: 1608–1613*, edited by Andrew J. Power and Rory Loughnane, 243–61. Cambridge: Cambridge University Press, 2013.
– *Magic and Masculinity in Early Modern English Drama.* Pittsburgh: Duquesne University Press, 2009.
– "Renaissance Inwardness and Current Critical Practice." *Dalhousie Review* 76 (1996): 273–84.
– Review of *Early Shakespeare, 1588–1594*, edited by Rory Loughnane and Andrew J. Powers. Cambridge: Cambridge University Press, 2020. *Renaissance and Reformation* 43 (2020): 324–6.
– Review of Alan Shepard, *Marlowe's Soldiers: Rhetorics of Masculinity in the Age of the Armada. Renaissance and Reformation* 27, no. 1 (2003): 121–4.
– Review of Richard Wilson, *Secret Shakespeare: Studies in Theatre, Religion and Resistance. Early Theatre* 10, no. 1 [2007]: 179–82.
– "*The Spanish Tragedy* and the Politico-Religious Unconscious." *Texas Studies in Literature and Language* 42 (2000): 33–60.
McAlindon, T. *Shakespeare's Tragic Cosmos.* Cambridge: Cambridge University Press, 1991.
McCabe, Richard. *Incest, Drama and Nature's Law 1550–1700.* Cambridge: Cambridge University Press, 1993.
Menzer, Paul. "c.f. Marlowe." In *Richard II: New Critical Essays*, edited by Jeremy Lopez, 117–34. Abingdon: Routledge, 2015.
Miller, David Lee. "Temperance, Interpretation, and 'the bodie of this death': Pauline Allegory in *The Faerie Queene*, Book II." *English Literary Renaissance* 46 (2016): 376–400.
Moschovakis, Nicholas R. "'Irreligious Piety' and Christian History: Persecution as Pagan Anachronism in *Titus Andronicus*." *Shakespeare Quarterly* 53 (2002): 460–86.
Mulryne, J.R., and Stephen Fender. "Marlowe and the 'Comic Distance'." In *Christopher Marlowe: Mermaid Critical Commentaries*, edited by Brian Morris, 47–64. London: Ernest Benn, 1968.
Nardizzi, Vin. "Grafted to Falstaff and Compounded with Catherine: Mingling Hal in the Second Tetralogy." In *Queer Renaissance Historiography: Backward Gaze*, edited by Vin Nardizzi, Stephen Guy-Bray, and Will Stockton, 149–69. Farnham: Ashgate, 2009.
Nicholl, Charles. "Christopher Marlowe." In *Oxford Dictionary of National Biography*. Vol. 36:721–30. Oxford: Oxford University Press, 2004.

– *The Reckoning: The Murder of Christopher Marlowe*. New York: Harcourt Brace and Co., 1992.

Niclaes, Hendrik. *Terra pacis a true testification of the spiritual land of peace, or the heavenly city of Jerusalem*. London: Samuel Satterthwaite, 1649. Wing N 1131.

Orgel, Stephen. *Impersonations: The Performance of Gender in Shakespeare's England*. Cambridge: Cambridge University Press, 1996.

Pagels, Elaine. *Adam, Eve, and the Serpent*. New York: Vintage, 1989.

– *Beyond Belief: The Secret Gospel of Thomas*. New York: Vintage, 2003.

Palmer, D.J. "Casting Off the Old Man: History and St. Paul in 'Henry IV'." *Critical Quarterly* 12 (1970): 267–83.

Parker, Courtney Bailey. "'Remember Me': *Hamlet*'s Corrupted Host and the Medieval Eucharistic Miracle." *ANQ: A Quarterly Journal of Short Articles, Notes and Reviews* 28 (2015): 15–20.

Patterson, Annabel. *Reading Holinshed's* Chronicles. Chicago: University of Chicago Press, 1994.

Peele, George. *David and Bathsheba*. Edited by Mathew Martin. Manchester: Manchester University Press, 2018.

– *The troublesome reign of John, King of England*. Edited by Charles R. Forker. Manchester: Manchester University Press, 2016.

Perkins, William. *A Treatise of Mans Imaginations*. In *The Works of … M. William Perkins*. Vol. 2. London: John Legatt, 1631. STC 19653.

– *A Warning Against The Idolatrie of the last times*. In *The Works of That Famous and Worthy Minister of Christ … William Perkins*. Vol 1. London: John Legatt, 1612. STC 19650.

– *The Work of William Perkins*. Edited by Ian Breward. Appleford, Berkshire: Sutton Courtenay Press, 1969.

Perry, Nandra. "*Imitatio* and Identity: Thomas Rogers, Philip Sidney, and the Protestant Self." *English Literary Renaissance* 35 (2005): 365–406.

Piesse, A.J. "*King John*: Changing Perspectives." In *The Cambridge Companion to Shakespeare's History Plays*, edited by Michael Hattaway, 126–40. Cambridge: Cambridge University Press, 2002.

Pinciss, G.M. "Marlowe's Cambridge Years and the Writing of *Doctor Faustus*." *Studies in English Literature* 33 (1993): 249–64.

Plutarch. "The Life of Marcus Antonius," *Plutarch's Lives of the Noble Grecians and Romanes*, trans. Thomas North (1579). In *Narrative and Dramatic Sources of Shakespeare*, edited by Geoffrey Bullough. Vol. 5. London: Routledge and Kegan Paul, 1964.

– *The philosophie, commonlie called, the morals written by the learned philosopher Plutarch of Chaeronea*. Translated by Philemon Holland. London: Arnold Hatfield, 1603. STC 20063.

Pollack-Pelzner, Daniel. "The Radical Argument of the *New Oxford Shakespeare*." *New Yorker*, 19 February 2017. www.newyorker.com/books /page-turner/the-radical-argument-of-the-new-oxford-shakespeare.

Pollard, Tanya. "What's Hecuba to Shakespeare?" *Renaissance Quarterly* 65 (2012): 1060–93.

Poole, Kristen. *Radical Religion from Shakespeare to Milton: Figures of Nonconformity in Early Modern England*. Cambridge: Cambridge University Press, 2000.

– "Saints Alive! Falstaff, Martin Marprelate, and the Staging of Puritanism." *Shakespeare Quarterly* 46 (1995): 47–75.

Potter, Lois. "The Antic Disposition of Richard II." *Shakespeare Survey* 27 (1974): 33–42.

Potter, Lucy. "Ekphrastic Catharsis: Christopher Marlowe's Mural of Troy's Fall in *The Tragedy of Dido, Queen of Carthage*." *Word & Image* 34 (2018): 310–21.

– "Marlowe's *Dido* and the Staging of Catharsis." *Journal of the Australasian Universities Language and Literature Association* 107 (2007): 1–23.

– "Shakespeare, Marlowe, and the Fortunes of Catharsis." In *"Rapt in Secret Studies": Emerging Shakespeares*, edited by Darryl Chalk and Laurie Johnson, 287–303. Newcastle upon Tyne: Cambridge Scholars, 2010.

Proctour, John. *The Fal of the Late Arrian*. London: William Powell, 1549. STC 20406.

Reid, Robert L. "Spenser and Shakespeare: Polarized Approaches to Psychology, Poetics, and Patronage." In *Shakespeare and Spenser: Attractive Opposites*, edited by J.B. Lethbridge, 79–120. Manchester: Manchester University Press, 2011.

Riggs, David. *The World of Christopher Marlowe*. London: Faber and Faber, 2004.

Roberts, Gareth. "Marlowe and the Metaphysics of Magicians." In *Constructing Christopher Marlowe*, edited by J.A. Downie and J.T. Parnell, 55–73. Cambridge: Cambridge University Press, 2000.

Rogers, John. *The Displaying of an horrible Secte of grosse and wicked Heretiques, naming themselves the Family of Love, with the lives of their Authours, and what doctrine they teach in corners*. London: George Bishop, 1579. STC 21182.

Rosendale, Timothy. *Theology and Agency in Early Modern Literature*. Cambridge: Cambridge University Press, 2018.

Rutter, Tom. "*Hamlet*, Pirates, and Purgatory." *Renaissance and Reformation* 38 (2015): 117–39.

Schoenbaum, Samuel. *William Shakespeare: A Compact Documentary Life*. New York: Oxford University Press, 1987.

Schwartz, Murray. "Leontes' Jealousy in *The Winter's Tale*." *American Imago* 30 (1973): 250–73.

– "*The Winter's Tale*: Loss and Transformation." *American Imago* 32 (1975): 145–99.

Schwartz, Robert. "Rosalynde among the Familists: *As You Like It* and an Expanded View of Its Sources." *Sixteenth Century Journal* 20 (1989): 69–76.

Scot, Reginald. *The discoverie of witchcraft*. London, 1584. STC 21864.

Shakespeare, William. *Anthony and Cleopatra*. Edited by Michael Neill. Oxford: Oxford University Press, 1994.

– *The Complete Works of Shakespeare*. Edited by David Bevington. 4th ed. New York: Longman, 1997.

– *Henry V*. Edited by Gary Taylor. Oxford: Oxford University Press, 1982.

– *Henry VI Part One*. Edited by Michael Taylor. Oxford: Oxford University Press, 2003.

– *Henry VI Part Two*. Edited by Roger Warren. Oxford: Oxford University Press, 2003.

– *King John*. Edited by A.R. Braunmuller. Oxford: Oxford University Press, 1989.

– *King Richard II*. Edited by Peter Ure. Arden Shakespeare 2nd series. London: Methuen, 1956.

– *King Richard III*. Edited by Antony Hammond. London: Methuen, 1981.

– *The New Oxford Shakespeare*. Edited by Gary Taylor, John Jowett, Terri Bourus, and Gabriel Egan. Oxford: Oxford University Press, 2016.

– *Othello, the Moor of Venice*. Edited by Michael Neill. Oxford: Oxford University Press, 2006.

– *Richard II*. Edited by Anthony Dawson and Paul Yachnin. Oxford: Oxford University Press, 2011.

– *Richard III*. Edited by John Jowett. Oxford: Oxford University Press, 2000.

– *The Riverside Shakespeare*. 2nd ed. Boston: Houghton Mifflin, 1997.

– *The Winter's Tale*. Edited by Stephen Orgel. Oxford: Oxford University Press, 1996.

Shannon, Laurie. *Sovereign Amity: Figures of Friendship in Shakespearean Contexts*. Chicago: University of Chicago Press, 2002.

Shapiro, James. *Rival Playwrights: Marlowe, Jonson, Shakespeare*. New York: Columbia University Press, 1991.

– *A Year in the Life of Shakespeare: 1599*. New York: HarperCollins, 2005.

Shell, Alison. *Shakespeare and Religion*. London: Methuen, 2010.

– "Why Didn't Shakespeare Write Religious Verse?" In *Shakespeare, Marlowe, Jonson: New Directions in Biography*, edited by Takashi Kozuka and J.R. Mulryne, 85–112. Aldershot: Ashgate, 2006.

Shepard, Alan. *Marlowe's Soldiers: Rhetorics of Masculinity in the Age of the Armada*. Aldershot: Ashgate, 2002.

Shepard, Alan, and Stephen D. Powell. Introduction to *Fantasies of Troy: Classical Tales and the Social Imaginary in Medieval and Early Modern Europe*, edited by Alan Shepard and Stephen D. Powell, 1–12. Toronto: Centre for Reformation and Renaissance Studies, 2004.

Shepherd, Simon. "A Bit of Ruff: Criticism, Fantasy, Marlowe." In *Constructing Christopher Marlowe*, edited by J.A. Downie and J.T. Parnell, 102–15. Cambridge: Cambridge University Press, 2000.

Sherman, Donovan. "'What more remains?': Messianic Performance in *Richard II.*" *Shakespeare Quarterly* 65 (2014): 22–48.

Shirley, Christopher. "Sodomy and Stage Directions in Christopher Marlowe's *Edward(s) II.*" *Studies in English Literature* 54 (2014): 279–96.

Shuger, Debora. "'Glums of Glutinous Heat' and the Stream of Consciousness: The Theology of Milton's *Maske.*" *Representations* 60 (Fall 1997): 1–21.

– *Habits of Thought in the English Renaissance: Religion, Politics, and the Dominant Culture.* 1990. Reprint, Toronto: University of Toronto Press, 1997.

– "'In a Christian Climate': Religion and Honor in *Richard II.*" In *Shakespeare and Religious Change*, edited by Kenneth J.E. Graham and Philip D. Collington, 37–59. Basingstoke: Palgrave Macmillan, 2009.

– "The Reformation of Penance." *Huntington Library Quarterly* 71 (2008): 557–71.

– *The Renaissance Bible: Scholarship, Sacrifice, and Subjectivity.* Berkeley: University of California Press, 1994.

Simpson, James. *Permanent Revolution: The Reformation and the Illiberal Roots of Liberalism.* Cambridge, MA: Belknap Press of Harvard University Press, 2019.

– "The Reformation of Scholarship: A Reply to Debora Shuger." *Journal of Medieval and Early Modern Studies* 42 (2012): 249–68.

Sinfield, Alan. "Hamlet's Special Providence." *Shakespeare Survey* 33 (1980): 89–97.

Skura, Meredith. "Marlowe's *Edward II*: Penetrating Language in Shakespeare's *Richard II.*" *Shakespeare Survey* 50 (1997): 41–55.

– *Shakespeare the Actor and the Purposes of Playing.* Chicago: University of Chicago Press, 1993.

Smith, Nigel. "'And if God was one of us': Paul Best, John Biddle, and Anti-Trinitarian Heresy in Seventeenth-Century England." In *Heresy, Literature, and Politics in Seventeenth-Century English Culture*, edited by David Loewenstein and John Marshall, 160–84. Cambridge: Cambridge University Press, 2006.

Snow, Edward. "*Doctor Faustus* and the Ends of Desire." In *Two Renaissance Mythmakers: Christopher Marlowe and Ben Jonson*, edited by Alvin Kernan. Baltimore: Johns Hopkins University Press, 1977.

Spenser, Edmund. *The Faerie Queene.* Edited by A.C. Hamilton. London: Longman, 1977.

Stanivukovic, Goran. "Beyond Sodomy: What Is Still Queer about Early Modern Queer Studies?" In *Queer Renaissance Historiography: Backward Gaze*, edited by Vin Nardizzi, Stephen Guy-Bray, and Will Stockton, 41–65. Farnham: Ashgate, 2009.

– "'Kissing the Boar': Queer Adonis and Critical Practice." In *Straight with a Twist: Queer Theory and the Subject of Heterosexuality*, edited by Calvin Thomas, 87–108. Urbana: University of Illinois Press, 1999.

Stapleton, M.L. *Marlowe's Ovid: The Elegies in the Marlowe Canon*. Farnham: Ashgate, 2014.

Steane, J.B. *Marlowe: A Critical Study*. Cambridge: Cambridge University Press, 1964.

Stevenson, Jane. "The Plot Thickens." Review of David Riggs, *The World of Christopher Marlowe*. *Guardian* 18 April 2004. http://www.theguardian.com /books/2004/apr/18/biography.christophermarlowe.

Stewart, Alan. *Close Readers: Humanism and Sodomy in Early Modern England*. Princeton: Princeton University Press, 1997.

Stewart, J.I.M. *Character and Motive in Shakespeare*. London: Longmans, 1949.

Streete, Adrian. *Protestantism and Drama in Early Modern England*. Cambridge: Cambridge University Press, 2009.

Summers, Claude J. "*Hero and Leander*: The Arbitrariness of Desire." In *Constructing Christopher Marlowe*, edited by J.A. Downie and J.T. Parnell, 133–47. Cambridge: Cambridge University Press, 2000.

Sweetnam, Mark S. "*Hamlet* and the Reformation of the Eucharist." *Literature and Theology* 21 (2007): 11–28.

Taylor, Charles. "Foucault on Freedom and Truth." *Political Theory* 12 (1984): 152–83.

Taylor, Dennis. "Introduction: Shakespeare and the Reformation." In *Shakespeare and the Culture of Christianity in Early Modern England*, edited by Dennis Taylor and David Beauregard, 1–25. New York: Fordham University Press, 2003.

Taylor, Gary. "Forms of Opposition: Shakespeare and Middleton." *English Literary Renaissance* 24 (1994): 283–314.

– "Shakespeare and Others: The Authorship of *Henry the Sixth, Part One*." *Medieval and Renaissance Drama in England* 7 (1995): 145–205.

Thomas, Vivien, and William Tydeman, eds. *Christopher Marlowe: The Plays and Their Sources*. New York: Routledge, 1994.

Tuggle, Bradley. "'Barbary' in *Henry IV, Part 1*: Another Shakespearean Allusion to 1 Corinthians." *Explicator* 70 (2012): 39–43.

Tyacke, Nicholas. *Anti-Calvinists: The Rise of English Arminianism c. 1590–1640*. Oxford: Clarendon Press, 1990.

Urry, William. *Christopher Marlowe and Canterbury*. Edited by Andrew Butcher. London: Faber and Faber, 1988.

van Es, Bart. *Shakespeare in Company*. Oxford: Oxford University Press, 2013.

Vickers, Brian. "The Two Authors of *Edward III*." *Shakespeare Survey* 67 (2014): 102–18.

Virgil. *The Aeneid*. Translated by Robert Fitzgerald. New York: Vintage, 1984.

Waldron, Jennifer. *Reformations of the Body: Idolatry, Sacrifice, and Early Modern Theater*. New York: Palgrave Macmillan, 2013.

Wall-Randell, Sarah. "Marlowe's Lucan: Winding Sheets and Scattered Leaves." In *Christopher Marlowe, Theatrical Commerce, and the Book Trade*, edited by Kirk Melnikoff and Roslyn Knutson, 11–25. Cambridge: Cambridge University Press, 2018.

Walsham, Alexandra. "William Hackett." In *Oxford Dictionary of National Biography*, edited by H.C.J. Matthew and Brian Harrison. Vol. 24:396–7. Oxford: Oxford University Press, 2004.

Webster, Richard. *Why Freud Was Wrong: Sin, Science and Psychoanalysis*. London: HarperCollins, 1996.

Weimann, Robert. "Mingling Vice and 'Worthiness' in *King John*." *Shakespeare Studies* 27 (1999): 109–33.

Wells, Robin Headlam. *Shakespeare on Masculinity*. Cambridge: Cambridge University Press, 2000.

Wells, Stanley, and Gary Taylor. *William Shakespeare: A Textual Companion*. Oxford: Clarendon Press, 1987.

Westerholm, Stephen. *Israel's Law and the Church's Faith: Paul and His Recent Interpreters*. Grand Rapids: William B. Eerdmans Publishing, 1998.

Wiggins, Martin. "Marlowe's Chronology and Canon." In *Christopher Marlowe in Context*, edited by Emily C. Bartels and Emma Smith, 7–14. Cambridge: Cambridge University Press, 2013.

Wilkinson, William. *A Confutation of Certain Articles delivered unto the Familye of Love, with the exposition of Theophilus, a supposed Elder in the sayd Familye upon the same Articles*. London: John Daye, 1579. STC 25665.

Wilson, A.N. *Jesus*. London: Sinclair-Stevenson, 1992.

– *Paul: The Mind of the Apostle*. New York: Norton, 1997.

Wilson, J. Dover. *What Happens in Hamlet*. 1935. Reprint, Cambridge: Cambridge University Press, 1962.

Wilson, Richard. *Secret Shakespeare: Studies in Theatre, Religion and Resistance*. Manchester: Manchester University Press, 2004.

– "'The words of Mercury': Shakespeare and Marlowe." In *The Cambridge Companion to Shakespeare and Contemporary Dramatists*, edited by Ton Hoenselaars, 34–53. Cambridge: Cambridge University Press, 2012.

Womersley, David. *Divinity and State*. Oxford: Oxford University Press, 2010.

– "The Politics of Shakespeare's *King John*." *Review of English Studies* n.s. 40 (1989): 497–515.

Wootton, David. "John Donne's Religion of Love." In *Heterodoxy in Early Modern Science and Religion*, edited by John Brooke and Ian Maclean, 31–58. Oxford: Oxford University Press, 2005.

– "Reginald Scot/Abraham Fleming/The Family of Love." In *Languages of Witchcraft: Narrative, Ideology and Meaning in Early Modern Culture*, edited by Stuart Clark, 119–38. London: Macmillan, 2001.
Wraight, A.D. *In Search of Christopher Marlowe*. New York: Vanguard Press, 1965
Yang, Albert C. "Validating the Enlarged Kyd Canon: A New Approach." *ANQ: A Quarterly Journal of Short Articles, Notes and Reviews* 33, no. 2–3 (2020): 189–97.
Žižek, Slavoj. *The Fragile Absolute – or, Why Is the Christian Legacy Worth Fighting For?* London: Verso, 2000.
Zysk, Jay. *Shadow and Substance: Eucharistic Controversy and English Drama across the Reformation Divide*. Notre Dame: University of Notre Dame Press, 2017.

Index

Donatists. *See* Brownists
Donne, John, 50, 73
Downie, J.A., 245n5
Dryden, John, 230
Duffy, Eamon, 19
Duncan-Jones, Katherine, 274n25
Durkheim, Émile, 39
Dutch Church Libel, 32, 47, 140

Edward II, 4, 11, 24–5, 70, 86, 90, 93,
    116–22, 123, 126, 132–3, 135, 146–7,
    177, 179–80, 182–4, 187, 188, 190,
    191, 264n14, 268–9n19, 271n60
Edward III, 265n34
Edward III, 11, 145–53, 156
Edward VI, 33
Egan, Gabriel, 36, 232
Egan, Michael, 267n14
Elizabeth I, 47, 50, 145, 208, 263n2
Ellis, Jim, 214–17
Empson, William, 50, 73
Engle, Lars, 250–1n54
Erasmus, Desiderius, 10, 26–8, 29,
    74, 97–8
Erlich, Avi, 255–6n21
Erne, Lukas, 264n14
Essex, Earl of, 44, 92, 208
Etherington, John, 52–3, 55, 194
Eucharist, 23, 24, 37–9, 54, 65, 72, 79,
    80, 98, 119, 132–4, 159, 202, 221,
    270n37
Euripides, 78

Family of Love, Familist doctrine,
    10, 12, 48–55, 73, 142–3, 159, 165–6,
    171, 172–3, 194–9, 210, 220–1
femininity and effeminization,
    33, 87–8, 255n10; in *Antony and
    Cleopatra* and later Shakespeare,
    227, 229; in *Dido Queen of Carthage*,
    61–2, 69, 226; in *Hamlet*, 77–81,
    226; in *Henry VI* plays, 91, 107–10,

112, 119, 181; in *Hero and Leander*,
    215–16; in *King John*, 155–6, 163–4;
    in *Richard II*, 185; in *Richard III*,
    125, 137; in Spenser, 263n2; in
    Venus and Adonis, 191–2, 205–6;
    in *The Winter's Tale*, 236, 240–1,
    275n39
Findlay, Heather, 199–200, 202–4,
    210, 216
Fineman, Joel, 204
Fisch, Harold, 274n19
Fleming, Abraham, 50
Florio, John, 269n24
Forker, Charles R., 86, 120, 262–3n60,
    264n16, 268–9n19
Foucault, Michel, 204, 247n16
Freebury-Jones, Darren, 85–6
Freeman, Arthur, 251n55
Freud, Sigmund, Freudianism, 37,
    46–7, 56, 237–8, 252n85,
    255–6n21
Frizer, Ingram, 212

Gatti, Hilary, 93
Gifford, George, 10, 39–44, 54, 55, 63,
    197–8, 210
Gillies, John, 75
Goldberger, Ary L., 258–9n2
grace, theology of, 10, 16, 21, 26–7,
    80, 92, 94, 98, 100, 107, 116, 141,
    181, 235. *See also* atonement
    theology; Original Sin
Graham, Kenneth, 48
Grant, Patrick, 45, 247–8n17
Greenblatt, Stephen, 14, 21–2, 72–4,
    86–7, 251n64
Greene, Robert, 118, 167
Groves, Beatrice, 194–7, 200–1
Guenther, Genevieve, 256n32
Guy, John, 105
Guy-Bray, Stephen, 237–9,
    275n40